THE OTHER
AMERICANS

THE OTHER AMERICANS

HOW IMMIGRANTS
RENEW OUR COUNTRY,
OUR ECONOMY, AND
OUR VALUES

Joel Millman

VIKING

VIKING
Published by the Penguin Group
Penguin Books USA Inc., 375 Hudson Street,
New York, New York 10014, U.S.A.
Penguin Books Ltd, 27 Wrights Lane, London W8 5TZ, England
Penguin Books Australia Ltd, Ringwood, Victoria, Australia
Penguin Books Canada Ltd, 10 Alcorn Avenue,
Toronto, Ontario, Canada M4V 3B2
Penguin Books (N.Z.) Ltd, 182–90 Wairau Road,
Auckland 10, New Zealand

Penguin Books Ltd, Registered Offices:
Harmondsworth, Middlesex, England

First published in 1997 by Viking Penguin,
a division of Penguin Books USA Inc.

1 3 5 7 9 10 8 6 4 2

LIBRARY OF CONGRESS CATALOGING-IN-PUBLICATION DATA
Millman, Joel.
The other Americans / Joel Millman.
p.   cm.
Includes index.
ISBN 0-670-85844-7 (alk. paper)
1. Immigrants—United States.   2. United States—Emigration and
immigration—Economic aspects.   3. United States—Emigration and
immigration—Social aspects.   4. Americanization.   5. Acculturation.
I. Title.
JV6465.M554   1997
305.9'0691—dc21   96-49265

This book is printed on acid-free paper. ∞

Printed in the United States of America
Set in New Caledonia

PREFACE

The discussion of immigration involves many different issues—
everything from social statistics and economic models to political
opinion on such matters as community values, human rights, and
national security. It involves us, as citizens and participants, in
many different ways. No American, no matter how opposed he or
she may be to the current tide of inbound migration, is completely
without sympathy for the plight of the world's poorest or without
pride for the successes of its most ambitious. No American, no
matter how pro-immigrant, is completely without concern for what
negative impact world labor competition may be having on America's native-born poor.

For these and many more reasons there is no single "correct"
way to frame the issue of American immigration. Nor is it possible
to decide which segment of American immigration is the "best"
one to examine. Immigration is a numbers game, a morality play,
a legal debate, a market model. No book can possibly handle the
entire spectrum of immigration issues, and this book makes no
claim that it does.

What the book does attempt to do is to establish what aspect
of immigration at the close of the immigration century constitutes
the "crisis" generating so much rancor today, and to defuse the
fear. For that reason the immigrants profiled in the following pages
are largely newcomers from what was once known as the Third
World—Latin Americans, East Asians, Caribbeans, and Africans.
While America has also experienced a recent surge in immigration

from Eastern Europe, Israel, Ireland, and the former Soviet Union, seldom does this population of new Americans generate controversy. California, after all, did not pass Proposition 187 in 1994 to restrict the flow of Armenians to Fresno County or to reduce the number of Irish in San Francisco. We see ourselves as a majority European society; thus most of our concerns about immigration are generated by arrivals from the non-European world.

The Other Americans also does not attempt to measure the "negative" or "positive" effect of immigration in macroeconomic terms. Although this is largely a profile of the immigrant economy, it is mainly a look at new business strategies and business synergies brought on by immigration, and how they emerge in our culture. It is, then, a look at how America's twin promises of human freedom and market transparency combine to draw talent from overseas, and how that talent improves all of our lives. The immigrant, in other words, functioning as input—consumer, investor, manager, saver, deregulator, developer.

All of the stories recounted here are based on the author's own reporting. All quotes, except where noted, are from original interviews. No names have been altered.

November 29, 1996

ACKNOWLEDGMENTS

Writing a book like *The Other Americans*, like writing any book, is a collaborative effort. Without the aid of dozens of people, the research effort likely would have foundered. The writing itself would have been abandoned.

And, as with all books, there are so many details that had to be left out of the telling. I traveled three times to Puerto Rico and twice to the Dominican Republic with the intention of writing on Dominican "boat people" and their impact on U.S. border control policy. Alas, space considerations eliminated all mention of this issue, which is an important one. Similarly, months were spent visiting Seventh Day Adventist churches and schools in Brooklyn, the core of a ghetto renewal program being carried out by West Indian immigrants. Yet the stories and comments of the Seventh Day Adventist parishioners are largely absent from these pages. Visits to Nigerian enclaves in Houston and Washington, to a community of Chinese Ecuadorians in Queens, New York, to a gathering of Senegalese traders in Detroit, to Senegal itself—each yielded images largely omitted from the finished work.

However, even where the images are missing, traces remain. For example, I spent a fascinating afternoon in New York's Chinatown with a *Forbes* magazine intern, Linus Chua, in June 1993. We were trying to dissect the supply-and-demand economics of underground employment agencies, then flourishing with the arrival of Fukienese immigrants being smuggled in on "slave ships" like the infamous *Golden Venture*. Linus, a native Fukienese speaker, proved invaluable in gaining access to what we discovered was an elaborate caste system of job providers working out of tiny tenement cubicles—a world spread among a few square blocks. Climbing the job escalator (and rickety staircases) in search of the Big Boss, we ended our day with an unassuming Vietnam-born Cantonese, who received us graciously and explained the business from his clients' point of view. Any one of those clients could have been Linus or, in a different time, my own grandfather. Linus left *Forbes* for a stint at the *Los Angeles Times*, where he became an accomplished financial journalist. Later, from the *Palm Beach Post*, where he covers Florida real estate, Linus again became my willing accomplice, offering tips and clips for the book's final chapter, on the renaissance of Delray Beach.

The list of people like Linus who offered key advice, key documents, key places to work or to sleep while I traveled the country is a long one. Omitting those who are quoted in the text or in the end-notes, I wish to thank the following:

In New York—Dame Babou, Jim Barry, Peter Benda, Darwin Berry, Aubrey Bonnett, Esmee Bovell, Ying Chan, Allan Chase, Muzaffar Chishti, Rachel Cobb, Barbara Cohen, Kim Conroy, Jorge Costa, T. J. English, Nancy Foner, Alma Guillermoprieto, the Reverend Lloyd Henry, Bordes Henry-Saturne, John and Karen Hess, Ken Hodges, Laura Jereski, Kewulay Kamara, Peter Kwong, Wayne Lam, Robert Lipsyte, Michael Massing, Sydney McIntosh, John Mollenkopf, Melchor Monk, Sylvia Moreno, Gerson Nieves, Valerie Oltarsh, David Peterkin, Alejandro Portes, William K. Rashbaum, Jerry Resnick, Julio Rivera, Saskia Sassen, Charles Seaton, Ronald Shiffman, Robert Smith, Noel Spencer, Emanuel Tobier, Charles Walker, Lawrence Weschler, Kathryn Wylde, Enid Winn, Louis Winnick, Aristide Zolberg. Also, special thanks to the parishioners of the Hanson Place Seventh Day Adventist church; Roy L. Hoyte, senior pastor; and the students of Lynda Straker's eighth-grade Hanson Place Seventh Day Adventist School class: Pia Baptiste, Dayna Joi Bashette, Aaron Bernard, Kervin Boyce, Kemi Desalu, Keisha Eastmond, Keith Elcock, Lyssandre Emmanuel, Samantha Fleary, Tricia Goring, Kristopher

Haughton, Monique Hutchinson, Justin Ian, Ruben James, Monique Jardine, Vaughn O'Marde, Valerie Pierre, Nicole Rhem, Marshana Ritchie, Tiffany Roberts, Richard Romain, Kalmira Romeo.

In California—Mark Arax, Efrain Bajaras, Elias Bermudez, Efrain Castillo, Clare Christiansen, Bruce Clayton, Sandy Close, Lourdes and Rodolfo Gonzalez, Craig Himmelwright, Susan Humphreys, Commander Edward Jewell, Manuel Jimenez, Sam Kuramarohit, Cher Chou and Vilay Lee, Jerry Lorastein, David Mas Masumoto, Noel and Daniel Melendez, Daniel Mountjoy, Juan Vicente Palerm, Humberto Ramirez, David Riggs, Steve Rosenbaum, David Runsten, Spencer Sherman, Adrienne Waite, Miriam Wells, Jennifer Yang.

In Massachusetts (or Brazil)—Phil Bennett, Sandy Buentello, Indira Desai, Amarildo de Souza, Peter Ditami, Maureen Dunne, Jeff Edges, Peter and Raquel Gordon, Jose Eduardo Mendonca, Nelson Merced, Matt Moffet, Carlos Perreira, Roger Rice, Nicholas Sanchez, Jonathan Sarna, Christine Taylor, David Whitford.

In Senegal—Roland Billecart, Padraig Declan Byrne, Thomas Edward Cairns, Mouhamadou Dia, Gary Engelberg, Djibril Fall, Famille Gueye, Arame Lo, Aziz Makward, Asatou Niang, Mamadou Niang, James Pollock, Mourtala Sall, Ousmane Sembene, Seydina Senghor, Babacar Touré.

In Florida—Freddy Breilleur, Art Bullock, Lula Butler, Douze Chiro, Jacques D'Espinasse, Dorothy Ellington, Fred Griffin, Dr. Jacques Guiteau, Madeleine Hart, Carl House, Ermithe Jean, Oliver Kerr, Frank Kunf, John Lewis, Dan Marfino, Clarice Peterkin, Elsie St. Félix, Alex Stepick, Otis White, Tom Yee.

In Washington, D.C.—Jodie Allen, George Anders, Calvin Beale, Toyo Biddle, Paul Donnelly, Rosemary Jencks, Budd Kerr, Teresa Lara, Robert McGuckin, Sulayman Niang, Jeffrey Passell, Ambassador Mamadou Mansour Seck, Frank Sharry, Daniel Stein, Valerie Strang, Roberto Suro, Bernard Wysocki.

Several people deserve thanks for seeing this book to its completion. First, my agent, Lisa Bankoff of International Creative Management, and my Viking editors at Penguin USA—Kathryn

Court and Marion Maneker, as well as their assistant, Laurie Walsh. Thanks, too, to Patricia Kelly and Roel Torres. Two mentors at *Forbes* magazine, where I launched this book with their enthusiastic blessing, were generous in giving me the time I needed to start, then later the outlet to present some emerging themes. Thanks, always, to Lawrence Minard and James W. Michaels. Thanks, too, to my editors at *The Wall Street Journal*, John Bussey and Craig Torres, who agreed to postpone my arrival in Mexico City until I completed the manuscript. Special thanks go to Peter Bird Martin and the Institute of Current World Affairs, whose funding a decade ago planted seeds for this project, and to Margaret Engel and the Alicia Patterson Foundation, whose generous 1995 fellowship kept my household intact during the home stretch.

Finally, I want to thank all the members of my family: my parents, George and Joan Millman; my brother, Josh; and my sisters, Jennifer and Julia. Thanks, too, to my stepdaughter, Madeleine Schwartz, who I can truthfully say spent more time sharing the research and reporting of this book than any other person in my life. Whether we were attending a Brazilian carnival in Framingham, Massachusetts, or the annual Caribbean parade in Brooklyn; "interviewing" Senegalese peddlers on the streets of New York or food shopping in Los Angeles' Mexican barrios; visiting the mosque in Harlem or ordering dim sum in Chinatown, Madeleine's enthusiasm for the immigration beat never flagged. Her questions, her observations, her precious joy in encountering the new and, to her, natural, made working on this project my joy too.

CONTENTS

THE OTHER
AMERICANS

Introduction

One thing we have going for us is the curious love affair most villagers have with America; they can even be a bit possessive about it. America is becoming everybody's second country . . . America as a symbol, an idea, of the good life, of oomph and vitality and freedom and fun.

Richard Critchfield, the author of *Villages*

★

In the summer of 1994, I went to Mexico to meet my new neighbors. I wasn't moving to Mexico yet. Instead, Mexicans were shuttling back and forth to New York. Thousands of them, many deciding to reside in *El Norte* permanently, with or without legal status. I traveled to the southeastern state of Puebla to find out why.

By the summer of 1994, some 100,000 Mexican nationals had settled in New York City, always in the most blighted neighborhoods of Brooklyn, the Bronx, and Manhattan. While that number was still small by New York Latin standards—more than 700,000 people migrated up from the Dominican Republic since the mid-1960s—it was, given the distance they traveled, an impressive migration. Impressive, too, was the speed with which the Mexicans had fashioned their underground expressway. By the summer of 1994, migrants from Mexico could travel from an adobe shack in Puebla to an apartment in New York City in less than forty-eight hours, at a cost of about a thousand dollars. I could scarcely make the reverse trip as quickly, nor, once I factored in the cost of taxis, hotel rooms, and meals, as cheaply.

A migration that was only a trickle at the beginning of the decade was a surging flood. Peasant farmers, many of them illiterate, now had the ways and means to cross two large countries in pursuit of employment. And they had done so by themselves, without government planners, without labor contractors, without even the certainty of ripening grapes to harvest, or apples, or sugar beets—any of the other edible magnets that for decades drew temporary workers to California, Michigan, and North Carolina. They were coming for urban jobs: delivering pizzas, cleaning offices, and preparing salads. They harvested dirty silverware from tabletops or sprayed the neat pyramids of fruit stacked at the Korean groceries. Thousands were self-employed, rising before dawn to gather flowers in the wholesale florists' district. Carting fresh roses and baby's breath to tenement apartments far from Midtown, they would bundle bouquets while their children were being bundled off to school. After a few hours' sleep, these flower children were back on the street, peddling from shopping carts outside hospitals and subway stations.

Mexico in the summer of 1994 was a time of NAFTA fever, a brief period of euphoria over Mexico's prospects for prosperity. Only a few months before, the U.S. Congress had approved the North American Free Trade Agreement, which was designed to open markets with Mexico. In the tempestuous debate leading up to the vote, "jobs" was the buzzword. NAFTA, its supporters said, would create an employment boom on both sides of the border. Or else, said the anti-NAFTA forces, jobs would drain the U.S. workforce south. Opponents and supporters alike seemed to be seeing Mexico through a rose-tinted lens.

Despite the reports of humming new factories, climbing stock-market indices, and soaring consumer spending (this was Mexico at the height of its supercharged peso party), job creation was hopelessly deficient. Throughout Mexico, jobs that had existed for centuries were disappearing. This was true particularly in the "Mixteca," Mexico's poor southern half. In states like Puebla, "jobs" meant hacking weeds in cornfields that any week now would be baked to dry stubble. Or it meant hawking soda pop and chewing gum in the plaza for pennies a day. Even these jobs were getting harder to find. Jobs that never could pay as well as the dirtiest job in *El Norte* were the jobs that were quickly disappearing as Mexico modernized and restructured. In the afterglow of NAFTA's passage, before a boom turned to bust, Mexico stood on the brink of disaster. And, compared to all the places the rest of my new neighbors were coming from, Mexico had it good.

From Mexico and the Dominican Republic, from Peru and Nigeria and Cuba and Thailand, individuals were on the move. They were leaving for jobs, but arriving as colonists. By the summer of 1994, 100 million world citizens were said to be living and working in countries other than their homelands. Welcomed as "guest workers" in some places, denounced as menacing "illegal aliens" in others, these colonists were said to represent the largest mass migration of humanity since the end of the Roman Empire. That this migration was linked to the end of the Cold War largely went unnoticed. In effect, the great cities of the West were receiving the Cold War's last refugees. Even places that had never been either side's pawn, places like Mexico, were affected by the end of Cold War competition. Foreign aid programs that drove international relations on both sides of the Cold War were quickly losing their purpose. "Tough love" was the mantra, no more winning the Third World's hearts and minds with a willingness to forgive debt, grant aid, or build industry. These had been life-support systems that allowed dying economies to sputter along, even after brain death. Now the plug was being pulled. "Compassion fatigue," some called it. "Restructuring" was another name.

Immigration is both a symptom and a cause of Third World restructuring. On a political level, every immigrant is a vote for change. In China, El Salvador, Haiti, and Mexico, places with no tradition of democratic change, these are the only votes that matter. Immigrants are the brain drain but also the brain support: their absence lets bad rulers perpetuate bad policy while their overseas earnings, remitted home to their families, keep cities fed, farmland

planted, and stores stocked. Salvadorans in the United States remitted dollars at a rate of nearly $3 million a day during the 1980s.
It was arguably only their money that kept the Salvadoran government solvent during its civil war, which makes that war the first in
history to be funded by its own refugees. And in El Salvador, as
everywhere else, that funding creates the savings needed to finance
the flight of the next generation.

Yet by the summer of 1994, this support system was beginning
to unravel. Now that poor nations were unable to petition world
governments for economic relief, they were losing control of their
own economies. Unable to foster growth or end inflation, much
less raise cash to pay interest on their mounting international debts,
states everywhere restructured. All over the world, assets were being sold to help governments ride out the crisis, which still would
not go away. The loss of state jobs sent a ripple through the shrinking job base, and sent more immigrants abroad.

Simultaneously, Third World economies were becoming "dollarized." In Brazil, in Poland, and in Beirut, newspapers routinely
listed apartments for rent in dollars. In Mexico, and throughout
Central America and the Caribbean, millions of common people
routinely used dollars for every type of transaction. Dollarization
also meant democratization, at least in the marketplace, as peasants
enjoyed what only elites had once had: a leg up on the runaway
inflation that crippled dreams. By the summer of 1994, even Cuba
had to decriminalize dollars-in-pockets and accept that its closed
economy had joined the world system. As dollars supplanted pesos,
baht, cruzeiros, and the rest of the Third World's artificial curren-
cies, the performance of the immigrant became ever more crucial.
Immigrants earned dollars. Their earnings, like their votes, were
soon the only ones that counted. Their earnings were making the
entire Third World new neighbors for us all.

Zapotitlán Salinas, a village in the southeast corner of Puebla, lies
about an hour's bumpy drive outside the resort town of Tehuacán.
Tehuacán is a bustling crossroads famous for the mineral springs

nearby. Nearly four hours by bus from Mexico City, a journey there leaves ample time to contemplate the arid "cornfields" bleached chalk white in the summer sun, and to imagine the hundreds of New York–bound migrants who had ridden north on these same roads.

Tehuacán is famous for more than mineral springs. Nearby is a dank cave where archaeologists believe they have found the oldest grains of cultivated maize, what Americans call sweet corn. About three inches long, a prehistoric corn cob was uncovered there in 1963, preserved for thousands of years in a thick shell of mud, grass, and human dung. In terms of North American history, that discovery was almost like finding the first wheel or embers from the first campfire. Maize cultivation lies at the root of American civilization. Once aboriginal man learned to grow corn, he was on his way to leaving his precarious hunter-gatherer existence. Surplus corn made Teotihuacán—the precursor to Mexico City, in ancient times and today the world's biggest metropolis. Mexican peasants believe the kernels are ancient men, and that when they are eating corn they are eating their ancestors. And they are right.

Zapotitlán Salinas was one of several villages being investigated by the reporter Richard Critchfield, one of the world's experts on migration, and a longtime collaborator and mentor of mine. Based for the summer in Tehuacán, he was studying the life of peasants there on behalf of the Ford Foundation, which had hired Critchfield to evaluate one of its programs. The Ford Foundation was paying Critchfield to determine whether a project it was funding —the promotion of amaranth, a high-protein grain that had been grown in Mexico since precolonial days—was working. Amaranth grown in sufficient quantities could be a new source of nutrition, the foundation hoped, breaking a cycle of hunger and poverty that was responsible for sending so many Poblanos north. Richard was less presumptuous. "Since the Cold War ended, groups like the Ford Foundation have to dream up these projects to justify their jobs," he confided with glee when we met in Tehuacán. "And people like me have to go along so we can keep studying peasants."

That was vintage Critchfield: cheery and cynical at the same time. Studying the world's peasantry had been Critchfield's passion for over thirty years. In books like *Villages,* a sweeping panorama of peasantry's present, and *Shahhat,* an up-close-and-personal study of a family in one Egyptian village, Critchfield gave the developed world a portrait of its own past, and thus a glimpse of its future. First in his native North Dakota, then in India, then covering the Vietnam war, then all over Africa, the Middle East, Latin America, and, most recently, rural post–Cold War Eastern Europe, he had made a career of chronicling The Great Change. That was what he called traditional cultures assimilating the challenges of a modern world, which he also called the story of the twentieth century. He called immigration—traditional culture released from villages on a global scale—the story of the twenty-first.

Villages feed cities, Critchfield never tired of explaining, not just by producing food, but by producing culture. Villagers are the embodiment of our shared human values: family loyalty, religious faith, the work ethic. "Urban societies," he warned in a letter he circulated earlier that year, "when they no longer have a sufficiently large rural hinterland to draw upon, have to cross cultural and political boundaries to draw in villagers to swell their bottom ranks if they are not to move toward slow biological and cultural extinction."

Some warning. Rural migrants feeding cities was what tempered the decadence of the cosmopolitan world, fresh blood pumping fresh oxygen into our smoggy, polluted lives. It is only in our time that the villagers in our midst are foreign-born. Thus, Critchfield explained, immigration is not only inevitable, it is essential. The current wave, to him, represented a burst of freedom and hope for us all.

From Tehuacán to Zapotitlán Salinas, the road climbs through a mountain pass, rising beside one of the last great cactus forests in North America, then along the cliffs that hide the Cave of the First Corn. "Mexico is an authentic culture, like India or China," Critchfield said. "And in that way it is unique in America." Peasant culture had endured here, he explained, unlike in Brazil, where indigenous tribes were beaten into the interior, later to be replaced on the coast with black slaves. Or unlike the United States, where the traces of premodern life endure solely in museums. But tradition lives in modern Mexico. Tehuacán's sprawling farmers' market is surely in the same place it was when Aztecs and Olmecs ruled this valley. Tehuacán's town square is in the same spot it was in a thousand years ago. Authentic culture is the embodiment of village tradition, the values Mexicans were now exporting to New York.

Zapotitlán Salinas is the principal "sender" town in the area, one village among dozens that seemed unique in exporting its children to *El Norte*. Most were going to the Northeast, as they were from most "sender" towns in the Mixteca. The men and women of this southern region are relative latecomers to the migration sweepstakes and had to find new destinations. Beaten to places like Houston, Los Angeles, Phoenix, and Chicago by countrymen living closer to the U.S. border, these *mixtecos* were guiding their ships toward new beachheads: New York, Philadelphia, Boston, even Montreal. Out of the town's total population of 3,500, more than 700 had gone abroad.

Why they were heading to the East Coast was a matter of job availability—everywhere else had been saturated. Why they were leaving Zapotitlán Salinas—and not another, equally impoverished settlement nearby—was a mystery. It could have something to do with the truckers, Critchfield mused. Police were always demanding bribes here. At a cantina the counterwoman complained that the *mordida,* the "bite," was so persistent, fewer of her regular customers were stopping in town. Deleted from sales routes, trade was drying up in Zapotitlán Salinas.

Another explanation was simpler. The counterwoman's sister, who lives in Tijuana, is Zapotitlán Salinas' *pollera,*—literally, a chicken-coop tender. Greenhorns crossing the border are called *pollos,* or chickens; the "chicken watcher" works on the Mexican side, guiding her chicks to a smuggler, or *coyote,* entrusted with getting her brood across. Zapotitlán Salinas, then, enjoyed a strategic advantage neighboring towns didn't have.

Across Puebla, little migration eruptions were beginning to appear. Calipan, a larger town about twenty miles from Tehuacán, had become another sender. Sugar, not "chickens," was the reason. The town's biggest employer, a government-owned sugar mill, had been privatized. That also was the reason in another Puebla town, Izúcar de Matamoros, about a hundred miles to the southwest. Under the old system, when sugar was a state enterprise, losses were guaranteed at state-owned mills because the price of sugar paid to farmers was subsidized. It was bad business, but served as the underpinning of a gigantic rural welfare system, which in turn served Mexico's all-controlling Institutional Revolutionary Party, or PRI, which had run the country since the 1920s. Party members within the sugar mill, negotiating with party members in the sugar growers' union, negotiated with party members at the secretariat for agriculture to set a price for sugar. The formula was simple: make sure the mills produced enough to satisfy Mexico's needs, and make sure the farmers received enough compensation to keep growing sugar in the valley. And keep voting for the party hacks who controlled their lives.

Privatization transformed the mammoth processing facilities, then changed life in the surrounding countryside. Instead of paying the farmers subsidized prices, new owners paid the world price for sugar. The world, particularly Latin America, is awash in sugar, so prices fell, and growers simply stopped growing. The Izúcar and Calipan mills, now the property of Grupo Escorpión—the Scorpion Group—were components of Mexico's biggest Pepsi-Cola bottler, Grupo Mexico, the new boss directing the peasants of Sugar Valley into the global economy. Restructuring had rendered their centuries-old economy obsolete. But the same forces that ended sugar subsidies were imposing a similar restructuring up north. Now Puebla's immigrant sons and daughters were in U.S. cities, competing for service jobs. In this way, immigration was neither the peasant's revenge for NAFTA nor NAFTA's consequence. It was its complement, a symptom of globalization, at once a cause and an effect.

The sons of tiny Zapotitlán Salinas were still pioneers in 1994, but were learning quickly. The signs were everywhere: the new cement-block homes, and newer ones under construction. Although home telephones still were unavailable, the people of Zapotitlán Salinas were making plenty of long-distance calls to relatives in *El Norte,* lining up at the local Telmex office to patch a line through. The most compelling bits of evidence that migration was surging were seen at rooftop level. More than thirty *parabolicos,* satellite dishes, were spotted on hillsides and near the town plaza. In some places, the inverted metal spiderwebs stood on cement foundations, taller than the shacks nearby. The signals they transmitted—major league baseball games, porno movies, game shows—were drawing the children of Zapotitlán Salinas closer to the escape hatch. Technology was also temptress, and all of Mexico her prey.

The Martinez family had sent two sons together. They had returned for a brief vacation a few weeks before. Such a rapid return indicated they had met with success, earning enough cash to finance their homecoming, as well as a new home in Zapotitlán Salinas. Of course, they kept some money in reserve for the inevitable trip back to New York. That would happen at the end of the summer, sometime after the drenching rains and the planting of the corn crop.

"That's up to Julio," said Antonio Martinez, at twenty-three the older of the two brothers. In a crisp checked shirt and straw hat, Antonio dressed who he was, *puro campesino,* the hick from the sticks. He wore dusty jeans and scuffed boots and shoulder-length hair, black as a raven's plumage. *"Puro indio,"* the Mexicans call it, pure Indian. He fingered pearl snap buttons before answering a question, responding carefully with as few words as possible. His gaze barely left the tops of his clunky workboots, which shifted nervously, kicking up clouds of yellow dust.

The Martinez family was in the capital-accumulation stage, and their sons were going to New York to do the accumulating. The Martinez family enterprise was onyx sculpture. Antonio worked with an uncle, fashioning wind chimes from bits of colored stone. Success would depend on their ability to market their wares to consumers more prosperous than their neighbors in Zapotitlán Salinas, and to keep a stream of family accumulators traveling north. Their new cement-block home housed their workshop, humming with the sound of an electric drill in the sleepy siesta afternoon.

Getting to New York was a breeze, Antonio recounted. The *pollera* in Tijuana hooked the brothers to a *coyote* who took them to Los Angeles for just six hundred dollars, or three hundred dollars apiece. Once inside California they paid three hundred dollars each for a plane ticket to New York's Kennedy airport, a domestic flight, free from inspection by immigration officials. "I arrived at night. We went to a friend's house," Antonio continued. "We went by subway. It seemed very strange."

The next day they went looking for jobs. Antonio started as a messenger, working for an Ecuadorian immigrant who ran a delivery service on Wall Street. Later he found restaurant work. An agency in New York can find you a place in a Greek restaurant, Antonio explained, but he didn't care much for the work. "The Greeks have a restaurant on every corner," he said. "But Mexican people prefer to work for Koreans, because you can save more."

The Greeks, Antonio explained, were more scrupulous about work rules, paying five dollars an hour. They also kept to a tight work schedule. The Koreans paid less, just $120 for a six-day, ten-hour-a-day week. That came to just two dollars an hour, less than half what the Greeks paid. Yet Korean stores have advantages the restaurants can't match. The four thousand Korean groceries in New York, many open round-the-clock, offer families like the Martinezes a chance to multiply their employment. A 24-hour workday meant more jobs for more members of the family; the pressure to sell a perishable product meant that workers could also be paid in food. Certainly they could eat on the job, something that would be discouraged in a crowded coffee shop where every table must be a profit center.

That was more business analysis than Antonio needed to know. He only knew that you go to New York to work, eat, and sleep. Considering the alternatives in Zapotitlán Salinas, it wasn't too different from what he would have known if he had stayed. Except that here, in Mexico, no one earned dollars. "The people who have problems are those who go to dances and get drunk and maybe get into fights," he declared firmly. "People who go to work don't have trouble." Antonio fit easily into the immigrant economy: dependable, docile, hard-working. Don't make waves or blow your pay at dances. Anxious to get back to his wind chimes, he politely referred any further questions to his brother.

Julio is everything Antonio is not. Younger, brasher, he lounged in his new house as Critchfield waited an unusually long time for Julio to grant an interview. Julio's home was built on a knoll overlooking the town. Chickens scratched his scrubby front "yard." Gray rain clouds gathered north of town, and the chill that comes before the torrential rains was already in the air. His toying with Critchfield was not only impolite, it was un-Mexican.

But then, Julio had no intention of being Mexican anymore. He emerged shirtless, wearing a pair of smudged white sweatpants and a Pittsburgh Pirates baseball cap, turned backwards. His barrel chest was solid, but a roll of flab across his waistline betrayed a fondness for the easy life. Unlike his brother's long Apache tresses, Julio wore his hair in the short style of an East Los Angeles "homeboy." When he spoke, he exposed a steel wire brace across his lower teeth, another souvenir from *El Norte*. He padded up in floppy sneakers without laces, another ghetto fetish, and used a homeboy's salutation: "What up?"

Julio bantered, but he wouldn't play the simple peasant. Whereas Antonio spoke only Spanish, Julio was an English-only adherent. If Antonio was intimidated by reporters' questions, Julio was indignant. "I already told you that, man," he would snap, then sigh and answer.

Julio was a sharp operator, the kind of quick-thinking leader a family needs to establish itself up north. Between the sneers and glares, Julio revealed himself as an apt student of New York's survival school. After he and his brother were settled in their first jobs, he explained, they plotted a path to their next goal: a place of their own. As any salaried worker knows, it's not what you make but what you keep, and as "guests" in another's apartment, Antonio and Julio knew they were paying more than their fair share of the rent. It was a cost they accepted as newcomers. They expected to surmount these barriers to entry, then pass them on to other rookies as they moved up the ladder. Thus a $500-a-month apartment in Brooklyn's Bushwick section cost the brothers three hundred dollars apiece. That allowed their "host," the senior immigrant, to pocket about a hundred dollars. But out of that he paid the telephone bill and stocked the refrigerator. Before they could rent their own apartment, the brothers decided, they had to find work together. They got lucky with Koo-Koo's Bistro, a yuppie bar on Manhattan's East Side. Turnover is always high in restaurants, particularly for the dishwasher and busboy jobs Julio and Antonio landed. The pay, off the books, was three hundred dollars a week for each man. But the best part of the job was the apartment: a two-bedroom flat on Harlem's 125th Street just west of Fifth Avenue.

Koo-Koo's owner, a Frenchman named Gilbert, owned the building at 125th Street and was happy to install the brothers as tenants. The rent was stiff—nine hundred dollars a month—but the synergy was unbeatable. First, location. Now the brothers could walk to work. That saved the household some five dollars a day on subway fares, or thirty dollars a week. Second, by adding tenants, they reduced their share of the rent to four hundred dollars. Then there was the inherent job security that came from working for their landlord. Gilbert, should he ever have a reason to fire the brothers, would be jeopardizing his ability to collect rent. Worse, he would have embittered tenants, who might destroy his building or complain to the authorities about poor living conditions, or worst, thanks to New York's housing laws, live in the Frenchman's house rent-free, perhaps for months, as he labored in court to have them evicted. The Martinez brothers, of course, were as good tenants as they were workers. By the end of their first year in New York, the brothers were earning close to four thousand dollars a month, and saving almost three thousand of that to send home.

While Antonio the drone concentrated on plates and silverware, Julio was out in the dining room, where his improving language skills allowed him to graduate from busboy to food preparer.

With his promotion came a raise. It was only fifty dollars a week, but there was a bonus: it left his busboy job open. Julio filled it with a cousin newly arrived from Zapotitlán Salinas. He assigned Antonio to keep an eye on the trainee, while he watched both. Julio, in a sense, had become a junior manager, responsible for three jobs in the kitchen: his own, his brother's, and the new guy's.

As the details spilled forth, Julio was describing the making of an entirely new market, one in which so many Mexicans were participating that New York now had defined "market" prices for much of what they bought and sold. Rents, apparently, had stabilized at three hundred dollars a month, no matter what the nominal rate on the lease. Koreans, no matter how flush or spare their enterprise, paid their Mexican help $120 a week. Their own labor had a value stratified in hundred-dollar increments, rising from grocery boy to dishwasher to kitchen manager. The parameters had been set by the mass.

After three years at Koo-Koo's, the brothers were ready to return to Zapotitlán Salinas. Antonio was still washing dishes, but Julio had acquired enough skills to fill a variety of restaurant jobs. He also had contacts: one of the chefs was planning to open a place of his own in Brooklyn, where rents were cheaper and the Mexican community was growing. That's where Julio would go when he returned, knowing a good job was waiting.

Returning to Tehuacán, Critchfield pondered the exodus from Zapotitlán Salinas. "Wages are now six times in New York what they are in Puebla," he calculated, comparing the three hundred dollars Julio and Antonio earned at Koo-Koo's with the fifty dollars *campesinos* were earning each week as farm laborers around Tehuacán. "When it drops to three times," he concluded, "they'll stop coming."

But immigration, while it is very much a numbers game, is much more than numbers. One of Critchfield's early books, *Villages,* describes America's magnetic pull: "One thing we have going for us is the curious love affair most villagers have with America;

they can even be a bit possessive about it. America is becoming everybody's second country . . . America as a symbol, an idea, of the good life, of oomph and vitality and freedom and fun." Thus the numbers don't account for things like teeth braces and laceless sneakers and the lure of being a homeboy.

Critchfield's warning on urban societies having to "cross cultural and political boundaries" for immigrants "to swell their bottom ranks" describes what is happening all over the world. It will happen whether America welcomes or impedes, just as it always has. Walking the streets of New York today, one can't help but feel sympathy with those who say America needs a break, needs some time to assimilate all these strange people, these strange tongues, this strange newness. It's hard not to wonder, with all the unemployed inner-city teenagers, whether it is fair for poor youngsters to have to compete for entry-level jobs with full-grown adults, who are hungrier and more determined to succeed at "the bottom ranks." It's natural to wonder whether the immigrant sea is water lifting our boats to prosperity or an inundation swamping our crafts at their moorings.

It is natural to wonder, as many Americans wonder, whether with all that is being gained by immigration, anything might be getting lost. Traveling to Tehuacán to meet my new neighbors was just one journey in pursuit of an answer to this question. There is an answer, and it is as simple as the relationship between Julio and Antonio, and their ability to work as a team to turn three-hundred-dollar restaurant jobs in New York into an onyx shop four thousand miles away. Their family unity, in other words, lends value to their efforts, which result in real wealth.

And the Martinez family is not unique. This pattern is being repeated by immigrants all over the world. Whether in Brazil, Africa, or Asia, the pattern of family unity is repeated in every immigrant success story. Yet it seldom seems to be part of the growing debate over immigration in America. Given the emphasis in America on family values, on traditional beliefs in right and wrong, it is more than ironic that immigrants are despised as part of the problem, not hailed as the solution.

Across the country the collapse of the family is being answered by new families arriving to share life in a new land. "Collapsed" inner cities are being reclaimed, as neighborhoods that have expelled their middle class for decades are suddenly full of life. Crime declines, and the drug culture begins to wither away. Failed schools become model institutions. What city daily has not written about the refugee valedictorian or the immigrant scholar winning first prize at the science fair? Immigrants don't just renew themselves. They renew us.

In the meantime we are bewildered. Watching another bunch of my new neighbors, Senegalese street peddlers, I can easily see the exotic as chaotic, the initiative as anarchy. They deploy their carts and baggage right in Midtown, on a street corner two blocks from the New York Hilton. First one, then another, then a third rolling rickety tables out on wheels, each choosing a spot beside a pay phone and a subway entrance, where each sits on his haunches. They sit five or ten feet away from their table, perhaps out of some Saharan custom, perhaps only to fool the vendor police who sweep Midtown now and again, trying to contain a scourge that has only grown bigger with each passing year. One peddler has a New York Bureau of Consumer Affairs tag pinned to his chest, and from his "licensed" table the other two draw their wares. All three were selling bootleg "I Love New York" T-shirts, the same ones ground out in dusty lofts by Mexican girls working over silkscreen presses, watched over by Sikh wives always scowling. The one with the license was having a fine afternoon, selling shirts for six dollars, two for ten, or three for fourteen to happy tourists. Anyone who paused long enough to hear his singsong pitch would be smitten. "What is it for you today, beautiful?" he chirped in syncopated, French-inflected street cool. "You love New York? It loves you, too."

At noon, in tune with the Midtown throng, the three black men threw canvas sheets over their tables, and the two outlanders joined their licensed chum for a council. Lunch. As a Chinese kid rode by on a bicycle—obviously a delivery boy from a nearby restaurant—the Africans waved him down. Within a very few minutes, they were munching chicken and fried rice. Suddenly the corner of Fifty-fifth and Sixth could have been the casbah in Senegal, or Haiti, or medieval Europe.

It's that kind of image that makes today's immigration so bewildering. What conceivable good can come from this scene? One man has a license, sure, but he is using his entry at the margins of legitimacy to support two more illegal vendors. And they're selling counterfeit T-shirts, for cash, made by people who probably don't pay the help minimum wage. What's more, they're blocking the pay phone. And leaving chicken bones all over the sidewalk.

How to defend this anarchy? It offends, it flouts our authority on every level. Except to say that it is essential. This, in microcosm, is the entry level that immigrants seek in order to join us. Those T-shirts earn the dollars that are reclaiming whole neighborhoods, reclaimed by the Mexicans whose wives and sisters print T-shirts for scowling Sikhs, and by the Senegalese who peddle them. Think of the tourists paying a tax that is delivered directly to the neighborhoods where the peddlers and the printers live—neighborhoods where jobs are rare and the ability to decipher the means to bring Midtown dollars home is rarer still. Then think of the Senegalese accountants, real estate brokers, taxicab owners, and restaurateurs who began life here as street peddlers. If they didn't find this place to start, they'd never go forward. One day they'll be among those complaining about the chicken bones, and much sooner than most people realize.

Every wave of immigration, including this one, yields its heroes: A. P. Gianini in turn-of-the-century San Francisco; Albert Einstein in the 1930s; An Wang, the computer visionary, in the 1960s. It is through these success stories that many argue in favor of immigration. Yet what endures is the contribution of the mass. Call it the "critical mass," which creates the environment that allows success to happen. Either by pooling savings or by founding schools or by providing credit, the immigrant mass is the rich soil the best of the new Americans root in. Immigration represents the triumph of the community over the individual, yet is the base from which each individual success story springs.

Immigrant families are the building blocks. Today, for nearly 85 percent of all legal immigrants, and probably as many illegal ones, family unification is the primary motive for coming to America. Yet family unification is derided by anti-immigration "restrictionists" as a pernicious loophole, nay, a gaping chasm. They are mistaken. The family unit is the most efficient engine of enterprise. Families manage resources equitably and balance competing needs without losing sight of one basic goal: the survival of the unit. New York is being reborn by immigrant families, who manage scarce earnings effectively. As they manage, they repopulate desolate communities, starting with apartments like the one Antonio and Julio Martinez shared. Immigrant families save better than American-born families do, educate their children better, and raise their living standards faster than the native-born. It is no accident that almost every successful company started as a family business, as an idea hatched around the dinner table. It is no accident that so many current American success stories began in an immigrant household. The immigrant family, when compared with the many divorced, dysfunctional, and disintegrating families among native-born Americans, is the embodiment of an "authentic" village culture, exactly as Richard Critchfield predicted in Tehuacán.

Julio and Antonio returned to New York shortly after our visit. It is sad that Richard Critchfield was unable to follow their progress. Shortly after returning to the United States later that year, he suffered a stroke while visiting Washington. He died the first week of December. His Tehuacán mission was his last and ended too soon for him to test his theories about the villager's rebirth in the city.

The villager's desire to be here is not, as he wrote, the "one thing" we have going for us, but the many. This book is about the many things immigrants import to America—in a sense, importing America itself. They are Julio Martinez and Marcia Holness in New

York. They are Hermes Reis, a Brazilian building a family business cleaning other families' homes in Framingham, Massachusetts. They are the Amins, a clan of Gujarati Indians running motels in eastern Tennessee, and Thomas Lam, a Chinese farmer in Oxnard, California. They are Senegalese peddlers, Haitian hotel workers, Filipino postal clerks, and Pakistani cab drivers.

Their stories make this book. Their stories make us.

CHAPTER ONE

New York:
The Critical Mass

This is a city where you can make money. The people are buying because they have jobs here, and money to spend.

Adolfo Soto,
Tortilleria Buena Vista, Brooklyn, New York

★

The four corners where Bushwick Avenue meets Flushing could be a movie set for quintessential New York blight. The 360-degree view offers the sweat-beige brick of a public housing project, the charred black of a burned-out liquor store, and the smoky gray of a 24-hour discount gas station, its attendants attending behind thick yellow-toned Plexiglas. This is the neighborhood that police have dubbed "The Well," for the depths of drug-induced depravity. It is bounded by the Bushwick Houses projects to the west and abandoned lots to the north, many razed after rioting in the mid-1970s.

The brightest corner belongs to a gaudy Dominican restaurant, whose major traffic on a frigid Saturday afternoon is provided by the homeboys in hooded sweatshirts, who have staked out a piece of nearby sidewalk. They pass in and out of the restaurant to make quick calls from a public phone by the entrance. Lookouts, no doubt, for the local drug lord. Brooklyn, New York, in the 1990s.

Down the block, at 913 Flushing, a line of customers snakes into the gutter, silent figures waiting for their daily fix.

Crack cocaine? Heroin?

No, *señor*. Tortillas.

They line up like this every Saturday at Tortilleria Piaxtla, Inc., and on Sunday, too. Brooklyn's first tortilla factory is one of five manufacturers of the Mexican staple to open in the city since 1986. In many ways, the tortilla wave is reminiscent of the 1880s, when the number of Brooklyn breweries peaked at forty-three. As the long line attests, business is booming for owner and founder Fernando Sanchez, despite the burgeoning competition. "A typical Mexican family, mama and papa and four kids, goes through two or three packages of my tortillas every time they sit down to eat," he says.

That's about a hundred tortillas per family, every twenty-four hours. Sanchez went from producing four thousand tortillas a week his first year to nearly four hundred thousand in 1992, processing roughly two hundred tons of corn flour into saucer-sized pancakes every month. And from just two co-workers when he started, Sanchez now employs fifty, virtually all immigrants like himself. "*Puros Poblanos,*" he said, waving his hand through a haze of corn dust, pure peasants. These are *paisanos,* like Sanchez from the Mexican state of Puebla. Tortilleria Piaxtla is named for his hometown.

Not too shabby for a man who entered the United States in 1968, unskilled and unschooled. Sanchez settled in the South Bronx, the notorious Burning Bronx of rampant arson and gang wars between the Savage Skulls and the pretenders to their turf. Sanchez lived in a tenement on Fox Avenue, the heart of the combat zone. "The first year the cops threw a Puerto Rican kid out a sixth-floor window," he recalled. "I think he died."

Sanchez eked his way through a series of factory, then restaurant, jobs, rising from dishwasher, to cook, to chef's assistant at a Midtown French restaurant. Along the way he staked two more brothers to their passage from Piaxtla, and brought his wife up from the neighboring village of Chinantla. In 1975, he got busted by *La Migra,* the Immigration and Naturalization Service, for working without a permit, and had to pay heavy legal fees to keep from being deported. Three years later, however, Sanchez was able to legalize his status.

By 1986, with ten thousand dollars in savings, he was ready to make his move, buying a used tortilla press from a company in Los Angeles, and shipping it east to an abandoned garage on Flushing Avenue. He called in some of the favors he had earned through a decade of money-lending to friends and relatives, and Tortilleria Piaxtla was born. Today, with $4 million worth of annual sales, he owns the building and a modest house besides. His six trucks bring product as far south as Philadelphia. On Saturdays, he ships product for long-haul deliveries, his men slipping French labels into the packs of tortillas bound for Montreal's growing Latino community. It's another example of New York's most enduring legend, that of the humble immigrant building a fortune.

They call Fernando Sanchez "El Gordo," "the Fat One," and the Fat One was his original brand name. A caricature of a fat man in a chef's toque and apron, surrounded by fresh corn, was the original logo. Over the years he has acquired other start-up brands, consolidating sales. But around Brooklyn, people still ask for the Fat One brand when they buy tortillas, so he kept the design. He kept the other brands' designs, too, which means at hundreds of tiny *bodegas* around town, customers have a choice of tortillas— even though many come from just this one factory. It's a kind of custom, he allows—people buy what they know. He still works as he did a decade ago, still wearing an old jumpsuit to the office, skinnier now than the fat chef on his packages. His new car sports vanity plates: GORDO.

Tortilleria Piaxtla has become a mini-empire: a chain of Brooklyn bakeries, a grocery store, and a satellite tortilleria in Providence, Rhode Island, run by El Gordo's younger brother. A cousin, Felix Sanchez, has a rival empire in Passaic, New Jersey—Puebla Foods. The two men grew up together, herding goats for Fernando's uncle before working as traveling salesmen around Piaxtla. But something happened to distance the two men—neither will say what—and since coming to New York, each has pursued separate business strategies. Sometimes Fernando and Felix duel for floor space—tortillas are always sold out of the carton, stacked near the cash register—in New York. Felix is also extending his reach into canned goods, sausages, and cheese. He scours farm auctions in places like Wisconsin for used dairy machines and rents space in idle processing plants to roll his spicy meats. Puebla Foods has gotten big enough for a profile in *Forbes* magazine.

Fernando likes lending more than managing, and builds his influence helping one *paisano* open a shop or another add an outlet to a chain of bakeries. But either way, both men are part of a rising tide of consumption that came from a valley back home, and that consumption is lifting New York. The line that stretches past Fernando's shop on weekends is part of that trend. How many *paisanos* are waiting in line, pinching pennies by paying the wholesale price, saving to be the next El Gordo? Sanchez knows who some of them are—he staked some of them or their brothers for their trip north. The best of the lot will be the ones he invests with, and the tide will swell once more.

And so, besides his own progress, Sanchez is responsible for at least three other tortillerias in New York, all operated by former employees who learned the business in his shop, then took a chance on their own. Usually they took customers, too, but always with Sanchez's blessing. Why not? They bought used equipment when Tortilleria Piaxtla was ready to upgrade to something better, letting Sanchez grow with the cash raised from the sale. Agronomists would see in the tortilleria proliferation a metaphor for growth—the leavings of one generation feeding the sprouts of a second. Every carton of Sanchez tortillas sold is like a burst of pollen, feeding the Mexicans who might one day dream of opening a business to feed others.

Economists, viewing the output of Tortilleria Piaxtla and Puebla Foods and the other new tortilla vendors, would see something different. Call it the Tortilla Index. From zero to over a million discs a day, all in less than a decade. On a bar chart the rise would be steady and straight up, like a steep staircase or mountain range. If the index were inverted to cover neighborhoods, it would show an expansion spreading out from New York's poorest quarters—East Harlem, Bushwick, and the South Bronx of the Savage Skulls—to less desperate but still poor districts, like Kensington, Corona, Sunset Park, and the Lower East Side. Every hundred tortillas, to use El Gordo's calculation, would be a family. Every family would have at least one wage-earner, and more likely two. Thus, every hundred tortillas would represent monthly rent being paid, baby clothes being bought, movies being seen, and wages being earned. In other words, a million tortillas a day would mean ten thousand households spending their incomes on the margins of the working class. Ten thousand families who weren't there ten years ago.

Fernando Sanchez is no economist. But he knows spending power when he sees it, and he knows what it can do to restore a blighted city. In 1992, Sanchez bought the building he had been renting since 1986 to make tortillas. The next year he bought the space next door for expansion. He also bought a vacant lot across the street, paying the city thirty thousand dollars while restoring what had been abandoned real estate to its tax rolls. He spent another fifty thousand dollars building a factory-outlet store for his customers, many now his neighbors. Sanchez saw them come. Many work in the no-name garment lofts along Flushing Avenue, dingy square hulks where the only signs of activity are the handwritten notices—*Se Necesitan Mujeres* ("Women Wanted," a sure indicator of garment work)—and clouds of steam venting from the windows where finished pieces are pressed before shipping. "When we started here, every night someone was robbed leaving my place," Sanchez recalled in 1995. Teenagers from the nearby projects preyed on the Mexicans who came to Tortilleria Piaxtla to work or shop. But as the block filled with new families, robbing got harder to do.

Mexicans filled The Well. By being there in ever-growing numbers, they made crime not pay. By filling the old garment lofts, they filled their pockets, which filled the apartment houses and filled Fernando Sanchez's dream to open his store, Plaza Piaxtla. A critical mass from Mexico brought safety in numbers. "Now the whole block is Mexican people," Sanchez said. "Everyone working, no one on welfare. That's why no more they rob my people."

The critical mass affects urban life in many ways, ways few of us can even imagine, much less see. In 1994, for example, the ten-cent phone call returned to New York. For the first time in almost two decades, a public telephone call in New York City cost less than a quarter. That same year, the price of a city bus trip actually declined. And while it wasn't quite the free lunch of the fin de siècle saloon, along one street in Manhattan something very similar appeared: the $2.95 all-you-can-eat buffet.

The ten-cent pay phone was not available citywide, nor would a dime (nine cents, actually) ring any party. It was a special line, connecting New York to the Dominican Republic. And nine cents only bought a minute. Nonetheless, the same lines connected calls anywhere in the United States for thirty cents, including anywhere else in the city. In New York, that was a savings of around 15 percent over any coin call made outside Manhattan, and a 200 percent savings over a coin-operated call elsewhere in the state. Calling New Jersey, Connecticut, or California offered even bigger savings: less than a third of the cost on MCI, the long-distance phone carrier that purports to be the cheapest in the nation.

The phones were available in practically every corner of the city, sometimes hundreds on a block. They could be accessed regardless whether the caller had ever owned a telephone or used a telephone credit card before. In neighborhoods where there were lots of phones—most neighborhoods—they offered a dizzying variety of prices and destinations. Mexico and Colombia for 29 cents a minute; Nigeria for $1.25 a minute, and Senegal for 99 cents; Haiti, Trinidad, Jamaica, and Peru for 49 cents or less. Customers simply walked up, paid cash for the number of minutes they desired, then entered a booth where a telephone might be ringing already as the call went through. A timer is regulated by a computer, the type used at self-service gas stations to run the pump until a prepaid total is met.

For the entrepreneurs running these services, start-up costs are as low as five thousand dollars—enough to rent a storefront, put a sign outside, and buy the computer software. By 1995, many phone parlors had dispensed with the computers to become little more than vendors of ten-dollar "tele-connect" cards, the same vouchers on sale at any newsstand or convenience store. By offering card and phone together, the parlors relied on someone else to access lines overseas. Their niche was providing on-site phones to cardholders, something newsstands and stores still could not do.

As for the buses, the fare reduction began with a few select routes in one borough, Queens. Beyond the reach of subway lines, in leafy neighborhoods like Cambria Heights and Laurelton, people rely on buses to catch the subway into Manhattan. Most mornings there are as many as a hundred thousand commuters waiting on street corners for slow-moving buses, which charge the same fare as the subway: at that time $1.25, one way. These commuters live in what New Yorkers call two-fare zones, paying twice what subway-only riders pay, even though both are served by one provider, the Metropolitan Transportation Authority. In other cities, a simple transfer slip evens the price for all. But the MTA runs a chronic deficit and doesn't issue free transfers for the subway.

Into this breach a guerrilla army swarmed—minivans following the same routes as the MTA's buses. Charging a dollar per ride, they cut the price of the two-fare commute by fifty cents a day. Faster and more numerous than the lumbering city buses, they also cut time. As with the telephone parlors, most providers (that is, the vans' owners and drivers) are immigrants, and so are most of the riders. Perhaps because they are fellow immigrants or because they are fighting for a piece of the city's business, the van drivers are flexible with their services. If a rider wants to get out somewhere that is not, technically, a scheduled bus stop, the driver complies. In a city bus? Forget about it!

Like the phone parlors, the minivans are a start-up entrepreneur's dream: four thousand dollars or so for a used but roadworthy vehicle, fifty dollars for a one-time registration fee, and ten dollars a year for an identification sticker. In 1992, the MTA estimated these "jitneys" competing with the city were siphoning off as much as a million dollars a week in lost bus fares. For years, the city had waged war on the guerrillas—deploying transit inspectors to harass drivers, barring vans from using the city's bus routes, issuing summonses. At one point the city tried to discourage vans from discharging their passengers by designating curbs near subway entrances no-parking zones. That most of the drivers were black West Indians cast another dilemma. No one wanted to add racism to the MTA's already poor image as an overstaffed, underperforming bastion of political patronage.

So, in 1992, the city blinked. For the first time in living memory, bus fares were reduced. For the Q4, Q5, Q42, Q84, and Q85 lines, the MTA offered its Fare Deal. Undercutting the jitneys, the new $1.50 fare bought a round-trip pass, good for either the day or any two-fare transfer. About ten thousand riders per day were lured back to the MTA—not enough to oust the guerrillas, but a step in the direction of profitable, peaceful coexistence. Three years into the Fare Deal policy, both jitneys and city buses were thriving, each having found ways to divide the market profitably. In 1994, the Bronx's Bx22 line from Castle Hill and Brooklyn's B46 in Bushwick were admitted to the Fare Deal family. Perestroika on wheels was spreading.

At the giant Jamaica Center transit terminal—where bus, jitney, and subway lines converge—commuters savor their choices. The jitney yard looks as if it has arrived whole from some Third World marketplace. Drivers park their vans in long rows waiting for passengers to fill their seats. Some send "shouters" into the throngs of commuters to corral the last fannies needed to fill their benches. Here everyone is a niche marketer, catering to a narrow route or a particular neighborhood. Abundant consumption leads to a proliferation of options. And everyone—driver, passenger, shouter, the food vendors who make a business selling to the others—is black. Jamaica Center might as well be Kingston, Jamaica.

The $2.95 lunch—that was for Bengali food, and only along Manhattan's Sixth Street. Like Chinatown, a mile to the south,

Sixth Street was one of those critical-mass districts that appeared unplanned in the mid-1970s, at the beginning of the city's immigrant boom. Like Dominicans in Washington Heights or the Jamaicans in Flatbush, so many had congregated so densely into one area, their mass could distort existing laws of supply and demand. A $2.95 all-you-can-eat lunch? New Yorkers can't buy a cheese sandwich at that price! But in 1995, the competitive price for the buffet special on Bengali Alley fell from $4.95 to $3.95 to $2.95. Every restaurateur knows the real money comes from marking up soft drinks and beer. Bengali owners decided profits depended on slinging enough spicy curry and *dahl* to keep drinks flowing.

The discount phone call, the cut-rate guerrilla bus lines, and the $2.95 buffet arrived in New York at about the same time, and for about the same reason. New York was returning to its immigrant past, restructuring itself as the mass of newcomers challenged business-as-usual. Throughout the city, the all-cash phone parlors became part of a visual tapestry capturing the diversity unfolding on every block. Phone-line "bundlers" jockeyed to win over dominant groups, offering special discounts to certain countries. A sharp-eyed pedestrian could measure the flow of immigrants anywhere in the city by watching for tele-connect bargains. Roosevelt Avenue was Queens's link to the Andes: Colombians, Peruvians, and Ecuadorians. Black Brooklyn's east-west artery, Eastern Parkway, became a lifeline to the Caribbean. Farther east, Nigerians joined Haitians and Egyptians along Utica Avenue. Asian enclaves rose in Brooklyn's Sunset Park and Coney Island, and in Queens between the two airports, in neighborhoods called Flushing, Rego Park, Kew Gardens, and Whitestone. French Harlem emerged next to Spanish Harlem, as Guineans, Malians, Ivorians, and Senegalese found homes between 110th and 125th Streets. Spanish Harlem now meant Mexicans and Central Americans, replacing the Puerto Ricans who came forty years before.

When new communities appear this rapidly, they become an engine of growth. Capital is raised, homes are bought, businesses are launched. The pattern of ethnic specialization, a New York trait of long standing, also plays a role. Ethnic niches make it possible for immigrants to be absorbed, trained, and launched toward better jobs, often without formal training. Be it pizza delivery or taxi driving, one brother showing another how is all a newcomer needs to unlock the mystery of employment.

Thus, Julio and Antonio Martinez entered a city where almost all the restaurant work was being done by Latinos and almost all the dry cleaners were run by Koreans. Koreans also had all the little stores peddling fresh fruit and vegetables, while Yemenites and Dominicans had almost all the little stores that don't. Almost all the newsstands were run by Gujarati Indians and Pakistanis. They found a city where English-speaking Africans worked as security guards, while French-speakers washed cars. West Indians dominated as nannies and home nurses; Filipinos ran the hospitals. So many Israelis launched so many car services—Haifa, Tel Aviv, Carmel, Jaffa, Sabra, Sinai, Shalom—a customer only had to recall an Israeli word to find one through directory assistance. The drivers themselves were invariably Muslim immigrants—invariably from places hostile to Israel, like Iraq, Iran, or Afghanistan.

By organizing by community, immigrants imposed brutal efficiencies on the delivery of goods and services. That is, they were able to bring the world price to New York. No one pays more than pennies for a public phone call in Latin America because no one can. The phone company's profits are minuscule per call, but the volume is enormous. With the phone parlors, immigrant Latinos proved that economies of scale work the same along Roosevelt Avenue and Broadway as they do in Mexico City or Santo Domingo. And all-cash transactions meant no bills to mail, no customer profiles to maintain. For phone calls, for bus rides, for construction work, pizza delivery, and a thousand other niche jobs, a new law of economics emerged: cash rules. But only efficiency makes cash profitable.

The evidence is all over Midtown—simple photocopied flyers fluttering from doorways, phone booths, and awnings. Along West Thirty-second Street, the heart of the Korean Gift District, twin sheets fly back to back off the steel casing of a pay phone. One, in English, beckons:

HELP WANTED!
We Need Bilingual People
Spanish, Italian, Chinese,
French, German, Hungarian
and Slavik [sic] Language

Then, in much smaller print, it says:

(*Or any other language!!*)
WORK AT HOME!
WORK AT OFFICE!
JUST WORK!
We Need Help Worldwide!

Along the bottom, a fringe of strips with a Queens phone number has been snatched almost bare. JUST WORK! turns out to be "an international manufacturer looking for distributors, consultants, supervisors," according to an answering-machine message, for an unnamed product. That means wholesalers and retailers, who are invited to be interviewed at a Midtown hotel ballroom later that week. "Distributors, consultants, supervisors" are all euphemisms for independent contractors willing to work without a formal salary.

"WORK AT HOME! WORK IN OFFICE!" In other words, a shipment has arrived, and someone is looking for "workers" to buy lots and move the merchandise.

The ad's twin, written in Spanish, offers work "STARTING NOW." Positions start at $420 a week, with "NO REQUIREMENTS, NO DOCUMENTS, NO EXPERIENCE" necessary. Free training. Here the contact is a voice-mail drop, an electronic receptionist asking for a name and phone number, a common recruiting device that renders the employer untraceable.

The amount of informal work being advertised throughout New York is astonishing. Sewing work is the most common, followed by bilingual telephone reception. Both types abound in Manhattan's Gift District, a historic manufacturing center between Thirty-fourth and Twenty-third Streets on the West Side. Since the early 1970s, this area had suffered steady decline, effected by the demise of the Garment District directly to the north. As the fashion industry steadily lost jobs to Asia and Latin America, the fringe businesses housed in lofts nearby withered. Along Broadway, stately old hotels grew shabby. Once frequented by the buyers who came from around the country to order inventory for department stores, they now housed homeless families, welfare recipients, transients, and prostitutes. The looming hulk of the Martinique, on West Thirty-second Street, was once a choice location. By 1981, it had degenerated into a poorhouse worthy of Dickens. Heavy steel doors replaced the once welcoming lobby entrance, to protect children inside from predators on the street, and to protect shoppers at nearby Macy's from the children. Everywhere outside, homeless men and women, many addicted to drugs and alcohol, crowded sidewalks and vest-pocket parks.

Koreans, in many ways the most entrepreneurial of the new immigrants, led the revival. As early as the 1960s, they discovered in Harlem a market for one of Korea's earliest export industries, the harvesting and weaving of women's hair for hairpieces. Harlem linked Koreans to African immigrants who, in the 1960s and 1970s, also were casting about for businesses. Many became traders, buying hairpieces from the Koreans—and later skin lighteners and other African-American cosmetics from Korean wholesalers. As the Koreans spread throughout Manhattan, they found other niches. By the late 1970s, the Harlem Koreans had moved downtown, many to the garment lofts west of Fifth Avenue, replacing Jews as subcontractors to the Garment District, just as many old-line garment manufacturers had been replaced by Korean firms back home. Eventually they would found the Gift District, a thirty-square-block grid bordered by Fifth Avenue on the east, the garment district to the north, Toy Avenue (West Twenty-third Street) to the south, and the wholesale floral district to the west.

The Gift District is the emerging Third World in microcosm: cheap manufactures from Asia unwrapped and stacked by Mexicans, bought and sold—rather resold—by every imaginable immigrant type. The Gift District is by the immigrant, of the immigrant, and for the immigrant, where the output of Third World industry meets a Third World salesforce, which sells to the same dishwashers, office cleaners, vegetable-cutters, and nannies who are their neighbors somewhere else in the city. By jamming every available space with their offerings—watches, hairpieces, costume jewelry, toys, flatware, perfumes—the Gift District merchants created the mother of all the little sales nooks that have turned Manhattan into a single sprawling casbah. Anything that can be bought quickly, and for cash, is warehoused in and distributed from the Gift District.

Working first with the Africans, then bringing in the Iranians, Iraqi, Indians, and Chinese, the Koreans turned these blocks into a gigantic warehouse. Whether at street level, below street level, or in an upstairs loft, what must be over fifty thousand doorways prominently display the admonition "Wholesale Only." Others insist that a taxpayer I.D. is a requirement for entry. But it's rare to see a paying customer produce such a document or even be asked to. White Americans, besides the few who already work here, are almost always turned away by the (almost always) Chinese or Korean proprietors. Yet Dominican women pick easily through stacks of cheap dinnerware sets. Ecuadorians fill shopping carts with jugs of shampoo. Jamaican teens buy single five-dollar hairpieces they braid into their own locks on the spot. Trade is brisk here, regulation merely a rumor.

At 1162 Broadway, floor space goes for twelve dollars per square foot on a 25-×-40-foot area. Take the whole thing and it's a little cheaper, nine thousand dollars. In 1992, the same space went for six thousand dollars, leased by Korean Plaza, a Korean realtor. "Costume jewelry, okay. Gold, okay," a Mr. Kim, the building manager, said when asked about the FOR LEASE sign, barely looking up as he swept a space against the back wall. No more than six feet high, he said it would go for three thousand dollars a month once the walls were in. "Perfume is a good business too. But we already have a perfume business here."

The goal, Mr. Kim explained, is to offer a one-stop shopping mall inside with a mix of retail stalls. Costume jewelry was on his list of acceptable items, along with clothing and cosmetics—anything to attract buyers without cannibalizing other tenants' sales. "Filipino jewelry is a good business too," he said, pointing to a man and woman hunched over a set of tiny tools behind a square of Plexiglas. "They have their own factory, importing from the Philippines."

Mr. Kim expected a high turnover, and he didn't care how long a tenant stayed. No proof of citizenship, no Social Security number was necessary to move in, just the standard two-months' rent plus security deposit—$18,000. In cash. First come, first served. "I got storage downstairs, you get your own bathroom. Open and close your own gate," he said, sweeping vigorously. "The whole building is wired with alarms. Good security."

Across the street, at 1225 Broadway, is the African building. The anchor store in this "mall" is Hair Zone, Inc., run by Koreans at street level. The signs are in French, the clientele in bright African *boubous*, wraparound gowns, and long Moroccan *jelabahs*. Senegalese tailors and traders, the Mexicans who work for them, and the Koreans who finance them speak a combination sign language and pidgin English. Upstairs are eight floors of storerooms, showrooms, packing rooms, and money changers to serve the merchants below. Kara International, a phone parlor catering to Senegalese peddlers, occupies three offices on the top floor. One shop has the phones, another a travel agency, and the third a money transfer service. According to Bamba Niang, the happy proprietor, his little corner of the Gift District handles $10 million worth of business a year, this from a space no bigger than two or three hundred square feet.

While manufacturing has declined with the withering of the Garment District, the area is arguably more viable as a jobs haven than at any time in the past two decades. The Gift District is where dozens of Korean accountants can be found at one address— 6 West Thirty-second Street—once a stack of garment lofts stretching a city block, now a Rubik's cube of one-desk cubbyholes. Private offices here go for $450 a month unfurnished or $499 with desk and chair. Either way, a pittance for anyone needing a New

York address to start moving product in from Asia. Tenants are obliged to share secretarial and mailroom facilities with others. But they can all use the plush conference room at the mezzanine level—turn right at the floor-to-ceiling fish tank, past the pool of receptionists. The hotels, many now owned by Koreans, are filled again with out-of-town buyers, even out-of-continent buyers. Along West Thirty-second Street, kimchee has replaced kosher at delicatessens. Oriental apothecaries—with their stuffed black bears, mounted elk heads, and other rustic fetishes—thrive where Judaica shops once lived. Between doorways, walls pucker with peeling layers of posters hawking next weekend's Miss East Asia pageant in Flushing, the KorBowl bowling league, and special dinners touting "investment strategies to be discussed." On side streets off Broadway, the little shops are humming again—not with sewing machines and steam presses, but with calculators and computers.

Somehow, in a way no one could have predicted, the mass rejuvenated a neighborhood. As the Gift District evolved into Supply Central for a thousand outlying shopping strips, those areas, too, began to stir with enterprise.

The New York that immigrants like Julio and Antonio entered was booming, rising on a tide of population growth that was bigger than any the city had experienced since the early years of the century. For these immigrants, the old frontier of wide-open spaces west of the Mississippi had been replaced by wide-open blocks— literally, after years of abandonment and arson—in the South Bronx, and in the Brooklyn neighborhoods of East New York, Bushwick, Flatbush, and Brownsville. The wide-open spaces left by businesses abandoning the city were among the first that newcomers rushed to fill. As just one indicator of immigrant enterprise, the Census Bureau recorded an enormous leap in minority-owned businesses in New York between 1987 and 1992. Black-owned firms jumped from 17,400 to almost 36,000. The number of Hispanic companies more than tripled, from just over 10,000 businesses to over 34,000. Asian businesses, the biggest slice of ethnic enterprise, almost doubled, from almost 27,000 to more than 46,000, with more than 90 percent of all businesses owned and

operated by immigrants. Most of the growth in all three sectors—
and for the Asians, virtually all the growth—came from immigrant
entrepreneurs.

By the mid-1990s the city was awash in independent contractors, many of them foreign-born. Everyone from the Mexican
dishwasher to the Haitian cleaning lady could be an instant entrepreneur. People, no matter how poor or uneducated, encountered
no difficulty managing themselves as businessmen. The long-
awaited Great Service Economy had come at last, replacing the
city's shrunken manufacturing base with a new class of worker.
Some enterprises existed at margins so meager few Americans
could imagine their appeal. But a foreigner could.

Consider Diarra, an immigrant from Mali, who delivers groceries for the Food Emporium supermarket on upper Broadway.
He is twenty-six years old and stocky, one of the coal-black, barrel-
chested Bambara people who have been coming to America since
the 1600s. His English is good, but his French is better. Diarra
makes just 85 cents per delivery, with no minimum guarantee on
the number of deliveries he makes each day. He says he never
earns less than three hundred dollars a week. And he pays taxes,
through a referral agency that places Africans in markets all over
the city. Chains like the Food Emporium, Gristede's, and Sloan's
pay less than a dollar per delivery to the "contractors," all of whom
anticipate that their grateful customers will match that payment or
perhaps double it with a generous tip. Few African supermarket
boys earn less than fifty dollars a day. For Diarra, it's an attractive
wage.

Living in Harlem, he earns more than many of his neighbors,
even though on the surface he earns less than the minimum wage.
In Diarra's case, the formal value of his labor—85 cents per work
unit—is little more than it would be back in Mali. Diarra is practicing a form of market arbitrage—moving his assets from a market
where values are depressed to where they can be deployed for
greater rewards. This is exactly what hundreds of Latin American
and Asian corporations did in the early 1990s by listing shares of

stock on U.S. exchanges. Instead of relying on local capital in Brazil, Mexico, China, and India to fuel growth, they made shares available in the developed world, where megasavers in the form of pension funds, insurance companies, and mutual funds had capital to spare. The developed world is just as generous rewarding immigrant labor as it is its capitalists.

Some, like Miguel Caceres, need not even be formally employed.

A short man shaped like a fireplug, Miguel Caceres left two children in Mexico to come to New York. On a frigid February day he was on the street, looking for work in Jackson Heights, another immigrant stronghold. In Mexico, he would be a *jornalero*, or day worker, allowed to make about three dollars for every ten hours swinging a machete in a field. In New York, he works construction.

Caceres shares a basement room in Richmond Hill, Queens, with three other young men from his village, Acatlán, in southern Puebla, each of the roommates paying two hundred dollars a month for rent and food. When work was scarce, as it was that winter, they ran an account with their landlady, a woman called Petra, who had emigrated from Puebla several years before. Miguel's day typically begins at 5:30 A.M., when he catches the subway to Roosevelt Avenue. There, under the rumbling subway cars, about a hundred men gather each morning. They are hoping for jobs paying anywhere from twenty-five to a hundred dollars a day. After working fairly regularly through the previous summer and autumn, Miguel found his situation had become much more tenuous by February, relying on jobs that lasted for two or three days at a time, often waiting a week between assignments.

An everyday scene from the immigration front in Texas or California, the "shape-up" line was a relatively new phenomenon in New York in the early 1990s. On Roosevelt Avenue, the hardest hour is between eight o'clock and nine, when the street fills with commuters, and vans pausing to pick up laborers have to dodge buses and traffic cops to gather their teams. Here the market is like a Wall Street trading floor, rewarding the quick and the daring.

Transactions happen so quickly there is no time for negotiation. "You don't ask what they're paying," Miguel explains as the trucks and vans rumble by, "you just get in."

Roosevelt Avenue is where three subway lines converge. It's also where many of the businesses that cater to illegal aliens are concentrated, such as the storefront phone parlors where undocumented Mexicans place person-to-person calls home. The remittance shops, storefronts that specialize in sending money home, are always closed at shape-up time. Theirs is an evening business— when cash is in hand. For those with lesser willpower, there are cut-rate brothels upstairs, where intimacy costs fifty dollars per half hour, punctuated by the pounding of subway cars outside. Miguel stays clear of the whores and proudly declares he saved five hundred dollars to send home to his wife for Christmas, before his current run of bad luck.

Roosevelt Avenue also is where immigrant New York mixes and mingles. The workers may speak only Spanish, but the employers are Greek, Chinese, Korean, Russian, and Israeli. Occasionally, even a white American will drive by, looking for a gardener or someone to help unload a truck. Chinese hire mainly for construction. Koreans seem to have a lock on demolition, painting, and asbestos removal. The previous summer, Miguel got three weeks' work from a Korean contractor, washing down apartment walls with acid. "It was a big job. Four hundred fifty-two rooms in a big apartment building," he recalled, crinkling his nose with the memory of the acrid fumes.

A white van with the name "Yoon Dam Construction" painted on one door appeared just before nine. From his seat behind the wheel, a foreman quickly waved three men into the back, where they took seats on buckets of masonry compound. "Painting," Miguel said with a sigh as he watched the van drive off. Across the street, in a blue van heavy with coiled electric conduits, another contractor interviewed two men for a job. The Korean knew enough Spanish to quiz each applicant on wiring circuits, eventually choosing the smaller of the two for the job. The also-ran crawled out through the sliding door as the van sped away. "Two weeks.

Fifty dollars a day," he reported to the cluster of disappointed but hopeful faces. "Good job."

It is a cliché in America that if you are willing to relocate overseas, you can live like a king on an American salary. In the case of Miguel Caceres, the same can be said for a Mexican living on a Mexican salary in New York. By his own reckoning, Caceres was working two or three days out of every ten, earning an average of fifty dollars each working day. That works out to $150 every ten days, or fifteen dollars per day. That's five times what a *campesino* makes hacking weeds in cornfields in Puebla. Now compare a day's pay in the United States with a day's pay in Mexico. The peasant's lot in Mexico is improved upon significantly in New York. Of the fifteen dollars Miguel Caceres earns each day, $3.50 goes toward rent, and about the same for the meals Petra prepares. Thirty tortillas cost him a dollar, a pound of dried beans slightly less. The immigrant can certainly eat better in New York than he can at home, and his apartment, even shared with three others, probably would be more spacious than whatever he left in Puebla—an adobe shack far from a town or even a paved road, where there would be no running water, no phone, and no electricity. As long as he saves three dollars more for subway fare to Roosevelt Avenue, he has all he needs to compete for another day's work.

That is not to say that at Miguel Caceres's level, life is bountiful. At this rung, work is hard and security is rare. Sometimes workers are told to wait for the last day to be paid for the job, then find out the last day was yesterday. Sometimes workers are paid with personal checks that bounce. Sometimes they are underpaid, working sixty- and seventy-hour weeks for the same two hundred dollars promised for forty. One winter, thirty Latinos struck against Michael Lin, a Chinese immigrant who ran a construction company. The thirty Latinos were joined by an equal number of Asian workers, trying to recover $110,000 in back wages Lin allegedly pocketed by paying his men with bad checks. The workers struck the Bank of Bogotá office on Roosevelt Avenue, halting construction until the bank's Colombian owners forced Lin to issue new checks. It was a rare victory, one that revealed another aspect of

American life: the pay and work conditions may be Third World, but the fringe benefits are world class. Get hurt on the job, and you are rushed to a First World hospital. Get screwed on the job, and you have the possibility of a First World labor action.

Thus, the Mexicans keep coming. Even with so many being disappointed, the supply of workers continues to grow. In fact, all of this was occurring at a time when New York, according to the statisticians, was losing employment, particularly in the manufacturing and construction sectors. The influx of *jornaleros* from Mexico would seem to be at odds with the laws of the marketplace. But the mass makes its own law: by keeping wages low, more employers were encouraged to bid for jobs where profit margins were small. In reality the construction industry was booming.

According to the 1995 edition of the New York City Current Employment Survey, the city lost fifteen thousand construction jobs from 1989 to 1990, and another thirteen thousand in 1991. Yet from 1989 to 1990, the number of nonresidential construction permits issued by the city nearly doubled, from 6,867 square feet to 11,691 square feet of new construction per year. Most of that rise came from outside Manhattan, in the boroughs of Brooklyn and Queens. Then, after dipping in 1991, construction jumped again. In 1993, the number of permits issued rose from 5,795 square feet to 7,905. According to the state's Department of Labor, New York lost three thousand jobs in this period as well. Were fewer people really doing more work? Probably not. Much of the work simply had gone underground, atomized into smaller units performed by operators like Yoon Dam Construction company. The statisticians simply were not counting the immigrant economy.

If we look at Miguel Caceres, then up the chain to the employers and the contracts filled, it is clear that cheap labor was one reason construction in the Bronx and other devastated neighborhoods was going forward. So, in a real sense, the mass of workers was creating its own demand. The mass also made it possible for newcomers (and only newcomers, it seemed, bothered with this market) to enter the industry. Forced to bond together, sharing expenses and profits equally, groups of three or four immigrants spread the risk of failure. Whenever one was lucky enough to land a job, he immediately paid any food and rent debt owed to his partners. Since most of these arrangements were based on family ties, even if only one *jornalero* in three was working, most likely all would still eat. For the luckiest, a job gleaned on Roosevelt Avenue would lead to permanent work. Like buying tickets in a lottery, the more *jornaleros* deployed by a family, the better the chances anyone's luck would become the life raft the rest could scramble aboard.

The dynamic growth of the immigrant job market is based on a new work frontier, that of the independent service provider. Time is another frontier. In grocery stores, pizza shops, child care, and home care, workers and entrepreneurs found hours of time going unexploited. Instead of imposing a burden, immigrants extended the city's workday, allowing professionals to work longer hours and still care for their children or get a meal delivered at home at midnight. In the 1970s and early 1980s, barely a handful of all-night delicatessens and coffee shops existed, catering mostly to night owls and a few off-shift workers. In the 1990s, barely a city block in any of the five boroughs was without the ubiquitous Korean greengrocer. And every one of those had a salad bar filled with fresh offerings, chopped and sliced by a team of Mexican workers. Immigrants arrived in a city that flattered itself with the delusion of 24-hour life and made that delusion real.

Complaining that these are "Third World jobs" misses the point. Of course they are. That's why Third World immigrants take them. What is truly extraordinary is the discovery, the immigrants' and ours, that Third World work earns enough in the First World for the worker to consume at a First World level. The immigrants proved something else: while some centers of employment shrink, for others the number of jobs available in a given industry is limited only by the number of job seekers.

Taxi driving is such an industry. Owning and operating a taxicab licensed with a "medallion" (the official seal of authenticity, issued to just twelve thousand yellow cabs citywide) was once a middle-class job in New York. In the 1970s, second-generation Italians, Jews, and Irish dominated the workforce. Many owner-operators lived in Queens or the suburbs, and worked a single eight-hour shift each day. They earned enough money to support mortgage payments on both a medallion and a home. Most could afford to send their children to college. Those lucky enough to have purchased or inherited a medallion before 1975 treated the driver's seat as a sinecure, literally an endowed chair. Since the city hadn't permitted additional concessions in almost sixty years, existing medallions were bought and sold on the open market at ever higher prices. And with every fare increase, their value soared.

The traditional "lumpen" drivers either worked as an employee of a fleet, or they contracted themselves to individual medallion owners. "Horse hiring," the practice was called. The economics were simple: as fleet employees, drivers took home about 30 percent of gross revenues. Their gasoline was provided by the garage, and their insurance was deducted from their paychecks, as were withholding taxes and union dues. Whatever tips were made were pocketed tax-free. For an independent contractor, the arrangement was reversed. Then and now, the independent buys his own gas and pays his own taxes, and pays the medallion owner about 25 percent of the gross. That leaves at least 60 percent for the driver.

As the horse-hiring system spread, some of the romance of taxi driving began to erode, replaced by cold economics. A musician or a college kid, or anyone temporarily "between jobs," could not simply acquire a hack license and find work immediately with a fleet. To lease, a rookie needed an initial investment of several hundred dollars. By the late 1980s, virtually all the old fleets were gone. Taxi driving had become, in the words of researcher Sheryl Fragin, "the latest version of an immigrant sweatshop."

The immigrant was hardly the cause of an industry's transformation, merely one beneficiary. Instead of an aging white ethnic owning his cab and garaging it at night, the same cab had become

a factory for as many as five or six men, often brothers or cou
usually from Pakistan, Afghanistan, Egypt, or Bangladesh. Whereas
a former generation of college-educated hacks had been linked by
bohemian pretensions and the inefficiencies of a recessionary labor
market, this generation was linked by a common faith, Islam, and
similar labor market inefficiencies back home. Immigrants, tied together by family in ethnic enclaves, were simply in a much better
position than individual Americans to lend one another money.
They could tap a bigger pool of new drivers to introduce to owners whenever openings occurred. As partners, they were better
equipped to buy a cab. Sitting on a hard seat for twelve hours at
a time, the standard New York shift, is as difficult as it always has
been—and in summer, literally a sweatshop. But it is not necessarily as exploitive as many outsiders believe.

Today's new driver is more likely to be a member of the family
that operates the cab business than he is to be a stranger, so "debt"
becomes more like a mortgage, jointly shared. Thus, if the "elite"
sinecures are gone, so is much of the exploitation. Less like a sweatshop, cab driving is more like any other immigrant family business.
The cost of leasing a cab, moreover, is actually less than it was in
1980. Then, drivers paid between fifty-five and seventy dollars a
shift, depending on the night of the week. In 1995, drivers paid
between seventy-five and ninety dollars, a rise of just under 2 percent a year, less than the cost of living increase. Meanwhile, because cabs are working around the clock, income per vehicle is
rising.

There is no mystery as to why a market as efficient as the
immigrant labor market would meld so effortlessly with the cab
business. Immigrants are drawn to self-employment, especially in
industries with no fixed hours. Russian drivers snapped up hundreds of medallions in the late 1980s, about ten years after immigrants from the former Soviet Union began driving cabs in New
York. Then came the Haitians. By the mid-1990s, the Pak Brothers
Yellow Cab Drivers Union of New York had become an organizing
force. The Pak (for Pakistan) Brothers began as employees of me-

dallion owners, then became contractors, then owners. In 1995, when the city finally authorized the issuing of four hundred new medallions, Pak Brothers were first in line to buy still more.

As the "formal" medallion-cab industry came to employ more drivers, something more remarkable occurred: the rise of an "informal" sector" comprising gypsy cabs and car services. The yellow cabs had created a second tier as dozens of immigrant providers emerged in the outer boroughs. A new kind of shakeout was taking place as drivers simply bypassed the closed, yellow-cab cartel and started new services of their own. "The medallions skim off the best business—Manhattan south of Ninety-sixth Street and fares from the airport," says Edward Rogoff, professor of management at Baruch College and a longtime student of the taxi industry. "Everything else is gypsy service or radio cars."

By 1993, some thirty-two thousand licensed "informals" were plying the streets, while the city's Taxi and Limousine Commission estimated another eighteen thousand roamed without licenses at all. Fewer than one in six taxis working in the city now are formal medallion cabs, the vast majority being unlicensed gypsies and second-tier car services. Most of these "companies" were little more than a man and his vehicle, sometimes with a Plexiglas partition between driver and passenger, sometimes with a radio dispatcher directing drivers to customers phoning in for rides. Dollars-a-ride cheaper than the formal cabs, and more plentiful in dangerous neighborhoods, the informals enjoyed ever-growing demand. This was due partly to the growing immigrant consumer base. Mainly it was due to the dynamics of the market: cruising cars, some charging as little as a dollar a ride, replaced the city's buses and subways, which were already inefficient in serving local commuters. Market segmentation was occurring. Buses and subways were exploited for their best service—long-distance travel outside the neighborhood—while livery cabs ruled for short hops around the block.

Dominicans, whose population in New York would reach almost 700,000 by the end of the 1980s, were the first to expand beyond their ghetto to streets in other neighborhoods. The

Africans followed right behind. By 1995, Harlem boasted three all-Senegalese car services and a spin-off company manned by immigrants from the Ivory Coast and Guinea. Each company boasted anywhere from twenty to fifty regular drivers, each driver providing his own vehicle, and linked together by no more than business cards with a dispatcher's phone number printed beneath a garish logo. Working requires almost no start-up capital, just a willingness to log time, cruising streets overlooked by the formal cab sector. And the car services spawned other, more substantial businesses. Small auto repair shops, restaurants catering to late-night diners (the drivers themselves), and the storefront offices of notaries and accountants would appear along Saint Nicholas, the western border of French Harlem. Middlemen worked out of their apartments, offering assistance in buying car insurance and registering cars, or selling used vehicles to the next wave of drivers.

Which gets us back to the guerrilla jitneys. All of this enterprise—formal, informal, and even illegal—worked to increase the market base of all providers. The more services were offered, the more consumers responded, the more they consumed. The MTA charged that five thousand illegal, mostly immigrant, van services siphoned business away from their buses. But when it released figures on transit usage, the same MTA revealed that while ridership had increased about 5 percent from 1990 to 1994, the increase along lines feeding immigrant enclaves was much higher. In fact, two lines increased ridership so dramatically that bus revenue for one section of Queens was up over $90,000 just in the year 1993/94. In a city where budget items are counted in the billions of dollars, $90,000 may seem a pittance. But it is not a decline. Rather than steal service from the city, the newcomers became new customers for the MTA. What is more, revenue gains on comparable lines in Brooklyn and the Bronx dwarfed the uptick in Queens. The Brooklyn B46 contributed to New York coffers an increase of nearly $400,000 after fares were reduced to compete with the immigrant jitneys. The Bronx gain was more modest, but still impressive: $184,178.

Something more dramatic was happening underground. The

jitneys were funneling hundreds of new riders into the subway. Jamaica Center, the terminus for the E, J, and Z lines, saw an increase of almost 680,000 passengers between 1990 and 1994; the station next door, Sutphin Boulevard, increased its ridership by over 225,000. Combined, those two stations in 1994 contributed over $1 million more in fares than they did in 1993.

The same trend was recorded in other immigrant neighborhoods. The number of turnstile clicks from the last six stations along the Broadway 1 line, an area in the heart of Dominican Washington Heights, was nearly eight hundred thousand higher per year in 1994 than it was in 1990. At $1.25 per fare, that's $1 million extra revenue—$2 million if you consider most of these fares returned from somewhere else. In East Harlem the increase was even greater. Between 125th and 103rd Streets, the contribution of four IRT stations went from about $8.5 million to over $11 million, a rise of better than 25 percent. In Jamaica, Queens, three stations clustered together showed the highest increase in subway use—an additional three million riders a year. The jitneys, whatever they were stealing from the buses, were certainly revenue providers for the subways. Commuters, apparently convinced at least one kind of vehicle was coming along soon enough, willingly fed everyone's change box. Rather than taking a bigger slice of the same pie, immigrants produced a bigger pie, resulting in a cash windfall that effectively subsidized the rest of the MTA.

Like the Tortilla Index, like the $2.95 Bengali lunch, statistics from turnstile use and bus revenue give us a day-to-day accounting of growth at the base of society. They also explain what seems to be inexplicable: how a city where the population of poor people is swelling can still be getting richer. They tell us that the immigrant tide is indifferent to the existing job market or to projections for job growth prepared by agencies like the Bureau of Labor Statistics. The mass rolls in, finds work, and its collective earnings attract new businesses. The ten-cent phone call, the dollar jitney, and the Bengali buffet are each something more than a discount consumer service—they are also job creators. Every new minivan that hits the streets represents three drivers, plus the incremental demand supporting gas stations, mechanics, auto-parts salesmen, and any other related services. The discount phone parlor is not simply competition forcing Baby Bell toward greater efficiency, it is also an outpost, what Latin Americans would call a *puesto,* a haven of employment that may shelter a dozen workers. If they are from the same family, and they usually are, the *puesto* is also a place to put their savings and consolidate their debts, from whence they will, working as a team, quickly add value and advance the family's progress—perhaps to a bigger *puesto* in a better spot. For New York, and for the country, this means there is no knowable limit to how many immigrants can enter and thrive in our midst, because there is no knowable limit to how many taxicabs, phone parlors, Chinese take-out counters, or Korean greengrocers consumers are prepared to support. What is sure is that whenever that limit is reached in one city, the tide will move onward, proving to the people of Harrisburg and Framingham and New Haven and Port Jervis that everything they never realized they needed before is being provided by immigrants, who are only too happy to serve and smile, and work cheap.

According to the Immigration and Naturalization Service, New York State is the number-two recipient of new immigrants, trailing only California. Between 1982 to 1993, over 1.5 million immigrants entered New York State, by which the INS means primarily the five boroughs of Manhattan, Brooklyn, Queens, Staten Island, and the Bronx. California, with 3.5 million entrants, more than doubled New York's intake. But California's count includes thousands, perhaps hundreds of thousands, of casual border crossers—"sojourners," immigration specialists call them. They are more likely to be day laborers or temporary workers than genuine colonists.

The INS figures, moreover, do not count the growing immigrant populations in New York's suburbs. Connecticut, the number-thirteen recipient, saw many of its immigrants clustered in the state's southwest "pot handle," in Norwalk, Stamford, and Bridgeport. New Jersey, number five on the INS list with half a million new arrivals, also lies within New York's immigration orbit. Elizabeth, East Orange, Union City, and Plainfield attracted large colonies of Asians, Africans, and Latinos through the 1980s, most pulled by jobs in New York. Jersey City, whose residents live closer to Midtown Manhattan than millions of New York City's own inhabitants, is the nation's third most "immigrant" city—behind Miami and Los Angeles.

New York was not merely receiving more immigrants than almost any other place, it also was receiving greater concentrations from the major sending countries. The flow of Mexicans to Chicago and Texas had flattened out by the late 1980s, but was surging into New York. Bangladesh, whose immigrants had previously been scattered, was sending about 85 percent of all migrants to New York, and adding about 2,000 new immigrants every year. The same was true for the West Indians, for whom Florida long had been an alternative destination. Between 1982 and 1989, nearly 700,000 legal immigrants entered New York—a third of them from just three Caribbean countries: Jamaica, Guyana, and the Dominican Republic. Haiti sent almost 41,000 legal immigrants during those years, while two Chinese provinces, Fuzhou and Guangdong, sent 70,000 more. Other big "senders"—Colombia (almost 23,000), India (20,000), and Ecuador (13,000)—were exporting minicities directly into New York's neighborhoods. After 1990, the immigrant flow became even more concentrated. Two groups, Dominicans and Russians, now account for more than a third of all legal arrivals.

The popular image of immigration as an out-of-control invasion ignores the tight organization actually taking place. Concentration, it turned out, was also good for the city's recovery. Like any business, a city prospers by increasing output while containing costs. Immigrants did both in New York. One way they do this is by managing each other, forming cliques of "co-ethnic" job specializations, which makes the exchange of information easier. At the same time, concentration keeps the cost of labor low by replacing advancing workers with newer, cheaper employees. Antonio and Julio Martinez at Koo-Koo's, for example. The most important way concentration builds prosperity is in consumption. Immigrant families earn like the poor but spend like the middle class, as figures from the 1990 census explain. New York's median household income in 1990 was just under thirty thousand dollars, with males earning slightly above the median and females slightly less. Household income, on a citywide average, was about even with what single wage earners were taking home. Although thousands of New Yorkers live in two-earner households, the fact that the median household income was so close to that of a single wage earner demonstrates the large proportion of inefficient earners—either "overpaid" singles or multiperson families struggling on a single income.

Census data reveal this correlation occurs in each racial subgroup of native-born New Yorkers: white, black, Asian, and Hispanic. But not among immigrants. The median household incomes of black immigrants are higher than the median incomes of either male or female earners as individuals. That is also the case for Asian and Hispanic households. What's more, five immigrant groups—Korean, Jamaican, Guyanese, Indian, and Filipino—had household incomes actually exceeding the city's median; in the case of the Indians and Filipinos, exceeding by nearly 50 percent. They did so even though their individual wages lagged behind the city's average. Almost without exception, immigrants earn less than their native-born counterparts, regardless of race. Yet they live in households that reported higher incomes than nearly two thirds of all native-born families.

Why? Because immigrants not only work harder for lower pay, they work more. Guyanese, for example, are among the lowest earning of all New Yorkers. Male or female, Guyanese earn about two thirds of the city's median salary, with men averaging less than $25,000 a year, women less than $19,000. These salaries are lower than those of any group of native-born New Yorkers. Yet Guyanese household incomes are higher than the median. That's because almost all Guyanese live in families with at least two wage earners; nearly a third live in three-income (or better) homes. Jamaican,

Indian, Korean, and Filipino families average two incomes or more per household. Therefore, even though as individuals they are earning less, as families they are spending more.

Another way of viewing this is to say immigrant families were doing better in 1990 than the mainstream because they were managing their resources better—putting more traditional families into family-sized apartments, using economies of scale in their own household purchases. "Households" comprising single men and women are inefficient users of the city's resources, as are families headed by single parents. These are "family values" of a sort anti-immigrant activists overlook. Anyone tracking immigration today sees a lot of reports that purport to measure the cost of too many immigrants. There is a racist point of view, which often boils down to a conviction that any additional nonwhite American would be "too many." Then there is the softer, New Age view that deals in other fears: overpopulation, environmental destruction, the "widening gap between rich and poor." Fortunately, none of these fears is even remotely justified, nor could any of them be proven conclusively. Immigration may be "driving" population growth, but that begs the question—Is this necessarily a bad thing? Without immigration, America faces the prospect of funding the growing needs of entitlement-worthy seniors from a shrinking base of working taxpayers. Are immigrants part of the entitlement problem or its solution?

The widening gap between rich and poor is equally thorny. Are immigrants the cause of a "widening gap" because they are poor or because they make poor Americans poorer by competing for scarce jobs, scarce housing, scarce opportunities? And if it's the latter, are jobs, housing, and opportunities truly scarce? As for jobs, figures on minority business creation, cited above, provide the best evidence that immigrants are job makers, not takers. As for housing, one merely has to drive through the charred blocks of Harlem or the South Bronx to realize there is no shortage of housing stock, just a shortage of renters and owners. Immigrants have driven through those same blocks, and hundreds have stopped to buy and renovate. Is that part of a "widening" income gap or a shrinking one? And if it is the former, how would restricting immigration reduce it?

In the mid-1990s, the figure of a $29-billion tax bill was widely reported as a defining "cost" of immigration, both legal and illegal. Concocted by Donald Huddle, an economist at Houston's Rice University, it has been challenged and, to some extent, refuted. Immigrants almost certainly generate more tax revenue—including federal and state withholding, but also sales tax, property taxes, and transaction taxes—than they take in services. Because immigrants are harder to count than native-born Americans (by definition, they are newcomers whose reporting on change-of-address status lags that of native-born Americans), federal disbursements lag behind local needs. The census makes an adjustment every ten years, but by then more immigrants have arrived, and a new generation goes undercounted. What Huddle proves, if anything, is that immigrants generate more short-term costs to states and localities that provide services than the federal government reimburses.

Statistical evidence of immigration's costs and benefits is elusive, but quantifies more easily on the cost side. Costs are counted in service institutions like schools, hospitals, and prisons. Benefits are atomized throughout society. "We measure what gets used in services, but we don't have data on what gets put back into the economy," says Joseph Salvo, an immigrant specialist with New York City's Department of City Planning. "The data picture is not balanced; you have all the negatives but not the positives."

A school district, for example, calculates how much is spent each year on each student by taking the entire school budget and dividing by the number of children. The district usually knows which of its students are foreign-born. Calculating the immigrant "cost" is a matter of multiplying the cost per student by number of foreign students. But even though the same school district relies on state sales taxes to pay some of the education bills, and an influx of immigrants leads to an increase in sales tax revenues, that immigrant "benefit" could never be quantified. Another example: New York City currently estimates the cost of owning and managing distressed real estate—apartment houses, abandoned storefronts, vacant lots—at between $200 million and $300 million a year. Over the past five years, more than four thousand structures left the city's hands and returned to the tax rolls. Immigrants were the biggest buyers. The immigrant benefit was twofold: reducing the expense of derelict properties and raising additional property taxes.

Counting immigration's benefits also can be done by assessing the costs of no immigration. "Just look at retail space," says Frank Vardy, who works with Joseph Salvo at the Department of City Planning. "There is nary a vacant space in Flushing anymore, an area [in Queens] that was dying in the 1970s. That was the result of the aging European stock. As populations grow older, usually there is only momma left, and momma is usually not a big consumer. She's sitting in three or four empty rooms and buying, what? A quart of milk and a loaf of bread. And the *Daily News*."

Focusing on immigrants' education, skill levels, or the types of jobs they fill misses Vardy's key point: it's not how they earn, but what they spend, and where. New York's prosperity depends less on high-tech industries and well-paid professionals than on mass consumption, particularly in neighborhoods where the cost of abandonment—crime, arson, drug abuse, children on public assistance—tax the wealth of the prosperous. Those immigrant families earn little, but spend loads more. Precisely because they are low-skilled and poor, they are forced to fill poor neighborhoods. In the process, they make those places middle class.

Salvo and Vardy have been tracking New York's immigration boom. In 1992, they gathered their findings in a thick volume called *The Newest New Yorkers*. By tabulating census data on employment, housing, health, and a host of other categories, they found New York has been blessed with a young, mobile, and ambitious new source of energy, one the city was lucky to have. Immigrants were not found to be entering the country to outcompete American-born workers in existing jobs but to build new industries and new families. Not only were immigrant families filling the old tenements with people—people who bought baby cribs, new refrigerators, personal computers—they also were evening the mix between overearning, overconsuming singles and the underearning, low-consuming poor. And, Vardy and Salvo found, most were at the beginning of their careers, with decades of earning power ahead of them. "Most recent immigrants fit the historic pattern of being younger than the city's general population," *The Newest New Yorkers* reports in its introduction, noting the "virtual absence of persons 65 or older," with the great concentration of immigrants falling between fifteen to thirty-four years of age. What's more, immigrants are more likely than the average New Yorker to be married and in families. In other words, fewer elderly immigrants on public assistance and fewer single "guest workers" remitting their earnings home.

As Joseph Salvo points out, costs are easier to identify than benefits; as Frank Vardy points out, the costs of not coming— empty storefronts and momma alone in a dying neighborhood— are costs diminished only by a continual stream of new consumers. As the city has come to rely on service industries rather than manufacturing for growth, labor becomes the central component. Immigrant labor is crucial. "There are two areas to address," Salvo explains. "One is the low end: what would have happened if immigrants had not been here? The lower-end service sector would have disappeared. Most people argue the garment center would have been long gone. What would female labor force participation have been had immigrants not provided child-care service? That is a key question."

Frank Vardy says immigrants willing to work on the cheap make it possible for native-born Americans to trade up, in the case of women, from housework to well-paying careers. "Women who work in Manhattan are bucked up in their earnings because of the services that exist in New York," he says. "Getting a pizza at midnight, getting laundry done. These didn't exist as available options ten, twenty years ago. Now you could have women working on Wall Street from eight in the morning to seven at night, women who have a child and also work. Without this labor force, maybe you couldn't do this."

Not that there weren't social ills associated with immigration. Crimes like tax fraud, the flouting of housing and workplace standards, illegal street vending, trademark counterfeiting, and the obvious crime of visa violation were all on the rise in the 1990s. These were largely crimes against the state's regulators. For all these sins, quality of life in New York was improving by nearly every measurable standard. Home occupancy was up, infant mortality rates were down. So was crime. Student test scores, once the shame of the nation's biggest public school system, began to reverse long years of decine. In the midst of a national debate about the costs and benefits of immigration, New York provides daily proof of the mass's power to transform. While anti-immigrant activists compile statistics to support fears of an impending apocalypse, New York confounds the doomsayers.

Public safety had improved so markedly by 1995, law enforcement officials were speaking of a "New York Miracle." After rising throughout the 1980s, violent crime—rape, robbery, murder, and assault—declined over 10 percent between 1990 and 1993. Crimes against property declined even further, about 20 percent. And the trend continued from 1993 to 1995, with reported crimes down almost 30 percent. "There's a miracle happening before our eyes and we don't know why," Columbia University's Jeffrey Fagan told *The New York Times* in July 1995, after statistics released for the first half of the year revealed another decline, which the *Times* called "simply breathtaking."

Immigration was not the sole reason for the change, but it was arguably the most important. Crime, above all, is perpetrated by teenagers and young adults, mostly male. The population of adult males between the ages of sixteen and twenty-five dropped by almost 10 percent between 1970 and 1990—some 110,000 men in that age group. What's more, the percentage of foreign-born males in that group tripled. Immigrants, of course, do commit crime, but may be less likely to do so than native-born youths. Thus New York not only shrunk its crime-prone population, it replaced it with a better class of *homo urbanus*. The net effect for the city amounted to replacing two hundred thousand native young adults with two hundred thousand immigrants, usually in the same poor neighborhoods. If it is true that immigrants, in general, show a greater propensity than their American-born neighbors to wash dishes and deliver pizza and then hit the books after working their "dead-end jobs," then this kind of "import substitution" would have a direct correlation to crime's decline.

Frank Vardy has a simpler explanation. "Immigrant neighborhoods, by definition, are dense. You don't have vacant stores and vacant homes, you don't have much of anything at all that is vacant," he says. "If you got people on the streets and people in their houses, and lights on in front of the houses and people watching over their property and their cars, it's just not a fertile ground for crime." What is certain is that crime didn't increase because of immigration. Throughout the peak years of immigration, arrests for rape, robbery, murder, and theft kept trending, stubbornly, down.

But does the youth that would rather pump gas than rob gas stations also have the effect of keeping gas-pump wages down? That is another part of the debate—the dignity of work and the lowering of an already low underclass. The immigrant tide, the restrictionists argue, does result in lower wages in some industries, or at least suppresses "natural" wage inflation. But there is little evidence that immigrants control wages outside the guest-worker community or even always within it. Koreans paying Mexicans $120 for a sixty-hour week don't force all grocery stores toward a $2-per-hour standard, only Korean ones. As the Mexican workers move up the chain, they leave positions to be filled by other new immigrants. The $2-an-hour job, then, serves as a paid apprenticeship, with meals.

Immigrants do not lower U.S. wages so much as confirm a global price. Manufacturing workers have understood this since the 1970s, when Third World manufacturers began to compete in automobiles, chemicals, textiles, electronics, and hundreds of other products. Immigration brings the same economics to service work. A dishwasher can be overpaid in New York only if his rival in Puebla or Hong Kong can't compete. A world price for sweeping floors and cutting fruit is being set, brutally, but not by immigrants alone. The consumer sets the price, too, because if he or she is not buying, the transaction doesn't take place.

Which brings us back to Fernando Sanchez and the neighborhood known as Tortilla Triangle. A decade after founding his Tortilleria Piaxtla, El Gordo Sanchez had over five thousand Mexican neighbors, most living within twenty-five square blocks of his tortilla plant. By the middle of 1995, two more tortillerias were operating in the neighborhood, Tortilleria Buena Vista at the corner of Flushing and Knickerbocker, and Tortilleria Chinantla at Central Avenue and Jefferson. The three factories—Chinantla, Piaxtla and Buena Vista—are named for three towns deep in the Mixteca, villages as close to each other in Puebla as the three factories are in Brooklyn.

Adolfo Soto, Sanchez's tortilla rival at the corner of Knickerbocker and Flushing, lived in California for almost thirty years. He was a legal, green-card–holding resident for more than twenty of those years, and saved a nest egg of several thousand dollars. In 1993, hearing that Little Puebla was rising from The Well, he crossed the country with his seven sisters, their children, and their children's spouses. He also brought a secondhand tortilla processor. For Tortilleria Buena Vista, Soto picked the ground floor of an old factory building, certain that the Mexicans and Central Americans working in the lofts upstairs would make his space their first stop on their way home. As word spread, he drew customers from other factories nearby. Soon he was making enough money to buy a truck, to take more of his tortillas to stores farther afield. In short, to repeat the success of his neighbor, El Gordo. "This is a city where you can make money," he explained, shortly after opening Tortilleria Buena Vista in 1993. "The people are buying because they have jobs here, and money to spend."

Two years later, Soto was running a second truck, and, like El Gordo down the street, had opened a factory outlet store across the street from his plant. Tortilleria Buena Vista added ten thousand tortillas a day to the city's growing Tortilla Index, representing the spending power of a hundred more Mexican families.

One of them, no doubt, was the Martinez brood, grown to four since Julio and Antonio left Zapotitlán Salinas, Puebla. As promised, they returned to New York after planting the family's corn, and quickly resumed their jobs at Koo-Koo's. But by the following April, they were ready to move on. They went to Brooklyn, this time with two more family members—Julio's forty-five-year-old father, and his younger brother, Fernando. Julio and the other young men were working again in restaurants, the older man took a job at the old Maxwell House coffee-roasting factory in Hoboken, New Jersey. By that winter Julio had located Koo-Koo's French chef in Brooklyn's Bay Ridge section. As promised, he offered Julio a *puesto* in his kitchen. "That boy, he never rests," the father, Domingo, said. "If you want to talk to Julio, you'll have to go to the restaurant."

In less than five years, "that boy" led a family to the Promised Land. Although the money they earned continued to flow south, the balance of their assets—the Martinezes' "family value"—had shifted north. Julio was thinking about going back to school, maybe even buying a house or starting a business.

Can a thousand Julios save a city? That's the immigration question. The answer is, of course they can. The evidence is the city without immigrants, the subject of the next chapter.

CHAPTER TWO

The City Without Immigrants

There was a time when the country just opened its arms to people and they were used to build the roads and the cities. And after that use had been fulfilled, they immediately decided to cut them off.

Pelegrino (Peter) Rodino, Jr., former congressman

★

America, strictly speaking, is not a nation. It is not a German *Volk* or a Russian *narod*. Americans, even American Latinos, are not *la gente* or *el pueblo*, words Latinos use for "the people." Even African Americans, speaking of The Race, do not mean a single, pure race, with a common past. We have no common culture stretching back to caves or to tiny grains of prehistoric corn. What's common in America is the now.

America is also not an empire. In most countries, a single ethnic group rules over a variety of sub (for "subjugated") tribes. The former Soviet Union was such an empire, and still is. India is an empire, and so is Brazil. So is tiny Guatemala, whose "tribe" of Spanish-speaking, mixed-race Ladinos rules over minority tribes of their own living ancestors. So is even tinier Rwanda—as we are reminded each time Hutus ethnically scour Tutsis. Yugoslavia is an empire that disintegrated.

In America, ethnicity is a condition, not a goal. Other nations treasure their common past, either as a bulwark against the encroachments of the Über Tribe, or as a means to become one. Ethnic supremacy is certainly the goal of Yugoslavia's Serbs and Croats, just as it is everywhere empires are hewn. America is the anti-tribe. Admission here is open to everyone, which is the reason we are everyone's mother country.

This is by our design, not by accident. In Africa, for example, U.S. embassies sponsor Black History Month every February to extol the contribution of Africans in America. Many Senegalese believe that America's slave past grants them a kind of repatriation status on the basis of family unification. Many even believe the majority of Americans are black. During the 1990s, the United States inaugurated the Diversity Lottery, specifically designed to promote immigration from nations underrepresented in the current wave, especially Africans. In Senegal, lottery rules were posted on billboards to accommodate the enthusiastic mob that flocked to the consulate. "I want to go to America because my roots are there," wrote one visa applicant. "My people had the chance to change and develop in the U.S. Despite the turmoil they've been through, they've succeeded and provide a model for us to learn from."

When immigrant restrictionists denounce nonwhite immigration as a threat to American culture, they suggest America has a definable ethnicity. It does not. America has been Latin since the 1830s. Indeed, it went to war to become Latin, absorbing half of Mexico before 1850. America became Asian later in that same century, bringing Hawaii (and for several decades, the Philippines) into its territory. In short, years before the mass of migrants began arriving from Southern and Eastern Europe, America already had millions of citizens who traced their roots to Africa, Mesoamerica, and the Far East. Many had been here for generations.

If the mother country is not a race or a tribe or a fixed territory, what is it? That's simple. America is an economy. More precisely, it is a market.

Think of the medieval fair, teeming with shouts and strains and the crunch of wooden wheels hauling produce from the countryside. Peasants load their carts and travel all night to be there by dawn. Why? Because at home the bale of hay and the squealing pig have only that value the individual peasant can give them. He can eat his output, trade it with a neighbor (who, chances are, is raising the same thing), or let it spoil. Its value depends on its presence in the marketplace.

Now think of America as that great fair. Today, the peasant is isolated in the stagnant backwater economies of the Third World. He is traveling all night to come here, but now in a plane. His wares are his willingness to work, his initiative, his ideas, his literacy. At home, these are undervalued assets, worth whatever the *patron* or the Party or the warlord says they are worth. With immigration, assets in an undervalued market achieve immediate currency, value that can be traded on and improved. Mexicans arrive knowing they are worth $120 a week at the Korean store or $5 an hour washing dishes for Greeks. Our market is more refined than the one at home, but also more flexible, giving the newcomer the opportunity to add value to his assets and bid up his price. The smartest *campesino* in Tehuacán is still a *campesino,* and will be paid the same as the dumbest one. But in a developed market, the smart one becomes the foreman and someday, with luck, the owner. In this way, immigration is a kind of alchemy, converting labor that is leaden in the old country into gold here.

In 1993, the United Nations Population Fund estimated that worldwide remittances from laborers working outside their homelands approached $66 billion. If so, immigrant labor is the world's most traded commodity after petroleum. Counted among the remitters were Turks in Germany, Palestinians in the Gulf States, Mexicans in the United States, and Filipinos everywhere. But only America among the great receiving countries has a tradition of converting guest workers to citizens, which means over time it has the best chance of converting a multibillion-dollar remittance pool into domestic spending. Actually, it already does.

What the United Nations did not estimate was the value of what foreign workers spend in their host countries. Where workers are housed in company dormitories, as in the Gulf oilfields, they spend very little. But in the United States, where an informal guest worker system rules, they spend a lot. Among New York's Mexican migrants no more than 20 percent of earnings are remitted home, even by the most conscientious of workers. The commitment to remit diminishes the longer immigrants stay. Bankers in the town of Izúcar de Matamoros in 1992 reported that they were receiving nearly $2 million every week in wire transfers from New York, not counting what was deposited by individual returnees or their families. So these same migrants, just from one town and the outlying *campo,* were spending between $5 million and $10 million a week in New York.

What was the total amount Mexicans were spending in the city? According to the 1990 census, Mexicans earn an average of fifteen thousand dollars a year. Therefore, the value of a hundred thousand Mexicans working in New York would be something over a billion dollars a year, at least 80 percent remaining in local circulation. Immigration not only allowed the peasant to sell himself for top dollar, but channeled most of those dollars into the local economy, into neighborhoods where it is needed most.

Even a so-called excess of immigrants—something difficult to define, much less prove—does not alter the underlying economics. The market is not a boat at sea, fragile in its buoyancy, but an expanding mass. It is the fair at the edge of town. If every new participant enters the market looking to buy, he is bidding up the price, thus the value, of what the rest of us own. It's the way a neighborhood is "gentrified" when more people want to live there, or how a university is deemed "more competitive" when more students apply for admission. For the alumni and anyone already attending, more competitive means more value for the diploma. For anyone trying to get in, it means more difficulty.

Because America is not an empire, the market is fair—competition is not distorted by advantages one tribe wields over another. But like ethnicity, competition is a condition not a goal. That's why immigrants, as antitribe as America itself, are an enduring dilemma. And why every generation repeats the conflicts of its parents.

The generation that tackled immigration reform in 1965 fashioned the debate in terms barely recognizable today. Border control, the obsession of immigration reformers for the past twenty years, was hardly an issue in 1965. Nor were employer sanctions, asylum fraud, or national identity cards, all troublesome side issues that cloud the immigration debate whenever it comes before Congress. Unemployment was low in 1965, and the economy was booming. Immigration was argued almost as a humanitarian issue. Formally known as the Hart-Celler Immigration Reform Act of 1965, the law the anti-immigration activists blame for a thirty-year immigration "predicament" rose out of the parochial concerns of big-city Democrats. "Containment" in this era related to Eastern Europe, and the desire of congressmen from Buffalo, Cleveland, Chicago, and Milwaukee to see that any Eastern European refugees who arrived in their districts be given status as legal residents.

The law immigration critics view today as the Trojan horse of the Third World had a purely American agenda. Philip Hart, the act's sponsor on the Senate side, came from Michigan. Emmanuel Celler of Brooklyn sponsored the legislation in the House. Celler, then serving his twenty-first term, was a freshman congressman in 1924 when the National Origins Act was passed. In 1965, he was the last congressman still serving who had cast a vote—in his case, against—on National Origins more than forty years before. That earlier law's quota system, which assigned immigration visas based on country of origin, had been under attack for years. Celler and other Jewish leaders blamed its quotas for trapping Jews in Europe before World War II, and for keeping many refugees out afterward. Yet quotas were fiercely defended in Congress, and strengthened by the McCarran-Walter Act in 1952. The debate reflected the generational conflict between the genteel politics of the country club set and the clamor of the more rough-and-tumble politics of the city machines. Celler would spend his entire career fighting to repeal quotas, emerging victorious only as his machine allies gathered power, rising as they accumulated seniority.

Hart-Celler's provision exempting visas issued for family unification from the overall quotas allotted to individual countries is the key component that led to what today is called "post-1965" immigration. It is Hart-Celler, in the view of restrictionists, that is responsible for nonwhite immigration surging out of control. Family unification, the restrictionists argue, allows Third World immigration to increase the minority population exponentially. It allows anyone who arrives and becomes a legal resident to sponsor other family members until, literally, everyone and his brother enters unchecked.

But in 1965, Hart-Celler was not seen as legislation that would have real impact on the developing world. Indeed, the "developing world" was barely known in 1965. Many countries that would become immigrant senders had only recently become independent. Bangladesh was still East Pakistan and most of the Caribbean was still the British West Indies. Americans were on their way to Vietnam, not the other way around. Mexico was the Amigo Country. "Red" China was our implacable foe. In 1965, the terms "affirmative action" and "multiculturalism" were not yet coined.

Although Hart-Celler was about immigration reform, like most legislation it had almost nothing to do with international affairs. It had everything to do with domestic politics. Civil rights was the overriding domestic issue, and became the context surrounding immigration reform. For the generation that came of age during World War II—the American sons and grandsons of the immigrants of the last great wave—reform meant abolishing quotas, period. "There were some people considered more desirable, and some were not," recalls Congressman Peter Rodino, Jr., a leading proponent of the 1965 act. "Frankly we saw it as a question of discrimination, pure and simple."

Anyone who remembers the Watergate hearings remembers Peter Rodino, Jr., the chairman of the House Judiciary Committee, which opened the probe into the scandal that doomed the Nixon White House. Rodino rose in the era of the big-city Democratic machines that ruled wards in Boston, New York, and Chicago for most of a century. His city was Newark, New Jersey. The machines brought the immigrant hordes into politics, then forged ethnic coalitions to push through New Deal legislation for Roosevelt, and later the Great Society programs for Lyndon Johnson. When President Johnson sent his own immigration bill to Congress, later to be incorporated into Hart-Celler, it marked the end of the eighty-year struggle between the WASPs and the ethnics.

Immigration was Rodino's bailiwick long before, and well after, Watergate. He did yeoman work for the Democrats in passing the 1965 act, then sponsored two more landmark bills in the 1970s and 1980s. The Simpson-Rodino Immigration Reform and Control Act of 1986 was probably the most far-reaching of all legislation passed after Hart-Celler, marking the high point of liberal reform. It permitted more than three million illegal aliens to qualify for an amnesty and begin new lives as legal residents. Among Mexicans, beneficiaries were known as *los Rodinos*.

Watergate and immigration reform notwithstanding, few Americans realize that Peter Rodino, Jr., is not really "Peter," but "Pelegrino," the oldest son of an Italian immigrant. Pelegrino Sr. left the hilltop village of Atripaldo, about a hundred miles east of Naples, the port he sailed from, in 1898. "He came here with a tag on him, identifying him," the retired congressman recalled in an interview. "He was just sixteen years old, and he had no one when he came. No one."

Pelegrino Sr. arrived at Ellis Island and went to work in a leather factory in Newark. He eventually married and raised three children, one of whom, the elder of two sons, became a famous congressman. But in the beginning he was just a face in the mob. "With a tag on" usually meant an employer or labor contractor had paid the passage from Europe. The tag was put inside the greenhorn's lapel or coat collar, and had to be hidden from inspectors at Ellis Island. It was revealed only after the immigrant was waved through, so that the contractor's representative, the factory foreman or whoever was sent to meet the new man at the dock, could identify him among the bewildered, blinking rabble. The practice was illegal, indentured servitude having been outlawed in 1885. But it was widespread nonetheless. In fact, this seduction was occurring all over Europe. Walk to Odessa and board a ship. Or find your way, somehow, to Liverpool, Piraeus, Bremen, Rotterdam, or Lisbon. Once in America, fresh hands were needed everywhere. Newcomers "with a tag on" were seized at the dock in Hoboken and whisked off to factories somewhere nearby, or put on trains bound for Pittsburgh, Detroit, Chicago, or Minneapolis. Just like today, any peasant who was willing could find his way to America.

Pelegrino Sr., who never left Atripaldo for more than a day before 1898, walked to Naples. His son says it took him two or three days, and agrees that if Pop couldn't afford a wagon ride down to the port, he certainly wouldn't have been able to pay for ship passage. In many ways, Pelegrino Rodino was leaving an Italy in turmoil, a turmoil much like the Mexico and China that peasants are fleeing today. The modern market economy was finding its way down the peninsula, beginning to penetrate villages like Atripaldo. Just as in places like Puebla, Senegal, and China today, modern methods made agricultural labor redundant, leaving a surplus of unemployed young men. The young villager had to have somewhere to go, so for the generations caught between the end of traditional farming and the start of the Industrial Revolution, that somewhere was America. In many ways, too, Italians came the same way Mexicans or Fukienese do today: in hock to the *coyotes* and the "snakeheads," the smugglers who front the cost of the trip and arrange menial jobs to work off the debt. Poverty was no barrier to entry. Work was plentiful in America, and the community's own enforcers—La Cosa Nostra, later known as the Mafia, or the early Chinese "tongs"—were just as efficient in ensuring compliance in nineteenth-century Newark as they are in Chinatown today.

The "snakeheads" of Pelegrino Rodino's time were in league with the agents of the shipping companies. Through a labor boss, or *padrone*, berths were paid for by the factories clamoring for more able-bodied peasants to introduce to the modern world. Immigrant banks, often run by these same *padroni*, allowed workers to put money away each week to pay for a relative's passage. They might also lend money—in effect, swapping the price of a ticket in return for the promise of another worker. It was up to the shipping companies to screen out anyone who might not pass inspection at Ellis Island—anyone who was too old, too sick, or too feeble-minded. Cargo rejected in New York was shipped back to Europe at the line's expense, so that part of the process was self-correcting. Occasionally a *padrone* would swindle the bank's assets, absconding with thousands of dollars in immigrants' savings and fleeing the city. In those instances, official law was powerless to intervene. The "banks" weren't chartered or regulated by any state agency, and few cities had resources to police what was obviously an underground economy. Thus organizations like La Cosa Nostra also protected the interests of the immigrants, even as they preyed on the community.

But abuses were relatively rare, and got rarer still after 1900, by which time so many Italians had emigrated to America very few came without having some family member waiting. In 1898, Pelegrino Rodino, with his tag, would have been among the last of the pioneers. Arriving at the Naples piers with his steamship ticket, however paid for, he was welcomed with hot soup, a shower, and a cot to rest on before boarding ship. After three days trudging down the mountain from Atripaldo, Pelegrino Rodino would have fallen on these offerings as the first samplings of the luxury that waited in America. By arriving in Naples, Pelegrino Rodino, like a million other migrants across Europe, was stepping out of the feudal past and into the modern age. Then, as now, neither distance nor poverty nor dependence impeded the migrants. Nor did law.

But that era was long gone by the time the National Origins Act was passed in 1924. The act set quotas for "Nordic" and "non-Nordic" immigration, with a preference for the former at the extreme expense of the latter. Although the great wave was largely spent by 1924 (World War I interrupted the flow), the 1924 legislation was a master stroke of revanchist design. Led by Southern Democrats and Midwest Republicans, Congress attempted to roll America back to a simpler ethnic composition. Quotas set by country were not allotted according to how many had arrived by 1924, but by the number that had arrived prior to 1890. In other words, before more than 270,000 Slavs, Jews, and Italians had crossed the finish line.

"The exclusion of the Southern European and the Eastern European and the preference for the Anglo-Saxon, this was quite evident," Congressman Rodino notes today. "Remember there was a time when the country just opened its arms to people and they were used to build the roads and the cities. And after that use had been fulfilled, they immediately decided to cut them off. The numbers [in 1924] were allocated to the English-speaking, the WASP, as you say."

In 1965, Congressman Rodino represented a district in northern New Jersey that included Newark and the towns of Bloomfield, Bellville, Glen Ridge, Nutley, Harrison, and Kearny. He represented almost five hundred thousand people, almost entirely white, mainly of Italian descent. The other Newark congressman, also a Democrat, was Joseph Minish, a former organizer in the electrical workers' union, who also traced his roots to Italy, although not all voters knew it.

What Congressman Rodino remembers as a moral struggle against discrimination had a strong political component. Districts like Rodino's and Minish's were turning from white to "colored" in the mid-1960s with whites fleeing to the suburbs. In 1962, Newark's congressional delegation had been cut during redistricting from three seats to two. All the Democratic machines across the Northeast and Midwest faced the same predicament, and the same prospect of being redistricted out of office. Thus, the fight for immigration reform in 1965 was not solely a fight for right, but also a fight for whites. The core constituencies of House Speaker John McCormack of Massachusetts, of Cleveland's Michael Feighan, of Chicago's Dan Rostenkowski, and of Rodino in Newark, were derived from immigrant stock. Many constituents still had family in the old country, many of them waiting for visas. Thus, immigration reform was also good constituent service, one that not only kept voters loyal, but kept them in the district.

"I remember the Italian visa number had maybe five thousand or so, and that was the extent of it," Rodino says today. "And there were maybe twenty or thirty thousand waiting for visas." The actual quota for Italy in 1965 was 5,666, the level set in 1952 by the McCarran-Walter Act. The actual waiting list was nearly 260,000 applicants—the twenty thousand to thirty thousand Italians Rodino remembers being only those waiting for visas to join families in his district. There were over seventy thousand Portuguese waiting, for just 438 slots each year. Greece was allowed just 308 spots—and had more than a hundred thousand waiting. The backlog for visa applicants throughout Europe had surpassed five hundred thousand by 1965. That would have been enough to fill every "non-Nordic" slot through the end of the century, yet had these been "Nordic" applicants, the backlog would have been mopped up in just five years. At the time, however, there was almost no demand for visas from "Nordic" Germany or the United Kingdom. Their quotas went unfilled year after year.

There were many in Congress who saw nothing wrong with letting non-Nordics wait in the old country. Most Republicans, and many Southern Democrats, supported quotas. "The President either fails or refuses to understand that America is not hurting for population, job seekers, or illiterates," Georgia Democrat Maston O'Neal told House colleagues during two days of debate in August 1965. Reviving the rhetoric of 1924, he added, "The supporters of this legislation also refuse to accept the fact that human beings differ in their desire to maintain stable governments, their levels of ambition, and their degree of morality."

In the Senate, Georgia's Sam Ervin, Jr., later to share Watergate heroics with Rodino, predicted if the president's bill passed, "the country will be drastically changed." Ervin called the bill a new form of discrimination, against white Americans. The bill, Ervin warned, discriminated "against the people who made the greatest contribution to our country." He then listed those contributors as immigrants from England, Scotland, Ireland, Germany, France, Holland, and Scandinavia. If the 1965 Hart-Celler Act became a Third World Trojan horse, that concern was not part of the debate. In 1965, Rodino's subcommittee on immigration heard testimony from representatives of the American Committee for Italian Migration and the American-Hellenic Educational Progressive Association. If the supporters of Hart-Celler can be attacked today, it would be for caring too little about nonwhite immigrants, not too much. Looking back, Rodino does not view Hart-Celler as a tool for stemming white flight. It was a more optimistic time in America, he says, when white ethnics were as enthusiastic about civil rights as black leaders were about lifting immigration quotas. "They were the ones who knew discrimination here," Rodino says of the black congressmen he worked with. "They realized there was this other kind of racial barrier in the present immigration laws."

Democrats had an overwhelming majority in Congress, and there was little doubt that immigration reform would pass. Family unification was smart politics in 1965. Restoring Democratic strongholds like Newark's Ironbound, Boston's South End, or New York's Bensonhurst was a way to shore up support for the machine. It was a way for old Democratic ward heelers to stanch the hemorrhage of white voters to the suburbs, and someone else's district. In late September, the bill passed by a voice vote in the Senate, and by a 320-to-69 roll call in the House. President Johnson went to the Statue of Liberty for the signing. "This is not a revolutionary bill. It does not affect the lives of millions. It will not reshape the structure of our daily lives or add importantly to our wealth and power," the president told the assembled crowd. "This bill says simply that from this day forth those wishing to emigrate to America shall be admitted on the basis of their skills and their close relationship with those already here."

So what went wrong? For one thing, American prosperity in the 1960s masked the deepening decline of the cities. It is no coincidence that the period when the cities began to fall apart was the same period during which immigration hit its lowest level. What demographers describe as the post–World War II trough (it actually began in the 1930s) was not the golden age immigration restrictionists believe it was. America may have been spared the difficulties of assimilating new waves of foreigners, but at the cost of a hollowing out of its urban centers. The aging and abandonment of the old ethnic enclaves would not have happened had the immigrants come, or at least not as severely. Today, the Ironbound remains Newark's only stable neighborhood. It has gone from Italian to Portuguese and, most recently, to Brazilian since the passage of the 1965 Immigration Reform Act. That it is an exception suggests that there were other Ironbounds that could have saved themselves—if only the people had come.

The tragedy of the 1965 act is that it came too late. From a Europe devastated by war, there would have been millions of families eager to relocate with relatives in Newark, Chicago, New York, anyplace where older brothers and cousins and uncles had an apartment to rent, a candy store to operate, or a bread route to run each morning. Even to a neighborhood "going colored" after the war, Italian, Greek, and Polish families would have come. We can be sure they would have done so then because so many new immigrants do so now—in neighborhoods a lot worse today than they were in 1965. But from 1945 through 1965, they could not.

By the late 1960s, Europe was on the verge of an economic take-off. Northern Italy was booming, drawing excess labor from the south. Portuguese went to Germany and France. The Greeks went to England. The half-million Europeans still waiting in 1965 were also beginning to age out. By the time their visas were ready, many of the twenty thousand to thirty thousand Italians waiting to enter Peter Rodino's old district were too old themselves. When they came, and a few did, it usually was to live with relatives in the suburbs. Everything they would have gone to in the old neighborhood was abandoned.

And that's when the cities began to crumble in earnest. White flight accelerated, tax bases eroded, schools decayed, business fled. By the mid-1970s, cities like New York, Newark, Hartford, Cleveland, Chicago, Detroit, and Philadelphia—all places where thousands of *paisanos* might have settled and thrived—had deteriorated into war zones. The great American market was thus abandoned and assets that would have changed hands, even at a discount, were worth more destroyed. So, after the abandonment came the wave of arson. After the arson came the demolition, until the urban landscape became synonymous with blight and loss. Eventually, city leaders, unable to restore life to the dying neighborhoods, resorted to mocking the survivors, displaying flimsy promises on flimsy billboards, or painting flowers and curtains onto sheets of tin to be installed in empty windows—anything to pretend that people who were long gone would return.

The 1965 act was not a mistake but a seed. People did return, eventually. It took a little longer because they came from farther away. From new places like Hong Kong and the Dominican Republic and Jamaica. Whenever a new group came, it found space in ghettos already carved out by predecessors most like themselves. In New York, the Vietnamese crowded into streets just east of Chinatown. West Indians flocked to Bedford-Stuyvesant, Brooklyn's "Little Harlem." Dominicans went to the Bronx and upper Manhattan, where the Puerto Ricans lived. By the 1980s, family unification was bringing more new colonies to New York, often from places that had no tradition of American immigration. The city of neighborhoods had a place for every new family.

The critical mass came too late to save Newark from yet another redistricting, which occurred in 1972, shrinking the delegation to just the one seat held by Pelegrino Rodino, Jr. It came too late for some of the other veterans of 1965's reforms.

But it came.

CHAPTER THREE

Brownsville, Brooklyn: Mass Plus Energy Equals Upward Mobility

West Indians are convinced, more than other folks, that a turn-around is going to happen.

Ken Thorbourne, housing activist,
East Brooklyn Congregations in Brownsville

★

"To write the story of Brownsville without mentioning Pitkin Avenue," an old-time labor organizer told author Alter Landesman in 1968, "would be like telling the story of the Pilgrims and omitting Plymouth Rock."

Pitkin Avenue is named for John Pitkin, an 1830s real estate developer who dreamed, like Pierre L'Enfant of Washington, D.C., of establishing a perfectly planned city. Selecting the farmland lying between Jamaica Bay and Central Brooklyn, Pitkin envisioned a city that one day would rival Manhattan, which he called East New York. The area was also known as the New Lots, squares of farmland which had been carved out of the old Van Siclen plantation, one of the early Dutch homesteads. Today Van Siclen is remembered with Van Siclen Avenue, a boulevard crossing Brownsville and East New York, two of the poorest neighborhoods in the country.

Pitkin's dream was realized as Brown's Village, the original name for Brownsville, from a parcel of land purchased in 1861 at public auction by a Vermont Yankee named Charles Brown. Pitkin never lived to see a second Manhattan, but by the time Brooklyn was swallowed by New York, in 1898, Brown's Village and the bucolic New Lots tracts nearby had filled to become a teeming immigrant neighborhood. Escaping from the tenements of Manhattan's Hell's Kitchen, Little Italy, and the Lower East Side, the most successful of the new New Yorkers were thrilled to ride the new Interborough Rapid Transit line east into the open fields of Long Island to homes they only could have dreamed about in Europe. These were the white ethnics later vilified by the drafters of the 1924 National Origins Act, and the parents of white Brooklynites who would flee to the suburbs after the Second World War.

From 1900 to the end of World War II, however, Brownsville boomed. The combined Brownsville–East New York area was considered to be the world's single biggest Jewish neighborhood. Brownsville was *die Goldene Medina* ("Golden Land") of shops, synagogues, yeshivas, and delicatessens. The men and women who toiled for pennies an hour in Manhattan's garment lofts, then forged the powerful garment unions, bought homes in Brownsville. Their savings built the schools and social clubs, the famous Betsy Head Swimming Pool, an opulent "natatorium" once the biggest man-made bathing facility in the United States, and the Hebrew Educational Society, a settlement house for new immigrants still arriving from Europe. Their children became the elite of U.S. arts and letters. Writers Henry Roth, Alfred Kazin, and Norman Podhoretz come from Brownsville. George Gershwin was born there, three blocks south of Pitkin Avenue on Van Sindren Avenue. Sol Hurok, later a Broadway producer, staged his first productions at the Brownsville Labor Lyceum. Lepke Buchalter, the Jewish gangster who founded the notorious death squad, Murder Incorporated, operated from a Brownsville candy store at the corner of Livonia Street and Saratoga Avenue.

More than a cradle of celebrities, Brownsville was a glittering commercial center. Eight neighborhood banks served home-buyers and small businessmen. On land once graced by rows of sweet corn, rows of three-story brownstones rolled out on a grid spreading over a hundred square blocks. The glorious Loew's Pitkin movie palace was built for a staggering (at the time) $3 million. It accommodated three thousand patrons inside and was the landmark structure that anchored the fourteen-block Pitkin retail strip. Stretching from Stone to Ralph Avenue, at its peak in 1942, the Pitkin strip trailed only downtown Brooklyn's Fulton Street as the borough's most important shopping district. Gross sales were reportedly over $90 million for the year—some $400 million in today's economy.

Tracing this storied past is not easy today. The Zion Square war memorial, just west of the Loew's Pitkin, calls the roll of Jewish war dead from World Wars I and II. The theater itself is a shuttered hulk, abandoned since the early 1970s. An African hair braiding salon operates out of a tiny storefront under the old marquee. The rest of the lobby is leased to a liquor store owned by a Pakistani immigrant. And don't bother searching for a plaque at the Gershwin birthplace, 245 Van Sindren. The entire block is an open field. There is no plaque, either, at 46 Amboy Street, the address where Margaret Sanger opened the country's first birth-control clinic in 1916. Running north to south through the heart of Brownsville, Amboy Street, too, became a desert in the decades after World War II. Its decline was foreshadowed in Irving Shulman's 1947 novel *The Amboy Dukes,* which shocked postwar America with its tale of brutal "juvenile delinquents." Today Amboy Street is remembered, if it is remembered at all, as the birthplace of boxer Mike Tyson, not birth control. Like Tyson, Brownsville is a symbol of black rage, by the 1970s synonymous with "black ghetto" and arguably the toughest neighborhood in America.

Marcia Holness remembers that time. On a Friday night in 1986, she was the victim of a mugging. She talks about it today with a kind of impatience, with herself mainly, for not knowing something or not doing something that would have averted the robbery. A lot of crime victims act that way. It's part of their coping process. Was it the knife or the darkness or the helplessness? Marcia Holness gave up her money and ran home.

It happened again almost exactly a year later, another Friday night under the same subway station. "Van Siclen station. Two Decembers I had a knife to my throat," she recalls, sounding angrier with herself than with her attacker. "Now I go to Pennsylvania Street. It's two blocks away, but it's much safer. There are people dealing drugs but they don't bother you."

Looking at a subway map, it's not readily apparent how Pennsylvania Street would be safer. Pennsylvania is one stop before Van Siclen on the Number 3 Interborough Rapid Transit line, the IRT, which dips and rises in soft swells over Brownsville and East New York like a kiddie roller coaster. No more than six blocks separate the two stops. Which means both are in full view of each other, high over the neat rows of two- and three-story townhouses. From Eastern Parkway, where the underground train emerges into the air, the IRT rolls over large swaths of borough real estate, much of it abandoned and empty, where only the hulks of twenty-story New York City Housing Authority projects stand against a lonely sky. "Ghettos in the air," people call them. And in between row upon row of those famous Brooklyn townhouses—more space than any Manhattanite could ever hope to live in, yet surrounded by such blight few would want to. Ghettos in the air to live in, and ghetto streets below to die on. At least in the old days.

The reason Pennsylvania is safer than Van Siclen has to do with those rows of houses and who lives in them now, people like Marcia herself. Marcia Holness is part of a corps of antipoverty workers, one of nearly half a million new black immigrants who have swept through Brooklyn over the past two decades. They are poor people entering poor neighborhoods intent on becoming rich. Individually, they are minimum-wage jitney drivers, nurse's aides, and security guards. Together they are a mass of renewal, reviving the urban corpse. They are black and they are willing to stay, something no ghetto could claim during the "Golden Age" of depressed immigration. They are the great returnees—the urban pioneers that Pelegrino Rodino, Jr., longed for, *paisanos* to America's lowest caste.

The emergence of a new middle class in black Brooklyn runs counter to popular misconceptions about the antagonism between blacks and immigrants in the inner city. Black immigration—from the West Indies, from Haiti, and from Africa itself—may well be the single most promising example of a critical mass investing value in a depressed market. Certainly the transformation of neighborhoods like Brownsville supports that view. And while gentrification of neighborhoods like Tortilla Triangle and the Gift District demonstrate the power of the global marketplace to direct individuals to opportunities in a global city, the experience of black immigrants in black New York demonstrates how wealth can be enhanced just from the resources at hand. Most important, black immigration creates the possibility that all Americans may begin to think differently about the "intractable" problems of the ghetto, and realize that solutions to crime and poverty are not only available, they already are taking hold.

Sadly, a good part of America's uncertainty about immigration can be attributed to its shame about conditions in America's inner cities. There is an erroneous assumption that black America has been unable to improve itself, and that only an interventionist state can "protect" poor blacks from their own inability to compete and thrive. Immigrants, by entering the poorest neighborhoods, confront black America's weakest families and often outcompete them. In the process they reinforce the negative stereotypes of both groups. The truth is the problems of the inner city—drug addiction, illiteracy, dysfunctional families, the inability to form multiple-income households (certainly the biggest handicap blacks have in competition with immigrants)—exist whether immigrants arrive or don't. The notion that black neighborhoods need to be protected is not only wrong, it is dangerously counterproductive.

On balance, blacks in New York and other cities with large immigrant populations do better than blacks in cities with few immigrants. By every important measure, blacks in New York, Los Angeles, and Miami live better than blacks in cities like Cleveland, Saint Louis, or Detroit. This is partly because these are "gateway" cities with many immigrants whose vitality tends to raise all economic boats together. It is also because many blacks in gateway cities, particularly New York and Miami, are themselves immigrants.

Blacks constitute New York's biggest immigrant community, be they Spanish-speaking Dominicans, French-speaking Haitians, or English-speaking Jamaicans. Of the nearly 1.25 million legal immigrants who came to New York City since 1982, about a fourth came from just five Caribbean states: Jamaica, Guyana, Trinidad and Tobago, Haiti, and Barbados. Several thousand more came from smaller islands, or from Central American countries like Panama, Honduras, and Costa Rica whose black citizens, although counted as Hispanics by the Immigration and Naturalization Service, have historical ties to the anglophone West Indies and have settled in Caribbean enclaves.

Marcia Holness, a Jamaican immigrant, works in a ward in Manhattan's New York Hospital. Actually, it is one of two jobs she holds. She works at New York Hospital from 6 A.M. until 10 A.M. when her real job starts, downtown at the Board of Health. From before dawn, when she leaves East New York to ride into Manhattan, until midmorning, she walks the corridors of the city's prestigious East Side hospital, taking care of patients. "Time to give me some blood," she sings in the cheery greeting that begins most patients' days. She hums to herself as she works, wrapping the taut yellow cord around arms, swabbing skin with an alcohol pad, then plunging forth with her needle. Besides her winning smile, she walks with a determined gait, silent but solid in rubber soles on the polished floors. She looks like she was built for country work: neither stout nor sinewy, just solid, moving from bed to bed with the quickness of a wrestler, flicking trays and using her strong wrists to push aside the heavy plastic curtains that guard one patient's privacy from all others. Privacy is for well people, her no-nonsense attitude seems to say. I'm here to fetch me some blood.

The Board of Health job is less strenuous. There, Marcia works as a health advisor in a tuberculosis program, respectable white-collar work that most of her neighbors in Brooklyn would be lucky to have. She works the extra job at the hospital in order to raise tuition for a master's degree program at City University. Her long-term goal is to serve as a public health educator, teaching preventive medicine in schools and clinics in neighborhoods like East New York.

With the hour's commute home, she seldom gets to bed before 10 P.M. That doesn't leave much time for a social life, yet she has one. She plans to marry as soon as her boyfriend, also from Jamaica, finishes school. He's in the nursing program at New York City's Hunter College. Both Marcia and her boyfriend are studying to become citizens, another long-term goal, and after that, move into a house of their own. The Board of Health job, like the one at the hospital, is a union job, but the pay is hardly lavish. Her full-time job pays her $28,000 a year, and she earns another half-salary, $12,000, drawing blood and coding urine samples at the hospital. With the extra work, she outgrosses the rest of her family—father, brother, and her mother, who receives a disability check—but after city and state taxes bite into her pay, Marcia is by no means rich. "I am taking care of my mother," she says, matter of factly. "I am like the right hand for my family."

Hospital work is a particularly strong magnet for West Indians, both men and women. At New York Hospital, dozens work as nurses, nurse's aides, technicians, orderlies, and cleaners. It is the modern equivalent of factory work for at least two generations of Caribbean Americans, and quite logical in a country that has seen manufacturing decline while the business of health care delivery has exploded. You can find immigrants from every nook of the Caribbean working in some capacity with health-providers across the city: Saint Vincentians working at Saint Vincent's Hospital in the Village, Saint Lucians at Saint Luke's, and Montserratans at Montefiore.

If Marcia Holness's choice of a profession is not unusual, neither is her work ethic. Jamaican immigrants are considered so enterprising that they are viewed with a measure of respect that borders on awe in Brooklyn's black community. However, among other West Indians, Jamaicans sometimes are stereotyped as slackers—rude bumpkins with Rastafarian ways, their hair in shaggy dreadlocks, their fingers smelly with marijuana stains. That's the stereotype, but only to other West Indians. Barbadians, by contrast, consider themselves the model immigrants—founders, in 1913, of the Sons and Daughters of Barbados Benevolent Society, the city's first West Indian organization. Saint Lucians brag about their tiny island's three Nobel laureates. Then, of course, there are the Arubans—the "black Dutch." Erudite linguists, the typical Aruban is usually fluent in four languages—Dutch, English, Spanish, and Papiamento, a Portuguese/Dutch patois, which serves as lingua franca on three Caribbean islands and Suriname on the South American mainland. In a reprise of New York's first overseas colonists, so many Dutch Caribbeans have entered Brooklyn recently they have even begun to recolonize the original Dutch settlement of Vlackebos—today's Flatbush. The stately Reformed Protestant Dutch Church, built by Peter Stuyvesant back in the 1650s, rings again with Dutch hymns, with a certain island syncopation for style.

No immigrants embody America's ethnicity-as-condition-not-goal creed the way the Caribbeans do. They are every shade of black and white, yellow and red. They speak English, French, Spanish, Dutch, and Creole. Four kinds of Creole, in fact, depending on who colonized their island, or even which coast of the island. Their religions are Anglican, Baptist, Catholic, Muslim, Hindu, and voodoo. There is even a small congregation of black Barbadian Jews occupying an old synagogue in East New York. Yet no other immigrant group has proved so resilient in the face of endemic American racism. Their legacy within New York's black community is one of high-tone achievement. Civil rights leaders as diverse as Ralph Bunche, Roy Innis, Marcus Garvey, and Stokely Carmichael all were born or trace roots to the islands. Shirley Chisolm, America's first black congresswoman, was born in Brownsville of mixed Barbadian-Guyanese parentage. General Colin Powell, raised in the Bronx by Jamaican immigrants, may be the most prominent African American in public life today. He is certainly the country's most respected Caribbean American. Even Louis Farrakhan (whose pre-Muslim fame derived from performing as The Crooner, a Calypso singer) traces a Caribbean heritage.

Caribbean immigrants trace their entry back to before the 1900s, when many emigrated as British subjects. Despite the 1924

National Origins Act, many continued to enter the United States on the underutilized British quota. After the 1965 Immigration Reform Act, with family unification the new raison d'être of immigration, West Indians were drawn as never before. As each of the Caribbean islands gained independence from Britain, each former colony earned itself a place on the new immigration quota list, allowing thousands of islanders with no existing family tie to North America to begin their exodus. In 1960, just over 125,000 black Americans were foreign-born, mainly Caribbean. By 1980, there were over 800,000 Caribbean-born black Americans, more than half of them in the Northeast. In 1990, Caribbeans represented one in five black New Yorkers, and by 1995, they would be the majority in two boroughs, Brooklyn and Queens. Counted along with the Haitians, Caribbean immigrants and their children number nearly a million in New York City and its suburbs. By the year 2000, if current migration numbers hold, foreign-born blacks will be a majority among blacks citywide. The biggest single group comes from Jamaica, some 200,000 being the most reliable estimate.

Marcia Holness and her family emigrated from Jamaica in the early 1980s. Typically, Marcia's clan was part of an extended family, a village actually, that emigrated in stages. Both her mother and an aunt had come to New York in the 1970s looking for work. The aunt stayed, eventually finding permanent work as a nurse's aide. Marcia's mother felt homesick and went back to Jamaica. Over the next ten years, she came back and forth, more sojourner than immigrant, paying for vacations and then extending them by hiring herself out to clean private homes. Marcia's mother married her stepfather, Alexander Greenwood, in Jamaica. For a few years, the united Greenwood-Holness clan farmed together in a village near Thompson Town in the parish of Trelawny, one of Jamaica's fourteen counties located in the cool mountains south of Ocho Rios. "We raised pigs and goats and planted yams and things," Marcia remembers, a smile creasing her face. "You know, ethnic foods."

Marcia's description of rainbow mists rising over dirt roads, and clapboard churches and mangos free for the picking everywhere, well, it sounds so bucolic it's a wonder why anyone would give up such a life to settle in East New York. But in the 1980s, Jamaicans did not have to ponder reasons to leave. Jamaica had been independent for barely a decade when the OPEC oil shock hit, and sent an already struggling economy into the fiscal equivalent of a coma. The worldwide OPEC oil embargo raised crude oil prices astronomically, and devastated weak, energy-importing nations like Jamaica. The "ethnic foods" Marcia's family raised could not be raised without petroleum-based fertilizers, nor could the tractors be powered without gasoline, nor brought to market from those cool Trelawny hills. Jamaica had neither the roads to service family farms, nor the funds to build them. Isolation doomed rural folk like the Holness-Greenwoods to subsistence farming.

Where an earlier generation flocked to Britain and, to a lesser extent, Canada, Jamaicans with relatives in the United States had an easy time gaining legal entry to the United States. Thanks to the changes brought by the 1965 Immigration Reform Act, common people like the Holness-Greenwoods had a choice of destinations. Marcia's aunt, now a legal resident, sponsored her sister and her new husband, as well as their son and two daughters, Marcia and Delmarie. After a two-year wait for visas, the family arrived in Brooklyn in April 1983. Sponsorship by a legal resident meant Marcia and her siblings were automatically legal residents, too. Her parents were automatically eligible to work; the kids were eligible to attend any public school that accepted them. Finding work or a school to go to was not a problem: in 1983, Brooklyn was an empty place.

Cities seldom shrink to prosperity. As population declines, so does quality of life. Virtually by definition, it's the most mobile who leave a declining city. Therefore, the same self-selection process that guarantees that the best of the world enters through immigration also functions in reverse. And that is what happened to New York.

From the end of World War II until the mid-1970s, when a fiscal crisis pushed the city to the brink of bankruptcy, a city was bleeding to death.

During the 1970s, New York City lost over eight hundred thousand residents, and it was losing them everywhere. Census figures compiled in 1980 reveal that population drained from four of the five boroughs, Staten Island being the sole exception. Even Queens, traditionally the most prosperous of the outer boroughs, lost nearly a hundred thousand residents over the decade. In other places the flight was so massive—tens and even hundreds of thousands of residents—evacuees could only be compared to war refugees. White flight is one term for the exodus, yet after 1970, whites were hardly alone. The two Harlem districts represented by Manhattan's Community Boards 10 and 11 lost a combined 93,719 residents between 1970 and 1980. Across the river, in the Bronx, another 97,000 fled from the adjoining neighborhoods of Morrisania and Crotona Park. Altogether, the Bronx lost more than 300,000 people, more than a fifth of its 1970 population.

Yet for all the lurid tales of gang violence, "the Burning Bronx" was not the borough most abandoned. That distinction belonged to the original city of immigrants, Brooklyn. In a single decade, Brooklyn lost 370,000 people, enough refugees to create in 1980 the nation's thirty-fifth largest city, one slightly larger than Minneapolis. And Brooklyn's decline was boroughwide. Fifteen of eighteen Community Boards reported population decreases; of those fifteen, eight lost more than 10 percent of their households. Three neighborhoods—Bushwick, Brownsville, and Bedford-Stuyvesant—lost over a third. Although whites continued to flee Brooklyn (and, in many neighborhoods, still do), it was the black middle class that was leading the exodus in the 1970s.

By 1970, East New York and Brownsville were already majority black districts, yet their population loss was stunning. East New York, Brownsville, and Ocean Hill combined to lose fifty-five thousand people over the next ten years. To the northwest, the neighborhoods of Bedford-Stuyvesant and Bushwick lost more than twice that many—over 115,000 people all told. The two black ghettos that remained stable—Crown Heights (which lost only five thousand residents) and Midwood-Flatbush (which actually gained seven thousand)—survived because new immigrants were arriving, mainly from the English-speaking Caribbean and francophone Haiti. Thus, a self-fulfilling cycle was already in progress: middle-class blacks escaping left vacancies for the immigrants who would become the next middle class, who in turn attracted enough new investors to create a recovery.

But first Brooklyn had to bottom out, which happened on July 13, 1977. The time was 9:32 P.M., the moment when an accident at the Consolidated Edison plant near Indian Point in the northern suburbs interrupted power to New York, plunging the city into darkness. Immediately, throughout the city, chaos ruled. In the gathering darkness, with subway trains struck, literally, dead in their tracks and traffic lights extinguished, the city disappeared into an eerie ether. People poured into the streets, anxious to learn what had happened, when it would be fixed, and how soon they could go back to their air-conditioning and T.V. Many carried flashlights, and when they learned the outage was citywide, spontaneously fanned out to street corners to direct traffic.

As the streets filled, a festive mood prevailed. Greenwich Village restaurants coaxed drivers to pull their cars onto the sidewalks so the headlights shined inside and waitresses could serve their boisterous patrons. Candles lined window sills and bars, and the liquor poured. It was all so ingenious, a terrific demonstration of New Yorkers coping.

There were festivities all over New York that night, not all of them so benign. In every poor neighborhood, looting began as soon as the electricity sputtered out. No act of violence provoked the spree. There had been no outrageous court ruling to protest. No altercation with a policeman had gotten out of hand. People just started looting. Along Broadway, Pitkin Avenue, and Eastern Parkway in Brooklyn, under the Third Avenue elevated train in the Bronx, along 116th Street in East Harlem and on Delancey Street in lower Manhattan, and in Corona, Queens, throngs took to the streets to steal. Everywhere, police and merchants stood by, watching helplessly as shelves were stripped bare. In the Bronx, looters "liberated" more than fifty new cars from a Pontiac dealership's showroom. With their computers down, police couldn't even process the many men and women apprehended—more than three thousand by dawn. Rumors spread as wildly as the looting: of cops pitching teenage thugs from rooftops, of gangs targeting the affluent white suburbs for tomorrow's pillage. These were fantasies, of course, but they reflected the depth of the anger, black and white, seething across the city.

This was an example of New Yorkers coping no one could be charmed by. In 1965, a bigger blackout swept the Northeast, but these same neighborhoods were calm. Perhaps it was the colder weather—the 1965 outage was in November—or maybe it was just a different city. The shudder this time was of a city gone mad. Looters were laughing and chanting as they pulled their own cars onto sidewalks to light their way into stores. They used trucks with chains to drive up and, as *The New York Time*'s Francis X. Clines wrote in a postriot postmortem, "yank the steel security gates away from plate glass windows like baby teeth."

Blackout Night, 1977, brought the end of innocence for many, especially liberal journalists. "The darkness this time was blood on the window shards of Kiddie Bargain Town on Pitkin Avenue," the *Times*'s Clines wrote after surveying the wreckage of Brownsville. "Where looters wadded themselves in, slashing their own vanguard and popped back out with a ludicrous inventory of baby carriages and strollers and infant paraphernalia. There was a glittering, slithering carpet of broken glass and hydrant water stretching down the Pitkin strip, cordoned off by the police who witnessed a kind of vague darting, a cynical frenzy by crowds watching one minute, pushing into a store the next."

Besides abandoned storefronts, the 1977 riots left another permanent stain on the ghetto. It was a new term, "the underclass." The underclass was whoever remained in the ghetto by 1977, whoever didn't leave despite the gains of the civil rights struggle, whoever continued—despite the opening of American society—to be angry and black. Few seemed to realize that if the underclass hadn't gotten with the program—hadn't "bettered themselves" or simply hadn't followed the middle class out of the city—it was because its members were the ones least equipped to succeed. They were the old and infirm, the young and fatherless, the illiterate and the mentally disturbed. But that was not what the underclass meant after 1977. The underclass became a code word for "abandoned."

From 1977 forward, the image, and reality, of the ghetto only worsened. As refugees continued to flee, now even faster than before the rioting, government policy became one of containment, a determination that the ghetto's plagues not leave the ghetto. It was a futile notion.

After Blackout Night, West Indians were just about the only Brooklynites, white or black, moving in. They came much like the Greenwood-Holness family.

The five new immigrants crowded into an apartment on Miller Avenue, a block west of the Van Siclen subway station where Marcia was later mugged. The apartment belonged to Marcia's aunt, and actually they crowded into a single room, which the aunt rented to them for thirty dollars a week. The rest of the four-room flat was rented to another family, plus a couple of temporary boarders. It stayed that way for two months, until Alexander and Myrtle Greenwood found jobs and began receiving regular paychecks. By summer Auntie was leasing them the whole apartment for four hundred dollars a month. "We got three more rooms then," Marcia recalls, "two more bedrooms, plus the living room. And our original room we shared."

Auntie wasn't a skinflint. She was generous with old clothes, extra food, and information she picked up about work nearby. It was generosity of a paternal sort. Auntie was the executive director of this family enterprise, whose "product" amounted to getting as many of her people up from the island, and employed, as she could.

She needed Marcia's family to start working immediately to help make her own house payments. She needed them to be on the way to owning their own home so that they, too, could rent rooms out to in-law/boarders, and thus double the amount of production. Luckily, she learned the Wartburg Lutheran Home for the Aging was hiring, and sent her sister and brother-in-law to apply. They were hired immediately as "dietary aides"—Alexander as a pot washer in the kitchen, his wife as a food server, wheeling carts through the dormitory. Marcia entered George Wingate High School, joining a swelling majority of Haitian, Jamaican, and other Caribbean-born students. By 1985, she was working, too, as a clerk for the Board of Education. In 1988, she started working at New York Hospital, squeezing in part-time hours as a medical techni-cian's aide between classes at Hunter College, where she would earn her degree in health sciences.

While Marcia was educating herself into the middle class, her mother and stepfather provided a secure anchor at Wartburg Lu-theran. Located at the corner of Sheffield and Atlantic Avenues, the nursing home has been in operation since 1875. In many ways it was an ideal workplace for Mr. and Mrs. Greenwood. For one thing, the demand for labor was continual. Like many nursing homes, Wartburg Lutheran had more staff than residents—about three hundred full and part-time employees for just 225 beds. For another, the job was no more than a ten-minute walk from their new home on Miller Avenue. Salaries, of course, were low. Myrtle and Alexander Greenwood started at a base annual salary of just over $13,000, although one of the perks of their employment was membership in Local 144 of the Service Employees International Union, which offered generous health care coverage and a savings plan.

Even in 1983, $13,000 a year was appallingly low pay. But it was more than adequate for an immigrant couple with little education—neither Mr. nor Mrs. Greenwood had gone past the sixth grade—and few marketable skills. The Greenwoods had little contact with the residents, mainly impoverished white ethnics with disabilities. And since meals are served every day, there was real job security. From 6 A.M. when the cooks arrived, to 8 P.M. when the last pots and pans were dried, work went on almost without a break. There was enough work, in other words, to employ three staggered shifts, which allowed one of the Greenwoods to see their younger children off to school, and for the other to bring them back. Thus, when treated as a "couple's" job, $13,000 apiece was actually quite lavish. Instead of thinking of two Greenwoods with two bad jobs, the family "split" a factory worker's income of $26,000, plus benefits.

In many ways, Wartburg Lutheran was even better than the factory: it was cleaner, it was less dangerous, and it had no grave-yard shift. Indeed, as light manufacturing began to disappear from the New York jobscape—something that had been happening steadily since the late 1940s—nursing homes, hospitals, clinics, and home nursing *became* the new factory for many new immigrants. West Indians flocked to this industry and quickly came to dominate the low end of the job spectrum. In many ways, West Indians filled niches no other immigrant could, or would, fill. English-speaking immigrants fit well into positions that were essentially industrial in nature—scrubbing bathrooms, preparing meals, moving patients— but also required an ability to communicate urgent news. Such as: "that patient is having trouble breathing," or "Mrs. Johnson has fallen from her bed." Other immigrants, no matter how dedicated, might not be able to do that. It is no accident that today, in all of New York's hospitals, the two biggest groups of workers are West Indian and Filipino immigrants.

The West Indians fit neatly into health work for another reason, their race. "There is a fundamental demographic fact: Southern blacks are not coming to New York in the numbers they used to," explains Dr. Waldaba Stewart, a board member of Kings County Hospital in Brooklyn, and former New York state senator. Dr. Stewart, who was born in Panama, adds that hospital and nursing-home work always attracted the unskilled, but usually not better educated New York natives. "The typical immigrant is willing to take any job, many times jobs that other Americans are not willing to take," he says. "In hospitals, they end up taking janitor jobs, disposing medical waste, or lifting a two-hundred pound patient. These are hard jobs."*

Hard and increasingly unacceptable to many black Americans. The same mid-1960s politics that brought immigration reform also brought choice to American-born blacks, nowhere more than in the workplace. Hospital work, previously among a handful of respectable jobs available to adults, suddenly became second rate. Now there were new opportunities to join the building trades' unions, or the civil service, or to go to college. The growing public bureaucracy, which would one day employ Marcia Holness, sucked thousands of talented black New Yorkers out of the menial-job sector. As a consequence of this sudden upward mobility, the old jobs looked worse than they were. Yet those members of the community who could best appreciate that fact no longer had to. That led to a second consequence: with the rise of black consciousness, service jobs were perceived as servile positions, beneath dignity.

Sadly, as one sector of talented black Americans rose into the mainstream, another at the margins of the job market began its decline. While American-born blacks were chafing against jobs cleaning white houses, watching white children, and sponge-bathing the white infirm, whites were growing uneasy hiring what they saw as angry young blacks. Through the 1960s and 1970s, as race relations everywhere deteriorated, immigrants in New York were the beneficiaries of two widening gaps. One was the gap between black and white; the other, the gap between the black middle class above and the growing welfare class below.

Sullen hostility, which wouldn't disqualify an otherwise able worker for a factory job, would be deadly to employment prospects in a job requiring at least some interpersonal skills. But factory work was disappearing. In the fifteen years following the passage of the Hart-Celler Immigration Reform Act, New York City would be drained of more than a million residents, and lose half that many

* Material quoted from or information developed for a story appearing in the February 12, 1996, issue of FORBES Magazine entitled "Ghetto Blasters," reprinted with permission of Forbes Inc.

manufacturing jobs. That deepened the dilemma of the unemployed, but left immigrants in an enviable position: doubled and tripled up in cheap rental apartments, they swarmed toward low-paying service jobs. Throughout the ghetto, American-born blacks watched with anger as the growing West Indian community in its midst climbed into the middle class. Thus, by the time the Holness-Greenwood family settled in East New York, a self-fulfilling cycle of racial pride mixed with racial hatred had forged a demographic change.

It had also forged the beginnings of renewal. In 1983, Brooklyn had about 2.2 million residents, around a half million short of its 1950 peak. The number of factory jobs had declined from 237,000 to fewer than 100,000. And yet a substitute workforce had begun to emerge, and with it a replacement for the old ethnic "working class" that had walked to work, toting lunch buckets to Brooklyn's many factories. It had been replaced by a new corps of workers commuting to the hospital. The old neighborhoods that had grown around those factories were being replaced by new ones, rising within a short bus or car-service ride to the hospital.

If you look at a map of Brooklyn, it will be no surprise to you that the neighborhoods that came back first, the West Indian neighborhoods, rose around these new work sites. The most obvious spot is Hospital Row—eighteen blocks of health-care facilities along Winthrop Street from New York Avenue to Utica Avenue across the heart of Brooklyn. Bounded by the Flatbush corridor on the west, Hospital Row is within walking distance of two major subway lines and about a dozen bus lines. More than that, Hospital Row is surrounded by row upon row of Brooklyn's classic two-family wooden houses, as well as brownstones and apartment blocks and, just to the south, blocks of well-tended, detached homes. All this housing made Hospital Row a factory within walking distance, and an opportunity for all the Myrtle and Alexander Greenwoods looking for a beachhead. By the end of the decade, the neighborhoods surrounding Hospital Row—Wingate, Flatbush, Crown Heights, East Flatbush, and Brownsville—had become the heart of West Indian New York, and had even begun to spread south and east.

To stand in the middle of Winthrop Street today—and see hundreds of cleaners and nurses and technicians and drivers and secretaries and all the other facilitators of the modern health establishment file past each morning, almost all of them local residents, almost all of them black—is to see the rebirth of Brooklyn. Like Henry Ford's great River Rouge plants, Hospital Row is the factory at the heart of a thriving working-class community. Serving white patients (and, with the aging of New York's native population, serving blacks, too) translates into jobs for black America, and savings to rebuild its neighborhoods.

Between 1980 and 1990, Brooklyn recovered seventy thousand new residents, its first gain in three decades. Another twenty-five thousand returned by 1995. These numbers are small yet important, since it was black Brooklyn that accounted for almost all of the increase. The neighborhoods most affected by middle-class flight were also among the first to be gentrified. Bushwick posted a net gain of ten thousand new households in the decade following the blackout riots. Bedford-Stuyvesant posted a gain of over five thousand. Crown Heights, the epicenter of a Caribbean population explosion, added over twenty thousand households from 1980 to 1990. Midwood-Flatbush contributed another sixteen thousand. West Indian immigrants accounted for as much as two thirds of rejuvenated Brooklyn's measurable population growth.

And while many West Indians started as the servile class of the new ghetto, they, too, were reborn. Their children became Marcia Holness, studying for her master's degree. Gradually, the West Indians began replacing the old, prewar middle class. And, by the mid-1990s, they were replacing something else: the pre–civil rights black middle class. Yet this time history would not repeat itself. This time the middle class would stay.

If it were only a matter of people and jobs, the story of the Caribbeans in Brooklyn would be quite unremarkable. They came, they stayed, but were they really any more important, say, than the Turks in Germany, or France's North Africans? The reason they are more important, much more important, is their willingness to forge a community. What mattered was not that they came and worked, but that they came and invested—that they felt welcome enough, even as black immigrants, to become black Americans. Confidence defines the market, and nowhere have market forces been more telling than in Brownsville, especially along the old Pitkin Avenue strip.

Today, twenty years after Blackout Night, most New Yorkers would be surprised to learn that home ownership is on the rise in all of Brooklyn's black ghettos. So are household incomes, and test scores in ghetto schools. Most New Yorkers would be surprised to discover Pitkin Avenue is a thriving commercial strip again and that blocks leveled to open fields in the aftermath of the riot are today filled with tidy two-family townhouses. Most are owned and occupied by West Indian immigrants. Out of the ashes of Blackout Night a new community rose, and West Indian immigrants were its vanguard. Young Jamaican students, many taking advantage of affirmative action slots to gain admission to the city's many university programs, began acquiring homes in the old ghetto. Some paid as little as $1.50 for their first properties—in those cases often abandoned shells or even abandoned lots. Some made fortunes restoring houses and selling them to fellow West Indians.

The West Indian invasion reversed Brownsville's long decline, from what had been the city's biggest Jewish ghetto to city's most desolate black one. The renaissance of Amboy Street, Margaret Sanger's old home and later Mike Tyson's, represents just one success story among hundreds. First abandoned, then burned, then bulldozed, Amboy Street's two-family houses disappeared during the 1960s and 1970s. Eventually, whole blocks stood bare, leaving illegal garbage dumps and the hulks of stripped automobiles. But in 1980, the rowhouses started to return. The city launched a multibillion-dollar restoration to lure working families back to Brownsville. Starting with the Nehemiah Housing Partnership at the corner of Livonia Street and Mother Gaston Boulevard, the pioneers were placed by local churches, and included a few West Indian families. By 1987, when the developers reached Amboy

Street, hundreds of new homes had been erected in Brownsville, and Caribbean owners were a solid majority. Many of the new homes have campers or motorboats on trailers parked out back. Two or three cars are usually parked inside the iron-grille gates, often sporting decals or rearview mirror ornaments in the design of flags from Guyana, Jamaica, Barbados, or Aruba. Sold for $50,000 each in 1987, they are worth upwards of $120,000 today, according to area realtors. Most of the original owners are still on-site. "As the program became a success story, we saw an increasingly West Indian population," explains Ken Thorbourne, a housing activist with the East Brooklyn Congregations, himself the son of black Panamanian immigrants. The East Brooklyn Congregations were the original Nehemiah Housing sponsor. "West Indians are convinced, more than other folks, that a turnaround is going to happen," Thorbourne adds. "And, more than a lot of folks, they are able to come up with the down payment for a house."

In some developments, almost every home is occupied by an immigrant. Elon Gibson, a Barbadian who heads the block association at Amboy and Blake Avenue, estimates 75 percent of the development he moved into in 1990—eleven hundred homeowners—are Caribbean-born. The city does not keep statistics on ethnicity in the owner-occupied projects, but officials agree that at least half of the eight thousand or so homes built in Brooklyn and the Bronx are occupied by immigrants, mainly West Indians. A stroll down any of the partnership streets in Brownsville reveals the obvious: every car in every driveway sports a Jamaican flag, an "I ♥ Guyana" bumper sticker, or a fender reflector fashioned in a red-black-red design: the colors of Trinidad and Tobago. Mailboxes are stuffed with copies of the *New York Carib News* and Kingston's *Daily Gleaner*. Yet few homes are occupied by native-born blacks because few U.S. citizens are conditioned to treat home ownership in the ghetto as a middle-class achievement. Immigrants do. "I know who I am and I do not make a decision on where to live based on a perception," sniffs Bob James, a native of Guyana. "It's clean here," he boasts. "Every yard is fenced in. This has been a great investment."

Brownsville will never again be Jewish, but it will be middle class. Where nearly fifty thousand had fled the neighborhood in the 1970s, over eleven thousand returned to the community between 1980 and 1990. According to the census, twenty-four thousand new black residents came into the community, more than half of them foreign-born, accounting for the eleven thousand newcomers, and replacing thirteen thousand more old-timers who left. The immigrants brought their earnings from jobs on Hospital Row, and their middle-class household incomes, the output of three and four jobs per residence. Native-born blacks who achieve middle-class status don't have to live in Brownsville—they make too much money. But immigrants, especially black immigrants, are among the lowest-paid wage earners in New York. Yet Caribbean household incomes are well above average—over $32,000—considerably higher than those of American-born blacks citywide. The explanation is simple: virtually every Caribbean home has several wage earners.

Buying a home in Brownsville is not only possible, it is necessary. Families need space to accommodate so many workers. Workers need to be close to the subway to get to their jobs. In a sense, the West Indian wave represents a mass choice by foreign-born blacks to invest in a lifestyle most Americans, black and white, have tried to avoid. If owning a home in Brownsville amounts to failure, so does holding the kind of "menial" jobs West Indians use to buy those homes. Menial work is greening the ghetto, however, with Caribbean immigrants earning the green.

"You have brother and sister buying the same two-family house together," Elon Gibson explains. "He occupies one half, she has the other." Elon Gibson's home, a neat three-bedroom just a few blocks from the subway, costs him less than five hundred dollars a month in mortgage payments and property taxes, well within the reach of most working New York families and a lot cheaper than nearby rentals. In 1980, fewer than one in every ten Brownsville homes was occupied by its owner; today it is nearly one in every six.

Marcia Holness and her family bought their home in 1989. After just six years in the country, they had saved enough for a two-story house on Vermont Street between Blake and Dumont Avenues. The house, Marcia recalls, was occupied by an Asian couple from Guyana. The asking price was $140,000, but no bank would issue a mortgage for anything over $125,000. To make the down payment and pay all closing costs, the Greenwood-Holness clan relied on special leverage, widely available in Caribbean enclaves, derived from savings circles called "su-su hands."

Su-su—or "partnership"—as the practice is called in Jamaica, is an informal savings plan. Some are decades old, and rarely admit newcomers into the circle. Others are ad hoc, run by a "banker" holding savings for dozens of "partners" depositing whatever sum has been agreed upon each week. Hospital wards have them, so do construction sites, schools, restaurants, and factories. Partners then take turns "winning" a "hand." Su-su hands of up to five thousand dollars a week are not unusual. Each partner selects the week he or she wants to take the pot, often timing the windfall to pay for school tuition, Christmas gifts, or a down payment on a house. Once every partner wins a hand, the circle dissolves or spins again. Some people use su-su to pay for a vacation trip back to the island, or just to make sure they save part of their salaries. It is peer-induced savings that bears no interest to the depositor putting money in or the borrower taking it out. "I know if it was up to me, I might miss a week," says Gloria Nelson, a Jamaican teaching at a Brooklyn elementary school. "This way I never miss a week."

Su-su in New York, as in Africa and the Caribbean, tends to be the province of women. Some su-su bankers are famous, and new members wait years for an invitation to join the circle of loyal savers. Marcia's aunt was in a circle of forty partners, who invited Myrtle Greenwood to join. Her husband joined the su-su at Wartburg Lutheran. Together they put two hundred dollars a week into su-su, and soon saved ten thousand dollars toward their house. When it was time to buy, they got ten thousand dollars more for closing costs by timing two winning su-su hands together.

Today the clan's two-story townhouse on Vermont Avenue is almost at the outer edge of Brownsville's growing Caribbean enclave. It was not lavish when they found it in 1989 ("It was basically a shell," Marcia recalls), but after renovation, it is the envy of the block. Its clean red bricks fairly glow next to the drab, peeling paint of some of the neighboring homes. The white doorjamb and matching windowsills are scrubbed to a bright shine that twinkles as sunlight picks up the bits of mica embedded in the stone. Now, the wheel of progress turns anew. Just as Auntie hosted the clan twelve years ago, the house on Vermont Street is a mix of cousins and nephews newly arrived from the old country. One new arrival lives in the basement, and works as a janitor at Wartburg Lutheran. Another Jamaican family recently moved in down the street; someone from Trinidad has been visiting the block, itching to buy.

The gentrification of Brownsville and other recovering ghettos is not an accident of immigration, but immigration's essence. Immigration to Brownsville means more than a ghetto on the mend, but something all of society shares: the immigrants' savings, their home mortgages, college tuitions, and all their new businesses just waiting to be dreamed up and tried. It means, too, the beginning of the end of racism—the end of an age when "black" meant "poor," and only the underclass lived in Brooklyn.

And New York is not unique. Some one hundred thousand Africans and Afro-Caribbeans live in the District of Columbia. Houston, Chicago, and Atlanta all have growing black immigrant communities. Miami, a city already in the Caribbean, may have the country's fastest-growing immigrant 'hood—Little Haiti, nearly a hundred thousand strong. And that's not even mentioning another hundred thousand West Indian "replants," mainly Jamaicans, who settled first in northern cities then remigrated closer to home.

Wherever they come from, and wherever they settle, black immigrants are doing what immigrants do everywhere. They build families, they open churches, they save neighborhoods. Like immigrants from everywhere, they take low-paying, entry-level jobs, then build on family ties to save money and buy homes. Black immigrants may be America's most essential new citizens, because they are the only immigrants who can unlock the value lying fallow in ghetto real estate. When Nigerians or Jamaicans gentrify, quality of life improves via a mass transfer of one community for another.

A black neighborhood stays black. Instead of fleeing to middle-class neighborhoods, immigrants discover they have made prosperous enclaves of their own. The working class becomes middle class simply by staying put.

Anyone can see the process simply by walking the streets of Brooklyn, streets where walking, at least without an escort, was unadvised just a few years ago. Halsey Street in Bushwick, like the area south of Pitkin Avenue, was reduced to open plain following Blackout Night. Today, neat rows of townhouses with blue and white siding fill the blocks south of Broadway. Almost all the new residents come from one country: Guyana.

"Got new people coming into the neighborhood, and new housing," says Stanley Henry, who owns a business nearby. "The older folks buy to improve their properties, the new folks buy to decorate." And he should know. Guyana-born Stanley Henry has been in Brooklyn for over ten years, operating a hardware store and buying property while waiting for a turnaround. He owns Henry Distributors, a spanking new, 1,300-square-foot home improvement store erected in 1995 on land purchased at the city's abandoned property auction. Henry enjoys brisk trade selling electrical switches and linoleum, and cement, Sheetrock and floor tiles— literally the bricks and mortar of urban renewal.

More than two hundred would-be Stanley Henrys crowded into an auditorium at police headquarters for another property auction in May 1995. Here and there sat a turbaned Sikh, or a coterie of Hasidic men clicking calculators. A lone white Yuppie in a blue blazer and open shirt worked the phones outside. Almost everyone else was black, either West Indian or West African. Bidders were flush with cash and ready to deal.

Bidding for Brooklyn parcels began at 10 A.M. Albert Appleton, a plumbing contractor from Antigua, bid $68,000 for a lot in Crown Heights. He said he needed space for his trucks, but a second business, car-leasing, would work out of the same location. A congregation of Guyanese Hindus paid $55,000 for a corner on Liberty Avenue in East New York. The community was growing, they explained, and needed a bigger place to worship. Again and again, street names synonymous with urban blight brought excited bids from the hopeful.

A Haitian family sitting up front had its eye on Parcel 30, a three-family apartment building in the Fort Greene section. It had been abandoned for over fifteen years. That, and a brownstone on Amboy Street, were the choice parcels of the day—the only ones the blue-blazered Yuppie abandoned the phones for. After opening at $5,000, bids for the Fort Greene lot quickly reached $20,000, then $25,000, then $30,000. The Haitians dropped out at $32,000, as the winner, the Ayinla family of Nigeria, took the decrepit shell. Final bid: $35,000.

The showdown for 355 Amboy was even more spirited. Blue-blazer dropped out at $33,000, leaving a Jamaican bidding against two Barbadian brothers. The winning bid was $70,000, to the Jamaican. Sitting on the edge of a weed-strewn lot, its windows boarded up, and its brick covered with gang graffiti, 355 Amboy gave new meaning to the term "fixer upper," and sent a shudder of fear through some of the prospective bidders who visited on guided tour a few days before the auction. The winner's vision was clear: he saw his dream house. The city raised over a million dollars in under three hours. At a second auction in October, it raised over five million.

Far from displacing American-born blacks, these millions restore life in the black community, rejuvenating all the institutions —black-owned stores, black-run schools, black churches, black sports teams, black block associations—that withered during the years of the great exodus. While it is true that most of the beneficiaries of this renaissance are also foreign-born (and, some would argue, less deserving of the fruits of urban renewal), a sizeable minority is not. The benefits of black gentrification may not devolve equally to all blacks, but without immigrant enterprise, few might benefit at all.

Consider the Holness-Greenwood family. Shortly after they took possession of their new home, they learned that the corner grocery was fronting for drug dealers. The family organized other homeowners on the block to force police to close it down. Today, a West Indian grocer occupies the space. The clan expects to join thousands of Caribbean immigrants who have become citizens, and a powerful voting bloc demanding services for black neighborhoods.

Every new storefront regained from blight is a benefit to all of Brownsville's people, just in the way that every street lamp that stays lit makes that patch of sidewalk below that much safer for every pedestrian. In this way, Caribbean immigrants are restoring prosperity. The number of new businesses launched in Brownsville grew by a hundred a year in the 1990s, from six hundred to just over a thousand by the end of 1994. By the mid-1990s, Pitkin Avenue had been reborn. Payless Shoesource, a discount shoe store, Martin Paints home supply, and Dunkin' Donuts have opened new outlets along the strip. Global Link, a discount long-distance telephone kiosk, Caribbean Electronics, and the Golden Krust Caribbean Bakery are on the same block where Kiddie Bargain Town was pillaged.

Golden Krust, a West Indian fast-food shop, is the Pitkin Avenue outlet of one of New York's most successful Caribbean enterprises. Founded in 1990 by a family from the town of Saint Andrew in eastern Jamaica, it was launched with an investment of just a hundred thousand dollars. Today Golden Krust operates in three states, with annual sales topping $10 million. Its key product is meat patties, the spicy stuffed pastries West Indians consume almost as a staple. Its market niche is the emerging West Indian neighborhood. Rather than compete with a frozen product distributed through wholesalers, Golden Krust sells in its own bakeries, letting the aroma of fresh-baked patties draw customers in from the street.

In a sense, they're following the smell all the way up from Jamaica. Lowell Hawthorne, Golden Krust's chief executive, is one of the "Sons" in Hawthorne & Sons, an industrial bakery founded in Jamaica in the late 1940s. Altogether, Hawthorne had eleven sons and daughters, but by the time they were ready to take over his thriving business, Jamaica was on the verge of collapse. It was the mid-1970s, Lowell recalls, when many customers were already heading north to New York. "My dad's factory was state of the art," he says. "But the economy was a shambles. The only way we could expand was to go abroad."*

Not right away, of course, or not right away with meat patties. Few Jamaican enterprises could have exported directly to the United States in the mid-1970s, and certainly not a perishable, highly regulated product like processed food. But anyone can export know-how, and that is what the senior Hawthorne did. He sent Lowell north in 1981 to join his older sister Laurice and enroll in the City University of New York. Four more brothers followed: Lloyd, Charles, Raymond, and Milton, as well as sisters Jacqueline and Lorraine. Lowell married Lorna, a girl he knew in Jamaica, and, thanks to su-su, Lowell and Lorna bought their first home in the Bronx in 1983, just three years after Lowell arrived. Their combined salary was $19,000 a year.

Su-su also bought a house for Lloyd, and for Milton, Laurice, Charles, Raymond, and Jacqueline. By the end of the 1980s, the Hawthornes had joined a growing colony of Jamaicans along the Gun Hill Road corridor in the North Bronx, most solid homeowners and potentially good customers. In 1989, the family launched Hawthorne & Sons abroad, taking out second mortgages on the various homesteads, and pooling their management talent to sell meat patties. They started with one bakery on Gun Hill Road, then a second nearby. Within two years they expanded into New Jersey and Connecticut, and within three they moved into an abandoned factory in the Bronx's Bathgate area. They opened on Pitkin Avenue in 1993, right around the time West Indians reached a critical mass in Brownsville, and the neighborhood began to turn around.

Like a lot of West Indians, Lowell Hawthorne is mystified, and angered, by the failure of native-born African Americans to rise out of poverty. He is baffled at their willingness to live in housing projects when home ownership is so closely within reach. His own

* Material quoted from or information developed for a story appearing in the November 6, 1995, issue of FORBES Magazine entitled "Imported Entrepreneurs," reprinted with permission of Forbes Inc.

employees, many in the country less than a year, run a su-su that pays out six thousand dollars a week. "Just three times around," Lowell says, "you can buy a house. Three hands, that's all you need for the down payment."

Unfortunately, many Americans, white and black, treat the rise of the West Indians as proof of the inferiority of American-born blacks. It's an unfair comparison. Over the past thirty years, talented African Americans have enjoyed the means of escape from the ghetto and many, many thousands have done so. When they did, they took a sense of community with them. Black immigrants, on the other hand, arrived with more than simply their determination. They also brought their institutions from the islands, their churches and banks and business networks, even informal ones like su-su circles. Black Brooklyn today hosts the Caribbean American Chamber of Commerce (the Haitian American Chamber of Commerce is across the border in Queens), and the Caribbean Women's Health Association. Brooklyn also boasts the Guyana Ex-Police Association of America (talk about a deterrent to crime!) and the Jamaica Progressive League.

More important, at least for restoring the city's housing stock, are the Jamaican building societies, two of which now have permanent offices in Brooklyn. Jamaica National Building Society, founded by the Baptist church shortly after slavery was abolished on the island, dates back to the 1840s. Like its younger colleague, the Victoria Mutual Building Society, it is essentially a savings and loan association, a thrift, designed to finance the homes of its depositors. For years, branch offices in Brooklyn served as collection points for immigrants determined to save for a retirement home in Jamaica. In the past five years, they have changed missions. They still send money home, but they are also making home mortgages for Jamaicans living in New York.

Then, there are the schools. Thanks to the West Indians, years of decline have been reversed at the City University of New York, or CUNY, for over a century a legendary incubator of immigrant success. Schools that foundered on the 1960s' "open admissions" policy (which allowed any high school graduate to attend college, regardless of performance) have been bolstered by a new wave of determined and academically gifted immigrant children. Not all of the immigrants are black, but on campuses where fights over Afrocentric curriculum have eroded racial tolerance and academic integrity, no other group has done as much to dampen the tension. Immigrant students, many of them educated into high school in the West Indies, have been drawn to CUNY because the admission process in island schools is so onerous. New York, then, becomes the beneficiary of a windfall of talent, much of which will stay in the black community and contribute to the growing black middle class.

Ultimately that contribution becomes self-fulfilling, bolstering the efforts of strivers within the U.S.-born community by adding strength to their number.

Consider someone like Crystal Giles, a "minority" black at the all-black, and private, Northeastern Academy in upper Manhattan. In 1995 Giles graduated as senior class president at the competitive school, one of only a handful of African Americans at what has become a majority Caribbean school. Seventy-three years old, Northeastern is the jewel in the crown of Christian schools ringing the ghetto, where black-run institutions that are equal parts religious, competitive, and affordable are a rarity, at best. More than 95 percent of Northeastern graduates attend four-year universities, with many alumni going on to earn degrees in the professions. Northeastern is run by the Seventh Day Adventists.

Tuition at Northeastern is less than two thousand dollars a year, and the waiting list for each entering class is long. Although the school was founded decades before Caribbeans began their current surge into the city, it surely would have closed its doors years ago if immigrant families had not been determined to preserve it as a cheap alternative to the city's deteriorating public schools. That determination dovetailed with African-American parents searching for havens for their own children.

Giles, who had to commute from across the city by subway each morning to attend Northeastern, recalls girls from her Queens neighborhood who brought babies to the local high school. She knows many more who used pregnancy as an excuse to drop out and collect welfare. "Northeast was a place you don't have to be afraid to be abstinent," she recalls. Drug use and gang violence were unknown.

Racism's strings were not unfelt—particularly on field trips away from New York—nor were students spared the perils of upper Harlem's streets. But Northeastern's dedicated staff gave comfort and confidence to students of all backgrounds. "We were an all-black school, and our teachers really wanted us to make it," Giles concludes.

In this way Caribbean New York has raised the standards, or at least the opportunities, for all blacks. Across Brooklyn, Caribbean immigrants have started dozens of private church-based elementary schools, all of which accept students from African-American homes. A few grant scholarships to children from homes receiving public assistance. The Caribbean parishes of the Seventh Day Adventists, run fifteen schools in New York, administering a $6 million annual budget. Virtually the entire amount is covered by students' tuition, including some 20 percent who are American-born. African-American families are delighted to pay just two hundred dollars a month for a competitive, religious-based education. Elsewhere, Haitian and Jamaican parishioners have swelled the rolls of Catholic and Episcopal parochial schools, in some places saving schools from extinction.

Even more impressive is the impact on the public high schools. When the Board of Education released test scores for city high schools in 1995, three of Brooklyn's top schools "belonged" to West Indians. The top school, Midwood High, has more Russians than Caribbeans, but it also has the city's only bilingual medical science curriculum taught in Haitian Creole. The other winners, Clara Barton and East New York Transit Tech, are almost 100 percent black, with some two thirds of their students foreign-born.

"Ten years ago this was a failed school," Jesse Lazarus, the principal of East New York Transit Tech, said before the June 1995 graduation. Not too many years ago, he added, commencement was held in his office, so few students managed to graduate. East New

York Transit Tech was a dumping ground in the 1980s. Despite training students in electronics, machinery repair, and other skills geared to put them into jobs with New York's Metropolitan Transportation Authority, there were few takers. In 1986, Lazarus had four hundred applicants for four hundred freshman spots and had to accept everyone who applied. Tough and black were the surrounding streets, and tough and black were those who went to school at Transit Tech—often discipline cases from other schools. In 1995, Lazarus fielded five thousand applications for the class of 1999, allowing Transit Tech to screen out ten of every twelve applicants. Many of those accepted come from Caribbean families where one parent already works for the MTA. Instead of, as one student expressed, "waiting for college to tell me what to do in life," Transit Tech students enter planning for $15-an-hour jobs on the trains. Many, if they are Caribbean, are intent on being the third or fourth wage earner that will enable the family to buy a house.

Transit Tech raises expectations, however, and most graduates attend four-year universities. A similar alchemy occurs at Clara Barton, a vocational school for medical specialties dominated by West Indian women. Like the boys at Transit Tech, Clara Barton's students enter expecting to go to work, even to follow their parents into the hospitals and nursing homes. Once exposed to a rigorous academic climate, many thrive in an all-black school. Foreign and native-born Clara Barton graduates garner millions of dollars in college scholarships every year—and are heavily recruited for spots at the University of Pennsylvania, Duke, Cornell, and Brown.

Clara Barton's 1995 valedictorian, Michaelle Jean-Pierre, is part of a new generation of black Brooklynites waiting in the wings. Born to Haitian immigrants, Michaelle is the youngest of seven children. Four older brothers hold engineering degrees, one sister teaches in the public schools, the other is a microbiologist. What makes the Jean-Pierre family remarkable is how well it thrived in public institutions, and at how little cost to the public.

All six of Michaelle's older siblings are products of the City University of New York. And all six still live and work in the city.

Their parents have been in New York since the 1960s, yet none of the children burdened the public elementary schools. The first six were raised in Haiti, returning for high school. Michaelle was raised in Brooklyn, but attended Crown Heights' Saint Francis of Assisi school through the eighth grade. In September 1995, Michaelle became the seventh Jean-Pierre to enter CUNY, starting a premedical program. She hopes to be practicing pediatrics, back in Brooklyn, by the beginning of the next century. "Being Haitian gave me a lot of motivation," she says. "We were the first black republic to win independence. It's something to live up to."

CHAPTER FOUR

California:
"Land and Liberty"

California is Paranoia Deluxe.
Senator Alan Simpson, in New York, June 1995

★

The latest Mexican revolution is being fought in tiny Carruthers, California. Carruthers is a farmtown of two thousand people located in the center of America's richest agricultural district, Fresno County. The revolution here is not one of high-tech agriculture, or of NAFTA-inspired international trade. It is the Mexican revolution started almost a century ago. For *guerrilleros* like Alberto Solis Casillas, it is the same Mexican revolution Emiliano Zapata promised in 1910. *"Tierra y Libertad!!"* was their rallying cry. Land and liberty.

Today, Mexican agriculture lags decades behind the rest of the developing world, in many villages even less productive than before 1910. However, thousands of Mexican farmers are thriving in America. It took a revolution in U.S. immigration law to give Mexican farmworkers what was promised to their grandfathers—the end of peonage. In California, where Mexicans are numerous and proud, Zapata's promise is being realized. If the land isn't free, the peons are.

A thirty-year veteran of the struggle, Alberto Solis is Mexico's "consul" in Carruthers. It is not an official title, rather one he holds by affirmation, a kind of honorary title to go with his three trucks, two *ranchos*, and the 140 acres of flat California soil Solis works with his family. "I am known here," he says modestly. Which means, among other things, that Alberto Solis is a soft touch. He's the one newcomers know will be ready with a handout, a meal, a job, or a tip on where jobs go begging. Fresno, a city of almost four hundred thousand, has an official Mexican consulate downtown. That office—with its seal, Social Security forms, and cashier's counter fronted by Plexiglas—is for the *compadres* who have business with Mexican authorities back home. Mexico has forty-three consulates in the United States, more than any other nation. Mexico, of course, has more of its citizens living here than any other country. But as patriotic as Mexicans are, no government can dictate loyalty. Mexicans like Alberto Solis, who have seen the future and know it speaks English, are consuls to another Mexico, the hybrid Mexico rising out of the California fields.

By the year 2020, there may be as many as 60 million people in gringo America who were either born in Mexico or who have parents who were. Most will either live in or enter the United States through California. That's the future Mexicans laughingly call *La Reconquista*, the reconquest. It's the present that Californians call "the immigration crisis." And most native-born aren't laughing.

Both Solises, Alberto and his wife, Maria, come from tiny villages. Alberto was born in Guadalupe Victoria, in the northwestern state of Zacatecas. Maria was born farther south, in a village called Tepamas in the state of Colima. They met in 1967, on the U.S. side of Mexico. "Under the wire," as Alberto puts it, meaning after both had entered illegally. It took them almost twenty years to emerge from the underground economy, but the rewards seem worth the wait. Between the ranch house, garage, and two trailers for temporary employees, they have built the kind of Mexican home most Mexicans have had to do without. The traditional adobe *horno*, a beehive-shaped bread oven, sits behind the house, next to the deep black barbecue pit—greasy and redolent with the aroma of singed avocado leaves. Their *rancho* even sounds like Mexico, thanks to a neighbor raising fighting *gallos*, or gamecocks. He has them billeted in identical shelters of whitewashed plywood spaced like miniature Quonset huts around a clean green lawn. In Fresno, where every available acre heaves with grape, cucumber, eggplant, or squash vines, a chicken yard seems frivolous. Not so, says Solis. Cockfighting may be illegal in California, but raising gamecocks is not. "*Gallos* make money," Solis says with a note of admiration in his voice as he strides past the gladiators' colony. They also make noise.

Solis's yard was a wreck September 16, 1995, the morning after an all-night fiesta. Since the beer was still flowing at 11 A.M., and the last band was only then packing its instruments away, "the morning during" might be a better description. Solis's oldest son, Alberto Jr., was hosing down the driveway where there had been dancing. His daughter, Marcela, stripped plastic from the picnic tables. Being consul, even an informal consul, carries certain responsibilities, one of which is making sure all the *compadres* celebrate *el 15 de septiembre*, Mexican Independence Day. Solis's responsibility ran into the thousands of dollars to fire up the *horno* and buy beer and sausage. He spent about two thousand dollars paving the stretch of dirt road running past his fields to accommodate the many cars, minivans, buses, motorcycles, pick-up trucks, tractors, and diesel cabs roaring up to his ranch. He also hired the three *conjuntos*—two "tropical" dance bands and a *mariachi* group. All told, nearly five hundred people crowded into Solis's barnyard.

"Eight hundred dollars for beer, six hundred for all the food," he calculates with a laugh, shaking his gray head and grinning at the wonder of his own beneficence. A sunburned forearm swipes dust from bleary eyes as he removes mirrored sunglasses to squint at the wreckage. He stiffens slightly and taps the visor of a red Oklahoma Sooners cap as he examines the latest bill for payment: $250 from the satellite company, for an antenna to pull in a pay-per-view broadcast of boxing champ Julio Cesar Chavez's Independence Day bout from Las Vegas. Add that to the Solis's party expenses, too.

"*Mujer!!*" Solis brays, calling his wife *ranchero* style, "Woman!!" A head darts from an open window, followed by five fifty-dollar bills from an open blouse. The Anglo kid smiles as he pockets his pay.

Sometime after dawn, with revelers still reveling, Solis had gone off to examine his squash vines. Another of the consul's responsibilities is to stay solvent, to make sure next year's celebration is even bigger. Their spread is the biggest around any of their kind has cobbled together in this era of the disappearing family farm. Their kind? They are *los Rodinos,* the Mexican farmhands who were *Rodinozado'*d ("Rodinocized") as beneficiaries of the 1986 Immigration Reform and Control Act, or IRCA. That act, the last great piece of legislation undertaken by New Jersey's Pelegrino Rodino, Jr., contained amnesty provisions for many illegal aliens living in *El Norte. Rodinos* had to prove they had lived in the United States continuously since 1982, a condition thousands of Mexican farmworkers met with ease. Like the historic 1965 immigration reform, in which Rodino also played a key role, the 1986 act is seen today as among many immigration surrenders that we are paying for a decade later. Yet the rise of new farm communities, like Carruthers, suggests that such a judgment is premature. If anything, the reforms of IRCA complemented the 1965 legislation by freeing farmworker productivity. If the 1965 Hart-Celler Act is the Trojan horse that allowed an army of undesirables to sneak onto our shores, then IRCA hitched a plough behind that steed and let the most lumpen of farm employees hope for something better.

Like many urban Democrats, Rodino backed amnesty as a way to recognize the fact that thousands of perfectly law-abiding immigrants had been criminalized for entering the country illegally. They had toiled in the United States for years, yet suffered from wage and other workplace discrimination because of their underground status. By entering the country illegally—or by entering legally and overstaying the time authorized with their visas—these workers were often badly exploited. They created a second tier of employment, Rodino believed, that depressed living standards for the country. Rodino's co-sponsor in the Senate, Alan Simpson of Wyoming, bitterly opposed amnesty in 1986, and spent the next ten years until his retirement from the Senate opposing any new measure that duplicated IRCA's surrender. Simpson considered amnesty for illegal aliens a mockery of border control, and predicted that amnesty would create even more criminality—in the form of a booming illegal documents industry, as thousands flocked to "prove" their long-standing residency. These fears were downplayed during hearings, however, after witnesses from the Immigration and Naturalization Service predicted no more than two hundred thousand aliens would qualify for the amnesty, and that not all of them would choose to do so. In the end, well over three million undocumented aliens applied for amnesty, more than seven hundred thousand of them in California.

Simpson's fears were not only prescient, they continue to be validated today. "Proving" residence with "documents" as fungible as library cards, phone bills, and pay stubs invited massive abuse. In the ten years after IRCA's passage, thousands of immigrants legalized their status using borrowed or fabricated records of long-term residency. In this respect, IRCA proved successful only in inflating the caseloads of immigration lawyers, who filed hundreds of thousands of amnesty requests, effectively overwhelming the Immigration and Naturalization Service—and obliterating the INS's capacity to process each one thoroughly. Such critical mass ultimately guaranteed that hundreds of thousands of undeserving *Rodinos* would be waived through. It also encouraged millions more to start planning their own exodus north, confident that, eventually, the United States would enact another "one time only" amnesty to soak up the excess.

But was amnesty necessarily a mistake? If the 1965 act had a component of urban policy—the repopulation of cities abandoned by the middle class—then the 1986 act worked a similar theme in rural districts.

In fact, the arrival of immigrants to rural places is neither strange nor new. What is new, and controversial, is a willingness to open a road to citizenship. IRCA did that, forcing newly amnestied aliens on communities on a permanent basis, instead of the transients who once filled labor camps or shabby hotels during harvests, then left. For California cities like Fresno, Oxnard, Watsonville, and El Centro, this meant entirely new demands for city services—schools, welfare, health care.

Now consider amnesty from the point of view of someone like Alberto Solis. Before IRCA, Solis was *mojado,* a "wet." Before IRCA, the Solis family lived underground. For almost twenty years, they worked in Fresno's vineyards, picking grapes, packing grapes, and stacking grapes for poverty wages. Every *Rodino* knows what those times were like—the way wages were withheld and there was nothing you could say about it, the way white kids taunted you, the way you felt every time a police car came up behind your car, that you were just moments away from incarceration.

Of course, even in those unenlightened times, an underground *mojado* might save his money and dream of buying respectability. In 1978, despite their undocumented status, Alberto and Maria Solis made a $2,000 down payment on their Carruthers homestead, a steal at $21,000. "I bought a ranch even though I was here illegally," Solis explained. "But I walked around with a fear that at any moment I could be deported and lose everything."

For the next ten years, while still undocumented, the Solis family continued to work as migrants, now saving for the chance to buy more land. For ten years they waited, putting as many as five pairs of hands in the fields during peak harvests. "That girl there," Solis says, pointing to his daughter, Marcela, "she worked from when she was eight years old. She put the paper in the bottom of the eggplant boxes. My wife packed, we all packed." Then came the Rodino amnesty, and suddenly the world changed. "I was able to work better after that, when I was legal," Solis continues. "So, with papers I felt better, I could buy what I wanted: machinery, a new pick-up, anything I wanted. And without fear. Before I was afraid to do anything, to buy anything, to plan. So we bought two more ranches. In 1986, and then, in 1989, I bought another one. I have no fear of anything, so I can spend money."

As legal residents, Alberto and Maria Solis worked to bring Alberto's brothers over from Zacatecas. That added to the weight of newcomers flooding Fresno County, but gave the Solis family more weight in the fields. By concentrating their efforts this way, the family survived the first hard years as farmers, and thrived. Today their $2,000 investment has grown to an estate assessed at over $150,000, while they have risen from underground pariahs to gentry.

Agricultural extension agents from the University of California know of dozens of *Rodino* farmers who regularly seek their advice. Many *Rodinos* are still quite marginal, renting small ten-acre plots around the valley, tending them at night or on weekends, and selling their produce within the neighborhood. Solis knows all the established growers: Manuel Ramirez, from Michoacán, who has vineyards on forty acres just west of Conejo Avenue; Edison Garcia, at the corner of Conejo and Del Rey; Sergio Garza near the corner of Walnut and Mount Whitney, also *michoacano,* also growing squash behind a tiny white house. "Garza is one of mine," Solis says, smiling weakly, then wincing at a reminder that he had been responsible for creating some of his own competition this tough season. "But he won't make it."

Like Solis, most of Garza's land is planted in squash and eggplant, two products where yields are high and the demand for fresh product is steady. He says squash can bring out about $8,000 per acre in good times. Eggplant, especially the smaller, Asian varieties, pay slightly better. Times were not so good in September. Between July and September, a glut of fresh squash drove the wholesale price to the grower down to $2.50 a box. Between renting land, paying for water, and paying a few outside laborers to pick and pack, Garza can't bring squash to the shed for less than $3.50 a carton. Now losing a dollar for every carton in the fields, he was faced with the unhappy choice of losing money on every box he brought to the packing shed or plowing the whole crop under.

Part of the problem, for both Solis and Garza, is that there are too many *compadres* doing what they do. But it's also part of a solution. As Solis explained, one of the functions of an unofficial consul is developing a kind of *peón* system among the expatriates. He had sponsored Sergio Garza's attempt to farm independently, lending him a little cash and a lot of know-how. In profitable years, that was good for Solis and all the *Rodinos,* a way for erstwhile wage-workers to share the bounty of capitalism. In losing years, it meant a glut in the market. But always there was the safety net— wage work was bountiful. Many "growers," in fact, straddled both roles as employer and employed. Beyond that was the original safety net: going back to Mexico. Thus, in good years or bad, the system was flexible. Solis, by renting one of his properties to Sergio Garza, then marketing Garza's crop, freed himself of the responsibility of managing an outside crew. More important, he freed himself from paying a crew—in effect, laying off the cost of bringing in twenty acres of squash to Garza. For Garza, renting from Alberto Solis freed him from having to commute from Fresno to work. Renting Solis's farmhouse keeps the family close to their job. It grants the extended Garza clan—five families, arriving from Michoacán over the past decade—a *puesto* in the valley. Moving up from migrant picker is a gamble, but win or lose it's a way to spread limited resources. In a winning year, they might make enough to save for a permanent farm of their own. In a losing year, like 1995, they would still be together. Even if, as his *patron* predicted, Garza would not be raising squash next year, he might still rent Solis's farm for living quarters, then hire out to another grower nearby.

Manuel Gomez plays the odds differently. Born in the town of Pabellón de Arteaga in Aguascalientes, he is a little man with weathered skin and tiny feet. His hands are strong as vises, and thick with calluses from a lifetime of squeezing dirt. Manuel Gomez farms three hundred acres of prime strawberry land in Watsonville, near Salinas. Legal since 1972, he remains a citizen of Mexico, although several of his children and grandchildren are gringos. All work on his ranch. "Farming gives work for the whole family," he says. "In the city, everyone has to find their own job."

Gomez first went "under the wire" in 1957, when he was just

nineteen years old. In 1959, he was recruited in the Bracero program, a federally sanctioned guest worker program that began during World War II. The Bracero program was phased out over the next fifteen years, but Gomez kept commuting. "I was in Texas, California, Florida," he says. "I was making forty dollars a day in 1966, and I thought I was rich, working in tomatoes. Then I got a job in Homestead, Florida, worked for a landscaping company. I drove a ten-wheel truck on Nixon's house in Key Biscayne. I put all the grass there in the president's house."

In 1972, he arrived in Watsonville, picking strawberries for the Nisei Japanese who had thrived in the industry since the 1920s. The Japanese, some of whom had been interned during World War II in concentration camps, were ruthless with their Mexican workers. "Every morning you come to the fields to pick and they give you a piece of gum and a whistle," Manuel Gomez recalls. "The whistle you kept in your mouth while you worked, and if the boss didn't hear the breath coming out through that whistle, he'd whack you on the back with a piece of heavy rope." The gum was for the counter. "You take your berries up to the truck on a little tray," Gomez continues, "and the counter says 'Show me you gum.' If it was red, or had little strawberry seeds in it, he knows you been eating their berries. So they don't pay for that tray."

Since first coming to California in the late 1880s, Japanese farms were among the most productive in the state. Over the decades, an elaborate system of credit, mutual aid, and family enterprise had evolved in the strawberry patch. Federal and state laws forbade Japanese from owning land along the coast, so Japanese families formed elaborate self-help societies—the forerunners of some farm cooperatives—to rent and work land for horticultural production. Japanese used sharecropping as a way to employ new immigrants just off the boat. Often members of extended families, the stigma of "shares" didn't bite as deeply. Few Anglos knew, in any case, who was kin and who wasn't, and the system rarely reached beyond the community. However, after the passage of the 1924 National Origins Act, when Japanese were no longer able to emigrate directly from Asia, they used Filipinos. By the 1960s and 1970s, older Japanese farmers were looking for new blood to take over the industry. They found it in Manuel Gomez.

Strawberries are the ultimate labor-intensive fruit—its short plant life (usually two years) means it must be replanted frequently. But the harvest is easy to sell fresh or for processing. By the early 1970s, Mexican farmworkers began hiring themselves out to small Japanese farms, taking a share of the crop as payment for their efforts. Gomez says he never had to share crops with the Nisei, but their farms were his training ground. He says he taught himself the strawberry business, on his knees, wheeling his little *carreta de fresa*, strawberry cart, through dewy plant rows while trying to bite a whistle and chew gum at the same time. By 1980, he had saved $36,000 and purchased his first farm, ten acres.

Fifteen years later, Gomez's spread is among the biggest of any Mexican grower in Watsonville, itself one of the centers of a state-wide boom in Mexican farming. Now the Japanese he meets are buyers, taking orders from fruit wholesalers in Tokyo. Japanese walk his rows clutching calculators and choose the bushes they want picked—guaranteeing top quality for shipment. They call Manuel and Manuel Jr. "Mister Gomez," and never inquire as to how they got into the strawberry business. "They sell a berry for a dollar each," Gomez says, not quite believing it himself. "The big ones, for decorations in cakes."

Most of the three hundred or more Mexican growers in Watsonville are sharecroppers, not owners, and the turnover among them is enormous. Gomez is often criticized by the smaller growers as a selfish turncoat—he battled against Cesar Chavez's United Farm Workers union in the 1970s. He himself admits he has no interest in joining their co-op, arguing, reasonably, that as the most successful Latino in the valley he can only tax himself trying to lift an army of rookies into profitability. Besides, he has his own public-uplift project, and this one is based in Mexico.

Like a lot of ex-migrants' operations, Gomez Farms depends on present-day migrants for harvest workers. Unlike others, Gomez recruits directly from his home village, Pabellón. His brother,

David, serves as labor boss. "They come every year," he says. "They arrive in March, about a hundred twenty, a hundred thirty people. Maybe fifty of them come from Pabellón. Some are my relatives, some my old friends, some the sons. They got papers, all of them, *Rodinos*, people who got amnesty in 1986."

The "papers" claim seems specious (later Gomez says, "You can't find a legal worker anywhere in the fields"). But Gomez's workers cross the border effortlessly, making their way to the same farm each spring, just as Gomez himself did from 1959 through 1972. What this prosperous son of Pabellón offers his village is steady work in a friendly environment, at U.S. minimum wage, minus what he deducts for housing and food. Most of his men take home between $7,000 and $8,000 for the season, enough to support their own families in Mexico.

"I tried to help the people from my town, they follow me all the time," Gomez says, denying he is exploiting anyone. "Right here in this area, you have a lot of crooked people. They don't pay their workers, they rip them off. At the end of the year when those people want to go back, they never have the money to get back. Sometimes people work all year round, and they don't get paid. They steal from their own people, their own family."

That is harder for Gomez to do because his brother, David, still lives in Pabellón. David is the link to Manuel, something of a legend in Pabellón: Strawberry Superman with lots of jobs. David says he is happy to spend half the year in Watsonville working with Manuel to raise cash for his fifty-head herd of dairy cows, $15,000 most years. "I'm his bank," big brother Manuel says.

David Gomez, who is ten years younger than Manuel, was Rodinocized in 1986, but chose not to stay permanently in California. Both brothers enjoy the best of two worlds—David earning the kind of pay Mexicans long for, Manuel exploiting the kind of cheap, loyal help Americans have just about forgotten. What the gringos can't duplicate is his village connection. Gomez's best workers leave to start their own plots in Watsonville, another reason Gomez feels he doesn't need to join any mass growers' group. He already gets them started. "Farming is like poker," he says. "You stay with it.

Sometimes you sleep in the fields. But the one who stays in the game longest wins."

A shrewd businessman knows that when an important shift occurs in an industry, some parties will be exquisitely well placed to profit, while others will be exquisitely clobbered. IRCA provided such a shift, and migrant farmworkers did profit. The revolution that happened to the Solis and Gomez families in California was repeated in hundreds of other rural towns. Former *mojados* were now free to spend.

For the first time since half of Mexico was absorbed into the United States, the legal status (thus the value) of Mexican-born workers achieved parity with the gringos. This wholesale revaluation occurred on such a massive scale, it effectively eliminated what had been a trade barrier between the United States and Mexico. Now, as a commodity free to seek its own compensation in the marketplace, labor was liberated. For laborers like Alberto Solis, this not only meant the freedom to spend money on things like additional land, but also to spend his mind, his ambitions, and whatever other inputs he brought to the marketplace in an open, transparent way.

Agriculture itself was transformed by IRCA, in a way no one could have predicted. There was a temporary displacement of labor streams (something that was predicted), as thousands of ex-*mojados* sought better jobs in the cities. But they were immediately replaced by new *mojados*, who continued to flow into California's lush fields. The real change came from the thousands of former wage-workers, many with decades of experience, suddenly marketing their skills at levels higher than simply picking fruit or operating machinery. These were men and women, thousands of them, who had spent their entire adult lives in California agriculture, the most advanced in the world. Their talents now translated into an explosion of enterprise.

By the mid-1990s, it had become apparent that something big was happening across rural America and that immigration was at the root of a tectonic shift. A new element had entered farming—youth. Suddenly, unexpectedly, a younger generation of farmers arrived. They had been there all along, but illegally. Now, after nearly a century of decline, the family farm showed signs of a comeback.

The Census of Agriculture (taken every five instead of every ten years) has recorded increases in the number of Hispanic-owned farms since about the mid-1980s. Between 1982 and 1987, the number of Spanish-surnamed individuals farming increased in state after state, while a much smaller number of Asians (categorized as "Pacific" growers, to include Hawaiian islanders and others) increased as well. From 1987 to 1992, the rise was even more pronounced. The number of Hispanic farmers grew from 17,496 to 20,956, an increase of nearly 20 percent. For Asians, who qualified for the 1986 IRCA amnesty in smaller numbers, the population farm families grew just 3 percent, from 7,900 to 8,096.

In the context of 1990s agriculture, a multibillion-dollar-a-year industry, these are minuscule numbers. Just to make one comparison, among African-American farmers the numbers declined from 1987 to 1992 by over four thousand farm families, from twenty-three thousand to under nineteen thousand. Those four thousand "missing" farmers would have accounted for less than 1 percent of total farm output for just one of the larger farm states. And yet this comparison is revealing. Against the overall trend of decline and consolidation, there has been a pronounced rise in the number of Hispanic and Asian family farms since 1986, the year of IRCA. The fact is that for all three groups—black, Asian, and Hispanic—decline was continuous from the 1950s through the early 1980s. It is only after 1986 that the numbers began to go up, and only for two of the three groups—the two that include a sizeable immigrant contingent.

What is even more remarkable is that revival was recorded everywhere, not only in the so-called gateway states. Hispanic farming increased in forty-four states from 1987 to 1992; in thirty-six states for Asians. Much of the Asian growth came in two states, Texas and Florida, which each gained over fifty Asian farms, increasing in Texas from 82 to 134, and in Florida from 118 to 192. In three more states, the Asian farming community grew by at least 50 percent—New Jersey's, which grew from thirty-seven farms to fifty-seven; Tennessee's which grew from twelve farms to twenty-seven; and Oklahoma, which had twelve Asian farms in 1987, and twenty-two in 1992.

In some ways, the gains in these last three states say more about the countertrend than similar growth in traditional farm states like Florida and Texas. Adding twenty Asian farms in New Jersey over five years is significant because it supposes a link to growing local markets—particularly those of the Chinatowns in New York and Philadelphia. The case of Tennessee—when examined next to similar gains in Alabama, North Carolina, South Carolina, and Georgia—suggests something similar is happening in the Southeast. The gains in Oklahoma, coupled with rises in Kansas, Arkansas, and Missouri, suggest the same for the Midwest. Family farming, then, is linked not only to immigrant producers, but also to immigrant consumers.

That is clearly the case in New Jersey, where new Asian farms compete with suburban sprawl. It's not that urbanization makes farming unprofitable (if anything, just the opposite occurs), but that as development encroaches, few traditional farmers can resist the temptation to sell their land. Ray Samulis, a cooperative extension agent in New Jersey's Burlington County, explained that the rise of the Asian farm is due partly to a shift from commodity to what he calls "retail" farming. Commodity farms, the majority in Burlington County, grow grains or hay. These are low-value commodities that would gross no more than $250 an acre at current prices. An eighty-acre farm, then, might yield twenty thousand dollars a year—perhaps enough to support a marginal, bucolic lifestyle, but one in which farming essentially would be a hobby. As land values increase, that hobby becomes more expensive, as the "opportunity" cost of not selling out to developers rises. Few farmers can resist the lure of the cash—as much as five thousand dollars an acre for empty land, perhaps another quarter of a million dollars for buildings, equipment, and livestock. However, retail farming, particularly of fresh produce, provides an alternative. Samulis says he knows of Asian-owned farms yielding seven thousand to eight thousand dollars an acre. Thanks to Burlington County's mild climate, these farms are harvesting through Thanksgiving, and often well into December. Compared to the "hobby" farms that rely on the summer trade, Asian vegetable farms are lucrative commercial ventures. Thus a farm selling for three hundred thousand dollars—or fifteen years of corn harvests—could conceivably cost less than the gross revenue from a single year's harvest of Oriental vegetables.

Of course, there's a catch. Oriental vegetables require a lot of labor—family labor or hired hands. Again, the immigrant connection is crucial: larger immigrant families breed their own workforce or rely on the informal contribution of an extended clan, much as Manuel Gomez does in Watsonville. Many Asian entrepreneurs begin farming as financiers, relying on veteran *Rodinos* to provide technical skills. More important than cheap labor, retail farming requires a consumer base, either a knowledgeable upscale clientele, or a burgeoning "co-ethnic" community. The Northeast has both. "Retail farming has the need for hundreds of thousands of people in a market close by," Samulis concludes. "From the outside, it looks like it isn't worth the hassle. But it is."

Consider the Changs, who work thirty acres of rented land in Burlington County. Neither Miri nor Seikun Chang grew up farming. Miri was born in Pusan, on Korea's southern coast; Seikun came from Seoul. They came to the United States in 1980, during the peak years of the great wave of Korean immigration. Miri Chang worked as a nurse before coming to New York; Seikun was an electrical engineer. Like many Korean immigrants, the Changs came as university students, entering tiny Wagner College on New York's Staten Island. They met in class, fell in love, and soon were married. After graduating, with twin degrees in business administration, they joined the army of Korean immigrants entering retail trade. Their *puesto* was a dry cleaner's near the Wagner campus, purchased from an elderly Italian American in 1984. In 1993, the Changs decided they needed a change. "Business was bad, we wanted to try something new," Miri Chang explains. "I was born in a city, I grew up in a city. Both of us went to college in the city. We didn't know anything about growing vegetables, but my husband always dreamed of being a farmer."

But even if the Changs were ignorant about raising vegetables, they knew how to sell. Working from textbooks Seikun's father sent from Korea, seeking advice wherever they could, the Changs started with Oriental cucumbers and zucchini. That first year was a bust—but by year two the Changs were harvesting regularly, and moving Korean produce through wholesalers in Flushing, Philadelphia, and Fort Lee, New Jersey. They added Korean cabbage and melon to their inventory, and doubled their acreage. "I don't have the experience to handle more than thirty acres, but I am learning," Seikun Chang explains. "Now wholesalers come to me, or sometimes I drive myself to Korean restaurants and groceries."

Miri and Seikun Chang are part of a growing network of Korean farms spreading along the Midatlantic coast from Delaware to Long Island. They attend the Korean Presbyterian Church in Trenton, undoubtedly along with the end-users of their produce. As the Korean presence expanded within the cities, a chain of Korean grocery stores rose to cater to their needs. Those stores needed fresh produce; farmers like Miri and Seikun Chang were able to oblige. Like the old immigrant farm communities of the 1800s, their's is a community of mutual interest. All share a common market in the cities; all draw on the same pool of Latino farmworkers. Together, a transplanted Korea is taking root.

Michelle Infante, the extension agent in New Jersey's Monmouth County, sees a similar pattern. She says as many as twenty Chinese farmers are currently operating in Monmouth County, where retail farming is even more refined. "Farmers will work with local restaurants and make new markets," she explains. "Before they would sell to a wholesaler. Now they sell right to restaurants in New Jersey. What will happen is a group of Chinese restaurants will form a co-op, say fifteen to twenty restaurants, to buy product from the farms. You go to any strip mall around Trenton and you see a lot of Chinese restaurants. That's their customer base."

Harvesting each day, a Chinese grower might deliver boxes of fresh bok choy, daikon, and mustard greens six times a week to twenty restaurants. He might charge each two hundred dollars for the food and the door-to-door delivery. That's a gross of four thousand dollars a day just from this niche market. The restaurateurs get freshness and dependability—they may also be relatives or investors (or both) of the farmers—and none of the hassle of contracting from wholesalers in Chinatown. Similar deals are arranged with poultry and swine producers. With every new strip mall restaurant, the farmer's life gets a little easier.

As dynamic as the new Asian farm communities are, their progress is dwarfed by the explosion of Hispanic farming across the country. For this group of immigrants, USDA demographer Calvin Beale found a total of eight states where their number more than doubled between 1987 and 1992: Missouri, North Carolina, Virginia, Montana, New Jersey, North Dakota, South Carolina, and South Dakota. The two most populous states, Texas and California, saw the biggest net increases: 694 and 412 new farms, respectively. Five more states witnessed net increases of over a hundred new Hispanic family farms: Colorado, Florida, Idaho, Oklahoma, and New Mexico. Other states with impressive growth included Kentucky, which registered more than sixty new farms, Virginia (74), Oregon (68), and Iowa (82). In all of these places, the Hispanic family farm was increasing at a rate of at least a dozen new farms a year. This, against a background of hundreds of older, native-born farmers quitting the business.

Throughout the country, a pattern repeated itself: former farmworkers newly legalized were becoming upwardly mobile. Where farming was in decline, new growers were emerging, in some cases reviving dormant farms, in others creating new industries whose rise reflected a sudden availability in manpower. Ginseng, for example, has become a boom crop in Wisconsin and Minnesota, in part because of the availability of Hmong and other Southeast Asian immigrants. In eastern Washington, Christmas tree nurseries thrive on the availability of *Rodinos*. Tracking the census numbers down to the counties, this formula—newly legal immigrant labor creating opportunities for dynamic new businesses—reinforces the theory that enterprise follows a critical mass of risk-takers. Thus, in Idaho's Canyon County (where the Hispanic grower population has more than doubled in ten years), high-tech seed farms are becoming an important niche. This kind of farming is tailor-made for the newly legalized: stoop labor, to be sure, but for a high-value crop grown on tiny plots of land. Along the levees east of New Orleans, dozens of small gardens, cultivated intensively by resettled Vietnamese refugees, feed a local market now spreading into Texas and Mississippi. Just as in Watsonville, California's Santa Barbara County is a haven for strawberry sharecroppers—the volume of the harvest soaring from under a thousand acres per year in the early 1980s to over five thousand today, as former *mojados* make the transition from picker to wholesaler under a wide range of sharecropping or co-production schemes.

Another immigrant niche is farm management, often a farm the immigrant has been employed on for decades. "Many older [native-born] farmers are really farm managers," says Mir Sayed, a cooperative extension agent in Idaho's Elmore County. Sayed, him-self an immigrant from Iran, says Mexicans have emerged as own-ers or operators in the sugar beet, soy, and potato fields as older, Anglo growers switch into easier lines of work, such as selling real estate or farm insurance. "Farmworkers know problems at the farm level, how things are at ground level. They know how long it takes to fix something, how to put in the irrigation, how to fix a pipeline; they have a depth of knowledge of how to do this," Sayed explains. "They can't get money from the banks, but they get known around the community, and growers share costs with them. They give them seed and fertilizer and offer to split the harvest, then they help them get loans." In Elmore County, Mr. Sayed has seen a division of labor where newly legal immigrants fill a gap between older farms that lack an extended family to take on the physical work of raising a crop and work-ready immigrants who lack the funds to farm on their own.

As important as the aging factor is, the real surge in immigrant farm activity comes from innovations in production which require younger farmers working their way into management. In North

Carolina's Sampson County, on the coastal plain south of the state capital, eight new Hispanic-operated farms emerged between 1987 and 1992. The new farmer rising here is in the swine industry. As in commercial poultry, independent growers are contracted to raise hogs for slaughter, a cost-effective way for packers to share the costs of production.

Ernesto and Ricky Morales, two recent immigrants from the Mexican state of Tamaulipas, are typical of the new breed. Like Alberto Solis and Manuel Gomez twenty years before, the brothers went "under the wire." Ernesto came first, entering Texas in 1987. He came without work papers, but with an agronomy degree from Mexico's Universidad de Tamaulipas. Two years later Ricky, also a university graduate, entered the country. In 1992, they learned that the quota for "emergency" farmworker cards was going unfilled. Armed with temporary papers, they began looking for better work.

As *mojados*, the Morales brothers were prized employees, cheap to pay despite their university degrees. With documents, they were able to leverage their skills into management jobs. Their gringo partner, Murphy Farms, handles financing, licensing, and marketing tasks. The Morales brothers are the on-site managers. "My brother is the chief of production," Ricky Morales says. "The gringo owns the business."

The Morales brothers take newborn "weaner" piglets (seventy-five thousand of them in a normal year) and fatten them to 12-pounders, a process that takes about three weeks. From there, the hogs go to nurseries, where a second crew raises them to 45-pounders and sends them on to "finishers" who bring them to slaughtering size. A farm like the Moraleses' represents an investment of between $2 million and $3 million, an unimaginable sum for a new immigrant. But Ernesto Morales doesn't rule out the possibility of launching his own operation one day—with or without gringo partners. "Obviously it's better to be stable, working in one place," Ernesto says. "For people like us, who grew up on the border, to come from Mexico and to work in the U.S. is like for someone to be from Chicago and go to Georgia, we are used to being around, always."

Another Morales clan emerged in southern Iowa. Rodolfo Morales's purchase of a 5,000-acre farm in Adams county, a community where most farmers were battling bankruptcy, brought whispers that Morales (no relation to Ernesto and Ricky) was laundering drug money for criminals back in Detroit. The facts are less dramatic. Morales says he fell in love with the rolling hills of Iowa while driving Iowa corn from Council Bluffs to a tortilla manufacturer in Detroit. After surviving the 1967 riots, Morales made a small fortune in real estate in Detroit's emerging Mexican barrio. He struck gold with Mexican Town, a 300-seat Latino "theme" restaurant that clicked with tourists, then a second one called Xochimilco. After retirement, he decided to raise cattle.

While Morales's neighbors couldn't help resenting a newcomer paying cash, they grew to accept Morales for his hard work and willingness to learn. In time he bought a second farm, as a wedding gift for his son and daughter-in-law, who grew up on a farm in Mexico. Compared to the mean streets of Detroit, neighbors' gossip doesn't rile Rodolfo Morales. "They always think a Mexican should be working the fields, he shouldn't own the fields," Morales says. "Everyone thinks a Mexican rides a donkey. It's unfortunate people think that way, but they got blinders on."

The Morales clan brought an advantage to agriculture few locals could appreciate. Wages in the city are high, and informal credit advanced within families makes financing available. Just as the Changs rely on Korean wholesalers to make farming viable in New Jersey, the Moraleses were able to leverage a predictable revenue stream from Detroit to avoid debt, the scourge of grain farmers in Iowa. What Rodolfo Morales is doing is no different from what surgeons or attorneys do when they buy land for hobby farms; it is only because Iowans are used to seeing Mexican immigrants as laborers that they suspected corruption. "They think, 'I work all day and I make only thirty thousand dollars a year.' But on the land you don't make any money," Rodolfo Morales explains. His fortune is in the city, which gives Morales another advantage his neighbors know nothing about. "Most farmers I've met live very frugally and die wealthy," he concludes with a laugh. "This is marginal land [for grain], but it's fine for running cattle."

The rise of the immigrant family farm, quite common in earlier eras of massive immigration, is surprising during a time when the death of the family farm seems so inevitable. It is unexpected; in fact, it has yet to be recognized for what it is: a rural revival. Because many of the practitioners are former farm laborers, there is a common belief that the immigrant family farm is an illusion, one that masks naked exploitation by agribusiness. The "proof" of this exploitation is the fact that few immigrant farmers actually own their land. Land ownership is thought to be the true indicator of independence; thus, a farmer who leases cannot possibly control his destiny. For many academics and activists, particularly those who came of age during the rise of Cesar Chavez's United Farm Workers union, entrepreneurship seems politically incorrect, especially while so many co-ethnics, the new illegals, continue to toil in the fields for wages.

Don Villarejo, director of the California Institute for Rural Studies in Davis, disagrees. "Most produce growers in California today, including the biggest growers, don't own their land. More than ninety percent of the ground where fresh tomatoes are grown is rented ground," he says, obliterating any notion that "real" farmers are homesteaders. "It's a high risk and low margin business, so a foolish thing to do is invest a great deal of capital in land. You want to minimize that risk: rent land and not have that money tied up. So the small farmers are not that different from the large growers. Tenant farmers were seen as people on the margins of society, and when they could finally buy land, that was seen as having made it into society. Today people are just looking for ways to make farming profitable. And one way to do it is not to tie up capital in property."

In modern farming, land is just another input, one reason the immigrant farm family can be successful. There is no mystical attraction to "ancestral" land, thus no locked-in prejudice for or against a traditional method of farming or a crop. Squash, eggplants, strawberries—maybe next year an exotic Oriental mushroom. Flexibility makes markets; it also protects farmers from overproducing, then suffering when prices collapse.

The classic example in California is the strawberry industry. Since IRCA, strawberry production has soared in the state, from fifteen thousand acres before the act was passed, to twenty-three thousand acres in 1994. Productivity gains were also impressive. Thanks to the new family farms, mostly Mexican, yields per acre were almost seven times the national average, some twenty tons per acre per year. The wholesale price for strawberries barely budged, however—from 20 cents to 29 cents per pound for frozen strawberries (second-year crops, mainly used for processing) and from 49 cents to 54 cents for fresh berries. Factoring inflation, strawberries were probably cheaper in 1994 than they were in the mid-1980s.

Mexican sharecroppers accounted for the bulk of the labor deployed in the strawberry fields in the mid-1990s, as much as three quarters of all farms by some estimates. It is a brutal system where a single bad crop can wipe out years of savings. However, since almost all the sharecroppers work rented land and have little investment in machinery, few are exposed to risk the way larger growers are. Strawberry sharecroppers play in an enormous natural casino—they may win thousands of dollars a season by bringing in a good crop at a time when competitors fail; or they may sell at a loss when there is a glut in the market. The fact that hundreds of farmers have managed to remain debt-free and sustain themselves season after season indicates that the rewards are adequate to satisfy the aspirations of anyone who wants to step up from migrant picking.

Still, there is a stubborn belief that the immigrant is being exploited. The image of brown *peónes* farming land owned by whites becomes identical to the Alabama sharecroppers of *Let Us Now Praise Famous Men*, or the Okies of John Steinbeck's *The Grapes of Wrath*. In these eyes, class and race, not markets, seem to define farming. And Rodinocized farmworkers, however productive they may be, are seen as today's lucky exception. "What's worse than being exploited in the United States?" asks Philip Martin, an agroeconomist at the University of California at Davis. "The answer is: not being exploited in the United States. That's always the argument. But in the long run, are you going to have to pay catch-up costs?"

Martin sees the rise of independent farmers as a logical outgrowth of the IRCA amnesty, but not necessarily as a means of assimilation. Eventually the immigrant grows weary of hard work, he argues, and if he fails to carve out a successful niche, he will simply demand more in the form of social services. In other words, welfare. The risk is that the immigrant farm boom will be short-lived, and a new generation of busted tenant farmers—call them "Mexies"—will swarm into the cities' poor barrios. "In the past we shoved that cost back to Mexico. So long as they are not U.S. residents on whom we have a future 'uplift' obligation, it doesn't really matter," Martin says. "But now, the big issue for the 1990s is, who is going to pay? In the short term, if you don't have these people you'll lose the production and have higher prices. But will we look back and say this was the most expensive thing we ever did?"

Others are even more skeptical. The independent grower is not independent at all, they argue, thus cannot "succeed," and welfare would be an improvement over peonage. "Independent contractor, sharecropper, self-employed, whatever they call it, this is a hoax designed to enable cheapskate farmers to avoid paying the minimum wage and taxes. They all are hoaxes," says Marc Linder, a professor at the University of Iowa who specializes in migrant labor practices. "These are migrant workers masquerading as sharecroppers."

That depends on the point of view. There are sharecroppers who used to be migrant workers, and may well be again. Many "independents" do return to wage work, as pickers or packing-shed employees or labor contractors. And many of those "failures" rotate back into independent growing. Because land is available on a short-term basis, anyone who "fails" can go back to salaried work. And those who choose to, and hundreds do, can save money again and return to the game. Farming is very much like poker, and also an elaborate sorting process. Winners rise to the top, learning more with each season, but "losers" are no worse off than they were when they started. Sharecropping may exploit, but it is not a hoax. It offers Mexicans upward mobility that is impossible back home.

The rise of the immigrant family farm does not mean the old ways Steinbeck described are disappearing. If anything, they endure. Indeed, it is the continuation of exploitation that makes the new enterprise possible. A day after Alberto Solis's Independence Day fiesta, the flat fields east of Fresno are heaving with activity. September is grape harvest season, and thousands of men and women are hard at work picking, sorting, packing, and piling crates of grapes the color of ginger ale, white table grapes grown on vines stretching chest-high for acres. Beneath them, sometimes crawling, sometimes stooping, sometimes a skip-and-stretch combination of the two, Mexicans swathed in old clothes snip away at the clumps of fruit. A good worker can fill a fifty-pound tub in less than forty seconds, for which he will earn about eight cents. Repeated thousands of times, this process yields a daily salary of seventy-five dollars, after deductions, a mountain of wealth in the mountain villages where most of these pickers come from.

All of the workers are Mexican, most illegal, all with false green cards—*micas chuecas,* they are called—all real-looking enough to satisfy the labor contractors who cart them from job to job. The labor contractors, too, are Mexican-born, usually *Rodinos* who have leveraged their new status into a management position. The labor contractors are Mexican, as are the foremen working for the big grape-growing concerns, as are the truck drivers waiting impatiently next to their rigs as fresh grapes are heaved up in mammoth bulldozer scoops to tumble like clumps of dusty moss into the trailers. Most of the state agriculture inspectors poking around the crop are of Mexican descent, too, usually the sons of *mojados* who came in the 1950s or 1960s. So are the two representatives of California

Rural Legal Assistance, making their rounds of the grape vineyards in the town of Kerman.

From top to bottom—labor, management, regulator, and litigator—the California grape harvest is a *mundo mejicano,* a Mexican world. Rufino Dominguez and Teresa Ramos, the two CRLA field-workers, are part of this world's regulatory mechanism. That is, they act as checks on the truly awful abuses that are occurring in the immigrant labor market, or at least they try to. "See what they do to harass us?" Teresa sneers as a pick-up truck roars past Rufino's ancient Buick, sealing the car in a cloud of dust. "The growers do anything to keep us out of the fields."

It is a ridiculous assertion that speaks more of Teresa's politics than any real hostility. In fact, organizations like the CRLA are probably the growers' best friends, especially at harvest time. By counseling workers, visiting the vineyards, and cataloguing their lists of "infractions," they become part of California's ritual of permitting illegal farmworkers to work. On this particular day, the "infractions" at the Viedel Company's forty-acre ranch include one missing women's portable toilet (there has to be an equal number for both sexes, even though men outnumber women in the vineyards by some twenty to one) and a lack of paper towels in the dispensers outside. These complaints, once reported and filed, open the growers to further inspection and the possibility of fines of up to $750 per violation. Their real purpose is to give the CRLA an excuse to enter the fields at harvest time to talk with the pickers, and to make sure they are earning at least the country's minimum wage. Grapes are lucrative and regulations are well established, so payment has not been a problem in the big vineyards. Workers at this vineyard are paid by check, $210 for a five-day week, and taxes are withheld. Most send their wages home via certified check. Packers make more than pickers, between $250 and $300 a week, and most are permanent residents. Their positions are a lot more desireable, standing under awnings as they fill the crates consumers see in supermarkets. If the vineyards are an assembly line, then the packing stands are the loading dock.

It is notable that what the CRLA does not police, or even report, is the widespread use of false documents, all of which are presented by pickers upon request. The pickers are also not shy about revealing where fake green cards are currently being sold (in downtown Fresno, in Modesto), and for how much (sixty dollars). The CRLA doesn't bust workers, and neither does the Immigration and Naturalization Service, which seldom sends agents into vineyards during harvest time. About the only policing done by anyone is by the growers, who station private security guards at the crossroads at the edge of the vineyards to make sure crates of packed grapes are not pilfered.

Rufino Dominguez is well known in California for a special expertise. A native of a Oaxacan village, San Miguel Cuevas, he speaks Mixtec, an indigenous Mexican dialect still spoken in the small villages of southern Mexico. Mixtecs have been coming to California in ever-increasing numbers over the past decade, establishing their own critical mass. In articles in the *Los Angeles Times* and *New York Times*, Mixtec Indians have been portrayed as the new Okies of the state's harvest, part of an historic chain of exploitation that links California's biggest industry to Mexico's oldest pockets of poverty. An estimated fifty thousand Mixtec-speakers are working the fields, and they are not hard to find in and around Fresno. Dominguez knows two places to look.

The first is the Skaggs Bridge County Park, a dry and dusty picnic area surrounding what looks like a stagnant creek. Inside, past the empty sentry box with the NO CAMPING sign, a small village of Mixtec migrants has established a bivouac. From ancient cars with Oregon and Washington license plates, eight families are living openly under the shade of fragrant cardamom trees. They have been here a week, arriving from Oregon where they tell Dominguez they were picking strawberries and raspberries. In a tableau worthy of Steinbeck, a whole world tumbles out of the old jalopies. Old women and naked kids feed twigs into the barbecue pits, grilling cheap chicken parts then dipping into kilo-sized bags of coarse salt for seasoning. These families have been living like this for eight days, sleeping on cardboard and "bathing" from a trickle of fresh water coaxed from a broken drinking fountain. Two older fisher-men, sons, perhaps, of the Okies who came to Fresno in Stein-beck's time, sneer as they hold their noses against the stench. They exchange disgusted looks as they drag an aluminum canoe onto a trailer. Bad fishing today, one says.

Bad fishing for the Mixtecs, too, they tell Dominguez. They have been driving around Fresno County every day looking for work, and their money is running out. Dominguez gives them his business card and the name of a local church that dispenses aid.

Things are better at Aulakh Farms a few miles away, if just barely. There, Dominguez and Ramos find Mixtecs living in a con-verted shed, three families with perhaps two dozen people all told. They share two rooms, but the rooms have working stoves and electricity, and they are right up against the vines, so there is no need to leave to search for work. Dominguez has been coming to the Aulakh farm for a year or so, proselytizing among the *peóns*. The village chief here, Miguel Luna, comes from Dominguez's na-tive village in Oaxaca. Some of the older workers here have green cards (they don't say whether they are legal or not), and everyone is sending money home to bring more family to California. The Aulakh family rents space in the shack for $120 a month, about a fourth of each family's income.

No one seems to mind that Rufino Dominguez and Teresa Ramos are visiting. At the farmhouse, the owner, a strapping man of thirty with a big grin and a hearty handshake, is happy to chat with visitors. "We'll do six hundred to six hundred fifty tons of raisins this year," Abe Aulakh says proudly, mentally calculating a profit of two hundred thousand dollars for his efforts. The Aulakh ranch is modern and plush, with a swimming pool and seven cars in the carport. If classic exploitation is what you're looking for, this seems to be it. But before anyone can ask, Abe throws a curve ball. "We did the same thing when we came here," he says. "We picked grapes, we hoed cotton, we drove tractors, we lived just like our Mexicans do now."

In one way, they still do. The seven cars parked outside rep-resent three extended families living inside. ("Four," says Kamaljit

Aulakh, Abe's wife, "if you count Abe's father and mother.") The Aulakhs came in 1976, from Amritsar, in the Punjab region of India. They are Sikhs, the dominant Indian group in central California, and they are prosperous. There is a large colony in Fresno County, where Sikhs run most of the convenience stores and gas stations on Highway 41. They're really strong up north, in Sutter County, where since the 1960s Sikh farmers have dominated the walnut and almond industries. There are even Sikhs in Nebraska, planting wheat, Abe (born "Abrasham") offers.

The Mixtecs are Abe's permanent workers, but Fresno is also their base to pick other farmers' crops—raisins, strawberries, and garlic in the county. They will also range as far away as Oregon, or go back to Mexico on brief visits. "We tell them what day we expect to start pruning, or picking," Kamaljit explains, "and they're here." Like her husband, she came as an immigrant, picking grapes with her parents. Abe and his brothers bought their first spread, forty acres, in 1984. Today they have two hundred fifty acres. "Back in India we do the farming, too," Abe says. "We like it here, same weather, good workers."

Good weather, good workers, and good profits. Fresno County, with $3 billion in annual farm sales, is America's richest agricultural center. It is also one of America's fastest-growing urban centers, its population rising from 165,000 to almost 400,000 in the last twenty-five years. With the growth has come traffic jams, ethnic gangs, drive-by shootings, and air pollution. It has also meant the depletion of thirty-five thousand acres of farmland in Fresno County since 1980, with a projection that another million may be lost by the middle of the next century, making America's farmingest county just another urban sprawl. Immigration, particularly from Mexico and Southeast Asia, is blamed for most of Fresno's growth.

"California is Paranoia Deluxe," agrees Senator Alan Simpson, an immigration restrictionist whose co-sponsorship of the Simpson-Rodino Immigration Reform and Control Act made it possible for so many *Rodinos* (not "Simpsoninos") to reside legally in the state.

California, on the subject of immigrants, *is* paranoid, seeing in every growing town the possibility of another Fresno, sprawling out of control and destroying a way of life that had endured for decades.

But as Fresno's population spreads, so does its way of life: farming. This is one of the ironies of the modern agricultural age and of immigration. Even as Fresno County loses more and more farm acreage to shopping malls and suburban tract homes, more and more farmers enter the farm economy. On the outskirts of town, sometimes right in town, the evidence is everywhere during harvest season. Besides Mexicans, there are Hmong, Lao, and Vietnamese, easy to spot in their *mok saona* straw hats, which look like baskets turned upside down on their heads. Tiny mothers with babies in slings behind their backs stoop and stride through fields of lemon grass, Chinese radishes, and, everywhere, strawberries. Fresno is home to thirty-eight thousand Hmong refugees, many of whom have lately discovered farming; that is, they have rediscovered it. For Hmong families, notorious for having as many as a dozen children, labor-intensive gardening is a growing occupation, one that appears to be breaking the terrible welfare dependence these refugees have suffered.

Fresno's farm proliferation is not unique. Across the country, a pattern is unfolding where the top farm counties are also among the nation's fastest growing metropolises. Don Villarejo started noticing the trend in the 1980s. By the mid-1990s, he reported that of the nation's top twenty agricultural counties, as defined by the value of their farm output, sixteen were in or near metropolitan centers. "By the year 2000," he says, "all twenty will be."

Compared to a century, or even fifty years ago, Villarejo explains, the big counties would have been in upstate New York, Wisconsin, Iowa, and Illinois, empty places where large farm operations concentrated on dairy and wheat production. They also would have had much lower values. In 1990, Villarejo completed a comprehensive study of the number-fourteen county, Ventura, and found that patterns of farming changed as its urban center, Oxnard, grew. "What happens," he explains, "is you have gone from dry land pasture to growing feed crops to growing vegetables and citrus, to growing strawberries and very intensive nursery crops, flowers, and even turf, so the average production per acre has been steeply increasing." He points to the paradox: fewer acres but more dollars, explained by the fact that the growth of the urban population provides a growing market for all these commodities. "What is rural in the country?" he asks. "The top ten agro counties in the country are metro. Look at San Diego, number twenty, it changes, but it actually increased its farm revenue."

All around Fresno, the process unfolds: large tracts of farmland come within range of urban sprawl and the farm moves. But in the new "marginal" land—an acre here, five acres there—niche players swarm in. They are almost always immigrants growing crops for the ethnic market. They are almost always more profitable as "marginal" enterprises than the original "traditional" farms they replace.

The key to any successful transition from *peón* to independent producer is access to markets. Asian growers, even the impoverished Hmong, have an immediate advantage in this regard, thanks to growing Asian communities across the state. Even the tiniest Hmong plots grow squash, winter melon, and other products that feed into a distribution system that takes their crops as far away as Vancouver and Toronto. In a reverse of the situation in Monmouth County—Chinese and Korean farming expensive land by catering to Chinese nearby—the Hmong do the opposite. They rent cheap land in Fresno, applying "free" family labor to raise products sold to Chinese far away. The link between Fresno and the world is Cher Ta Farm Produce, a Hmong-owned packing shed operated by Lang Lee. Lee worked as a bookkeeper for the last democratic government of Laos; his father was a Hmong mercenary on the Central Intelligence Agency's payroll. After the war, the Lees fled to Thailand, where they did their first farming together. "I raised sesame," the younger Lee recalls. "Some Thai people leased us land near the camp and told us what to plant. They said, 'Sesame seeds make money.' "

After four years in Thailand, Lang Lee received a refugee's visa to the United States and was placed in Des Moines, Iowa, where, while attending community college to improve his English, he worked as a janitor for a church sponsoring Lao refugees. Like most Southeast Asian refugees in the 1980s, Lang Lee survived through a mixture of menial work, government assistance, and family sharing. Like a lot of Hmong, he had relatives in California, and in 1981, moved to Fresno to be closer to his clan. He collected welfare even as he started gardening, the virtual "workfare" many Hmong have adopted in their search for a stable life. Cher Ta Farm Produce was launched by Lee's brother in 1988 as a distributor for Hmong produce. About fifty Hmong farms service Cher Ta Farm Produce regularly and another hundred Cambodian, Mien, Vietnamese, and Lao families as well. Some "farms" are smaller than a city block, and right in the city. "We have farmers with just two or five acres," Lang Lee says. "But some people quit. With all the regulation it's hard to make a profit."

Sounding like a born free-marketer, Mr. Lee ticks off the state requirements: compensation, taxpayer identification, insurance, portable toilets in the "fields." Even the tiniest growers must meet standards just like mammoth vineyards. Lang Lee knows, because one of Cher ta's biggest suppliers is his own spread, 220 acres only two miles from downtown, at the corner of Jensen and Martin Luther King, Jr., Boulevard. The Lees' spread is representative of many downtown operations: former alfalfa land no longer in service for commodity farming because it abuts too many people. For one thing, there is the potential threat of theft or vandalism of expensive farm machinery. More important, aerial pesticide spraying is forbidden, making it impossible to grow corn, cotton, or alfalfa. But niche players like Lang Lee can seize an opportunity. The Lees have five small tractors (three of them used); but their "machinery" is essentially the dozens of Hmong families—cousins and clansmen—willing to weed and hoe and pick by hand for a piece of the harvest. By rotating crops all year, the Lees always have some surplus to distribute to pickers as pay—pickers who are, after all, their own family. Down the street one neighbor, a Lao, has eleven acres sown with strawberries and persimmons. Another, a former Vietnamese air force officer, has twenty acres planted with Japanese pear trees.

The great advantage, besides cheap labor, that these and other growers have is cost of land. A tract across the street from the Lees' farm had been good pasturage but has lain idle since the area was zoned for development. One local realtor estimated the land would sell for $30,000 an acre for a shopping mall or condos. But the area around Martin Luther King, Jr. Boulevard is rather depressed, and so far no developer has offered to buy the land. So it can be leased, by anyone, for as little as $250 per acre per year.

The Lees were growing eleven different crops during mid-September: daikon radish, baby bok choy, green beans, eggplant, moqua, Chinese broccoli, napa cabbage, yu choy, gai lan, snow peas, and lemon grass. On some products, the Lees can draw three crops a year—and gross as much as $12,000 per acre each year. Chinese moqua (also known as "fuzzy melon") is harvested year-round, and fetches between seven dollars and eighteen dollars a box, or an average of about twelve dollars a box through the year. Lang harvested almost five thousand boxes of fuzzy melon in 1995, earning about sixty thousand dollars on eight acres. Unlike Alberto Solis and Manuel Gomez, who sell to brokers, Lee keeps some of the profit by brokering his produce through Cher Ta. But with demand for Asian produce growing across the continent, prices are generally high. "I sell all over the States," Mr. Lee says proudly. "And to Canada."

In the central San Joaquin valley alone, Don Villarejo says, there are between five hundred and eight hundred Southeast Asian farm operations. "Strawberries, cherry tomatoes, things like that. These are labor-intensive crops, so the farmers tend to rely very heavily on family labor and kinship relations," Villarejo explains. "We're talking two to ten acres in size, maybe done in addition to other work. It is a family business, and the innovations are amazing. There are restaurants and markets catering to these operations and entrepreneurs who jump in and grow for that market. There is cash generated, there is employment generated, but no one is getting rich."

But the state is. The same urban sprawl that is eating Fresno's farmland is eating land outside Jakarta, Taipei, Seoul, Kuala Lumpur, and Singapore. But as more Californians grow Asian crops, they become cheap enough to market overseas, despite the high freight costs. Among the consequences of a burgeoning ethnic market are burgeoning sales to those immigrants' "co-ethnics" in the old country. Billions of dollars' worth going back across the Pacific. Of the $12 billion of produce California exported in 1995, half went to Asia. In fact, the faster Asian cities grow, the more profitable California fresh produce becomes—for the simple reason that the farther Asian farms are from their core cities, the harder it gets to get their output to market. In short, it is now easier to fly broccoli to Hong Kong, then drive it overland to buyers in Guangdong (booming southern China's megalopolis) than to ship broccoli from anywhere in China. And that is making a man named Lamchop very happy.

Tom Lam was seven years old the last time he saw China. Born in the village of Sun We in Guangdong Province, Lam was a month old when Mao's Communists routed Nationalist forces from the mainland, and sent the Lams into exile in Hong Kong.

He can't remember why he returned, only that his mother took him to see her brother in their old village. He recalls walking most of the way, then being carried. "My uncle had one of those traditional poles with the two baskets," Tom Lam says over a burger and onion rings in an Oxnard, California, diner. "He put me in one of the baskets and found some rocks to balance the other one. That's how we walked home."

Four decades later, "Lamchop" (the nickname on his business card) Lam says the vegetables he raises in California are being sold along that same road—now a highway through Guangdong's booming industrial landscape. "Farmland disappears in China just like in California," he says. But prosperity means higher incomes, and opportunities for U.S. farmers. Tom Lam's Oxnard Vegetable Exchange is the biggest Chinese-owned farm in California. Among growers, Tom Lam is the legendary Man Who Made Crown Broccoli—an innovation that boomed. What started as a trial shipment to New York's Chinatown has blossomed into a $13 million (annual sales) business.

Arriving just out of high school, in 1968, Lam had previously been employed selling encyclopedias door to door in Hong Kong. While many immigrants trade rural life for the bustle of the city, Lam's passage was the opposite. In California, he became a farm-worker. "We left Los Angeles airport at midnight," he says with a laugh. "At six the next morning, I was picking cucumbers in the fields."

Lam learned fieldwork watching Mexican farmworkers. He learned the business side from other growers, including Japanese who had been in Oxnard since the 1920s. Lam became a natural-ized U.S. citizen and, by 1985, was working as a salesman for a local vegetable wholesaler, Seaboard Produce. For Seaboard, Lam handled distribution to New York's Chinatown. One night he got a call from a regular customer with a problem. "In those days," Lam recalls, "we shipped broccoli whole, bound in rubber bands. But in the Chinese restaurants they only used the tops, the flowers. Send them ten boxes of broccoli, ten boxes of garbage go on the street." Garbage haulage is expensive in New York, his customer complained, what can we do? Tom realized in Chinatown, where restaurants line every street, this was a common problem. So he thought of a common solution: ship flowers only, and charge a bit more. No one had ever shipped broccoli tops before, so no one knew what to charge. In Chinatown, no one knew what to pay. Rather than waste time marketing, Lam decided to give the first shipment away. "It started out, 'Try some, no charge,'" Lam says of that first shipment, three hundred boxes. "Within a week, it was, 'You got any more? I want to buy.'"

A box of whole broccoli sold wholesale for ten dollars, but Lam soon found he could go as high as twenty dollars a box for crowns and still not keep up with demand. Crowns packed wok-ready in Oxnard were irresistible. Besides cutting down on garbage ("now all they throw out is a carton,"), Tom Lam's broccoli cut kitchen costs, too, since most of the preparation was being done in the fields, at two to three dollars less per hour than restaurant workers made. Lam sent a second shipment of six hundred cases, then a third shipment of a thousand. A year later, he left Seaboard to start his own brand, Ho Sai Gai.

As with many start-ups, Lam quickly faced the problem of too rapid growth. He had purchased three thousand acres near Los Alamos to raise broccoli, but still couldn't meet demand. So he contracted packers along the coast. His "new" product was new in packaging only, so his subcontractors felt free to make their own deals with Chinatown wholesalers. The next season, Lam's emergency suppliers had become Lam's full-time competition.

Lam found other marketing problems closer to home, in the Los Angeles Chinatown. Even though this market was three thousand miles closer to his broccoli, the mom-'n'-pop truck farms serving Chinatown from Riverside and Long Beach were even closer. These are fifteen- to fifty-acre plots, Lam explains, that exist almost entirely on family labor. Against his own three thousand acres, mechanized and employing a well-trained workforce, these little plots should be unable to compete. Even though Oxnard, at the predawn hour when broccoli is shipped, is less than an hour from downtown Los Angeles, "momma and poppa" may be just five minutes away from their customers. The little truck farms earn top dollar selling direct to users in the suburbs, then dump any surplus in the big China-, Korea-, and Japantowns in the city. Lam complains some even scavenge garbage dumps for his discarded Ho Sai Gai cartons, selling them for a dollar apiece while eroding loyalty to his brand with an inferior product.

So he pulled back. He cut his sales staff in half, directing it to select customers who would enter exclusive supply arrangements. Although targeting a mass market got him started, Lam doesn't sell a mass product now. Lamchop Lam is one Chinese grower who avoids Chinatown, selling instead to gourmet brokers and exporters, tapping a higher-value market in Vancouver, Toronto, and, increasingly, Asia itself. Tokyo, Taiwan, and Singapore are all good markets for Oxnard Vegetable Exchange. So is Hong Kong, whose distributors ship onto the mainland. That's how Lam knows his eggplant and yu choy are being eaten near his birthplace, in restaurants and hotels frequented by budding millionaires demanding specialty crops flown in from California.

Tom Lam's next invention was baby choy mue, miniature bok choy seedlings picked almost as soon as they sprout. It takes a trained worker with a serrated knife an hour to cut a carton of choy mue out of the ground. Lam has just thirty-six hours to harvest a field before the sprouts outgrow their baby taste. The effort is worth it, earning Lam three to four dollars on each box of choy mue, as much as $10,000 profit per crop per acre. If the crunchy delicacy becomes a craze, each planting could be worth as much as $50,000 per acre, five times a year. On a sunny afternoon the fields look like an outdoor factory, which, in a way, it is. About a hundred and fifty Mexican farmworkers work Lam's fields on their knees, digging the baby plants free of the black soil. Lam's farmworkers are long-term employees ("turnover less than 5 percent," he says), many with him since he shipped his first box of Ho Sai Gai.

Lam's baby choy mue has become the rage among Guangdong's nouveau business elite, men who think nothing of paying twenty dollars for a salad to impress associates. The bubble will likely last, he adds, because as China's industry grows, its farmland gets farther away. Meanwhile, California's production will become even more efficient. He'll profit if he gets to the market first. Lam scans his fields and smiles. "Timing," he says, "is everything."*

---

* Material quoted from or information developed for a story appearing in the November 6, 1995, issue of FORBES Magazine entitled "Imported Entrepreneurs," reprinted with permission of Forbes Inc.

CHAPTER FIVE

Interstate Commerce

Together, the Future Is Ours.
Slogan of the 1993 Asian American Hotel Owners
Association Conference in Atlanta, Georgia

★

The southeast corner of Tennessee is among the prettiest corners anywhere. The Appalachian mountain chain rises steadily here from the rolling hills of Georgia. North Carolina is almost within walking distance. That is, if you feel like walking straight up, over peaks five thousand feet high. Here in this corner of the South, the mountains and river jumble in together, forming a cul de sac facing north, south, and east. In the middle is Chattanooga, a city with just under a million inhabitants and a century-long history as a commercial crossroads. It's a city that would have been big enough and rich enough to be a state capital had it been lucky enough to be situated in the middle of a state, instead of at the edges of four.

The Chickamauga Creek flattens out to a broad marsh outside town. The creek's natural flow would be to the northeast, into the Tennessee River. But today Chickamauga's rills flow by artificial impulse, rising and falling on tides selected by engineers at the mammoth Tennessee Valley Authority. The TVA's Chickamauga Dam backs the Tennessee River into Chickamauga Lake just inside city limits. Chickamauga—a Creek name meaning "dwelling place of the war chief"—was a famous Civil War battleground, dwelling place of war chiefs James Longstreet and Braxton Bragg during the bloody Chattanooga siege of 1863.

The Shallowford Road crosses here just west of the Chickamauga Dam. It continues southeast across a swamp for three miles, finally joining Interstate Highway 75. Here a traveler may decide to follow the river road downtown, then around north to Nashville, or he or she may bypass the city and head south, along the paved "river" that is the federal interstate highway system.

If you're driving on Shallowford Road today, it's easy to forget how it got its name. Shallowford Road presents a vista of fast-food joints, gas stations, and cheap motels. Two small strip malls lie north of the interstate, and a palatial shopping center, New Hamilton Place, lies directly south. Garish signs tout unleaded gasoline at $1.09 a gallon, 39-cent hamburgers, and Kids Stay Free Everyday specials. Seven gas stations with convenience stores built around cashiers' stations sit at this exit, and eleven motels. There are outlets for speedy check-cashing, video rental, eyeglass-fitting, and aerobic exercise. The Buckhead Roadhouse, a "real" restaurant that attracts more repeat customers than fly-bys, is the Shallowford Road exit's sole homage to permanence. Its outsized, barnlike angles look misplaced, squeezed into the parking lots of two neighboring motels—a Days Inn and a Hampton Inn. Buckhead's mahogany paneling and enormous rock fireplace, like the thick pork chops and steaming clumps of mashed potatoes that are its specialties, are meant to be out of place. They're meant to convey something old, something your parents or grandparents might recognize, and wonder how a place so traditional was spared the onslaught.

But that's an illusion. The restaurant goes all the way back to 1994, when it replaced the Italian restaurant that replaced the Mexican restaurant that opened on bare ground just five years before. Buckhead Roadhouse is a replica of a trendy Marin County, California, restaurant, the Buckeye Roadhouse, whose partners selected the Shallowford Road exit at I-95 as a testing ground for a national chain. Chattanoogans who never heard of Marin County believe the link is to Yuppie Atlanta, where the art-deco Buckhead Diner in the trendy Buckhead district caters to a similar nouveau taste.

Like everything these days, automobile travel makes any place as memorable as home. And as forgettable.

But Shallowford has a tradition. It begins with the Cherokee and Creek and Shawnee, who dwelled here in prosperous villages. Long before there was an interstate highway, the shallow ford was the perfect spot for an ambush. Chickamauga braves under the command of Tsugunsini, "The Dragging Canoe," waited there with evil intent in 1777. Their quarry was Tennessee militiamen fighting with George Washington's revolutionary army. Tsugunsini warned white settlers before launching his campaign: "You have bought a fair land, but will find its settlement dark and bloody."

That prophecy proved prescient nearly a century later in November 1863, as the Shallowford Road became the retreat route for forty thousand Confederate troops, crushed by Grant's armies in the battle for Missionary Ridge. Within a year, William Tecumseh Sherman selected the Shallowford Road area as a staging ground for what would be Sherman's devastating March to the Sea, the campaign that leveled Atlanta.

As it happened, Sherman left Tennessee for Georgia along a route that Interstate 75 follows today. For all but the coldest months, I-75 carries tourists up to campsites in the Great Smoky Mountains National Park, the country's most visited. Many tourists take an extra day to stop and visit the Chickamauga battlefield, the United States' most visited military park, receiving more annual visitors than Gettysburg and Yorktown combined. And, for all but the hottest months, I-75 carries thousands south toward Orlando and Disney World, as much a monument to our time's peace and prosperity as Chickamauga's shrines are to Sherman's epoch of destruction and despair. The Shallowford Road exit, Exit 5 on I-75, bisects the main north-south expressway connecting eastern Tennessee to Atlanta some hundred twenty miles to the south, rolling on another six hundred miles, through Macon, then Orlando and Tampa. Vacation Highway.

Today, interstate highways supplant railroads and riverboats. Eight highways—I-65, I-75, I-85, I-20, I-24, I-40, I-59, and I-81 —pass within a two-hour drive of Chattanooga, putting the city within a long day's drive of Dallas, Chicago, Detroit, Toledo, Cleveland, Washington, D.C., and Saint Louis. For the sheer number of interstates passing within a fifty-mile radius, Chattanooga dwarfs hubs like Dallas and Cincinnati. Most important for Shallowford Road, Chattanooga is the midpoint for thousands of Florida-bound tourists coming from up north. Interstate 75's Exit 5 is again an ambush spot, lying an even ten hours from Chicago, and exactly ten more from Orlando. That location puts Shallowford Road smack in the middle of a vortex spinning toward Disney World, which is to the tourism industry in the southeast United States something akin to a black hole in space—its gravitational pull is so great, it forces every moving vehicle into its orbit. That pull draws business to Exit 5, generating revenues well in excess of $200 million a year, enough revenue to support hundreds of jobs. Many are tailor-made for someone like Ray Amin.

Ramesh "Ray" Amin belongs to a new Indian tribe that has settled here. Amin first surveyed the Shallowford Road in 1982. Back then, Shallowford still looked much like it did when Sherman left, except for the six lanes of highway, service road, and feeder ramp running right through the old creek bed. Land was cheap in 1982, but expensive to drain and grade. There was a gas station, but the only other business operating within shouting distance was a truck terminal belonging to the Overnite Freight company, really no more than a parking lot attached to a driveway attached to Highway 153 and surrounded by a chain-link fence. The "customers" were empty Overnite trailers, parked in rows near a single pay phone.

When Ray Amin happened on Shallowford Road that day, he cared little for Shallowford Road's storied past. His interest was in the future—particularly in finding a suitable school for his oldest daughter, then about to turn nine. For the last three years, Ray and his family had been living in tiny Etowah, Tennessee, a railroad crossing about a hundred miles northeast, deep in the Cherokee National Forest. Etowah was too small to attract others of his tribe, and he fretted about his daughter's marriage prospects in hillbilly country. Ray's people marry young, and they plan for marriage early. Which meant if their daughter was to find a proper mate, the family had to move to a bigger town, Knoxville perhaps, or Chattanooga.

Ray Amin knew as soon as he saw Shallowford Road that it was ripe for development. He had a good feel for his customers, what they wanted to spend money for, and what they wouldn't spend money for. He knew if he moved onto Shallowford Road, pretty soon he would have neighbors. "MacDonald's had done all the studies," Ray recalls. Land fever as old as the pioneers flickered in his heart. "The highway was here. They knew it could be a good exit. I wanted that land. I told the realtor: 'I want that land.'"

Ray Amin's tribe is the Gujarati, a people descended from Aryan nomads who rose in the fertile valleys of the Indus River two thousand years before the birth of Jesus. They settled what today is India's most densely populated state, Gujarat, on the Arabian Sea between Bombay and India's border with Pakistan. With over 40 million inhabitants, Gujarat is the birthplace of many prominent Indians. Mahatma Gandhi, this century's greatest Indian, was a Gujarati.

Since the 1800s, Gujaratis have sent small colonies to East Africa, the Carribbean, and the South Pacific. Most were laborers for the British. Gujarati built the railways that linked Indian Ocean ports like Zanzibar to the East African interior. They remained to work, then manage, tea plantations. Throughout British Africa, they became tradesmen—opening general stores, trading coffee, running transport companies. In Trinidad and Guyana, they were shopkeepers and civil servants. In Fiji, they ran banks. They are a mobile people. There are over half a million Gujarati in America today.

All Gujarati, wherever they live, trace their roots to an ancestral village in India. Even in exile, many bond in arranged marriages with partners who trace their heritage to that same original village. Marriage is usually within castes—another reason Ray Amin was eager to leave Etowah. A bigger town meant proximity to other Gujarati, increasing the chances someone would know of a prospect somewhere else whose family matched the Amins' background.

Ray Amin in 1994 seemed the picture of the up-and-coming real estate speculator. Slamming the door of his BMW sedan, he hitched up baggy linen pants and stuck out a warm right hand. At five foot five, with an oversized blue blazer and a loud tie, he seemed like a man who has always looked younger than his years, and was only now growing into the successful adult he had spent a lifetime pretending to be. His black hair is longish, parted on one side. His teeth are straight and bright, his handshake rock-hard. Ray Amin, forty-eight years old in 1994, had spent just over half his life in America. With his twanging A's and dropped G's, Ray Amin sounds a little more like a Southern swampland salesman than he would care to. Then again, selling swampland has made him rich. He put $65,000 down on a Shallowford Road lot in 1982. Now he could bulldoze the Buckhead Diner to rubble and sell the land under it, his land, for half a million bucks. He owns the Shallowford Hill Plaza strip mall next to the Days Inn, and the Shallowford Corner Shopping Center around back, by the Hampton Inn. He owns two motels and one Shell station, too.

"Ray Amin," he says, offering his card as we cross the parking lot. "But you can call me Patel."

"Patel" means farmer or landowner in Gujarat, where Patels are the biggest clan. "Amin" is Patel, as is "Desai," but everyone was Patel before the British came. The British needed a handle on the arcane caste delineations—there are eleven Patel castes in America, and many more in India—to facilitate tax collection. Desais kept the books for the Patels, Amins were their farm managers. "Desais had a little better education," Ray Amin explains. "Amins were more like skilled craftsmen, a goldsmith or a blacksmith. Only a few Amins in a whole town of Patels. That was the way in old India."

Detaching Amins and Desais from Patels was one step in bringing Gujarat into the modern world. Immigration was another. In Africa or Trinidad or Fiji, many became Patels again. Starting in the mid-1970s, Patels from East Africa and Asia began immigrating to the United States and immediately entered the lodging business. Today, over ten thousand roadside motels are owned by Asian Indians, a community that has become a force throughout the industry. The "Patel motel" has become a cliché among lodging executives and customers alike. Within big national chains, the number of owners surnamed "Patel" is staggering. One company, Hospitality Franchise Systems, has over six hundred Days Inns, Super 8's, Howard Johnsons, and Ramadas managed by Patel partners. Yet Gujarati motels reveal more than an immigrant group entering a discrete niche. Rather, they represent the discovery of a vast American frontier.

Patels took a sleepy, mature industry and turned it upside down—offering consumers more choices while making the properties themselves more profitable. Motels that attracted billions in immigrant savings turned into real estate equity worth many billions more. That equity, managed by a new generation, is being leveraged into new businesses. Some are related to lodging (manufacturing motel supplies); some, to real estate (reclaiming derelict housing); some, simply cash seeking an opportunity. The Patel motel model is another example, like New York's West Indian jitneys, of the way immigrant initiative expands the pie. And there is another lesson: as the economy shifts from manufacturing to services, the Patel motel phenomenon demonstrates how franchising can turn an outsider into a mainstream player. The Gujarati model for motels might be copied by Latinos in landscaping, West Indians in home care, or Asians in clerical services. By operating a turnkey franchise as a family business, immigrants will help an endless stream of service providers grow.

Today Patels run motels in most states, but especially along the interstates of the Sun Belt, stretching between Virginia and California. Hundreds of Patels live in each of the states of Tennessee, Georgia, Florida, California, and Texas. Any town with a four-lane highway, it seems, has Patels. Patels own motels in Athens (Georgia, Alabama, and Tennessee), Burlington (Iowa, North Carolina, and Vermont) and Canton (Mississippi, Texas, Ohio, and Michigan).

They're in Grand Prairie, Texas, and Grand Island, Nebraska. And in Plainview (Ohio and New York), and Longview (Texas and Washington); in Fort Payne (Alabama) and Fort Wayne (Indiana).

Patels run motels in Gettysburg, Appomattox, and Yorktown; in towns named for Indian tribes—Cheyenne (Wyoming), Shawnee (Oklahoma), and Ogallala (Nebraska); and in towns named for Indian oppressors—Fremont (California), Jackson (Mississippi), and Sheridan (Wyoming). In the handful of American towns named for cities in India, Patels run motels. Mike Patel owns and operates the Relax Inn in Madras, Oregon. Cousin Jay Patel owns the nearby Budget Inn and, across town, Bakulesh ("Bugsey") Patel has a Best Western. Nina and Jay Patel run the Best Western off I-20 in Delhi (pronounced "DEL-high"), Louisiana, while Victor Patel has Delhi's only other lodging, an independent called the Hilltop. Even towns too small to have motels have Patels: Calcutta, Ohio, has Sam and Ari Patel, who arrived in 1995 to operate the local Dunkin' Donuts. But, Sam says, this is temporary. The brothers-in-law spent years learning the motel trade working for an uncle in Texas. Donuts are a toehold in Calcutta until they bring in a motel.

The community so dominates the business, it has generated its own folklore. "*Atithi Devo Bhava* means 'a guest is equivalent to God.' [It is] an ancient Sanskrit saying that incorporates the essence of Indian cultural ethos," gushed the *India Post* in 1992. "From times immemorial Indian mythology and scripture abound with examples of Indian heritage of respecting and honoring a guest. Perhaps this time-honored tradition is at the heart of the success of Indian-American hotel and motel owners in the U.S. lodging industry."

It is altogether fitting and proper that the Patels should do this, and altogether false. Patels in India never ran motels, and there is no evidence of a Patel lodging tradition in Africa or anywhere else. In fact, the lodging "tradition" in India is so scanty that American hotel chains entering the country have to bring in Patels trained in the United States to run them. Rather than the Indians bringing an overseas tradition to the American heartland, the heartland gave the Patels an instant culture.

The earliest Patel motels date back to the 1960s, although the phenomenon as it is known today traces to the 1970s and the brutal reign of Uganda's Idi Amin. His expulsion of Asians from Uganda made headlines around the world, but Gujarati were under similar pressure from Nairobi to Johannesburg. Motel-Patels today come from Tanzania, Zambia, Malawi, and Zimbabwe. While the Ugandan Patels surrendered their African holdings, others simply left them to other Gujarati before going abroad. Many Gujarati already were accustomed to leaving Africa to study in India or England. Thus Patels in America are a mix of African refugee, Indian villager, British scholar, and perhaps a dozen other subcastes, drawn together in marriage. And the motel business.

Patels would have immigrated to America eventually. But it took a sudden cataclysm, Idi Amin, to create the critical mass that became an industry. In the 1970s, any immigrant willing to invest at least forty thousand dollars in a business employing at least ten Americans could apply for permanent residence, the first step to citizenship. Gujarati had lived for generations in Africa as British subjects, and were punished for their loyalty when the British left. When the crunch came, a British passport brought only safe passage out of Africa—to Britain, where thugs called them "Pakis" (for Pakistani), beat their children, and torched their shops. As refugees in America, Gujarati wanted something better than residency. American citizenship meant instant respectability.

But with a forty-thousand-dollar investment, choice was limited—basically to diners or roadside motels. Few chose food service. Being Hindus, Gujarati were uncomfortable handling meat. Being foreigners, they were bewildered by the face-to-face interactions restaurant work requires. Seating the customer, taking the order, serving, revisiting the customer, bringing a check, and bringing change—every step delays the essential goal: getting the customer's money into your cash register. Indians who bought properties with existing restaurants often leased the space to other immigrants, usually Chinese. Anything to avoid food service. For forty thousand dollars, properties could be bought outright. Even after hiring ten locals to do laundry, answer phones, and clean the pool, there was still plenty of work left for a family.

Pre-Patel, the motel business was divided between small family-owned independents and corporate franchises. In time, the Patels would meld those two into a hybrid: small family-owned corporations controlling several properties, usually spread among various franchise brands. Unlike the big, centralized bureaucracies of a Holiday Inn or a Hilton, the Gujarati were nimble managers. Unlike the old mom-'n'-pop motel operators, many were highly trained, accustomed to transactions requiring much more sophistication than purchasing motel supplies. The new owners quickly adopted modern accounting formulas to guide their purchases, starting with a strict monitoring of cash flow. Wherever they are, motels have predictable cash-flow performance, a revenue-per-room history. Even fleabags have a known cash flow, especially when they are used to house indigent tenants whose rents are paid by the government. Thus, when buying a distressed property—the only kind Patels could get for forty thousand dollars—a good buy was anything that could generate at least ten thousand dollars a year. Four times cash flow became the mantra of the Patels, who realized even motels of ten rooms could be profitable. Once in possession, they worked to upgrade properties and improve cash flow to the point where, finally, they sold the property (often to another Patel) and traded up to a better motel.

H. P. Rama, a Malawi Patel, started in motels in 1973 with a forty-room independent in Pomona, California. Today his Greenville, South Carolina, company owns twenty-three hotels in the United States and India, and a factory that makes bedspreads and curtains for motels. Rama's father was a dry-goods salesman in Africa, but H. P. went to school in Gujarat in the early 1960s. He earned his M.B.A. from Xavier University in Cincinnati, then invested in his first motel. Rama says his study of operations research and "queueing theory," the efficient ordering of tasks, were easily applied to motels. Each time he acquired a property, Rama would break tasks down into the number of minutes each required. Then he matched employee "units" to each job. Thus, each night clerk was trained to record each guest's expected check-out time, then phone a supervisor before midnight for an hour-by-hour count of the rooms to be cleaned—and their order—the following morning. The supervisor then dispatched each housekeeper with a list. Instead of four chambermaids on staff, each waiting for her rooms to empty, each rotated through the property, cleaning rooms as guests left. "This is a detail business," Rama explains. "Say you have a hundred-room motel and six housekeepers. If you save ten minutes waiting time on each one, that multiplies to an hour of pay, every day. That's five dollars fifty an hour, plus insurance and payroll taxes, say up to seven fifty. With ten motels, that is seventy dollars a day."

When five guests arrive in bunches, say on an airport shuttle, Rama's clerks are trained to pass out registration cards to all five, then make them compete with each other to be the first to get a room. The desk clerk, meanwhile, is free to answer phones or attend to other guests. "No one is going anywhere, so no one feels slighted," Rama says. "Besides, each of the five feels his time is not being wasted." None of this is new to lodging—big city hotels and luxury resorts staff heavily from university programs that teach these skills—but they were practically unheard of in roadside motels, pre-Patel.

By buying, renovating, and reselling, the Patels did more than establish a foothold in the industry. Eventually, they would remake lodging in America, changing a centralized, highly leveraged "hotel" business into the lean-'n'-mean "hospitality" industry. They did it largely on their own, with their own family financing and their own on-the-job training.

"They own the interstates," says John Crow of Pannel Kerr Forster International, a real estate consultant who has worked with dozens of Patel-founded motel corporations in the Southeast. "I would guess fifty percent or more of all new franchises since 1992 are Indian. Altogether they have something like ten billion dollars in assets. The franchisers know they call the shots."

The motels John Crow is talking about are not the fleabag mom-'n'-pops, but the Rodeway Inns, Econolodges, Holiday Inns, and Super 8's Americans have been enjoying for years. By 1992, more than half the Days Inns were owned by Indians, and almost a third of the Howard Johnsons and Ramadas. The starter motels bought by the first immigrants had changed hands dozens of times, but seldom left the community, so by the mid-1990s, Patels had a virtual monopoly on properties of fifty rooms or less. As Patels gained experience in the motel business, they traded up to bigger properties and slowly forged a niche in their own image.

That image is "low service," an industry term meaning "no food." It also means no room service, laundry, or conference facilities. But in Patel hands, low-service hotels became star performers of the hotel business—with profit margins double those of full-service chains like Hyatt, Hilton, or Radisson. Patel success forced full-service providers to develop their own "low service," "budget," or "economy" niches. Then those niches developed niches. Budget for businessmen, budget for tourists, with kids and without kids. Budget for seniors. Every successful budget chain spawned offspring—Ramada offering Ramada Limited, Hampton Inn offering Hampton Inn Express. Choice Hotels International, a nursing home company, launched a new budget brand almost every year —Quality Inn, Choice Inn, Comfort Inn, Sleep Inn. The differences between each property were invisible to the naked eye—but not the price differences. Separated in each market by $5- and $10-per-night increments, the fragmentation allowed lots of players to troll for lots of different tourist fish. And wherever consumers wanted to squeeze extra dollars from their travel budget, they found Patels eager to provide.

The Indians who picked motels over restaurants chose wisely. Their goal was to meet the customer once, take his money, and not have to serve him again. Interstate locations were preferred, not only because land there was cheaper to buy, but also because the customer rarely spent more than one night. "You got your American plan, your European plan, and your Indian plan," P. J. Patel, owner of the Guest Hotel in Houston, joked once. "The Indian plan is: Here is your room. Here is your key. Goodbye."

Patels not only saved by shucking their restaurants and coffee shops, but by hiring other Patels. The African Patels, who had forty thousand dollars to put down on the property, found there were plenty of Indian Patels who arrived the same way Ray Amin did— with just a few dollars in their pockets. They went to work as night clerks and cleaners, sometimes trading a future stake in the business for their labor. For someone also attending a nearby college, a Patel motel was the perfect part-time job. Eat and sleep on the premises, and study during the night shift. Besides their minimal salary, the luckiest earned equity in the motel, usually a 25 percent share, which he could leverage into full ownership when his boss was ready to sell. In this way, the Patels built an empire. Cheap laborers became cheap partners, then on-site replacements as successive waves of owners passed through the motels.

Of course, there was a backlash. In town after town, the native competition erected billboards or lettered marquees with words intended to lure customers away from the ruthless Patels. "American Owned," as everyone knew, meant "No Indians." Banks and insurance companies refused Patel accounts. Throughout the 1970s and into the 1980s, franchise companies shunned Patel franchisees. "Patel meant the lowest end," says Gerald Pettit, chairman of a leading franchisor, Choice Hotels International. "People named Patel meant cooking in a curry pot and a kid getting her diapers changed on the counter, a poorly run hotel."

Media treatment was even less sympathetic. Ray Amin remembers small-town papers in Tennessee wondering what "tribe" these Indians all came from. Somehow a rumor spread that Native American "Indians" were behind the motel-buying spree, and were planning to burn all their motels on a national Day of Vengeance. "I don't like 'em," an anonymous motel broker in Newport News, Virginia, told *The Washington Post* in 1979. "They haggle, they maneuver, they do things not customary in this country." Another broker, from New Jersey, asserted, "They've got different business ethics."

The *Post* reported that the U.S. Department of Justice was "actively investigating" Gujarati Indians on a variety of violations. Patels were accused of arson for profit, of using their motels to launder stolen traveler's checks, and of using the same surname, Patel, to circumvent immigration laws. For a time, law enforcement agencies sought a unified "Patel crime family," modeled on the Mafia. According to the *Post*'s report, the immigrants were accused of buying motels in one family's name, then selling paper shares to others of the same name, thus allowing dozens of Patels to enter the country behind one investor's visa. Justice Department officials spoke of a "motel scheme," and other newspapers launched what amounted to a nationwide Patel watch.

And as daily newspapers peddled a Patel-under-every-motel-bed theme, the industry trades erected a solid barrier of prejudice. Since Patel motels were bottom of the barrel, "American Owned" was seen not as a slur, but a legitimate survival tactic employed by moteliers being overrun by unscrupulous foreign competition. "Foreign investment has come to the motel industry . . . causing grave problems for American buyers and brokers," *Frequent Flyer* magazine declared in an article in the summer of 1981. "Those Americans in turn are grumbling about unfair, perhaps illegal business practices: there is even talk of conspiracy."

The conspiracy, never clarified, seemed to point to a "mafia-like pool" of investors, either in New Jersey or California, which allowed these "Near Easterners" (sic) named Patel to "take over" towns like Tallahassee. A drawing of a businessman wearing a turban, with four Shiva-like arms juggling strips of motel rooms graces the jingoistic text. "Now the average person who saves up for fifteen years to buy a small hotel can't compete with foreign investors," complained one Chicago-area broker, who nonetheless was not averse to earning commissions as a broker in Patel motel deals. *Frequent Flyer*'s overall complaint was that Patels had triggered a buying frenzy—driving the prices of properties to two and three times their previous values. That was only bad news for competing buyers, and a windfall for the sellers. But that was hardly the point: "Comments are passed about motels smelling like curry and dark hints are heard about immigrants who hire Caucasians to work the front desk," the article concludes. "The facts are that immigrants are playing hardball in the motel industry, and maybe not strictly by the rulebook."

Patels laugh about such portrayals today, but at the time they were deadly serious. Even now anti-Indian prejudice is rampant in the lodging business. In truth, the American being done out of his sinecure was the reason the Patels excelled in lodging. Their competition in these early years was older, poorer, and quite a bit less educated than the Gujarati. He or she (usually both) was also childless, at least on-site. It wasn't Patel cash as much as Patel youth that made the community a success, and gave Patels the ability to expand holdings quickly. "We bailed those old operators out," H. P. Rama insists today. "Most of the small motels, I'd say eighty percent, were sold by people whose kids weren't interested in running motels."

"American" operators were also victimized by the expanding motel franchise companies, many of whom came to towns where no national motel brand had been before. Sometimes the new franchisee was a Patel. There were, of course, "pools" of Patels formed to back new moteliers wherever opportunity surfaced. They were hardly "mafia-like," and hardly restricted to one state.

Patels come from a culture of scarcity and thrift, yet have learned to be themselves within America's disposable present. Just like the traffic going by on Shallowford Road, Ray Amin is at sea in a culture in permanent flux. But family and community give him all the permanence he needs. He wouldn't give vials of shampoo away at his franchised motels if doing so wasn't required by the chain, nor would he take pains to make the Hampton Inn's free breakfast slightly more lavish than the one at his Days Inn next door. But he has learned that motels are simply a business, and going along makes him prosper. "I had never drinked a coffee where you could drink all the coffee you want for ten cents. I never done that," Ray says after the waitress filled his for the umpteenth time. "Why? Because I didn't have ten cents."

Ray Amin was born in India in 1946, in a village a hundred miles west of Baroda. His father raised cotton. Ray, the oldest son, was the first in his family to attend university, earning degrees in chemical engineering and biology in 1967. He answered an ad for a job in the laboratory of a fertilizer plant in Baroda. "They posted the job, and there were five thousand applicants," he recalls. "For one job. Whoever had the best grades might get a job. Or whoever had the best connections."

Twenty years after independence, India was training thousands of eager young men, but its economy was not growing fast enough to absorb the talent. Everywhere, it was the same. Connections mattered, and a country boy like Ray could hope for little. Ray's father was also being squeezed. With eighty acres under cultivation, he was relatively rich in a state where subsistence could be scratched out with fifteen acres or ten. But now, traditional methods were dying; to survive, a farmer had to absorb his neighbors. That meant borrowing money from a state bank for fertilizers, tractors, and the new miracle seeds of the Green Revolution. That, too, meant having the right connections. By the hundreds, then the hundreds of thousands, Indians migrated toward the cities or abroad. "I waited about three or four months," Ray remembers, finally learning by form letter what he already knew. No job for him in Baroda. "I decided to go abroad."

Ray's father mortgaged his property to pay for Ray's passage, and for tuition at the Northern Technical Institute in Toledo. There, twenty-two-year-old Ray enrolled to study die-cast engineering. He arrived in New York on February 5, 1968. Like most immigrants, he remembers the exact hour, 5 P.M., he cleared customs, and the feeling of the frigid New York dusk. Like a lot of first-timers, he also remembers how a taxi driver cheated him.

The "theft," if you can call it that, seems more like a misunderstanding. He had to switch planes to get to Detroit, where an old mate from Baroda was to retrieve him for the drive to Toledo. His English, suitable for university studies in India, wasn't adequate for the complexities of negotiating public space in America, let alone a busy airport. "Someone said, 'Take the red and white bus,' and I did," Ray recalls. "But I followed another Indian guy off the bus. He was going to TWA. When I presented my ticket, the attendant said I had to get back on the bus and go to Northwest. I had no idea each airline could have its own terminal! I panicked, and waved to the first cab I saw."

The driver offered to take Ray to the terminal for a set price: two dollars. The Northwest terminal, it turned out, was the next one over, visible from where Ray had been standing. "Two dollars!" he sputters, more than twenty years later. "When I saw how close I was, I could have walked!"

It wasn't the principle, but the money. For Indians emigrating in 1968, two dollars represented a considerable portion of their net worth. Strict currency laws kept common people like Ray from exchanging more than a few rupees before traveling overseas. Indian students usually arrived with ten dollars or less in their pockets. Ray Amin arrived with just seven dollars. By the time he arrived in Toledo a few hours later, he was down to his last five-dollar bill.

"I used to walk across the Maumee River Bridge in blizzard conditions to save the five cents for a transfer ticket," he continues, picking up speed and smiling with wonder at his own history. "I still remember that: for five cents I walked a mile in the snow, a foot of snow. O.K.? And my lifestyle: I got up, six in the morning, I got ready for school, made breakfast, ate, cleaned the pots and pans, went to school, came back, made the lunch, ate the lunch, packed the dinner and went to work. You know, in a ride. I didn't have a car. Then worked till midnight; came home, made the food, ate the food, went to sleep."

Of course he excelled, working two jobs and completing work toward another degree. He was living the stereotype of the Gujarati nerd, "Rammy" Glick. Ray's jobs were in restaurants, the stepping-stone immigrants typically favor for their flexible hours and one attractive fringe benefit: leftovers. His first job, scraping plates into the garbage pail at the Hillcrest Hotel, paid $1.25 an hour. The leftovers sickened him. He was pinching pennies to make his tuition and rent, and mountains of food were being wasted—meat mostly, which for a Hindu vegetarian added insult to hunger. Nausea choked his throat and tears filled his eyes as the pile of hamburger rinds, breakfast sausage, and soggy bits of bread filled plastic tubs. The vapor of peanut oil made his throat gag.

After graduation, Ray wouldn't see the inside of a restaurant again until he was the owner, but he was no less a workaholic. He traveled home to India for a brief vacation—and to marry Urvashi, a bride chosen by his father. Returning to Ohio, Ray joined Atech Chemical Coatings, a company that makes paints for aluminum siding. What Americans wasted in coffee shops, Ray soon learned, was nothing compared to the opportunities they were willing to forsake in the job market. While other engineers planned weekends on the lake or went hunting or visited relatives, Ray pushed. He was exploited, actually, working beyond mere "overtime" for seven years, putting in seven days almost every week. "All my bosses loved me," he says proudly. "I never, ever got laid off."

He doesn't admit it easily now, but Ray was lonely. When his co-workers came in on Monday, talking about the Ohio State game, or that great shot so-and-so made on the eleventh hole, Ray Amin felt isolated. Even now he feels a need to defend his record. "One job, I opened the plant in blizzard conditions. It was five degrees below zero but I went to work," he says firmly. "In 1974, I worked fifty-six days straight."

Even in Toledo, the Indian colony was growing. Men Ray had gone to school with in India were also starting families. Patels who had trained to become surgeons were working as orderlies in Ohio hospitals, waiting for certification. Others became teachers, some went into business. On religious holidays, Patels would gather in Detroit or Chicago. A few communities even built their own modest Hindu temples. There were weddings of Patels to attend in Ohio, Michigan, and western Pennsylvania. Social life was returning to Ray Amin. But work came first.

"One time we were going to go to Sandusky, to Cedar Point, an amusement park, my family and I one Saturday morning. My wife had all the food and everything loaded up, the van was all full, and we had some friends with us, and the telephone rang, just as I was turning the door knob. I said I better see what that is: who was that at eight in the morning? It was my plant supervisor. He said, 'Ray, those four thousand gallons of paint have to be ready and approved. And you're the only one who can approve the batch. I'm sorry but you have to come in.' "

Ray sighs his little shrugging sigh, and leans forward, explaining, in the bluff way what he wouldn't have had to explain back then. "I was the only one who could drive . . . ," he starts to say, suddenly looking away. The way he must have looked away from the looks Urvashi and his daughter were giving him that warm spring day. He looks down at a pair of pork sausages on his clean plate. Whatever once made Ray Amin sick has now made him strong. He spears both on his fork, sliding them quickly into his mouth as the waitress approaches to clear his place. He gave up vegetarianism around the time he began thinking about entering the motel business.

The Holiday Terrace Motel on Highway 411 in Etowah had a $220,000 mortgage. At that price, the motel had to be generating between $50,000 and $60,000 a year, or no less than $5,000 per month. Ray put $70,000 down, selling his house in Toledo for $15,000, taking $25,000 from his company profit-sharing plan and another $10,000 out of his savings account. He borrowed $20,000 from his brother and in-laws, interest-free. "I saw it and I loved it," Ray recalls. "Twenty-two rooms, mountains in the back, pool in the front. I said, 'This is heaven.' "

The astonishing key to Patel success was not that so many over-qualified immigrants settled for work in motels. It was that so many overachievers, many with established careers, chose to leave their professions to become motel owners. That's what Ray Amin did. It is hard to imagine the rationale that meant sacrificing a prestigious job in industry to wash toilets and make beds—and to risk life savings to boot! But Ray can imagine. "There are in India three things," he explains. "*Utum Vepar* is the first. It means that having a business is good. Number two is *Khiti*, that means farming, the second best thing. And number three is *Kaneest*, or service to someone else. That is considered the worst of all three."

It's partly the caste system, Ray says, and partly being an Indian in America. While thousands of Patels fit well at banks, hospitals, and every other type of American corporation, the longing of others to not be anyone's employee is strong. "People thought I was crazy," Ray admits. "I left a lot of fringes: thirty-five thousand dollars a year in salary, profit sharing, five to six weeks vacation every year. But my father had a saying: 'Better to live like a king for a day than live like a lamb for one hundred days.' That's how I felt."

Ray felt something else. He was afraid that being Indian, and being well paid, would lead to dismissal. Instead of seeing himself the way he does now—the Ray who worked fifty-six straight days once, the Ray any of his old bosses would take back on a day's notice—he sees the Ray who made too much money, who would be a target of downsizing. "I've seen it so many times," he said, "they work for one company all their life, and their job is in jeopardy. Instead of laying off the lower people, they go after the big fat cat, and save half a dozen jobs." After more than ten years in Ohio, Ray Amin felt insecure. In October 1979, he left for Tennessee.

The Holiday Terrace's natural customers were tourists visiting the Smoky Mountains, but when Ray came, he realized the most profit-per-room was being generated by locals. The Louisville & Nashville Railroad had a repair depot near Etowah. Ray could count on renting two or three rooms every night, and sometimes as many as ten, to railroad men. They would stay several days at a time, and leave at all hours—whenever their engine was ready to roll. The erratic schedule kept Ray Amin and his family active day and night, but increased profits. "We watched the costs on everything," he recalls. "I even got up at two in the morning. If that was when a railroad man left, we were in there cleaning the room up. Sometimes we would rent it again that same morning. I had days when I rented thirty-five rooms, even though there were only twenty-two in the place."

In the three years the Amin family lived in Etowah, he never came close to earning what he made in Toledo. But by the time he left, the Holiday Terrace was grossing between six thousand and eight thousand dollars a month, nearly twice what the property was earning when he moved in. By 1981, when Ray bought a second property nearby, he knew his *Kaneest* days—working for someone else—were over. The motel Ray Amin called "heaven" in 1979 was gone by 1982, flipped to another Gujarati, from New Jersey, for $325,000. Ray threw the Etowah Motel into the deal for another $200,000.

Before leaving for Chattanooga, the Amins took another motel, a 71-room independent called the Cascade in East Ridge, Tennessee. It belonged to Ray's brother Charley, together with three Gujaratis working with him at the Fermi II Nuclear Power Plant in Monroe, Michigan. Together the four pooled their savings to buy the Cascade, engaging Ray as arm's-length manager. Another Patel, a CPA named Harry Patel, was hired in Toronto to be on-site manager. Both sides, Amins and Patels, profited from the deal— Charley and Ray keeping costs low and Harry learning the motel business. "They paid me about a thousand dollars a month, plus the training," he says today from Kansas City, where he owns six motels.

Compared to Ray's job in Toledo, Charley's career at the Fermi II plant was even harder to walk away from. He was making over $100,000 a year, about three times Ray's last salary. Yet Charley, too, chafed under *Kaneest,* and soon left for Tennessee to join his brother on Shallowford Road.

The methods the Amin brothers pioneered in Etowah in the early 1980s became a national standard by the end of the decade. Clustering, or acquiring properties close to each other, was something motel-Patels did out of necessity, to husband scarce resources. By the late 1980s, clusters of Patel-owned motels—some independents, some franchised, some converted from one to another— were springing up throughout the South. Several things contributed to this trend. First, debt. With the building savings-and-loan crisis, and the bursting of the real estate bubble after 1987, bank financing for motel properties evaporated. According to Steven Belmonte, president of the Ramada Inn chain, by the end of the decade, seven of every ten properties in America were in bankruptcy, in receivership, or on the verge of a debt crisis. "These properties went back to the lenders," he explains. "That's one of the reasons service levels declined in the industry rather rapidly. Properties were being operated by asset managers and portfolio managers, rather than hoteliers."

Enter the Patels, many who now had ten or more years of experience in lodging. As reluctant as loan officers still were to lend to immigrants, asset managers were desperate to dispose of distressed motels. So the economics shifted from buying based on four-times-cash-flow to buying based on cost-per-room, which gave another advantage to the budget motels Patels were building. An economy motel on the Interstate costs as little as thirty thousand dollars per room, much closer to the $40 a night an operator can charge and still be competitive. Ultimately, the budget strategy became self-fulfilling. In essence, it created a swarming guerrilla army of fifty- and hundred-room units, sweeping the mammoth luxury hotels into bankruptcy.

Second, and also self-fulfilling, was financing. The more big hotels failed, the more pressure they put on all lodging properties, the harder it was to get bank loans to finance new hotel construction. Industrywide, the lodging business lost $10 billion between 1989 and 1992, yet Patels never stopped buying. Motel-Patels, by pooling their sources of cash, bought properties at pennies on the dollar.

Enter the third big change. As property values collapsed, a few smart entrepreneurs realized that detaching themselves from actually operating a motel meant they could reap a fortune managing hotel reservations and marketing. Thus the "hotel" business became the "hospitality" business. Savvy operators like Henry Silverman at Hospitality Franchise Systems and Gerald Pettit at Choice Hotels International were the first to realize that they didn't need to own motels to be profitable. In fact, they would be more profitable if they didn't. What they "owned" was brand-name identification, linked to toll-free, 1-800 reservation systems.

Gerald Pettit's Choice Hotel International sells franchise services to over three thousand Rodeway Inns, Econolodges, Comfort, Clarion, Sleep Inns, and Friendship Inns. Henry Silverman's HFS, the world's biggest franchiser, runs seven chains, with over five thousand properties. Like Gerry Pettit at Choice, he doesn't own motels either. Almost all of his Ramadas, Howard Johnson's, Days Inns, Villagers, and Knights Inns are independently owned properties. With market segmentation letting the franchiser attract lodgers along a climbing scale, hospitality companies soon found it didn't matter if two or three or seven of a system's properties occupied space at the same highway exit. As long as each has its loyal clientele, each could thrive. Thus, Choice's escalator climbs from Friendship Inns, priced under $35 a night, to Sleep Inns and Econolodges ($35 to $45), Rodeway Inns ($40 to $60), then Comfort Inns ($45 to $65), Quality Inns ($65 to $85), and Clarion Suites ($85 to $100).

"It's the classic case of a bar of soap," explains Morris Lasky, a consultant whose Lodging Unlimited tracks the hospitality business. "You have one bar of soap and have thirty percent of the market. Make five bars and you have forty percent of the market."

As the "hospitality" companies flourished, however, the market's brutal regime dictated that for any new brand to survive, it must grow quickly—no fewer than a hundred properties need to be up and running within twelve months of a brand's launch to be viable. Suddenly there was demand for operators who could learn quickly, relocate if they had to, and could raise cash for new construction. Instead of pariahs, Patels became the darlings of the lodging world. And just as the hospitality companies needed Patels, the immigrants needed the infrastructure of an established American corporation. To move beyond the drive-up trade, they needed the kind of steady business a toll-free reservation system creates. They needed to learn how to manage bigger properties. For immigrants, franchising provided instant training, with seminars and manuals to describe every motel nuance. Franchising also gave economies of scale in purchasing everything from disposable bathroom cups to towels, to television sets. No surprise, then, that as the hospitality chains grew, they attracted a disproportionate number of Patels. Today, of every hundred new low-service properties, about half of them are in the hands of Gujarati.

Ray and Charley Amin operate eight franchised properties in and around Chattanooga: a Days Inn and Hampton Inn abut the Buckhead Roadhouse at Shallowford Road; they also own a Hampton Inn in Cleveland, Tennessee; a Hampton Inn Express, a Holiday Inn, and two more Days Inns in Georgia. Besides his own properties, a total of eleven motels rose out of the swampland Ray bought in 1982, including four owned by Patels. Pete Patel runs Comfort Suites, Bob Patel has a Country Lodging, Navin Patel runs the Ramada Limited, and there is a Sleep Inn owned by Dinker "Dennis" Patel. By 1994 Dennis Patel had already broken ground on his next property, another Days Inn, and yet another Patel, Ashok, was building an independent motel.

Like that bar of soap, a motel room became a commodity. What is surprising, ultimately, is not that Indian immigrants thrived with thrift and enterprise, but that today—more than a decade after the budget craze began to accelerate—there are still new budget brands coming onto the market, and no sign that a saturation point has been reached. As long as Patels are buying, any new scheme has a chance to make it. "There's a point where a chain has to grow quickly, and that's where the Indians have been a huge benefit to the franchise chains," says Randell Smith, the country's leading roadside-lodging numbers cruncher. "A lot of other people don't want to put in the time and effort to bring these properties up— who else brings in whole families?"

The interstate exit has become the supermarket aisle—the longer it reaches, the more cereal boxes it offers. Smith breaks the budget business down into five categories—upper upscale, lower upscale, mid-scale, upper economy, and lower economy—and even charts subgroups into smaller categories. Smith says properties are selling for much more than they can possibly return, but owning a motel has become like owning a baseball team; as long as there is a hunger to own motels, the price of properties keeps going up, and more franchisers launch more brands. "This I never anticipated, but if you look at the fundamentals of American society, it makes sense," Hasmukh Rama says. "The consumer likes new things, different things. A simple idea is bought by the average American consumer, and a hotel is no different. Take the example of restaurants: you have Wendy's and McDonald's, and Burger King and Hardees. Everyone is selling beef, but still everybody is doing business. Because each has its own niche. People go for it. Hotels are not quite like that, and yet it works. I still marvel at that!"

Patel Inc. continues to grow. It even has annual conventions and trade shows under the banner of the Asian American Hotel Owners Association, or AAHOA. Besides the enormous caldrons of lentils, shredded coconut, and vegetable curd consumed, what impresses most is the speed with which the Patels have institutionalized their clout. In the speeches, in the vendors' booths, in all the diverse services sold to motel owners, Indian purchasing power is the tail wagging the dog. Franchises you've probably never heard of (and never will, if Patels don't buy) like Microtel and Key West Inns virtually exist to lure Gujarati immigrants. Some are willing to allow Patels with independent no-name properties to convert into franchised flag-bearers. Others insist on new construction. Others try flag-switching, convincing a motelier to switch out of one company's brand and into another. No matter how it's done, franchisers know if the Patels don't buy, the brand will disappear.

That impresses vendors. A typical 200-room motel costs between $1 million and $2 million, new, and depending on the brand, earns from $2 million to $5 million every year in gross room revenues. Thus, Patels attract vendors selling mattresses, cups, towels, bed linen, and all the other disposable items most guests barely think about. They also sell improvement. To extend the life of a building, there are wall sealants and faucet governors, and air-conditioning and heating systems. They also sell renewal, physical and spiritual. A San Francisco hotel liquidator is offering Complete Rooms, all furnishings, starting at $195, as well as lamps or those awful paintings for $5 apiece. Meanwhile, the M. K. Gandhi Institute for Nonviolence pitches from one booth, while followers of the Param Pujya Shri Rameshbhai Oza, an itinerant Hindu priest, passes out flyers for the swami's upcoming trip to Chattanooga.

Most vendors offer to save money, not souls. A 200-room motel can rake about three hundred dollars a month in "service charges" tying a customer's room phone to a preferred long-distance carrier. No wonder so many long-distance vendors offer motels discounts of as little as ten cents a minute for calls to India. You can beautify an ugly property with Rib-Roof, a lightweight canopy that promises, "Business as Usual—no disruption during application." Another gimmick, "The Smart Flapper" toilet tank stopper, uses 50 percent less water with every flush, saving "around $25.00 per year," per room, according to a brochure. In a 200-room motel, that's three thousand dollars a year into the owner's pocket, the cost of paying a night clerk for several months. Everywhere there is the appeal to thrift and ethnic pride. Buy bed linens and towels from Krishna International—toll-free orders at 1-800-KRI-SHNA. Other companies are called Devanshi, Tarsadia, and Shiva.

The Asian American Hotel Owners Association came together in 1989 and traces back to the mid-1970s, when Asian operators faced discrimination in applying for property insurance, troubles that began with the many newspaper articles alleging money-laundering and widespread visa fraud among the Patels. The catalyst to organize came in the early 1980s, when, at a regional fire marshall's convention, a Missouri delegate reported that he had found Patels burning their properties and submitting fraudulent claims. The story circulated throughout the South and Midwest, and suddenly hundreds of insurance brokers were refusing to sell property insurance to Indian owners. The blacklist led to the formation of the Mid-South Indemnity Association in 1986. Finding strength in numbers, Patels then formed the Indo American Hospitality Association, which later merged with AAHOA. AAHOA says it's open to all Asians in the industry ("no more than ninety-seven percent Indian," H. P. Rama insists), but it is foremost a Gujarati organization. Today it has over ten thousand members.

Well over half AAHOA's members are surnamed Patel. At the national convention, held on the first weekend after Thanksgiving, conference credentials are disbursed from two booths—one for names starting with the letters A through L, the other M through Z. A better system would be "Patel" and "not Patel." AAHOA, at this level, is a love-fest. Everyone knows everyone else through school, an old motel partnership, or the village back in India. Vijay Mesuria arrived with his rock band from London, fresh from a tour of Gujarati Africa. He marveled at his prosperous American cousins. "I've got an uncle 'ere, somewhere," he said in a Cockney brogue as thick as a pint of East End ale. "Got 'imself a motel in Waco, Texas."

P. J. Patel of Houston says joining AAHOA is no longer a matter of showing solidarity against rednecks who erect "American Owned" signs along the highways or even to celebrate cultural solidarity. It is to arrange marriages. "Families come to check out who might be available for their sons and daughters," he explained as he waited in the long M–Z line for credentials. His own marriage took place in 1980. While working as a medical technician, an uncle in England learned, from another Patel in Africa, of a third Patel from the ancestral village. He had a daughter, also a medical technician, living in New Zealand. After checking out P. J.'s future wife, the marriage was arranged. P. J. was six years old at the time. "We met for the first time at our wedding," he says.

Charley Amin sees nothing strange about this story. Charley says most of the people attending AAHOA conventions were married this way, and many of their children still are. Charley's wife, Kokila, was born in Tanzania in 1954. Charley was already established in America when they "met" in 1977. "She understands we are married to the business first, wife comes second," Charley says. "If I say because of business I am not going to go on vacation, or we made a plan and I cancel it, the wife doesn't hold it against me. She understands why I am doing it."

Like Charley, Kokila is an American citizen, but not Americanized. It is the twist to the Behind Every Great Man boast every great Gujarati makes when asked the key to success: My wife, she doesn't ask me nothing. Arranged marriages have helped Patels expand holdings, something the hospitality companies appreciate. "Say my son marries a daughter from a family in Zambia, or South Africa, or Kenya. Then she brings her family over, mom and dad could run a motel," Ray Amin explains. "A lot of owners, they get a couple to manage a property; if they manage it well, they get a stake. My son-in-law already owns his." Ray's daughter, Anu, the daughter the Amins moved to Chattanooga for, married a Patel from Zambia. Together, Anu and her in-laws run the Amins' Hampton Inn in Cleveland, Tennessee.

Charley Amin has enrolled his young children in something called the Charotar Patidar Samaj, an association of matrimony-minded Patels in Atlanta. A report of the CPS's Thanksgiving gathering in Atlanta one year can be found in the Atlanta edition of the *India Tribune*. Besides articles on Awareness Night (which featured "informal matrimonial talks"), there was a half page of classified ads under the heading "Matrimonial" for those who couldn't make the Atlanta gathering. "Six Gam Patidar parents invite correspondence from Patel boy," reads one box. "Caste no bar," reads another. Altogether, more than fifty "alliances" were sought. And, at the bottom of the page, one motel buyer.

"Americans fall in love before the marriage, but Indians fall in love after the marriage," Charley Amin explains. "We get married, then we fall in love. Our divorce rate is very low. I don't know how long we are going to hold on to this, but divorce in India is unheard of."

Of course, strong marriages make strong franchises, another reason why the hospitality companies sponsor the AAHOA conventions.

Although there is no technical limit to the number of interstate highway exits that could exist in America, and almost no limit to how many motels could be erected at each, there is a limit to how much Patels will pay others to bring them guests. While the hospitality business created an opportunity for the Gujarati to excel, they are now so powerful they no longer have to be followers in the industry.

The official slogan of AAHOA's 1993 convention in Atlanta was "Together, the Future Is Ours." Attended by about two thousand delegates, the gathering brought out the big guns from all the major franchise systems. CEOs of Hospitality Franchise System, Choice Hotels, Promus (owner of the Hampton Inn, Embassy Suites, and Homewood Suites chains), and Holiday Inn were featured speakers at an inaugural event. Patels sat respectfully as the presidents dished out the praise. "You people busted your ass, and made a profit when nobody else could," Steven Belmonte, the Ramada CEO, brayed to a rapt crowd. Texas Senator Phil Gramm, just beginning his 1996 presidential run, praised Asian-American enterprise, then made pointed reference to his own link to Asian-American life: he married into a family of Filipino immigrants.

A year later, the mood had changed. AAHOA met in 1994 in Nashville, at the Opryland Hotel, the country's biggest hotel outside Las Vegas, with almost two thousand rooms, almost all of them continuously booked. "I hear they have ninety-five percent room occupancy," Ray Amin marveled as he strode the complex's wide interior boulevards. As he savored those numbers, he ignored the fact that Opryland, at once both plush and tacky, is a living shrine to redneck culture. Opryland is just about the whitest theme park in America. Few blacks work there, and none stay as guests or patronize restaurants like Rhett's and Old Hickory. The average age of the guests has to be well past sixty, men and women shuffling along with the aid of aluminum walkers, wearing name tags that identified the many Christian tourist groups bused in each day. These are exactly the people attracted by an "American Owned" sign. As Patels schmoozed and cruised the carpeted lobbies, they couldn't help displaying a certain swagger.

In a year, AAHOA's membership had nearly doubled, and now over four thousand delegates listened to the presidents' stroking. But they were no longer silent. They cheered as Choice's Gerry

Pettit praised their recent victory in Washington, D.C., lobbying to retain a lucrative Small Business Administration program that has allowed hundreds of AAHOA members to apply for cheap "minority businessman" loans. They cheered the hype, then fired off a barrage of charges as the portly white executives squirmed onstage. What about franchise fees, aren't they excessively high? What about impact—aren't you pitting too much competition against our motels by adding all these "extension" brands? And what about bigotry, why are "brother" franchisees still erecting "American Owned" billboards on the interstate?

"I've been discriminated against all my life, and I won't stand for it," Yesvant Surati, a motelier from Youngstown, Ohio, railed at Gerry Pettit, spitting out his anger in a clipped South African accent. Surati owns a Comfort Inn, franchised by Choice, the same system franchising Rodeway Inns. "There are billboards on I-65 for a Rodeway Inn, American Owned. This is discrimination knowingly tolerated."

Another motel operator, Ray Dayal out of Nashville, stood to say he had seen the signs, too. Quaking with rage he bellowed, "This guy is making money at our expense, and we want him out of our system." Pettit gulped and told the assembly the sign would be gone "within twenty-four hours."

Ironically, a naturalized American citizen who chooses to leave an old sign erected by a native-born is seen as an operator with a sense of humor, not a bigot. Some AAHOA members delight in turning discrimination to their own advantage. But overall they despise the relics of bigotry and lobby every organization they can to remove them. The American Automobile Association no longer permits "American Owned" language for motels advertising in their guides. Days Inn and several other franchises explicitly forbid those two words in any property's advertising. "They've found strength in numbers," Pettit admitted later.

Another source of rancor was the fear that some chains are overstocking properties. Promus's Hampton Inn came to Nashville with a list of about two hundred locations to fill, each with an entry fee of $40,000. Those two hundred properties were to be opened in just thirteen Northeast states, thirty-five in Pennsylvania alone. At a cost of $40,000 to $50,000 per room, Patels were already growing wary of too many Hampton Inns. And if the driving public suddenly tires of Hampton, Patels would be the losers. So, the four thousand franchisees were in Nashville to pressure the hospitality industry to deliver more guests. More guests or a cut in franchise fees. Several speakers asked the presidents' reactions to Gujarati establishing their own franchise system. The question was an implied threat: cut fees, give us more, or we'll get our own guests. "We'll be in the bathroom, throwing up," answered Ramada's Belmonte.

The motel-Patels will prevail. Like the invasion of cookie-cutter motels into every crevice of the heartland, they are part of an intrusion on "traditional" ways of life. Which means, of course, they are fully assimilated. They are, in fact, part of an unstoppable engine of assimilation, but to what end? Do Americans really need to have a choice of six, or ten, or twenty motels at every highway exit, even if they want them?

Maybe not. But the long campaign of the Patels is about more than one industry. Interstate lodging serves as a *puesto* for immigrants seeking their footing; it also makes them employers, savers, and income generators for a broader community. Ray and Charley Amin left safe jobs to become entrepreneurs. Their net worth today is between $10 million and $15 million, which is thus the value of their decision to the economy as a whole. They still own dozens of acres of undeveloped real estate. More important, they launched a new company, American Plastic Industries, a factory grinding out plastic trash-can liners and cups—naturally, for the motel trade. It's perfect synergy: whatever they can't sell at a mark-up to other moteliers, they can use themselves. Altogether, the Amin brothers employ one hundred thirty-five people, no more than six of them relatives.

Thus, motels made it possible for Ray and Charley Amin to leverage two jobs in Ohio and Michigan into one hundred thirty-five jobs in eastern Tennessee. The plastics company is not even a decade old—and who knows where it will lead? "I intend to leave my son a one-hundred-million-dollar business," Ray Amin says. "My ambition is that he will run a Fortune Five Hundred company one day."

Wherever assets are undervalued and a transfusion of management talent is needed, Patels are poised to succeed. A pharmacist named Dilip Barot owned and managed half a dozen Florida motels before turning to subsidized public housing. Today, he manages two thousand low-income apartments in Las Vegas, Kansas City, Miami, and Norfolk, Virginia. Far from a slumlord, Barot does for run-down projects what he did for run-down motels: upgrade asset value and improve occupancy—in effect, trading out of gangs and drug abusers and into stable, working-class families. By running public spaces like private businesses, Dilip Barot has saved taxpayers millions of dollars and set a new standard for government lease programs. His first rehab, the Bahama Village project in Key West, Florida, was bought with money raised through the same Gujarati network that financed the purchase of his first motel. Could he have done it without a motel background? Probably not.

Another former motelier, Pradeep Patnaik, has taken his skills abroad. In 1989, he was part of a delegation of small businessmen who visited the Soviet Union. The next year, with perestroika in full swing, he was invited back to open and manage a $30 million tourist hotel in the city of Vladimir, about a hundred twenty miles northeast of Moscow. Hotel construction led to another venture, rehabilitating a state-owned poultry farm. Both of these ventures meant jobs, and wealth, for Americans, because they promote America's most exportable resource, innovative business techniques.

Other moteliers are leading their American hospitality sponsors back to India, opening profitable chains that benefit American shareholders. Next step: commercial and home real estate. In 1995, Henry Silverman's Hospitality Franchise Systems bought Century 21 from Metropolitan Life, with the intention of growing a network of franchised real estate brokerages the way he grew motels. As with motels, brokerages are just starting to attract immigrant entrepreneurs—including dozens of Patels. As with motels, HSF is in the position to profit by capturing the moment when undervalued immigrant businesses enter the mainstream. Just as pools of Gujarati risk-takers bought motels, they will go right on buying, and rebuilding our neighborhoods and cities. When the Patels say "Together, the Future Is Ours," they're right.

CHAPTER SIX

Boubous over Broadway:
The New African Americans

Every immigrant is committing cultural suicide.
Mame Kane Niasse, Harlem Senegalese

★

For six hours each week a corner of upper Manhattan becomes the casbah. It happens during July and August, along that stretch of Riverside Drive where traffic widens to accommodate the massive mausoleum of President Ulysses S. Grant. In the shadow of stately old apartment buildings on the western edge of Columbia University, an open-air market full of black vendors and their customers hums with trade.

The casbah started spontaneously several years ago, drawn by the free Wednesday-night concert staged at Grant's Tomb by New York's Jazzmobile series, an open stage-on-a-trailer bringing black culture to poor black neighborhoods. Jazzmobile visits spots all over New York, but only here, just blocks from French Harlem, has such a tumult of buying and selling taken root. The vendors arrive in the midafternoon, sometimes trailing elaborate, motorized pavilions. Some bring steam tables, ovens, and other kitchen facilities. Others erect aluminum-frame tepees open on four sides under canvas tops. Some simply flip open portable card tables or string a length of cord between two trees. There, beside dangling clothing, books, art prints, or T-shirts, they hawk their wares alfresco.

Soul food rules from paper plates: fried fish with yams, roasted corn, sticky honey cakes, and pork barbecue. The throng is a mix of solid family, college, and "gangsta." Older couples bring lawn furniture to catch the Hudson River sunset. Columbia coeds, smart sisters with Southern accents and straightened hair, stare dumbfounded at one sideshow: the two young men bearing twin albino pythons upon thickly muscled shoulders, flirting. Bootleg video tapes are sold everywhere, copies of films still running in Manhattan theaters. Elsewhere, homemade audio cassettes, also bootlegged, are on sale. Knowing fans can hunt for "master mixes" of legendary underground disc jockeys, stolen moments from the coolest party, the funkiest club. Some of the vendors have full sound systems, the better to advertise their musical menus. As the crowd builds into the evening, a din rises as volleys of recorded rap and soul and jazz riffs hover over the buzzing mob, sometimes drowning out the live sounds that drew them to begin with.

Grant's Tomb on Wednesday is a black thing. The food is Southern, Caribbean, or African. The music is soulful. Bow-tied vendors in sharp suits hawk *The Final Call*, published by Louis Farrakhan's Nation of Islam. Pamphleteers pass out self-published tracts denouncing the Jews, who, they claim, exploit Harlem. With a nod toward updating a neighborhood's traditional paranoia, they denounce the Korean, Yemeni, and Pakistani businesses lately thriving in their midst. Other pamphleteers are peddling some underground party going down either later that night or that coming weekend. Somewhere in Harlem or Brooklyn or the Bronx, an apartment will become a ghetto juke joint where the coolest fellows pay a twelve-dollar admission fee, but the hottest ladies get in free. Passes distributed in the crowd say where and when, but not for whom. Anyone, even Jews, can buy *The Final Call*, but party time is a black thing.

On the thickest nights the crowd is impenetrable and seems to surge on its own tidal rhythm. Steam rises from hot dinners mixing with the vapor from hotter bodies. Marijuana smoke marries menthol from a thousand lit cigarettes disappearing into leaves overhead. On Wednesday nights during summer, a cool breeze of smiles eases a city's tension.

Except when violence threatens. Like now, against a skinny

vendor of African-style clothes. Backed up against the table in his portable shelter, the skinny vendor is trying to look cool, suppressing a swallow of fear and blinking behind rimless eyeglasses as a bigger man with wild dreadlocks cocks an angry fist just inches from his face. This was a fight you could see coming a block away as Clifford, the man with the dreadlocks, strode quickly across Riverside Drive, a look of menace on his face. "You still don't got my stuff?" he barks, pushing the skinny vendor halfway into a rack of brightly patterned vests and billowy African pantaloons. "You take my money and don't have my stuff?"

"Clifford, I was traveling . . . ," the vendor begins evenly, controlling his fear. "I . . ."

"I don't care where you been," growls the bigger man, now coiled like a snake about to strike. "You told me last week you would have my stuff. And you're nowhere around."

The skinny vendor repeats his excuse, stiffening now that he sees the woman, Clifford's date, shuffling nervously at the edge of the crowd. Clifford's display may have more posture than purpose, he calculates. "I said I was traveling," the smaller man repeats. "You'll have your clothes next week."

"I'd better." Clifford glowers, straightening his back, then pressing his face into his quarry's one last time. "And you'd better know what trouble is. Because I guarantee that you're gonna meet it. You hear me? You're gonna meet it!"

And he's gone. Seizing a chance for a peace overture, the vendor dashes out behind him, tapping Clifford's shoulder and offering the beginning of one last assurance. Clifford wheels, but the anger is gone. Still, with his girl watching, he can't resist repeating his threat. "You better know trouble, my man, because you're gonna meet it!"

Once Clifford has disappeared into the throng, Aziz Diouf, his intended victim, flashes a knowing grin. "I know his brother," he begins by way of explanation, straightening his own back and declaring to anyone still watching, "I've got his money, and I've got his clothes. He's gonna hit me? What's he going to hit me for? If he wants his money, I'll give him back the money. Then he won't get his clothes."

The Senegalese word is *baol-baol*, marketplace, the place where Aziz Diouf learned his first lessons in customer satisfaction. Like roughly half the vendors who flock to Grant's Tomb on Wednesday, Aziz Diouf is an immigrant, part of a growing colony of peddlers entering the United States to exploit a most unique business opportunity. Aziz sells African clothing that he makes himself. He is also selling Aziz—his authenticity, his old-country realness. His OBT—original black thing. It is one of the most peculiar developments in immigrant America, as strange, in its way, as the Indian nuclear engineers who choose to run roadside motels. African youth—often privileged and protected at home—choose commerce in America's most impoverished black neighborhoods. Although the phenomenon has spread throughout black French Africa, the Senegalese dominate. Not all of the twenty thousand or so Senegalese living in New York are peddlers like Aziz. But almost all of them came here through peddling, either bartering African souvenirs for start-up cash, or exploiting the progress of relatives who did. For reasons having to do with American history, African colonization, geography, and religious faith, a community of Senegalese *baol* is slowly conquering black America, doing to places like Harlem and the South Bronx what their fathers did to Dakar a generation ago.

The Baol is also a region within Senegal, the dry "peanut basin" east of Dakar, where by tradition the country's premier barterers are born. Over time, *baol* (rhymes with "howl") has become the name for anyone, from any part of Senegal, with a head for street business. Aziz Diouf comes from Dakar. His father prospered in Dakar's premier *baol-baol*, the Sandaga, as did his brothers and all his cousins. While Aziz sounds vague about his family background—"we do business," is all he'll say—he isn't being evasive. "Doing business," to a Senegalese, means selling. It means bartering or transporting or searching for goods and the consumers to sell to. No government job, no driving a truck for an oil company, no milling peanuts, catching fish, or planting millet. "Business" can be street vending, owning a restaurant, owning a snack stand, or owning just a bucket of *bissap*, the sticky purple punch Senegalese brew from sorrel buds. It's being a middleman, a wholesaler, a money lender, a money changer. *Baol-baol*, in other words, means making it your own way, being responsible for your own livelihood and that of any extended family you are prosperous enough to extend.

In New York it amounts to selling trinkets to the natives, the culture-starved diaspora *baol* expatriates discovered about ten years ago. From June through October there is no shortage of black-oriented festivals to vend at; for regulars like Aziz Diouf, Grant's Tomb is just one of several stops during busy summer weeks. Aziz pays thirty dollars a week for his piece of Riverside Park. On good nights he can clear two hundred dollars from his designer pants and vests. It's a particularly advantageous spot since it saves him the cost of travel and lodging outside New York. It also gives him the chance to develop a regular clientele—not street toughs like Clifford, but any of the young Buppies, or black urban professionals, trolling the crowd for bargains. Senegalese have made killings meeting just that right buyer from Macy's, or the Home Shopping Network, or that upscale sister from Richmond who runs an African crafts boutique back home. At Grant's Tomb, at a black "Greeks" fraternity conference, at the Million Man March, the culture-starved buy Africa.

Aziz pays nothing for the spot in Harlem where he met Clifford. Harlem is the *baol-baol* for a growing number of Africans and their imitators among the Jamaicans, Haitians, and American-born. Aziz works a spot on 125th Street and Adam Clayton Powell Boulevard, joining the vendors who have become fixtures of Harlem commerce. Some market ethnicity with authentic Senegalese *boubou* dresses, some ride pan-African chauvinism with ersatz kentecloth headbands, caps, or umbrellas made in Korea. Some sell angry-slogan T-shirts stitched in Guangdong.

Aziz sells African textiles shipped from the Sandaga. He fash-

ions them into designer streetwear—Super Fly meets the Sahara.
He sells baseball caps made of "mud cloth," a fuzzy fabric that
comes from Mali in earth-tone browns and blacks stitched with
cuneiform triangles. Matching vests and balloon trousers complete
the look.

Thirty years old, Aziz seems much younger. His skin, the color
of caramel, suggests Arab blood. But his features are all African.
The men and women who enter his stall are effortlessly charmed
by his smile and his eyes, softened by the tinted eyeglasses and
baseball cap, a fuzzy, oversized dome of fudge-colored mud cloth.
The vest and trousers seem to accentuate, not obscure, his scrawn-
iness. Aziz is over six feet tall, yet weighs under 150 pounds, a
desert bird with sleek legs and a strong hunter's jaw. Long-limbed
and supple, he can fold himself at improbable angles to reach under a table for a piece of cloth, or into one of his blue plastic boxes
where his carvings and sandals are stored. He has all the essential
souvenirs: a simple African harp called a *kora*, primitive xylophones
called *balafons*, trinkets every *baol-baol* has.

But, wait, Aziz wants to show you something only he has. "Just
a moment, I have just the thing," he says with a flashing smile, not
in the bored, mechanical way of this world, but in gentle tones that
sound like genuine concern. Unfailingly polite, nothing is ever
forced on a customer. It is the way of the Sandaga, where vendors
so utterly outnumber consumers that a sales pitch is reduced to
Zenlike telepathy. God wants to you to buy from me, so there is
no point in me having to convince you. It is the same way Aziz
answers questions about his cloth, his designs, his origins in clipped
sentences that bespeak confidence: I know this is the best possible
price you will find in this *baol*, my brother. I know and God
knows, and if you walk away today, my brother, both of us know
you will come back to buy. *Insha'allah.* God willing. Such calm
assurance works hypnotic magic, and dollars fly from a buyer's
pocket into his.

Amid the Muslim pamphleteers, perfume vendors, and incense
burners, Clifford spotted the skinny African with his tableful of

shirts, vests, and trousers. He peeled off three hundred dollars in twenties and tens, accepting Aziz's promise to deliver a complete three-piece suit (trousers, vest, and cap) in two weeks, deliverable at this same spot. "Thank you, my brother," Aziz said as the wad of cash disappeared into his own wide pockets, not a trace of satisfaction on his lips. It was God's will.

And it is an act, this Sandaga shtick. Aziz carries a beeper and business cards and a slip of plastic that gives him 24-hour access to cash at more than a hundred New York locations. The business card shows a simple silhouette of Africa inside a triangle and the words "Aziz Fashions." The beeper is for another line of work, translating from either French or Wolof, in courtrooms where fellow immigrants need a hand. Aziz charges a hundred dollars per assignment, almost always at traffic court, where he assists Africans fighting a parking or speeding ticket. Some are peddlers, others gypsy cab drivers, of which there are at least a thousand in New York. Aziz caters to the browser at his table as some kind of link to West Africa. To the newcomers from Guinea, Mali, Niger, Togo, and the Ivory Coast, he is a link to America.

Aziz Diouf, like many *baol,* arrived overqualified for life in New York. Fluent in four languages—two of which, Spanish and English, make him conversant with virtually the entire local populace—and with a degree in accounting, Aziz hit the sidewalks running. Like most newcomers, he brought a load of souvenirs to sell, either on his own on the streets of Harlem, or to other *baol* hungry for new product. An aggressive salesman willing to work long hours in any neighborhood. Aziz soon discovered the clique of successful *baol* in the lofts above Broadway's concrete Sandaga, the Korean Gift District. Through them, he tried his hand at selling everything from T-shirts to umbrellas. By the time Aziz had been in New York twelve months, he was working almost around the clock—making his clothes at home, sometimes contracting work out to other immigrant tailors, on beeper call at all times. By the time he set up his first stall at Grant's Tomb, he had been in New York four years, just about ready for take-off. "It looks easy," he says, relaxing again after Clifford's disappearance. "But, believe me, it was no piece of cake."

Largely invisible to black and white Americans alike, the Africans who have arrived in America over the past two decades represent the first mass migration of Africans to this continent in more than two centuries. In sheer numbers, more Africans are landing annually at the end of the twentieth century than at any time during the height of the slave trade.

They come from two sources, English-speaking Africa—mainly Liberia, Ghana, and Nigeria—and French West Africa. The English-speakers compose the vast majority, at least a quarter million Nigerians alone. They have established defineable immigrant enclaves at least a decade old. The Ghanaians of East Orange, New Jersey, a suburb of Peter Rodino's old Newark district, number some three thousand. A tiny enclave of Liberians, mostly refugees from a bloody civil war, emerged in New York's Staten Island in the early 1990s. Georgia Avenue, in Washington, D.C., another enclave, hosts dozens of Nigerian businesses extending from the campus of Howard University north into the suburbs of Silver Spring and Takoma Park. That community, one of the biggest African enclaves anywhere in the United States, is dwarfed by Houston's Nigerian 'hood, perhaps one hundred thousand immigrants spread over several west-side wards. Like the West Indians, English-speaking Africans flock to the service industries. Ghanaians are big in taxi driving, Nigerians in health care. More than fifty Nigerians work at just one New York hospital—Manhattan Psychiatric on Ward's Island in the East River—almost all of them Ibo tribesmen from the same village in eastern Nigeria.

In that way, the passage of the English-African immigrant mirrors the tale of other groups—chain migration, built by family members carving out niches in specific industries. That is not true for the French-speakers, who number fewer than a hundred thousand. They arrived with an industry intact—peddling—landing as colonists intent on establishing a piece of Africa in the heart of darkest America.

Among all immigrants today, the French Africans' struggle may be the most inspiring. They have defied distance and poverty, as well as a formidable language barrier, to establish themselves in U.S. cities. The progress of the Nigerians and Ghanaians over three decades, to French-speakers like the Senegalese, is almost irrelevant. The Africans who preceded the Senegalese do not represent what sociologists think of as "authentic" immigration. English-speaking elites, many came as university students, remaining to pursue opportunities more lucrative than all but a handful could have enjoyed at home. More than immigrants, they are part of the "brain drain" phenomenon—educated cosmopolitans, often political dissidents, abandoning their own countries.

The Senegalese are also well-educated, certainly compared to their parents. Like Aziz Diouf, they tend to be young and multilingual. Yet, unlike the Nigerians or the Ghanaians, few come as students. And unlike their West Indian or Latino counterparts, they tend not to compete with native-born Americans in local job markets, but to be self-employed.

Also, unlike many of their Caribbean and Latino counterparts, they tend to arrive through legal channels. Coming by air from Europe or Dakar, the Africans almost never enter the country secretly. Some have remained years after their original visas expired, yet very few of them actually are here "illegally." Almost all have exploited international *baol-baol* to finance transatlantic trips, constantly updating their visas. Even with the overstayers, many manage to secure temporary authorization to reside in the United States—as students, Muslim clerics, even as agricultural workers. As with other immigrants, Senegalese have not been shy about acquiring work authorization documents through fraud.

In the wide range of immigrant figures, the Senegalese emerges as special: the Great Deregulator. Entering legally, working furtively, leaving harmlessly, the *baol* challenges every assumption about "controlling" our borders or "stealing jobs." No group is more attentive to the international rules of cross-border transit.

None is more indifferent to the local job market. "A human being does not live in one place, and one place is not for just one kind of human being," explains El Hadj Mouhamadou Lamine Mbacke Falilou, a Senegalese cleric with a huge immigrant following. "In America you had the Indians first. Then the Europeans, then the black slaves. Now it is my people's turn."

Like the Lebanese, Irish, or Cantonese, Senegalese consider themselves to be cosmopolitan. They have a long tradition of employment abroad—collecting Paris's garbage, or riveting panels at the Renault plant in Tours, harvesting oranges in Spain and Sicily. In the 1970s, when OPEC nations set the international price for crude oil, and coffers of member nations were filled, Senegalese flocked to Gabon, then boasting one of the world's highest per-capita incomes. There, assorted Diops, Niangs, Gueyes, and Mbayes worked as schoolteachers, postal workers, engineers, and servants. During the heady days of the Ivory Coast's dictator-for-life, Félix Houphouët-Boigny, when a massive foreign debt financed a lifestyle lavish by any African's standards, Senegalese *baol* flocked to Abidjan, paving the way for others. "A teacher could earn ten times in Côte d'Ivoire what he could make in Dakar," says Mame Kane Niasse, a New York Senegalese over a plate of *chebudiene* (or "*cheb*," the national dish—fish stew with rice) at Soumbedioune, a Harlem restaurant. Niasse spent his first three years out of teacher's college working in Abidjan, tutoring rich Ivoirians in Parisian-style French. Gesturing to a group ordering food at a nearby table, he adds, "They used to laugh at us 'poor Senegalese.' " Making eye contact with a bigger man, whose wide smile suddenly drops into a frown, Niasse continues, "I told my students, 'One day you will live like us.' I was right. That one over there was my student."

That same pattern—*baol* establishing a beachhead for other migrants—is unfolding in the United States. The first Senegalese who came to New York came from the Sandaga, arriving in the late 1970s. Unlike the permanent wave that would follow, these men were already world-class traders, moving merchandise *en gros*, wholesale. They came for a few days at a time, just long enough to unload a shipment. The first *baol-baol* brought gold from Guinea and diamonds from Sierra Leone, finding ready buyers for either in Manhattan's Jewish gem district along Forty-seventh Street. Other traders scoured the interior of the continent, going from village to village in Mali, Ghana, Benin, and Niger, looking for ebony carvings, original textiles, or ancient jewelry. For those who could evaluate truly important antiques, New York's art dealers, museums, and auction houses provided an eager clientele. The most enterprising *baol-baol* built on their successes, moving up to bigger shipments. Five or six or a dozen peddlers might join forces to send a container to New York by sea, each loading his wares carefully by hand, then flying ahead to meet the cargo docking in Brooklyn or Newark. A proficient *baol-baol* might make such a journey five times a year.

They returned to Africa with the made-in-America goods their customers craved. A new generation of Africans was growing up independent, free from French or British or Portuguese masters. African nationalism generated pride in African beauty, thus the sons and daughters of elites, whose parents looked to Europe for fashion, were starting to take their cues from America, that is, black America. Africa became enthralled with how the black Americans dressed, how their hair looked. James Brown, the African-American "Godfather of Soul," performed in Senegal in 1972, launching a craze for processed hair that, a quarter century later, has yet to abate.

So, on their return trips, the *baol-baol* carried hair, human or artificial, and the cosmetics to make authentic Africans look like authentic African Americans. More valuable than the diamonds and gold they brought out of Africa were the hair straighteners, wigs, and cosmetics the early traders brought home. By the late 1970s, the Sandaga knew New York as the place to go for wigs and hairpieces, mainly made in South Korea, available *en gros* along New York's Broadway, in the Gift District. Fluffy Afro wigs like the Jackson Five wore, or wavy "processed" hair like James Brown's, it was all there. An enterprising Korean even opened a store on

Thirtieth Street—the Sandaga, where Africans knew to go for the best price.

The *baol* still come, but by the mid-1980s what had been a closed cartel of Sandaga elite had been democratized. Any young Senegalese might cobble together enough to fly to New York and stroll enthralled along Broadway, his *boubou* billowing just as his heart swelled with certainty that here anyone can get rich. As the community grew, the cost of business dropped. There were more rooms to share on brief visits to Harlem, more containers going back and forth across the Atlantic. As Senegal's national airline, Air Afrique, added more flights, tickets were easier to get, they even got cheaper. Thus, since the mid-1980s, there has been a steady rise in nonimmigrant visas issued to Senegalese. From just over two thousand in 1984, the figure jumped to almost four thousand in 1986, and to over five thousand in 1987, below which it has not dipped. Since 1990, no fewer than thirty thousand Senegalese have been issued visas to enter as tourists, students, or self-employed businessmen, along with about two hundred others given immigrant visas, in most cases to join family members who were born in the United States, or who became naturalized citizens.

While technically law-abiding (at least in terms of visa law), the presence of the Senegalese on city streets is a naked retort to perhaps a dozen civil regulations. In New York, Washington, Atlanta, and many other cities, Senegalese are notorious for peddling without licenses, peddling counterfeit items, peddling stolen goods, and, of course, peddling without charging sales tax. They work door-to-door in dangerous housing projects, or work from a square of fabric on New York's Fifth Avenue, hawking fake Rolex watches or Hermès scarves, always ready to whip their wares into a bundle and scram the moment the antipeddling police arrive.

Coumba, all two hundred pounds of her, works a spot in Midtown. Coumba comes from Pikin, a Dakar suburb that has sent many *baol* to work the streets of New York. She sells handbags from a plastic bag, working with two partners, Cheikh and Omar, sellers, respectively, of watches and sunglasses. Coumba has been working since 1990, moving up from a shared room in *Le Cin-quante*—The Fifty—a cheap hotel many new arrivals come to on Fiftieth Street, to an apartment of her own in the South Bronx. With three kids and no husband, Coumba has a lot in common with other single moms in the ghetto. But, unlike those women, Coumba has her kids back home with grandma while she ekes out a living on the sidewalk. "Africa be very bad," she explains, using the same street English she began learning the day she arrived. A sigh rumbles two hundred pounds of girth, swaddled in layers of *boubou*, sweater, sweatshirt, and winter coat. "One person in twenty has a job, and the one takes care of all the others." When her husband left her, Coumba became that one.

Coumba's *puesto* is a blind spot on the east side of Lexington Avenue between Fifty-eighth and Fifty-ninth Streets. It's directly across from the cheery-bright leisure duds in the windows of The Gap, and a block from the main entrance of Bloomingdale's. Coumba, Cheikh ("shake"), and Omar lean against the inside wall of the closed Alexander's store, once a retailing giant, now abandoned. They press their backs flush against a plywood barrier, keeping their eyes straight ahead. Three pairs of feet tap a nervous beat on a carpet of crushed cigarettes, paper drinking-straw wrappers, napkins, and the other residue of pushcart cuisine ground into the sidewalk grime.

Coumba sells counterfeit handbags, twenty dollars apiece for copies of Yves St. Laurent and Givenchy. On this cold Thursday, a few days before Christmas, she is a target of the 19th Precinct's antipeddling squad, sweeping Lexington Avenue periodically all afternoon. Coumba is cautious, but nonchalant. She got out of the jug on Monday, and has already made eye contact with the officer, Patrolman Collins, who put her there. She kicks the black plastic bag concealing her wares, pushing it away into a corner of the dirty entrance, then stands with her shoes together to conceal the bounty. She's also watching Omar, who tends to be careless. Omar can't stand still, and his pacing makes Coumba nervous. Around and around he walks, stepping over a balled-up pink blanket on the ground. Inside is his stash of sunglasses.

Coumba's eyes are still darting between Omar and Officer Collins, when the policeman makes his move. Omar and Cheikh scatter. Coumba does a little dance, stepping away from her plastic bag then stepping back as Collins strides by. If she isn't within five feet of the handbags, she knows, she can't be charged with possession. And she knows Collins, without a backup, won't grab the contraband on his own. They will dance this way for the rest of the afternoon.

Cheikh returns first, trailing a white couple asking about watches. He opens his briefcase, revealing a row of fake Rolex and Pierre Cardin pieces, available anywhere in Chinatown for around seven dollars each. Cheikh sells four, and stuffs eighty dollars into his jeans. Omar reassembles his "stall," two folding chrome X-frames supporting a plastic tray, the kind bakeries use to deliver loaves to supermarkets. From under his flannel jacket comes the balled-up pink blanket, out of which Omar draws two dozen plastic sunglasses to arrange in rows on the bread tray. Sunglasses in December? An impulse buy, for the same consumer paying twenty dollars for an imitation Rolex with no working parts.

Besides Coumba, Omar, and Cheikh, an underground casbah has secreted itself along this stretch of Lexington Avenue. There are Senegalese in battered old vans, warehouses for contraband parked within a few feet of the peddlers. There is Mamadou, a species of pilot fish attaching itself to only marginally more respectable establishments, in this case the Pakistani newsstand on the corner at Fifty-ninth. Newsstand colonizers, numerous in Midtown, employ a cheap and facile way to avoid antipeddling sweeps. For a small monthly "rent," they avoid the potential expense of hundreds of dollars in summonses. Mamadou's partner, who won't give her name, mans another "warehouse" five feet away—a folding table littered with smudged greeting cards. Under the skirt of tablecloth are sacks of cheap polyethylene weave, mounted on luggage wheels. The greeting-card table is the mother ship, harboring the handbags, watches, sunglasses, and whatever else Coumba and her crew are selling this Christmas.

By rush hour, after a day of furtive glances, thrusts, and parries, the 19th Precinct will net exactly one pink blanket and twenty pairs of sunglasses. Collins will take Omar's goods, but not Omar. Nor will he write a single summons, nor remove a single *baol* from the streets, nor interrupt a single sale in progress. Omar will wander Lexington Avenue forlornly for perhaps an hour, until Ibrahima, a well-dressed black man stationed in one of the parked vans, leaves his *puesto* to replace Omar's lost goods, and slip the distraught peddler twenty dollars from his own pocket. Coumba will decamp to Fifth Avenue, Cheikh to Grand Central Terminal. Both will sell without distraction until midnight.

Versions of this Christmas tableau are being played out all over Manhattan, often in places the police don't even see. Like on Thirty-third Street, where Oseinu and Matar, two brothers Coumba knows from home, have a stall outside Kosta's Dry Cleaning. Call Kosta's and if a Puerto Rican kid named Manny picks up the phone, ask for Oseinu. If, for some reason, Oseinu isn't open for business—peddling hats, scarves, and gloves from a folding card table—Manny will take a message. Kosta's is his warehouse, where he stashes his inventory when he's not on the sidewalk.

Or like Alfa, downtown on Fulton Street. Like Mamadou, Alfa has a protector, Mr. Kim, who rents Alfa a piece of his variety arcade for $1,200 a month. It's a good location: six feet on the sidewalk, plus the door, plus the awning overhang at the top of the subway entrance where the numbers 2, 3, 4, 5, A, C, J, and M trains meet. Squeezed in between the Pakistani who sells perfumes and the Pakistani who sells neckties, Alfa peddles video cassettes for ten dollars apiece. Bootlegs? Sure they're bootlegs! Who sells Tommy Lee Jones in *Cobb,* or Wesley Snipes in *Drop Zone,* or the *Swan Princess* for ten dollars, the very week these films open in theaters? Alfa even shows previews from a monitor hidden behind some rags. He does a brisk business selling to commuters who don't want to go out again after they get home. Or who don't want to worry about keeping a cassette past the expiration day at Block-buster. Videos, in other words, costing only slightly more than a ticket to the theater or a rental, without the hassle. At $1,200 a month, he needs to sell just four tapes a day to cover his rent.

Another four tapes gives him another $1,200 for personal expenses. Another four and he can afford to deploy a friend, Ousman from Guinea, who peddles tapes on the street, from a briefcase.

Since Alfa and Ousman only pay for what they sell, theirs is a business with almost no capitalization. It is labor intensive, but labor is something Alfa has plenty of.

The economics of peddling—four tapes a day to make $1,200 a month rent—are what feeds the growing wave of immigration. *Baol*, like Alfa, Coumba, and the brothers Matar and Oseinu, have low fixed costs and one valuable asset that makes selling irresistible. The asset is themselves, their willingness to stand and wait, endlessly, to make a sale. Even in winter months the street business thrives.

In summer it's a gold mine.

Three days after confronting Clifford, Aziz is traveling south on the New Jersey Turnpike. On a Saturday in late July, the temperature has already passed 90 degrees. Inside Aziz's van, it feels like 100. Yet the windows are rolled tight and the air conditioning is turned off. "It never works, and anyway I don't need it," Aziz says matter-of-factly. He bought the 1986 Plymouth Voyager from the phone company, a source preferred by gypsy Senegalese. Because of what they were used for—carrying thousands of dollars worth of electrical equipment and replacement parts through urban streets— they are perfect for peddling, equipped with steel grates and latches for heavy padlocks on each of five doors. Nothing fancy, totally functional, and permanently filthy. Aziz paid twelve hundred dollars for the van, splitting that with a neighbor who used it briefly to run a messenger service. Visitor passes with the name "Diene," Aziz's erstwhile partner, still line the sun visors and dashboard. Diene is gone, and Aziz has moved on to bigger game.

Even in this heat, neither Aziz nor Saliou Niang, Aziz's new partner, are sweating. Aziz folds over himself, knees almost touching his armpits in the cramped passenger seat. Saliou—"Sal" as he likes to be called—stares straight ahead from behind the wheel.

The older of the two, Sal is a thoughtful veteran of New York life, having entered the United States in 1987 on a tourist visa. Now aged thirty-four, this son of a Senegalese truck driver is new to *baol-baol,* but learning quickly. Short and stocky, he has a square face and jaw, and skin the shade of black coffee; his closely cropped sponge of hair is even blacker. A black scar creases his chin, and he has worry lines appropriate for a man who seems deep in thought even when flashing his full, honest smile. An oversized printed T-shirt sails past his waist, ending almost at midthigh of his blue jeans. Both shirt and pants are spotless, as cool and dry as Sal's lips, palms, and brow.

Sal is an economics major in his fifth year at the Borough of Manhattan Community College on Chambers Street, where part of his expenses are defrayed by tutoring other African students. He is in the *baol-baol* for the money only, hoping to make enough cash during the summer to pay for fall's tuition. Like Aziz, he caters to a hybrid market, authentic African cloth fashioned to a casual urban style. His main item is a T-shirt and baseball-cap ensemble, with matching shorts. Sal buys a twelve-yard bolt of printed Ghanaian cotton for about fifty dollars. He pays forty dollars per dozen for plain white T-shirts, which he dyes off-white, beige, or tan. By stitching a six-by-ten-inch block of African fabric on the dyed T-shirt, he has a third of an ensemble—shirt, cap, and bermuda-length shorts—he sells for forty dollars. An initial outlay for materials of around $250 nets Sal just over sixty sets, valued at some $3,600, against which he must expense the cost of his rent and electricity, food, and any money he spends on the road.

At 10 A.M., both men already have been awake for six hours, Saliou preparing the bales of cotton T-shirts and matching shorts and caps loaded into Aziz's van, Aziz occupied with about a dozen van-related tasks: oil change, replacing tires, fill-up with premium unleaded. Although the van's sea-green and gray paint will still look scuffed and cracked, Aziz pops for the $7.95 car wash at the Exxon station at the bottom of 149th Street. Easing his way through the rolling brush wheels and jets of hot wax, he brakes to a slippery stop as a crew of men in blue jumpsuits—Africans all, either Gambians or Ivoirians—attack with black rags. Last week, while on their way to Detroit for the Afro-American Music Festival, Aziz and Sal spun out on bald tires. So Aziz has his brakes checked before speeding up onto the expressway and out of town.

The New Jersey Turnpike is a smooth and manicured highway with twenty-two exits, all well marked. Sal can take Exit 8 to Trenton, then cross the Delaware River north of Philadelphia and drive south, or else stay on the highway to Cherry Hill, Exit 4, and enter Philly over the Walt Whitman Bridge. Their ultimate destination is Penn's Landing, about a mile north on the expressway. Two choices complicate matters. Aziz squints with anxiety as he studies a road atlas in his lap. On their way to Detroit, Sal and Aziz took the New York State Thruway straight north, driving halfway to Canada before realizing they had made a mistake. They ended up riding to Buffalo, then southwest to Erie, Pennsylvania, picking up Interstate Highway 80, the same road they should have taken due west from Harlem, in Ohio.

Detroit's annual Afro-American Music Festival is but one of perhaps two hundred summer events the Senegalese flock to when plying their wares in the hinterland. New York may be a Senegalese gateway city, but the provinces, especially the black inner city, is where the gateway opens onto real profits. Harlem's 125th Street, even with its "regular customers," is the minor leagues compared to Detroit, Atlanta, Chicago, Baltimore, and Saint Louis, all cities within a day's drive from Harlem, all with big African-American ghettos where a real African is still something of a rarity. There, the hunger for authentic African products runs deep. Veteran *baol-baol* have been mining provincial ghettos for a decade. For Aziz and Sal, it is the beginning of a new opportunity, and they are still learning.

Besides the road atlas, Aziz consults a book called *Bandele's Annual Small Business Guide to African-American and Multicultural Events: Conferences, Festivals, Shows.* The book appeared for the first time in 1994, and immediately became a *baol-baol* bestseller. For twenty dollars, plus three dollars shipping and handling, subscribers receive over a hundred pages of listings, as well as the names, phone numbers, and contact names for about a thousand individual African-American organizations—everything from the National Conference of Black Political Scientists to the Sickle Cell Anemia Foundation of Greater New York. *Bandele's* lists of festivals includes Memphis's Africa Cultural Awareness Fest, which opens the *baol* road circuit every year in April, followed by Atlanta's Peach Caribbean Carnival, held in May. Washington, Chicago, and Miami each hold a Malcolm X Day. Chattanooga, Tennessee, sponsors the Bessie Smith Strut. Haile Selassie's annual birthday parade is in Chicago, while some festivals have a circuit, hitting several cities through the summer. The Bill Pickett Invitational Rodeo, named for a popular African-American wrangler, is one, staging shows in Kansas City, Oakland, Denver, and Austin. "Juneteenth" festivals are held in Tulsa, Cincinnati, and Fort Smith, Arkansas. Kwanzaa, an increasingly popular Christmas substitute among middle-class blacks, is marketed through Kwanzaa Holiday Expos held over three weekends in Philadelphia, Saint Louis, and New York. All these events permit street vendors, sometimes for fees so low an enterprising *baol-baol* can cover his costs of travel in just a few hours of heavy selling.

To be worthwhile—that is, to offer bigger sales than the two hundred dollars or so either peddler routinely makes on a Saturday on 125th Street—a festival also has to be in a city accessible by van, and it can't be too expensive. The River Blues Festival at Penn's Landing would seem to fit the bill perfectly: thirty thousand people for two days of free music, as with Grant's Tomb, always good for luring a free-spending crowd.

Still, there is the dilemma of which exit to take off the turnpike. "I have the 1994 book in my home," Sal says, somewhat defensively. "I could have brought it." Aziz pores over the 1992 edition of the Rand McNally road atlas, regretting that he does not have Sal's newer version. For something as basic as the New Jersey Turnpike, a six-lane expressway traveled by several million Americans each day, it is unlikely that very much will have changed in just two years. But how can Sal or Aziz know this? Sal's jaw hardens as he speeds up to pass a car full of teenagers entering at Exit 11. Aziz stares harder at the pages spread before him, trying to visualize the fastest and safest route to Penn's Landing, a place he has never seen, and cannot begin to imagine. Crossing at Trenton seems ill-advised, Aziz decides. Interstate 95 narrows to a single line on the Pennsylvania side of the Delaware River, then seems to disappear entirely somewhere in northeast Philadelphia. Taking the Turnpike south to Cherry Hill permits an easier arrival. Besides the small Philadelphia map in Aziz's atlas, there is an even smaller insert of the downtown area, including, in tiny red letters, the words "Penn's Landing" at what looks like just a few blocks north of the Walt Whitman Bridge. "Exit 4, Cherry Hill," Aziz says solemnly, glancing down at the map one more time and tracing the chosen route with his index finger.

However reassured he is by the thick blue line of turnpike, Aziz is baffled by the mysterious interstate numerology. The "95" continues until Trenton, then disappears inside Philadelphia, then reappears on the other side of Philadelphia, near a city called Chester. Meanwhile, the New Jersey Turnpike becomes Interstate 295, another north-south expressway, running parallel to the Turnpike. "Two ninety-five. Ninety-five, which is the Turnpike?" Aziz wonders aloud, staring once more at the pages spread upon his lap. "Which way do we go?" Panic rises in his throat, but it's all explained as soon as the van exits the Turnpike and slides onto New Jersey state road 689, the connector to the bridge into Philadelphia. Passing over I-295, Aziz sees it is exactly what the atlas shows it to be: an expressway running parallel to a stretch of the New Jersey Turnpike, essentially an identical road on which you could cover the same mileage, except at no cost.

Aziz tenses in anticipation of the drive through Cherry Hill, wondering if it really is a hill with cherries, or cherry farms, where he might yet lose his way to Philadelphia. Abandoning the comfort of six turnpike lanes for suburban sprawl, scrawny 689 is the quintessential suburban "Miracle Mile," with its cheap motels and package stores and dry cleaners. But living in urban America, the *baol-baol* partners know nothing of the suburbs. Aziz swallows hard, unable to shake his fear that, like last week on the trip to Detroit, he has just made a terrible mistake.

Sal, the driver, is the quicker to grasp the concept of the two highways. Two ninety-five, he decides, is the older road, perhaps replaced by the new one, the one where drivers must pay almost five dollars to ride from New York to Philadelphia. Another mystery of the road revealed, sort of. You can take the free road, he explains to Aziz, but you have to know it is there. No one is going to tell you. "I like that," he says breaking into his wide smile. "It's like doing business in America. You don't have to lie, you just don't tell everything."

Saliou and Aziz are doing business in America. They are part of a vanguard of entrepreneurs rising from what will likely be the last source of new Americans—black Africa. That Africa is one of the nation's oldest sources of citizens is, of course, ironic. By the mid-1990s, at least ten thousand Senegalese had permanently settled in New York's black ghettos, with perhaps ten thousand more migrants arriving from Mali, Guinea, Niger, and Côte d'Ivoire. They brought with them all the signs of a permanent immigrant enclave: the typical restaurants, the storefronts for making remittance payments, the little telephone "bundler" shops that charge less than a dollar a minute to reach Dakar, Conakry, Bamako, or Abidjan.

Hair and hair straightener might have brought the first *baol* to Harlem, but there were other factors at work as well. After decades of looking to France for social mobility, the flow of migrants north began to break down in the 1980s. Antiforeigner pressure, including the rise of militant racism, was one reason. Another was that Europe, no longer a creator of jobs, simply was unable to absorb Africans the way it could in the 1960s and 1970s. Africans, too, had changed. The generation of those born in the years just before and just after independence no longer had the urge to be French.

Sal and Aziz come from this generation. Like most West African emigrants, the dominant images of their childhood were of

American heroes, usually sports heroes, always black. When asked who was the first American they were aware of, and knew by name, each answers at once: Muhammad Ali. When asked if they know his original name, they also answer without hesitation: Cassius Clay. When asked why his name changed, again the answer is automatic: he found Islam.

In the full tapestry of American images planted in the minds of Africans like Sal and Aziz, none dominates like this black hero. Muhammad Ali, one of us, a black man who became a practicing Muslim, taking the religion of Senegal. Ali, in effect, renounced America for Africa, something that would have been unheard of for the elite of Senegal's colonial period, something that every African, no matter how elite, could feel proud of. Cassius Clay was the heavyweight boxing champion of the world, the most celebrated athlete on the planet. Muhammad Ali, believer in Islam, lost his title, his fortune, his ability to "do business." Yet he was redeemed and would thrive anew. As a Muslim. The triumph of this one black celebrity told millions of Africans that America is a place where risks are rewarded. And where you, a black follower of Islam, can belong.

In the thirty seconds it takes to leave the New Jersey Turnpike and turn onto Highway 689, Aziz and Sal pass no fewer than four law-enforcement units—two New Jersey state troopers in squad cars idling at the exit's brick station, the uniformed toll-taker and his supervisor, and two Cherry Hill cops cruising the Miracle Mile. In Paris, Sal says, police can stop any African any time and ask for papers. You're black African, they're white European, he says. You have to show you belong. "Here we belong," Aziz answers, nodding hard at the white policeman sitting alongside his van. "Our people built this country."

This is not just T-shirt wisdom learned at the festivals. Sal and Aziz arrived believing America is a black nation, a common perception among Africans. Even the Senegalese, who know that America has always had a white president, know the mayors of all the major cities are black, as are its sports heroes and entertainers. The fact that America is a white country and that blacks are neither powerful nor rich is a realization that comes hard. "America, I think, was also settled by Europeans," Aziz says, staring out at the Miracle Mile, sounding a little unsure that what he is saying, what he is seeing, is actually true.

What Aziz and Sal don't know about the New Jersey Turnpike is dwarfed by what they don't know about America. Needless to say, Aziz has not heard of either Ben Franklin or Walt Whitman, the Americans honored by the two bridges crossing into Philadelphia. Aziz guesses they are famous athletes, probably basketball players. Like most African immigrants, Aziz and Sal were stunned to discover just how poor inner-city blacks are. "I cried the first time I saw Harlem," a woman named Fatou says. Even professionals like Mame Niasse, who had earned a degree in France, were shocked by the depth of poverty and despair found in black ghettos.

Penn's Landing is shimmering with heat as Sal and Aziz arrive. A network of concrete ramps and steel walkways along the Delaware River, it is cut off from downtown Philadelphia by a four-lane expressway. By the water's edge, a stage has been erected under a black canopy, but none of the technicians checking lights and speakers seems to know where, or whether, vendors are allowed. In the early afternoon the only activity is garbage collection: speedy carts with flatbed backs, driven by red-faced civil servants dodging the handful of tourists, all white, strolling the riverfront. As Sal goes off in search of someone in authority, Aziz spots another Senegalese, a woman in a frilly red *boubou,* fanning herself at a picnic table. She waves, then grimaces. Same problem: no one knows where the vendors' tables are supposed to go.

By the time Sal returns, still without an answer, four more vans have arrived. Two are filled with Senegalese, the others with Malians. Altogether there are twenty men and women and their *baggage,* and no indication that this is a selling day.

It won't be. The River Blues Festival isn't allowing vendors this year, only the permanent food vendors, locals licensed for the season by the city. Everyone has a copy of the Bandele guide, where, on page 55, under space dimensions and booth fees, vendors are instructed only to "Call to Inquire." Neither Sal nor Aziz nor any of the other vendors have called. With so many Senegalese on the road during the summer, some festival organizers are cracking down on peddling. Or else they are bowing to pressure from local vendors, who want the movable caravans of Africans to stop coming, and outhustling them for their customers.

"I knew I should have gone to Milwaukee," says the driver of one of the New York vans, stuffing his hands into his pockets and sauntering off to stare at the river. He is Kone Cheikna, the leader of the Malians. Dressed in matching bronze-toned sharkskin shirt and trousers, Kone wears his hair very short, almost shaven. Beneath his flat nose, a pencil-thin moustache highlights a skin tone the color of *café au lait*. He stands just under six feet, but weighs over two hundred pounds, sturdy and soft at the same time. Smiling broadly, his eyes crinkling and lightening his round face to the color of honeyed tea, Kone comes from a mixed Arab-African lineage— what the Senegalese call *Narou Kayur,* or Moor—border people from villages near Mauritania. "I knew I should have gone to Milwaukee," he repeats, shrugging his disappointment to the river, turning his palms aloft and muttering. "Milwaukee is always good. Or at least we could have stayed in Brooklyn."

One by one, Sal, Aziz, and the rest of the peddlers drift into a circle around him. The Malians, some black and stocky, some tea-toned *mauritaines,* spread mud cloth on the concrete. Taking out boxes of Marlboros or super-long Benson and Hedges, everyone lights up, waiting for Kone to speak. "Or Milwaukee," he repeats. "We always make good money there."

According to the Bandele guide, the 21st Annual Inner City Arts Council Celebration of Community Arts Festival will only bring seven thousand to ten thousand patrons to Milwaukee. With those numbers, space fees are minimal, and latecomers are seldom turned away for not sending payment in advance. The reason to go to Milwaukee this week would be to get a head start on the next one: eighty thousand patrons expected for Milwaukee's annual African World Festival, the event every vendor in New York will be leaving for next Thursday. "I made three thousand dollars in one day in Milwaukee last year," Kone boasts. The younger vendors look at each other and nod. If they had left yesterday, as some had argued, they would be selling there now. Whatever they didn't sell this week would surely go next week, and if they needed more, the *baol-baol* in Chicago would have had plenty of goods, just a couple of hours away.

The Malians argue among themselves, Sal and Aziz stare at their Bandele guide, searching for a solution. Besides Milwaukee, the only other festivals this weekend are in Atlanta, Houston, Oakland, and Las Vegas. That someone like Kone has been misled by Bandele is reassuring, proving that anyone can make a mistake.

It's also catastrophic. Kone, whom Aziz calls "Babou" in an ostentatious show of respect, is something of a street legend in Harlem. He has been a *baol-baol* in America since 1978, when he arrived from Côte d'Ivoire. Like everyone, he sold first on the street, but never bothered with the low-margin tourist trade. He always sold authentic carvings and textiles, always directly to art dealers. He pumped gas at an Exxon station in Brooklyn, and worked at a car wash in Harlem. "But just for one day," he explains with his shrug and smile. "It wasn't for me."

As he worked, he saved. With his first thousand dollars, he bought a used postal van and drove to Los Angeles, taking two junior *baol* on as his apprentices, at a cost to them of five hundred dollars apiece. His vehicle now paid for and his own wares stuffed in back, he made it to California in four days. There he unloaded more than five thousand dollars' worth of carvings in just six hours. The apprentices did almost as well and, after settling with their "Babou" for the costs of the trip west, the three joined forces to buy wares for the trip home.

Kone got a tip on some blue jeans, slightly damaged seconds, available for twelve dollars a pair from a Chinese sweatshop in Long Beach. He makes an imaginary cut up the back of his thigh to explain the type of damage. "Great price, twelve dollars," Kone recalls wistfully. "You get originals, no mistakes, for twenty to twenty-five dollars. So, twelve dollars was a bargain in those days."

Pooling their cash, they bought three hundred pairs, all the Chinese had. Kone sold the car to his apprentices then flew, via

Paris, back to Abidjan. Blue jeans were prized in Côte d'Ivoire in 1979. Selling to wholesalers, Kone cleared eight dollars a pair pure profit, and discovered a lucrative new three-stop circuit. For the next three years his route was set: Dakar to New York with African art, New York to Los Angeles (or, occasionally, denim manufacturers in South Carolina or Georgia), then back to Africa, via Paris. Through the growing network of peddlers in Paris, Kone also learned what was selling in Europe: American suits and records, electronic gadgets. Whenever possible, he would stay in Paris long enough to sell there as well, always returning to Abidjan with profitable *baggage*. Sales begot sales, and soon it seemed every *baol-baol* in Abidjan was offering to front him cash to make sure his stall was on Kone's sales route the next time he came through with his jeans. Kone worked the route until the market for jeans got so big the top traders took notice, and began to import containers from abroad. "Then you couldn't do business anymore," Kone says and sighs. "So I decided to stay here."

Today he is partners with a Guinean in a Harlem store called Siguy Imports. He brought his wife and two daughters over from Mali in the late 1980s, and had a third child, a son, in America in 1992. His years of *baol-baol,* and his Harlem store, make Kone an elder statesman, but it's a mantle that lies uneasily on his pudgy frame. "Now they come, from my family and from all over Mali," he says, sounding a little exasperated. "They bring goods to my store. 'Sell for me, and pay me after,' they say. But so much! You can't sell so much in New York anymore! That's why we are on the road. They give me a hundred pairs of shoes, I agree to pay for eighty. The rest is mine. But, I have electricity to pay, rent, phone. I have to pay gas for the van. To buy the book [Bandele]. And sometimes you can't sell."

Some of the Malians want to go back. It is past noon, too late to get a good spot on 125th Street, but there is always a crowd in Brooklyn's Prospect Park on Saturday. On a hot day like today, they can be back by 3 P.M., and sell until midnight. Or, they can take their chances in Philadelphia. Kone has sold here before, on the campus of Temple University. Someone has heard of a party tonight, a reunion of Mande'ne Africans, from Sierra Leone, who have rented a hall in West Philadelphia. The suggestion is dismissed quickly: the Mande'ne, or Mandingo as they are known in Senegal and The Gambia, party late. No one will even arrive before midnight. Besides, why would a bunch of expatriate Africans want to buy mud cloth from them?

Kone settles the discussion—Brooklyn. He has charged eighty dollars each from the four junior *baol-baol* in his care. But he will probably offer a rebate, or at least a credit toward next week's trip to Milwaukee. He won't lose money today, but he won't make much of a dent in the pile of shoes, shirts, and *boubou* dresses he has carried down for his many "partners." Aziz and Sal bid farewell to "Babou," but decide to skip Brooklyn.

Sal wants to start early tomorrow, selling on 125th Street. Tonight he wants to join the Mourides celebrating *magal,* their annual pilgrimage to Senegal's sacred city of Touba. Aziz agrees. Better luck tomorrow. Today we learned, he says to Sal. They'll drive back on I-295 for as far as it takes them, saving a couple of dollars in tolls, and learning one more thing about doing business in America.

Senegal is, by African standards, a rich and prosperous country. In thirty years since independence, it has had just two presidents, both popularly elected and reelected. It has never suffered a military coup, it knows no religious strife. Deeply Muslim, it is also among the most tolerant of Islamic countries, so antifundamentalist, in fact, it sent troops to fight Saddam Hussein during the 1991 Gulf War.

And yet Senegal has become a major immigrant sender. Besides New York, dozens of cities have "a Senegalese peddler problem," among them Rome, Mecca, Johannesburg, and Bangkok. At least five hundred thousand Senegalese—one of every sixteen citizens—resides abroad, an immigration ratio as high as Mexico's. The reasons for their departure have been mounting for decades, spelled out in a cable prepared in 1993 for an incoming U.S. ambassador: "Young Senegalese, whether they be urban youth, working class university students, or rural-based adolescents, are increasingly disaffected. Third World nationalism, creeping desertification in the North, and continued decline in the economic sector have contributed to a youth movement which is increasingly frustrated and desperate. . . . A new class has emerged: the university graduate who can't find a job."

The combination of Europe's rejection and America's embrace made the Africans' passage to America inevitable. So does American history. Senegalese first came to America three centuries ago, from Gorée Island, a French concession off Cape Verde, where "captives" from the interior were sent to French possessions in the New World. The "captives" were largely Bambara people from Mali, seized by Wolof and Fulani knights, or Moroccan slavers. As slaves they traveled to Haiti, Guadeloupe, and Guiana. The majority were sold to Brazil, then a colony of Portugal, while others went to Louisiana, to be put to work clearing mangrove swamps and planting delta cane and rice fields. The first Senegalese left a rich legacy in Louisiana's Creole culture. In addition to words like "gumbo," and the "okra" used in its preparation, blacks arriving from Gorée are believed to have carried with them legends like the Tar Baby, tales that have endured as part of American folklore.

Gorée Island is the place all the black tourists from America come to see. It is Senegal's memorial to the African-American Holocaust, which is also the Senegalese *baol*'s first opportunity to exploit ethnic pride. American blacks were "co-ethnics" who came to Africa and were shocked to discover they were American. They hated the food and hated the heat and hated the smiling people who seemed only to want to hustle them for money. Yet, like Americans everywhere, they were faithful to the souvenir code. Senegalese first became aware of the black American market through tourism, and they also became aware of the Americans' apparently inexhaustible need to shell out dollars for trinkets any kid could buy for pennies in Dakar. Eventually the tourists fed a second diaspora, back across the Atlantic.

In its official propaganda, the Senegalese government presents itself as a world crossroads, a turning point midway between Europe, Africa, and the Americas. This is, historically speaking, accurate. Europe discovered America through Senegal. That is, it learned to exploit America's riches after learning to enslave Africans just off the Senegalese coast. The nearby Cape Verde archipelago, uninhabited when Portugal claimed it in the mid-1400s, was the first place where African slaves were used to cultivate sugar cane "offshore." From Cape Verde, the sugar industry jumped easily to Brazil, then to the Caribbean, Florida, and Louisiana. At each stage, sugar fed Europe's hunger for black souls.

While slavery was legal in the New World, West Africa held little appeal to the colonial powers. But the end of slavery brought the beginning of colonization. Britain established colonies in Sierra Leone and The Gambia, the former to repatriate Africans liberated by the British navy on the high seas; the latter as a listening post to "monitor" the slave trade in the interior. British moves inspired countermoves by the French. By the 1880s, when the last slave nation, Brazil, abolished human bondage, the race for West Africa was on.

Senegal's cosmopolitan capital, Dakar, lies detached from the continent on a *presque île* ("almost an island"), in the French term Africans still use for the finger of land extending from the coast. Under French rule, Dakar was almost France, sending representatives to parliament, and enjoying the many benefits of *liberté, egalité,* and *fraternité*. In metro Dakar, the people spoke French. Most of Senegal's eight million people, however, speak Wolof. Wolof speakers come from the Baol, the dry savannah that begins about a hundred miles east of the coast. France administered this part of its colony as something different from France, allowing a religious sect called the Mourides to rule in partnership with colonial administrators.

The Great Mosque of Touba, a city in the Baol east of Dakar, is ground zero for the Mouride Brotherhood. *"Touba"* means "sweetest" in Wolof, although it is also said to be derived from the Arabic word *"tawaba,"* which means "repentance." According to legend, the Wolof saint Ahamadou Bamba received a revelation there, "there" at that time being a single baobab tree surrounded by desert. With Bamba's blessing, an oasis grew. After Bamba died, Touba held his tomb and his mosque.

Today a city of two hundred thousand inhabitants, Touba lies on the edge of the great Sahelian desert, an area seared by the drought that plagued West Africa through the 1970s. Dozens of New York Senegalese—when asked what part of Senegal they came from—simply answer "Touba." Logic would presume that they are refugees from economic collapse and that Touba, like other "sender" villages, is a wasteland surviving on exported labor.

That presumption could not be more wrong. Touba is the richest city in Senegal, from wealth generated by trade and the alms of pilgrims. Touba confirms grace—Allah blesses those who praise Allah—in Africa's answer to Calvin. The immigrants mean they are "of Touba," that is, Mourides. Discipline and the Mourides' immense wealth make the brotherhood a state within a state —staffing ministries, running banks, and electing presidents. Rather than fleeing religious persecution, immigrants extend an empire, colonizing new lands as effectively as the Korean, Pakistani, and Chinese immigrants the Mourides do business with in America.

Mouridism began in 1886, with the battlefield death of Lat Dior, the last Wolof king. His court, an arcane hierarchy of nobles, knights, and slaves, was shattered by French rule. It reassembled in peacetime under Ahamadou Bamba, a charismatic Muslim cleric. In 1895, amid wild rumors of a desert uprising, the French decided to exile Ahamadou Bamba to its penal colony in Gabon. But instead of ending the resistance, France discovered it had created a martyr. Like that of Iran's exiled Ayatollah Khomeini, Bamba's cult grew. According to contemporary accounts, thousands of *baol-baol* marched with Bamba to the sea. A disciple, the dreadlocked bodyguard Ibra Fall, fell to his knees and screamed he would drink the entire ocean dry if that would halt the dreaded ship, symbol of the millions of martyrs sent away as slaves. "No one in the Baol had ever seen the ocean, it was a mystery," explains Ibrahima Thioub, a professor of history at Dakar's Cheikh Anta Diop University. "Thus, the one who had conquered the ocean was believed to have supreme power."

Thus, too, did exile create a legend filled with miraculous tales. Bamba was placed in a hot furnace, the bards (called *griot*) sang, or was left to die on an island inhabited only by snakes. He neither ate nor drank for an entire year, held in a cell reading the Koran. He is pictured in books and paintings swathed in his white robe, surrounded by human skulls in a den with lions who would not strike, part of the lore apparently lifted from the Old Testament. "The sailors would not let him pray," Abdou Xadir, another Bamba scholar, says. "He jumped onto the waves, and unrolled his rug. When he stood up, there was dirt on his forehead."

Bamba was returned to Senegal in 1905. He spent two more years in exile in the Mauritanian desert before being allowed to return to the Baol in 1907. The last twenty years of his life passed under house arrest in Djourbel, studying the Koran and composing a slim volume of poetry called the *Quasa'id*. When he died, the colonial government counted a hundred thousand disciples. They mourned peacefully, later petitioning authorities in Dakar for permission to build a mosque for their saint at his grave site. The site was Touba, just seven kilometers from Bamba's birthplace.

Bamba's legacy is mixed. He is revered as the patriot who resisted French hegemony. Yet after switching from exile to accommodation, France profited from the prophet. Thousands of francs were raised from the tax disciples paid to enter Djourbel; Bamba blessed hundreds of Wolof conscripts enlisting in France's World War I forces. In fact, by the time Bamba died, Mourides enjoyed a lucrative alliance with their masters. Touba, a holy city, was free from colonial taxes. As a duty-free entrepôt, the city quickly became a commercial hub and agricultural center.

Agriculture then, as now, meant peanuts, Senegal's chief source of foreign exchange. When peanut farming was extended into Senegal's interior, France relied on Mouride chiefs to sell the program. As a colony, the peanut industry was a profitable French monopoly. Today Senegal loses money on every peanut it sells, however, because the subsidy paid farmers (to keep farming and stay out of bursting cities like Dakar) exceeds what the harvest earns on the world market. Mouride peanut brokers compound the state's losses by using duty-free Touba as a launching pad to smuggle product to The Gambia, Mali, and Mauritania. Ultimately, peanuts impoverish the state but enrich the Mourides.

Ahamadou Bamba is credited with "Africanizing" Islam, that is, making the creed of the slaver acceptable to his quarry. In fact, Bamba's legacy was transforming clerics, or *marabouts*, into rulers. Mouridism, unique in Islam, binds disciples directly to a single *marabout*, even to the extent of disciples pledging their children's loyalty to children of their *marabout*. In other words, the traditional master-slave relationship. Most Wolof are Mourides and most Mourides are Wolof, thus Mouridism preserves an ancient caste system disguised as an Islamic sect.

If Bamba's tomb is considered the largest mosque in black Africa, Touba's annual *magal* pilgrimage—with over a million celebrants—is certainly, after Mecca's, Islam's biggest *haj*. During *magal*, street peddlers march through the casbah with arms full of perfumes and watches for sale. Many of these items are sold to pilgrims to give as gifts to the *marabout*. The *marabout*, in turn, distributes them to disciples, who sell them back to the peddlers. The watches and perfume are sold and resold, offered and reoffered to the *marabout*, then back to the pilgrim, over and over again in a great circle of Mouride devotion. In a way, Mourides spin that same circle as Senegal's economy: millions of hands moving a few scarce items, over and over again.

Like any underdeveloped economy, Senegal's exists in a precarious balance, actually an imbalance, of surplus manpower and scarce wealth. Thus, in Dakar's Sandaga, commerce is characterized not by consumers shopping for merchandise, but peddlers shopping for buyers. Every transaction sits on an immense pyramid of labor—literally dozens of salesmen deployed for every meager sale. Five or six men "sell" one radio in a casbah stall, but perhaps a dozen more chant the name of its merchant in the street. Similar redundancies flourish in procuring goods, moving goods, storing goods. It's sales ruled by the law of physics, not economics—the gravity of humanity, the inertia of a generation that can't find a job. And everything is dominated by the Mourides.

Beugue Bamba ("Love Your Bamba!"); *Wakeur Bamba* ("The Followers of Bamba"); *Serigne Cheikh Mbacke* ("Blessed Bamba"); *Cheikh Abdoulahi Mbacke* (roughly the same thing) are the names of every imaginable enterprise in the Sandaga. Fix your watch at Bijouterie Bamba, dupe a passport photo at Studio Alhamdoulahi ("Thanks to God"). Taxi dashboards bear Bamba's image; buses are marked with one word, "Touba," above the windshield, and the logo "Société Musulmane" (Muslim, Inc.) below.

The mosque-as-shopping-mall system works, essentially, because it is a slave system. Bosses pledge fealty to their *marabout*, employees are pledged to the same *marabout*. They "work" unstintingly for no defined wages but are fed and housed from their bosses' pockets. Profits are remitted to Touba—to build the glorious mosque but also to staff Koranic schools, buy seed and fertilizer for peanut farmers, and maintain an elaborate social services network. Dakar, in its way, was the first Wolof colony outside the Baol, a first step in the Mouride migration to New York.

Which is the other reason the system functions. Immigration is its built-in safety valve. Mourides seldom left the interior before 1965; within a generation they controlled all street commerce in Dakar. After Dakar was saturated, they moved to Europe. Then came the drought in the Sahel, devastating peanut farming. In the mid-1980s, with France tightening immigration from its former colonies, Mourides targeted New York. This new migration both enriches *marabouts* and liberates disciples, while reviving commerce in some of America's poorest communities. The same "Bamba" and "Wakeur" labels, imported from the Sandaga, are found on storefronts in Harlem and the South Bronx.

As part of this new migration, immigrants like Sal and Aziz struggle to reconcile ancient Africa with modern America. Confusions abound. Even immersed in African-American communities, they taste only one plate from the menu, the urban plate. Immersed in the stew of African America they taste its mixture, but can't always distinguish the different flavors. They see "Howard," "Morehead State," and "Grambling" not as schools, but as the decals on the back windshields of station wagons driven by middle-class buyers at Malcolm X or Juneteenth Day. They read posters declaiming "The Blacker the College, the Sweeter the Knowledge," sold alongside T-shirts with the legend "Danger: Educated Black Woman." Then they see suburban black teens, college kids, with their Alpha Phi Alpha scars—brands, really—burned onto chests and shoulders.

"No people have sacrificed more for America. You owe me," reads one T-shirt sold by the *baol*, who buy from the Asians in the Gift District. "Get out of here with your beggin' ass," reads another, in apparent contradiction. More confusion: fear and loathing of female liberation, alongside triumphant independence. In some ways, no African on earth is more enslaved than the Mouride, a slave to commerce. That Senegalese in the United States package the mythology of American slavery for profit—fifteen dollars a shirt, or two for twenty-five—at Afrocentric festivals is just one among layers of irony twisting the relationship between African *baol-baol* and American customer. Another is the way such selling makes blackness, for *baol* like Aziz and Sal, just one more vendor's trinket in a giant American Sandaga. Another is the way, by selling, they forge their own liberation from the *marabout*.

Twenty years after Senegalese began surfacing on Harlem streets, the Sandaga store on Thirtieth Street remains. Its Korean owners have decamped to, of all places, Senegal. Having made a small fortune selling strands of Asian hair to Africans, they were persuaded by the Senegalese government to relocate in an industrial park in the Dakar Free Zone. Their Sandaga is now a showroom only, where their samples, under warnings to *"Ne touchez-pas"* (don't handle the merchandise) still attract African buyers. Hair and cosmetics still finance rookie *baol* arriving from Dakar, but after two decades of contacts between Dakar and New York, trade has become more sophisticated. With more peddlers living here permanently, they no longer have to handle each aspect of cross-border trade themselves. Now, instead of importing his goods, selling them, then returning with U.S. products for resale in Senegal, a *baol* may specialize. He could peddle only—buying from any of the Gift District stores catering to Africans—or he could work in one of the cargo lofts, bundling goods for shipment home. Or he could run plates of hot *cheb*, couscous, and peanut-lamb stew from one of the new Senegalese bistros squirreled away on hot plates. He could work as a salesman for one of the Koreans.

With the growing business network, new avenues open for *baol-baol*, some even legal. Senegalese emerge as cab drivers, accountants, insurance salesmen. Since money and goods still go home to Senegal, there has developed specialization in dispersal. Now, the returning *baol-baol* might represent a dozen or more partners, and he wouldn't be returning with just a suitcase full of hair straightener or skin cream. By the mid-1990s, successful peddlers were shipping high-end products, usually electronic goods, usually from Japan and Korea. Facsimile machines, personal computers, and microwave ovens become the remittance tender. Bought for dollars, sold for francs, the *baol* profits not only from selling, but also from the currency conversion.

The most successful of the Senegalese anchored this permanent wave. Peddlers like Khadim Mbacke, another Mouride, became wholesalers with import-export companies of their own. Mbacke's "conglomerate"—one company is called Touba Trading Company, another Touba Airlines—is no more than a cluttered warehouse surrounding a cluttered desk, seven stories above Broadway. Touba is a museum of the new Senegal trade: hairpieces and full wigs strung along one wall, cosmetics in a dusty glass display case along another. Stacked in one corner, cartons of Panasonic color television sets, a hamper of unfinished blue jeans in another. Everywhere, Senegalese coming and going, making phone calls, leaving packages, signing documents. Mbacke makes most of his money as a facilitator, packaging the traders' goods going home to the Sandaga.

But as the ties between Touba and the United States grow, Senegalese on both sides of the ocean are changing. Aziz Diouf has not been home in four years, and he doesn't know when he'll go back, or if he ever will. Saliou, whose student visa allows him to work part-time, wants to marry a girl he knows in Dakar. In 1994, he applied for the special "diversity" visa lottery, but failed to win a slot. Winning would have meant a permanent green card, and a chance to become a citizen. Yet Saliou is ambivalent. "Every year you stay here it gets easier," he says. "But every year you lose more of yourself. In twenty years, you are all American, and not African anymore."

Senegalese have their own radio show on Sunday nights, and their own newspaper, *Xabaar,* written in French, Wolof, English, and Arabic. Its ads urge Senegalese parents to know their school districts and participate as "parent voters" in schoolboard elections, a right all immigrants have, even the undocumented. Another ad asks for a trilingual secretary—French, Wolof, English—for a business in the Bronx; an Air Afrique ad touts new Saturday service to Ghana, "home of colorful *kente* cloth." On the back page is an advertisement for the Senegal Housing Bank, and the promise *Avec nous vous financerez votre maison au Sénégal,* "With us you will finance your home in Senegal." But there is equal pressure to house Senegalese families in New York.

There is a Senegalese child born here every week, affirms Mame Kane Niasse, former head of the city's Senegalese Association of North America, now a kind of freelance *marabout* to expatriates. Little Senegal has moved uptown from the gift district, sprawling along 116th Street west from Masjid Malcolm Shabazz, Malcolm X's old mosque on the corner of Lenox Avenue. Just like Touba's Grand Mosque, it's the center of Senegalese life in Harlem, overlooking an open-air market across the street. Just like in Touba.

Mourides are also buying real estate, starting with an abandoned schoolhouse at 137th Street and Edgecomb, which they intend to reopen as a *masjid* and children's center. Across the country, in much smaller numbers, Senegalese colonies are also sinking roots. Besides New York, African stores named "Touba" can be found in Maryland, Atlanta, Los Angeles, Providence, Miami, and New Orleans, the city where the first Senegalese in North America were sent as slaves centuries ago.

Like all immigrants, Senegalese meet hostility from the very African Americans they came emulating. As they fill empty storefronts on 116th Street, then the empty apartments above them, older residents can't help feeling resentful, occasionally offering taunts neither Africans nor African Americans could imagine uttering a few years ago. "One guy told me, 'Your people are the ones who sold my people into slavery,' " a storekeeper named Selle Gueye says with a bemused smile. "What can he mean by that?"

Yet, like all immigrants, Senegalese find the freedom of American life irresistible. The freedom and the self-importance. Aziz, Mame, and Saliou are independent operators in New York, whether they are going to school, driving a taxi, or saving for their own business. At home they would be son, husband, cousin, in-law, and grandson. Whatever they had would be, by custom and by law, property of the clan. And so they would be condemned to serving others first. In time, any ambition they had for greater wealth or importance would be dissipated with the francs spread among an ever-growing circle of obligations. It's what Saliou says when he fears, after twenty years, he will no longer be African, or what Mame means when he sighs, "Every immigrant is committing cultural suicide."

With the Senegalese, it is a community committing suicide, if only to be born anew. In 1990, the Senegalese Association petitioned its embassy in Washington to bring a Senegalese bank to New York. The association had already proven its worth the year before, when it lured a consul to New York to service the thousands of expatriates who wanted Senegalese papers updated. The embassy obliged, but demanded a payoff—that the expatriates also would register as absentee voters for upcoming national elections, presumably to vote for the ruling party. In other words, constituent service, international style. Mame Niasse opened an office at the mosque, where three thousand Senegalese citizens were registered. "They saw how many we were," Mame says with a smile. From then on, the embassy is eager to lend a hand, he adds, "whenever they need us to vote again."

The bank opened in June 1993 in a suite of offices on the sixth floor of an office building at West Thirty-fourth Street and Seventh Avenue, just two blocks from the Gift District. Licensed to handle money transfers, the Banque de l'Habitat du Sénégal wired just under a million dollars home during the second half of 1993, a tiny fraction of the value of all the *baol-baol* wealth sent home in cash and merchandise. But in the first six months of 1994, the BHS branch remitted over $4 million, and by the end of the year, another $3 million. The bank also requested permission to offer its clients savings accounts, in dollars, paying regular interest. "A lot of our customers send money home for years, planning to build a house when they go back," explains Seydou Lo, the BHS manager in New York. "But sometimes when they go home the money has all been spent—on a new wife, maybe given to the *marabout*. In Senegal, what belongs to the son belongs to the father. No court in the country will rule that the son must be made whole."

So, the bank that began as a way for sons to send dollars home will soon keep their savings here, leveraged by small business loans and mortgages. "Our people know how to do business," says Ibrahima Diene, another bank official. "But they can't always raise capital. That's where we can help."

Along 116th Street in Harlem, the Grand Concourse in the South Bronx, Church Street in Brooklyn, slowly the storefronts are resuming their mission of commerce. Toubas are blooming from Harlem to Los Angeles. Every immigrant is committing cultural suicide, but from his demise a new African American will be born.

CHAPTER SEVEN

Typicalness: Massachusetts and Minas Gerais

God made the earth, and Man made the borders. To go anywhere in the world to better yourself is God's way. To not go
because of borders and law is Man's way. We follow God's way.

Father Roque Pattussi, Saint Tarcisius parish

★

In late October, months after the rains have stopped, the housing development called Bairro Vale Verde—"Green Valley"—
seems misnamed. Not greens, but washed-out yellows, pinks,
and gravelly browns abound—the colors of exposed soil, rich with
veins of clay and mica poking up where surface dirt has been
scraped away. Rust is prominent, too, orange-brown creeping up
like vines along pipes once bright silver, rickety scaffolding erected
alongside Green Valley's buildings. The houses are white-gray, the
color of unpainted cement. Dirty white litters the ground: crushed
Styrofoam and soiled toilet paper and other fluttering residue of
an end-of-the-day construction site. Which is what Green Valley is,
and has been for twenty years.

Up and down rolling hills on the edge of this Brazilian city of
Governador Valadares, along wide streets forming a tight grid, rise
dozens of new concrete buildings. Some are wide and long, palatial
even, of two and three stories with elaborate, pillared balconies,
massive gates, and carports for as many as half a dozen cars. Others
tower as high as ten stories. In some places, deep holes have been
carved, receptacles for new structures yet to be born. The finished

towers bear the names of their owners' far-off exile. No doubt alluring to the pedestrians and bicyclists who pass by, they seem rather bland to an American visitor. In fact the names seem boring: Edifício Newark, Edifício Marlborough, Edifício Framingham, as empty of romance as the buildings are empty of tenants.

Vale Verde is less than a neighborhood; rather, it is a community bank account whose depositors live offshore, in all those American towns whose names the buildings bear. Some homes have been unfinished for years, standing tall and lonely and waiting, not for residents, but for enough new cash to add another cubic yard of concrete, pay for interior fixtures, or install pipe and electrical wire. It has been this way in this corner of Brazil for almost a generation, as more and more men fly away to pursue their dreams. Vale Verde is a virtual ghost town, even less than abandoned.

In the study of immigration, Governador Valadares is a classic "sender" city. Like Naples in Pelegrino Rodino's time, like Tehuacán (Puebla) or Touba (Senegal) today, it functions as a kind of choke-point through which entire villages funnel their youth. Like Tehuacán and Touba, Governador Valadares is a proxy for one country's immigration. No Brazilian can hear its name and not think of *saudade,* that untranslatable word that represents a stew of Brazilian emotion—homesickness, yes, and longing, but also hope and freedom. *Saudade* means escape. Not the false escape offered to the poor who crowd into Rio's teeming *favelas,* or the false escape offered to the educated few, to join Latin America's biggest bureaucracy. But real escape, to where Brazilians break the strictures that suffocate individual ambition. *Saudade* to places where fortunes are being made, fortunes that build empty palaces in Vale Verde. Which in turn rise as monuments. To *saudade.*

After more than a generation of sending, Governador Valadares has become famous, a symbol for all Brazil of all Brazil did not become. Mention Governador Valadares anywhere, and see knowing smiles, hear gasps of hope. In 1993, Brazilians sat riveted to a popular soap opera, *Pátria Minha (My Country),* based on the adventures of returned *Valadarense* immigrants. Viewers everywhere saw the saga of Raul, Pedro, Flavia, and Ester—their enlightened countrymen battling the petty corruption and stifling disappointments—as a slice of life most Brazilians recognized as being exactly like their own. "There is a joke in Brazil," says José Carlos de Oliveira, a returned migrant. "When a plane flies north from Rio, the pilot passes over the town and says, 'We are flying above Governador Valadares—the southernmost part of the United States.' "

Valadares's chamber of commerce says "tourism" is the town's number one industry. Ibituruna, a large rock outcropping south of the town, is famous worldwide as the planet's premier launchpad for hang-gliding, occasionally hosting world-important gliding tournaments. But even Ibituruna does not attract many tourists. "Tourism" here is a one-way industry, sending Brazilians away to earn *dolares*. On the main street, John Kennedy Boulevard, money-changing shops outnumber all other businesses, most doubling as travel agencies and informal mail drops. At the Tele-Travel Store (rendered in English) the come-on is a poster-size photo of a stack of hundred-dollar bills. "My first million," it reads in Portuguese. On the first floor of the Plaza Center 700 shopping mall, three of the six shops are travel agencies, with names like Bras-USA, Cambitor (*câmbio* means "change," as in "change money"), and Giutur. A few shops advertise something new: a service to check if dollars are real. Valadares has become so thoroughly dollarized, counterfeit bills are everywhere. Imagine, in a country whose currency changes almost every year, Valadares has a stable currency, albeit one printed abroad. Across Brazil, people refer to the town by its new nickname, "Valadolares," Vala-dollars.

So many U.S.-based Brazilians look homeward to Governador Valadares, the local newspaper *Diário do Rio Doce* began a second paper in 1993, *States News*. Staffed by four reporters and two editors in Governador Valadares, *States News* may be unique in the global economy: an expatriate newspaper, written for and by immigrants, but published back home. Marli Gama, the business editor of *States News* in 1994, was, in 1980, Marli Gama of the Route 9 McDonald's in Framingham, Massachusetts. Like much of her staff, she came home to edit a paper—an unheard-of twist in the usual story of immigrant upward mobility.

More than forty thousand copies of *States News* are distributed weekly throughout eastern Minas, each issue full of news, not only of events abroad, but also of personal events. Messages like "Miguel, I just finished copying the video for Ana that you said she was asking me for. Cheers, Andre, Framingham." There are advertisements for homes and mall space in Brazil, and for Brazilian services in America. Dentists announce their services both in Minas clinics and American ones. An ad for a clothing store on Framingham's Concord Street faces an ad for Marcos Helenio, the Workers Party's candidate for Minas state deputy. On almost every page, there are offers of houses or condominiums in one of the new housing developments going up in Valadares or among the beach front resorts of Espírito Santo, newly flush with the cash immigrants send back to Brazil.

States News is more than anything a printed form of the traditional immigrant grapevine, a sophisticated effort to exploit the millions of "Vala-dolares" entering Minas every month. "The immigrant goes back and forth, or his family is here," Ms. Gama explains, "he wants to buy a house. So we run ads here."

The capital of Brazilian immigration is, officially, a city of 210,000. Governador Valadares sits in the heart of Brazil's great outback, in the northeast corner of Minas Gerais—the general mines—so named for its rich veins of iron ore, gold, and silver. Minas Gerais, its citizens boast, is the "real" Brazil, a vast territory of almost four hundred thousand square miles, with over 15 million citizens, one of every ten Brazilians.

Minas Gerais is Brazil's heartland, the country's third most populous state. *Mineiros,* the people of the state, think of themselves as the most typical of Brazilians, and most Brazilians agree. Traditional dishes like *frango com quiabo* (chicken stew with okra) or *galinha molho pardo* (black beans and rice, smothered in a chicken-blood sauce) are thought of as typical *mineiro* dishes, a country's

soul food. *Sertaneja* and *caipira,* species of redneck pop, also from
Minas, are thought of as the "real" sounds of Brazil. Milton Nascimento, Brazil's greatest folk singer, comes from Minas Gerais. So
does Brazil's greatest soccer player, Edson Arantes do Nascimento,
known to the world as "Pelé."

Minas dominates the map of Brazil. Its southern villages are
within a few hours' reach of Rio de Janeiro and São Paulo to the
south, while Brazil's capital, Brasília, is only miles from Minas's
northwestern corner. From Minas, only the Amazon seems far
away, although within the state itself; the distance between large
towns seems endless.

Outside its capital, Belo Horizonte, Minas is like a tropic Alaska
where small towns appear suddenly over the crest of highway,
then quickly disappear over the receding horizon. Barreling down
BR-381, the two-lane trunk road that connects São Paulo to the
northeast, a motorist crosses Minas at its widest point, whipping
two hundred miles past signposts naming places that sound magical
to a foreigner's imagination: Coronel Fabriciano, Diogo de Vascon-
celos, Raul Soares, Antonio Dias, Ipatinga, Jequeri, Caputira,
Caratinga, Bom Jesús do Galho, São João de Oriente, São João
Evangelista, Virginopolis.

From these tiny towns a trickle of migrants became a torrent.
Minas sends more emigrants—*brazucas,* as they're known abroad
—to America than any other Brazilian state. According to some
estimates, anywhere from 40 to 80 percent of the four hundred
thousand Brazilian immigrants said to be living in the United States
are *mineiros.* At first glance, this seems a bit of an anomaly. Minas's
immense territory defies any concept of overpopulation. Minas
lacks the desperate, grinding conditions of Brazil's northeast, the
black belt seared by drought, from which most of Brazil's internal
migration springs. Nor does it offer the cosmopolitan glow of Rio
de Janeiro or São Paulo, from which international flights leave a
dozen times a day, and where links to New York, Miami, Washington, and California are part of the ambience of an elite "world"
city.

If Minas is not impoverished, neither is the town of Governador Valadares. It, too, is a Brazilian anomaly—a bustling commercial center boasting the kind of vitality failed policies have destroyed elsewhere. Immigration, and immigrant dollars coming home to feed investment, is one reason for Valadares's well-being. The Rio Doce, the river on whose banks Vale Verde rises, is another. This is the same Rio Doce for which the world's biggest producer of iron ore, Compania Vale Rio Doce (or CVRD—$2 billion in revenues in 1996), takes its name. Supporting CVRD are extensive railroad lines, coaling stations, even a eucalyptus plantation sown in a joint venture between CVRD and Japan's Nippon Steel. Two massive steel complexes in nearby Ipatinga—the Acesita and Usiminas mills—provide thousands of high-paying jobs.

That's the paradox of Minas. Both its prosperity and its distance from international borders would combine, in theory, to make it one of the least likely "senders" of immigrants. But that is only if immigration is a function of material need. Governador Valadares is today's quintessential "sender," the kind of place that mocks theory about What Must Happen to keep the emigrants from continuing to emigrate. Valadares and Ipatinga have jobs, lots of them, and dollars and a well-educated population. Development is the reason Valadares is a sender. The more its people learn about the world outside and their own value in a global marketplace, the more they flee—from Tehuacán, Puebla, or from Touba in West Africa. That's the paradox of emigration.

The Reis family in Ipatinga is part of that global context. Their home in the heart of Novo Cruzeiro, a hillside *bairro*, is, typically, a three-story palace still under construction. It is also a shrine to the six missing children—Napoleão (Napoleon), Vitage, Hermes, Celina, Rafael, and Jehova—who have scattered across the northeast United States. A slim, vivacious woman with a short punk haircut, Isis Reis is only too happy to show a visitor photos of her siblings in America. "My favorite is Hermes," she says, sorting a stack of snapshots. One is of a slim boy against a backdrop of New England snow. Hermes at the mall in Natick, Hermes outside the

Registry of Motor Vehicles, Hermes with his girlfriend (later his wife), with friends eating at the Ipanema Restaurant in Southboro. Isis is devoted to Hermes, saving his letters and managing his interests here in Ipatinga, which amount to this unfinished house and two more properties he keeps for rental income. She loves the others, Isis explains, but they don't need her as much. Rafael is settled now in Newark. Napoleão makes regular trips back to Brazil. Celina just left and Vitage—Vitage drives a truck around the United States, sending home lots of cash and flowery greeting cards as testimony to extreme *saudade*. One is an enormous blow-up color photo mounted on a wall, a close-up of Vitage by a lake with the date: January 25, 1991. "Mommy and Daddy, Sisters and Brothers," his message reads, in English, scrawled in block print with a green crayon: "Please get close to me now. Would you? Let me Feel you! Let me Hug you! Let me Kiss you! I miss all of You so Bad!"

"That Vitage, he's so sentimental," sighs Isis, sounding a little embarrassed. America is for the tough, not the sappy.

The economics of the Reis family's migration can be explained as "labor futures," leveraging the sweat of service work into rental properties earning Brazilian *reais* at home. Under Brazil's arcane rent-control laws, any family has the right to develop property it owns land and title to. However, the maximum permissible rent is "three minimum salaries," or three times the sixty *reais* a Brazilian worker is entitled to each month. In U.S. terms, that comes to about two hundred dollars per month, which meant, in 1994, a permanent monthly income that would establish a family well within the middle class. Such a rental home could be had for around $40,000—about two years' worth of profits from America. By borrowing $10,000 to launch a first son's voyage north, the Reis family added—with monthly interest payments made in dollars— almost $30,000 to the cost of its first property. But once the wage earner was established, every subsequent migrant traveled nearly cost-free.

In 1994, Hermes returned for a brief visit, bringing $9,000 to cover property taxes and other costs of improving his holdings. He also brought hard-to-get items like circuit boards and electronic parts, helping his older brother launch a second family business— maintaining a dozen video games installed in Ipatinga bars. All told, Hermes and his brothers have invested over $50,000 in various ventures, enough to support another dozen members of an extended family with part-time work. In addition to building equity, the Reis properties were spinning off nearly $7,000 in annual dividends, more than enough to send a sixth child, Luiz, to the land of *saudade*.

"Dishwashing" is what Luiz says he'll do in Massachusetts, using one of the few English words he knows. "Landscaping" is another, along with "Holiday Inn," which he thinks is a type of job, not a place with several. Luiz knows only that New England offers snow and work. "I never thought I would have to go," Luiz says, his eyes locked on a videotape of an evangelical church service. He doesn't sound disappointed or scared, or even very excited about the prospect of joining his brothers in New England. It's just that ten years ago, when this mad dollar-rush started, no one in the Reis family could imagine they would need to send more than one son away. But what they didn't realize is that immigration becomes its own industry, a process of growing expectations validated by growing opportunity. First a house, then a business, then a transnational empire.

The men who built Valadares's Bairro Vale Verde and Ipatinga's Novo Cruzeiro began leaving in the mid-1960s, around the same time the Amin brothers left Baroda, Gujarat, and for roughly the same reasons. Brazil, like India, was producing more ambition in its postwar generation than its own economy could absorb. Claudio Parreira, a man with gray temples and a thick belly, says he was the first Brazilian to arrive in Framingham, way back in 1971. "I was the fifth person in Marlborough," he says with a snort. "But I was the first in Framingham."

Claudio Parreira is a legend in Governador Valadares, *o pai dos migrantes*, the father of the immigrants. Over a nineteen-year career in Massachusetts, he and his brother pioneered enclaves across New England, later claiming to be the first Brazilians to colonize

Nashua, New Hampshire, to buy a house in Andover, Massachusetts, to work at the Coach and Six on Route 1 in Peabody, or tend bar at JT's on Route 26 in Sudbury—$3.95 for all the lobster you can eat. "I worked a hundred ten hours a week at that place," Claudio says with obvious pride. "I worked for a Greek guy. On my day off he sent over a case of beer. 'You're a nice guy,' he used to tell me."

That same Greek was later sued by his workers for withholding more than thirty thousand dollars from his crew of dishwashers and cooks over four years. The father of the immigrants was one of the plaintiffs in a class-action suit, eventually receiving a check for a thousand dollars after the Greek settled. "He told me he wanted the check back," Claudio recalls. "I said, 'Joe, I would never be the one to take you to court. But this money is mine.' He fired me."

A neighbor, José Carlos de Oliveira, matches Claudio's tales with his own. Both men are famous for being among the very few *brazucas* to make a successful transition back to Brazilian life. Part of their success was luck, part work ethic. Neither can remember taking more than two days in a row off in what, combined, amounts to a sojourn of over thirty years in New England. Mainly their success came from being early visitors, getting to the gold fields first, then exploiting those who followed. "Claudio was my teacher," José says solemnly, without a trace of rancor. When his own brothers joined him, he did the same thing. "You see a better job in the restaurant," he explains. "You say to the boss, 'Take a chance on me,' and your ass is still covered because your brother can do your old job. That's how it goes." If anyone is exploited, then it is within the willing context of an apprenticeship.

Neither man fits the usual profile of the impoverished Third Worlder, now or before. Claudio Parreira's father was a building inspector for the town. José de Oliveira ran his own business, a small convenience store. Sender towns are places of commerce, where cash and credit are at hand. José de Oliveira sold his business to raise funds to travel to Ecuador, then to Tijuana, Mexico, where he crossed into the United States. Compared to some, travel for him was easy. "I know a couple that stowed themselves away on a boat in Vitória," he says with a shudder, referring to the nearby port capital of Espírito Santo. "They died."

Despite the horror stories, the experiences of early sojourners like Claudio and José sound like tales from a bygone era, as antique as all-you-can-eat $3.95 lobster buffets. Even though they were in Massachusetts illegally, neither man experienced any threat of being detected or deported. America was immigrant-friendly in that golden age. One time, Claudio recalls, a co-worker was picked up after a car accident. Word spread through the *brazuca* community. Claudio and his brothers decided, in an instant, to flee. That's how they became the first *mineiros* in Nashua, New Hampshire. Claudio says the community had grown to six hundred by the time the brothers returned to Massachusetts a few years later.

Brazilians choose New England for a variety of reasons. A booming service economy, a liberal electorate, and the tiny presence of the Immigration and Naturalization Service combine to create a safe haven. And, like the Senegalese, Brazilians share an indirect tie to early America. Starting with whaling, in cities like New Bedford, Mystic, and Fall River, then into the period of the great textile mills and shoe factories, New England has been a magnet for Portuguese migrants. Massachusetts is the United States' most Portuguese-speaking state, with an estimated eight hundred thousand Lusophones. Thus, even before Brazilians began arriving, Boston suburbs like Somerville and Cambridge, as well as Providence, Rhode Island, and all of Cape Cod, boasted sizeable Portuguese enclaves, immigrants from the Azores, Madeira, Cape Verde, even Portuguese Africa. These waves paved the way for the *mineiros*.

Although fewer *Valadarenses* are going to America these days, "tourism" has not ceased to be a major industry. The town does a thriving business serving would-be guest workers from other cities, particularly from the port cities of Vitória in Espírito Santo state, or from Salvador in Bahia.

Today, at least twelve thousand *Valadarenses* live in the two towns of Framingham and Marlborough. While some *brazuca* communities outside New England—in New York City, Newark, and Pompano Beach, Florida—may be more populous, there may be no greater concentration of Brazilian immigrants in the United States, per capita, than in these two suburbs twenty miles west of Boston. Just as Governador Valadares may be the southernmost part of the United States, Framingham is becoming the northernmost town in Brazil.

Framingham, Massachusetts, with its sixty-five thousand residents, is also America's biggest town. That is, it is the largest incorporated district still governed by the traditional "town meeting" form of government that began in New England in the 1600s. Situated exactly twenty miles west of Boston and twenty miles east of Worcester, Framingham epitomizes the 1990s model of the "edge city," a multiracial, multiincome, multiskill community that thrives beyond the limits of a traditional urban center.

The story of Framingham tracks "typical" America through four centuries. The original name was Danforth Farms, for the English nobleman to whom the lush woods and meadows were deeded; the first white settlers arrived in the 1640s. During King Philip's War, the first great conflict between the English and indigenous tribes, the Eames plantation, one of Framingham's oldest, was overrun by Pequot warriors. They massacred its inhabitants. Nearly a century later, in April 1775, royal engineers under General Thomas Gage passed through, scouting routes for a punitive expedition against restive colonials. Traveling the Worcester Road (today's Route 9) they encountered two companies of Framingham Minutemen drilling with muskets. Based on their reconnaissance, the British bypassed the direct route west to march through the nearby hamlet of Concord. A few days later, Framingham's Minutemen heard too late the "shot heard round the world" at Concord Bridge, and so missed the battle. Framingham Minutemen were on time, town historians later recalled, to harass the British in their retreat. Moreover, they say, five years earlier at the Boston Massacre, a son of Framingham—Crispus Attucks—was the first American to die for freedom. Attucks was born a slave in Framingham.

Besides Crispus Attucks, the Pittsburgh Pirates' Harold "Pie" Traynor, by some lights the greatest third baseman ever, also was born in Framingham. Horatio Alger, bard of America's self-improvement ideology, wrote *Ragged Dick* in Framingham. The country's first free academy was founded there in 1798, and in 1853, the nation's first teacher's college, today's Framingham State College. Although George Washington never slept in Framingham, during his birthday celebration in 1862, Framingham hosted the first public recital of Julia Ward Howe's *Battle Hymn of the Republic*. Shopper's World, America's first from-the-ground-up shopping mall, was erected in Framingham. To stroll beneath its quaint porcelain bubble, where Jordan Marsh was the "anchor" store, or down the cool concrete ramps to the lower quadrangle is like visiting an archeological dig, the birthplace of Suburbanus Emptor, the "typical" American of our time.

If Minas Gerais is "typical," so is Framingham. For Framingham, this is not merely an opinion, but scientific fact—or, at least, a medical one. Framingham has earned such status twice, first in 1916, then in 1948. No one completes medical school without hearing of the ambitious Framingham Heart Study which, over the past five decades, has tracked the dietary habits and other health indicators of five thousand Framingham residents. That study, which continues today, contributed enormously to science's knowledge of heart disease. Framingham, with its mix of working and professional classes, many ethnic and religious groups and nearby medical community, was considered an ideal setting and, by all accounts, the Framingham Heart Study has been a resounding success. What many people do not know is the reason Framingham was chosen was that, a generation earlier, a similar study was held. From 1916 to 1923, five thousand Framingham residents were examined periodically in the Framingham Health Demonstration, a study of tuberculosis funded by the Metropolitan Life Insurance Company. Just as with the heart study, the town was selected because it seemed so "typically" American.

Immigration, too, is a component of Framingham's typical pro-file. For a century and a half, Framingham has been a "receiver." It began in the 1840s, with the Irish. Framingham was hardly the only town in Massachusetts to experience an Irish influx. But it was the only town in south Middlesex County to permit the establish-ment of a Roman Catholic church. Saint George's, authorized by town meeting vote in 1844, was built in the part of town called Saxonville, so named for the Saxony wool processed at its mills. As an 1887 text, *History of Framingham, Massachusetts,* recalls, this initial parish, located "near the carpet Factory . . . at first took in Framingham, Sudbury, Wayland, Southboro, and Ashland."

Thus the town distinguished itself as a cosmopolitan town sur-rounded by uptight Yankee hamlets. Framingham attracted immi-grants because it was the first town to offer them free assembly in the 1840s, a place where "papist" Irish could pray without fear of harassment from the anti-Catholic activists like the Know Nothings, a political party which flourished in New England right up until the Civil War. The reference "near the carpet Factory" is also tell-ing. In the 1840s, Framingham was in the midst of an industrial boom that would last through the end of the century. Several textile plants rose in Saxonville, their looms powered by currents from the swift-flowing Sudbury River. Immigrant labor was desperately sought for these mills, so permitting a place where Catholics could worship was undoubtedly part of the town's strategy to lure work-ers. During the Civil War, Saxonville thrived on Union Army con-tracts, and its carpet mills became the most advanced in the nation.

For the next hundred years, factory work and Catholic worship forged twin rails upon which immigration rolled into Framingham. The second Catholic church, Saint Stephen's, opened in 1883. A few years later, Dennison Manufacturing moved to town from Brunswick, Maine, where a large part of its workforce, also Cath-olic, was French Canadian. Thus, in addition to an Irish constitu-ency, Saint Stephen's became Framingham's "Canuck" church, receiving parishioners with names like Deschamps, DuLac, Le-page, Fournier, Saint Andre, and LaFrance right through the 1940s. Dennison, the nation's first manufacturer of paper cartons, would become America's biggest paper products company. From 1900 to about midcentury, it would be Framingham's biggest employer, holding that distinction until just after World War II, when a massive General Motors plant opened.

Saint Tarcisius on Waverly Street was opened in 1906 by the Scalabrinian Fathers, an order founded in Italy in 1887, whose initial purpose was ministering to immigrants. Italian stoneworkers were particularly desireable at this time. To serve Boston's growing population, a chain of reservoirs was being carved out in Middlesex County, and Italian immigrants cut the quartz and granite that went into their retaining walls. Framingham was also developing into a transportation center—it would become the "Hub of New England" by century's end—and Italian road crews were pressed into service, spreading macadam and gravel on the new highways, and laying railbeds for the six rail lines crossing town. Once more, the Catholic church was a key component in attracting a desireable workforce. First from Boston's North End, later from Italy proper, a new wave of Catholic workers came to help America's typical town prosper.

From Italy came Bonfiglio Perini, whose construction company, Perini & Sons, began as a "wop gang" laying track for the Boston and Worcester Railroad in 1893. Since the 1950s, Perini & Sons (and grandsons) have been one of the country's biggest construction firms, owners at one time of the major league Boston Braves. Perini Corporation is still based in Framingham.

Starting with Saint George's of the textile mills, to Saint Stephen's, and then Saint Tarcisius, Catholic churches linked new Americans to American neighborhoods and American jobs. Even now, with the *brazucas,* migrants entering Framingham continue a Catholic tradition stretching from Ireland to Italy to Canada, Portugal, and Puerto Rico. And even after the factories began to close, churches continued their assimilating mission.

Roque Pattussi, the Portuguese-speaking priest assigned to Saint Tarcisius, is kind of a rarity in Framingham: a Brazilian who doesn't come from Minas Gerais. He comes from Mucum, a city in the southern state of Rio Grande do Sul, whose founders were largely Italian immigrants. Padre Roque (whose name the parishioners pronounced the Brazilian way, "hockey") is a tall, fair-skinned Italo-*brazuca*. Like Pelegrino Rodino, Jr., he is a Neapolitan just a century and a continent (or two) removed from the Old Country. He enjoys Italian food, but sucks *mate* from a silver-stemmed pipe, in the gaucho style of the Argentine and Paraguayan pampa. The fact that he, son of Italian immigrants to Brazil, should be sent by the Scalabrinians, an Italian order founded to serve immigrants, to minister to Brazilians in the church at the center of Framingham's Little Italy is no coincidence. For every immigrant committing cultural suicide, there is another reinforcing tradition.

Not that Padre Hockey is a square. He was but twenty-eight years old, newly ordained, when he came to Framingham in 1992. Today he wears blue jeans and sneakers under his white cassock, and a woven, multihued stole across his shoulders. The overall effect is Solidarity with the Oppressed, from the Nike footwear to the Central American refugee-camp vestments. His morning congregation hates that look. They sit uneasily before this young *pai,* and kneel even more uneasily. "They expect a priest to command, to look like a father," Padre Roque explains. "They got scared when they first saw me."

"They" are the Portuguese, the Old World Portuguese who come to Saint Tarcisius at 10 A.M., the third of four Sunday morning masses, all an hour long, all but one conducted in English. Saint Tarcisius' Portuguese mass is now twenty years old, but is not for Brazilians. In fact, they shun the morning mass, just as the older, whiter Portuguese—most heavy-bearded Azorians—avoid the *brazucas.*

The nighttime is for the *brazucas.* The mass starts promptly at seven, and ends who knows when? For many *brazucas,* Sunday night with Padre Hockey is the social event of the week, never drawing fewer than four hundred worshipers. Imagine, a mass of only an hour! Those morning Catholics don't know what they're missing. Instead of a few dozen bleary-eyed Azorians puffing cigarettes outside the church, the evening crowd is rocking. They're rocking their cars up and down Waverly Street (Saint Tarcisius' parking lot has long since been filled), filling the side streets and the streets behind the church. Inside, a twenty-person choir is shouting "*Aleluia*," while synthesizer, guitars, and conga drums pound something almost samba. This crowd not only seems young—it is young, in baby strollers, baby carseats, suckling breasts, stretched out snoring among the back pews. Two men pan the sanctuary with new video cameras. Even more than American television and movies, it is the immigrant himself who sells America to those still waiting to come. See, look at our terrific church! Like the "good news" about abundant jobs and cheap cars, this gospel is part of Framingham's lure.

The Portuguese who come in the morning want to be a flock led by its shepherd. The evening congregation wants to share power. For a week the liturgy group, all lay activists, script and choreograph an elaborate service, even down to editing Padre Hockey's sermon. Brazil, the world's biggest Catholic country, is also the country least served, per capita, by ordained clergy. So, for decades, Brazilian Catholics have been accustomed to running their own services, especially in remote villages where a priest may not visit more than once or twice a year. In Framingham, laymen manage the congregation with almost as much authority as their priest.

On this night, the last Sunday in August, the theme of Padre Hockey's message is the power of community to succor the believer in a strange land. But before the priest's sermon, the children lead an elaborate demonstration. The lights of the sanctuary are doused, leaving only a flickering kaleidoscope of color, "flames" from a cheap Christmas tree "burning" before the altar. One of the parishioners, dressed in biblical garb, rushes in a panic through the black room, his wails augmented by the crashing sounds of synthesizer chords and screechy guitar licks. He is Moses, fleeing the wrath of God. Now voices, in Portuguese, guide Moses to the bush, beseeching the wretched refugee to look at his flight, his life, seek solace in his faith, and prevail. The lights come up to the strains of Saint Tarcisius' rock choir. We are all frightened refugees seeking our way in a hostile desert, Padre Hockey tells the packed room. "Who feels *saudade*?" he offers, the congregation murmuring its longing. "We all do. We all feel *saudade*. For our families. For our community. For Jesus."

Padre Hockey, armed with a wireless microphone, begins to work the room. Like a talk-show host, he moves through the pews. Tell us a story, give us testimony. It's the part of the mass that makes the Portuguese cringe, but brings forth zeal from the Brazilians. Women rush forth to hug Padre Hockey, then burst into tears as they recite. My sister had a baby and I wasn't home, one says. Or, I got my driver's license and I felt so good this week. Or, my boss gave me a raise. I got my green card. Laughter, tears, sudden bursts of applause. By the time Padre Hockey returns to the sermon (or was this the sermon, "interactive," as it were?), the congregation has been standing for almost two hours. Yet, as the infants snore and drool and soil the pew cushions, a warm feeling bathes the room. "We are all Moses, and we are all the light from the burning bush," he concludes. "We are each other."

Padre Hockey will not leave the church until well after midnight. Besides the one-on-one consultations that keep him, *mate*-sucking and cassock-free in the rectory, the end of the mass is an exercise in community building. Framingham's *brazuca* church has come a long way in a very short time. There is a *brazuca* day-care center at Saint Tarcisius for kids with working mothers—which is just about every mother. And there is a new church "beeper" service, with a parishioner on call twenty-four hours a day. It can be for something dire, like a lift to the hospital in a medical emergency, or something relatively trivial, like a lift to the Department of Motor Vehicles for that all-important driver's test that, here in the suburbs, gives the *brazuca* the means to overcome his homebound *saudade* and start to climb the ladder to success. Most often the beeper beeps for something in between the dire and the trivial. Most often it has to do with a problem with the police. Almost all the *brazucas* in Framingham are relative newcomers, which means almost all of them are illegal. The church beeper means, if you get busted, your first phone call—a glorious right in America!—goes to your church, which can send a member, sometimes with an attorney, to get you out of jail and into an asylum petition. Brazilians, by and large, have no claim to political asylum, yet like most immigrants, they know they can stall detention and deportation by launching an appeal for asylum. It may be no more than a delaying tactic, but in Massachusetts—a jurisdiction where the Immigration and Naturalization Service has a minuscule presence—delay is a way to stay. Padre Hockey supports this and any other tactic that keeps his parishioners safe and his community intact. "I tell them, God made the earth, and Man made the borders," he says, relaxing in the rectory after the long mass. "To go anywhere in the world to better yourself is God's way. To not go because of borders and law is Man's way. We follow God's way."

If a trip to Shopper's World is like visiting an archeological dig, then attending mass at Saint Tarcisius parish is a journey back into childhood. I was born in Framingham, four years after my parents joined the great exodus of urban ethnics leaving Boston for the suburbs. That same exodus would swell Framingham's population from 28,086 in 1950 to 44,526 in 1960. The town's current level of around 65,000 would be reached by the early 1970s, after which growth would level off.

My parents, George and Joan Millman, were typical of the postwar couples building new towns outside cities throughout the Northeast. All four of my grandparents were immigrants from Russia or Poland. Typically, both grandfathers were small businessmen—one a grocer, the other a jeweler—while both of my grandmothers were homemakers. My parents' generation was the first in either family to attend college, and became the first to break out of the immigrant economy—my father becoming a civil engineer, my mother an elementary school teacher. They entered Framingham the way most World War II veterans did—buying a small Cape Cod–style home in one of the new tract developments, Cochituate Oaks, for $12,500. In 1956, the year I was born, Framingham Union Hospital had just opened its new maternity ward. Later, Framingham Union became part of an enormous health-care complex called the Metro West Medical Center, which sprawls well beyond the row of red-brick buildings I remember as a kid. My first school, Lincoln Elementary, is one of several buildings either owned by Metro West or housing the offices of the many independent doctors, therapists, home-nursing agencies, or consultancies living off of what has become the town's biggest employer.

For a hundred years, the South Side was essentially an Italian community, with the church as its center. Even now, a hundred years after the first immigrants came, South Framingham is still dominated by Italians. The shops clustered along Waverly Street —the Stefanini Bakery near the Stefanini Brothers' grocery, DeCollibus' TV Video just blocks from the DeCollibus' Auto Body shop—give the neighborhood a just-off-the-boat feel, despite the obvious suburban ambience.

Even during the "golden age" years of low immigration, Framingham received a steady stream of foreigners. Kevin Norton, my closest friend in the third grade, arrived from County Galway in 1963. He was the youngest of seven brothers, four of whom worked at Dennison Manufacturing, as did his father and two uncles. Every Sunday they attended mass at Saint Stephen's, usually in staggered shifts while Kevin's "mammy" prepared a hearty noon meal.

My memories now of their little apartment on the top floor of a typical "triple decker" are revived today when visiting the homes of current immigrants. There is the same acrid smell of old wallpaper glue, the same sound of a television set, always on. The little white porcelain house the Nortons kept on the coffee table in the living room—a replica of their whitewashed sod shanty in Galway —is practically the same size and same dimension and same whiteness as the little pottery homes Salvadorans and Guatemalans and Haitians have in their apartments now. The crucifixes hung in every room are the same ornaments hung by Mexicans and Vietnamese.

I remember, too, that Kevin's family had a color television set before mine did, and that his brothers drove cars newer than my father's. Kevin's older brothers bought comic books and boxing magazines—enthralling to a kid whose parents permitted only "educational" reading matter at home. That this was part of the immigrant creed—instant wealth in the Golden Land—being played out a few blocks from my school was something I could not know at eight years old. Even at sixteen, playing soccer on a team dominated by kids born in the Azores, all of whom worked and already owned cars, I still did not grasp that the most typical thing about my typical New England town was its steady influx of immigrants.

Today the South Side remains working class, and heavily foreign-born. Along Hollis Street, where the town's first Puerto Ricans and Portuguese settled in the 1970s, are all the signs of immigrant enterprise. As in Manhattan's Washington Heights or Brooklyn's Brownsville, there are the same storefront phone parlors (as in New York, operated by Dominicans), the same remittance shops and newspapers from home. Framingham has three Indian-owned saree shops on Concord Street where J. C. Penney and Woolworth's used to be. It has a Jamaican-owned Black Pride shop, filled with African trinkets and *boubous* from Senegal. It has a Russian delicatessen and a Korean store filled with martial arts toys and cheap dinnerware. All of these ethnic outcroppings are overwhelmed by the Brazilians.

There are said to be more than two hundred Brazilian businesses in town, many of them almost invisible to Framingham's Anglo residents. Yes, everyone sees D'Lima's coffee shop on Concord Street, the Valadares Express store, Amaral Jewelry, and the Vigo money exchange. They are obvious—with big Brazilian flags in the front windows, and tourist posters of sunny Rio on the walls. What they don't see are the tiny enterprises upstairs, off the street, where Brazilians sell soft drinks, magazines, and cookies imported from home, or rent bootlegged videos of popular soap operas. There are at least a dozen places where you can rent an eight-hour packet of Brazilian television for twenty dollars, four two-hour cassettes programmed by Globo Televisão in Rio. Globo, South America's biggest media company, airlifts hundreds of cartons of these summaries of its news and entertainment shows to the United States every week, where homesick *brazucas* snap them up eagerly.

In a way that is also hidden to most of the town's older residents, the *brazucas* have become part of an unstoppable wave. The lilt of Portuguese greets you buying coffee at Dunkin' Donuts, or paying for gas at the Sunoco station. Brazilians are plumbers and carpenters and nursing-home workers. They work as cashiers at the all-night convenience stores, or on the night shift at the print shop. Most are illegal. Their mass has grown large enough to support its own commerce—selling each other insurance, cars, property (both here and in Minas Gerais). They serve each other and hire each other and make a community. Even if the factory work that fed a century of immigration is gone, the two-family homes, the triple deckers, and the bungalows that rose within walking distance of Dennison's and GM are all still there. Their tenants are the same type who lived there a generation ago. The factory jobs are gone, but there is other work to be had, and they are having it.

The day Brazil met Italy in the cup final, Framingham met the mass in its midst. The town did the right thing, stationing extra cops and granting a temporary liquor license to let *brazuca* community leaders provide free beer—to toast Brazilian glory, or drown the worst *saudade*.

Fittingly, the game ended in a scoreless tie, with the fate of humanity decided by a series of penalty kicks—ten minutes of tense one-on-one duels that left the Brazilians watching the game at a bar called Ebenezer's, hugging each other with each attempt, sobbing on the verge of breakdown. At the crucial moment, João Viana, a dishwasher at Ebenezer's, fell on his knees and burst into tears when one of Italy's free shots flew wide of the goal. A few seconds later, when Brazil's last shot wrinkled the net, he hugged the floor, exultant.

Outside, almost immediately, the chanting began. *"Olé, olé, olé . . . Brasil, Brasil."* From everywhere came the pounding of samba drums and the shrieks of whistles. A pick-up truck flew past Waverly Street, its bed filled with shirtless youths, waving beer bottles and trailing a Brazilian flag. At the bar, the two beefy Irish mugs pointed glasses for refills and asked the bartender to switch the television to the Red Sox game.

As the *brazucas* marched and partied into the night, I worked the sidewalks. Illegal immigrants, normally suspicious of an American with a notebook, were eager to be interviewed. And why not? Brazil is the greatest country in the world after a World Cup triumph, and Framingham is Brazil! The next day's *Middlesex News* had a front-page color photo featuring five girls in matching green and yellow Brazilian uniforms, each with a letter spelling B-R-A-S-I-L across their chests. The headline: "Downtown Brazil."

By 1985, the year the *brazuca* wave began, Framingham was already a very different town from the one immigrants found even a decade before. In 1986, General Motors closed its South Framingham plant. Dennison Manufacturing was about to merge with a California company, Avery International, a deal which would shutter most East Coast operations, eliminating nearly a thousand Framingham jobs. By 1986, the venerable Bancroft Cap Company, which stitched headgear for U.S. military contracts, was already long gone. Its six-story block of lofts and loading docks housed tiny "micro" businesses—a printer, a computer parts store, a small plant assembling labeling equipment. In 1994, most of its space was vacant.

Immigrants coming to Framingham after the mid-1980s no longer work in industry because Framingham no longer makes things. There are exceptions, of course. Bose speakers, considered top-of-the-line by audiophiles, are made in Framingham, and immigrants work in their assembly. Wonder Bread has a plant just outside town on Route 30, and many immigrants work there. Instead of blue-collar companies like Dennison and Perini, service purveyors now dominate Framingham's corporate elite. TJ Maxx, the clothing retailer, is a Framingham company. So is Staples, wholesaler of office supplies. Many emerging companies are hyperspecialists, whose operations the average resident would be hard-pressed to describe. Microsystems Software Inc., which develops "cost-efficient management and filtering software for the Internet," is one. Genzyme Transgenics Corporation, another Framingham firm, is engaged in "the application of transgenic technologies to enable the development and production of recombinant proteins and monoclonal antibodies for medical uses." Connected Corp. calls itself "a leading provider of online backup and data management services," while Netlink is "a leading provider of performance-assured access to frame relay."

Framingham is still the "Hub of New England," even if what hums along New England's roads are human ideas, not products. Together with the many Boston-area universities, the rise of computer companies like Digital, Prime, and Wang in the 1970s and 1980s completed the transformation of Framingham into a new kind of bedroom community, one where schools and quality of life and shopping malls became the defining indicators of wealth. Which also means Framingham has a new kind of immigrant community.

Starting in the 1970s, Framingham became a "typical" American town in another way. With the emergence of the two-income family, the working wife, once rare, became the norm. Thus, even as factory work disappeared, demand for workers increased. Immigrants today do everything from landscaping and gardening to baby-sitting and house-cleaning. Fast-food service, the substitute for a home-cooked family meal, is another immigrant stronghold. And, as Framingham "typically" ages, immigrants are in great demand at nursing homes and hospitals, both enormous employers.

The same initiative that has Brazilians running their own mass at Saint Tarcisius has allowed this new wave of Lusophone immigrants to thrive in the suburbs. If the Azoreans and other Portuguese prefer to be led, they also prefer "guided" jobs in factories. Even after the Massachusetts Miracle became the Mirage, Brazilians ignored the contraction in the local economy. Brazilians, by concentrating on self-employment, found the home-cleaning business recession-proof. They not only expanded the house-cleaning industry, but spawned a spin-off industry, brokering lists of clients. Advertised in the local Brazilian papers, these are start-up kits, selling for about $200 per home. Established *brazucas* capitalize their business by spinning off homes to new arrivals, often from their own families. Thus, as the colony of *brazucas* grows, the house-cleaning radius spreads outward from the Hub of New England—to all the ritzy suburbs that don't have immigrants, but where two-income couples are desperate for reliable workers they can trust an empty home to.

Hermes Reis is a typical cleaner. Hermes arrived from Ipatinga in 1985, traveling directly to Boston after spending a couple of days with one of his brothers in Newark, New Jersey.

Thirty-four years old, Hermes is a slight wisp of a man who could pass for twenty-five, or even twenty. At five feet, six inches and weighing 150 pounds, dressed in a T-shirt and jeans, he could be the teenager who, twenty years ago, would have been hired to do the kind of work he does now. If Hermes Reis looks like the native-born worker he has replaced, there is a reason. Cleaning homes, baby-sitting, gardening—all part-time jobs teenagers did a generation ago—are done full-time today by immigrants. And not because teenagers don't want to, but because there are fewer teenagers around. Like many teenagers, Hermes's passion is music, but only religious music, the raucous *"Aleluia, Aleluia"* of Brazil's pentecostal revivalist church. Despite a punishing schedule that has him cleaning homes from dawn until late at night, six days a week, he almost never misses church on Sundays, and usually finds time several weeknights to practice hymnals on his portable keyboard at home or at another parishioner's apartment. Either because his religious faith does not permit him to lie, or because he is too naïve to know better, Hermes Reis was extremely generous with the details of his life in Framingham, neither defending nor denying that he, too, has broken "Man's laws" in pursuit of his new life.

A high school graduate in Brazil, he never seriously expected to stay in Ipatinga. One older brother, Rafael, preceded him to the United States, entering on a tourist visa and overstaying. Two more, Vitage and Napoleão, crossed from Mexico. A fourth brother, Jehova, arrived in 1986, followed in 1993 by a sister, Celina. Both Vitage and Napoleão exploited the farmworkers' loophole in the 1986 Immigration Reform and Control Act to get green cards. So did Hermes. Starting in 1985, Hermes worked days at a copying shop in downtown Framingham, nights at the restaurant at the Sheraton Tara on Route 9. By 1990, he had earned his own green card. A year later he married Jeni, a girl from Ipatinga who came on a tourist visa. They moved to a two-bedroom apartment in the Lord Chesterfield complex, a sprawling compound with over two hundred units, perhaps a third rented by Brazilians. In the shadow of Shopper's World, hemmed in by busy Routes 9 and 30, the Lord Chesterfield is a perfect launching pad for the cleaning business. The on-ramp to the Massachusetts Turnpike is less than a mile from the complex; from there, it's just fifteen minutes to the Route 128 beltway, the suburban freeway connecting dozens of affluent suburbs. Within the Lord Chesterfield, the many Brazilian families meant no shortage of available labor, greenhorns from home who would work cheap. For young couples with kids, there was also cheap day care, another consideration when launching a cleaning business involving two partners.

Hermes and Jeni began cleaning homes in 1991, exhausting six years of savings to acquire their first clients. "I had to pay seventy-five hundred dollars for fourteen houses," Hermes says, wrinkling a freckled nose with the memory. "That was a terrible deal. The person who sold them, he never told the people we were coming to their houses. We lost a lot of them. The ones we kept, they paid too cheap."

One of the remaining homes, in Wayland, would have been better lost. On his first day at the home, Hermes was blamed for damage to an expensive chandelier and dining room table. He claims it was poorly installed, which is why it fell and shattered when he tried cleaning the bulbs and crystal with a feather duster. The old woman who owned the house wanted him to pay for the damage on the spot. However, she realized that forcing Hermes to pay with money he didn't have risked him simply walking away. So they struck a deal: Hermes and Jeni cleaned her home free of charge every week for six months to compensate for the damage. After five months, or about twelve hundred dollars' worth of cleaning, the old woman told Hermes not to return again.

Still, even this bad start was a start. By the summer of 1994, his business was humming. The average house can be cleaned in two to three hours, usually for a flat fee of sixty dollars. Scheduled once a week, a good route of twenty homes yields gross revenues of seventy-five hundred dollars a month, the same price Hermes paid for his "terrible deal" when he started. Even after expenses —gas, two hundred dollars a week for a third hand—Hermes and his wife seldom take home less than a thousand dollars every week for themselves, all of it untaxed. It is a business that requires no more than showing up on time, and being quiet. "We use their stuff, people like their own cleaning things," Hermes says, explaining that even supplies are subsidized by the patron. "Some of our customers, they trust us so much, they let us into the house with our own keys." Some, the few mothers homebound with young children, use the cleaning teams as baby-sitting relief, escaping to do the shopping or even watch a movie while their bedrooms and bathrooms are being cleaned. Some Brazilians offer laundry service, but Hermes doesn't: too costly in time, he says, and too many complaints if something happens to the clothes. In some homes, another immigrant does the wash while Hermes and his crew clean. Usually Spanish-speaking Central Americans or Mexicans, they communicate in a pidgin called "Portuñol" (Portuguese and Español), the more experienced hand-tutoring the other on the quirks of the household.

By selling off excess clients to friends, Hermes was nurturing a self-sustaining business, a virtual service "nursery" where he tended the mother plant, selling off "cuttings" to newcomers. Like the Gujarati with their motels, Brazilians like Hermes apply themselves to growing a business many Americans would consider second-rate at best. Thus, every Christmas, a stack of cards went out from the two-bedroom flat at the Lord Chesterfield apartments, even to families Hermes cleaned for just once, or who long since had their services sold to another cleaner. "Anyone might tell a friend about me," he explains. "Or maybe they move to another town, and decide they want us back."

Afternoons, sometimes in the early morning, he and Jeni would be driving all over towns like Needham, Wellesley, Newton, Natick, Wayland, and Weston, looking for those long, wide streets with the older homes, colonials and Victorians. Wherever driveways were empty, that was a sign that both parents worked and would probably need some help keeping the house. Together they stuffed homemade flyers announcing their services into strangers' mailboxes. "One time a policeman said to me, those mailboxes belong to the post office, you can't use them," Hermes recalls, a little baffled by the concept. "So they say use the mail slot in the door. So that's what we did."

Hermes' ledger for one week in September reveals how lucrative home-cleaning can be. On Monday, he did six homes, two each in Natick and Wellesley, one in Sudbury, one in Wayland. On Tuesday, he had a cancellation, but managed to clean three homes in Sudbury. Two homes were visited in Wellesley on Wednesday, and two more in Needham and Lexington. Thursday he did four homes, all in Wellesley, Friday one each in Wellesley, Natick, and Framingham. Twenty homes in five days, for a yield of twelve hundred dollars.

It is not hard to understand why some Framingham residents resent the immigrants. Many used to make the kind of money Hermes and his family earn now, in the factories that are long gone. Although no jobs were "taken" by the *brazucas*, there is a sense that little is being put back into the community. Framingham's immigrant dilemma is this: although the Brazilians do play a positive role—not only serving workaholic Yuppies, but also spending millions of dollars each year in the local economy—they are regarded as transients, guest workers who earn thousands of dollars each month, and export them.

Hermes Reis has his own dilemma. His sister, Isis, may not realize it, but he is losing money. He owns three homes in Ipatinga, two rented for income, the third, and biggest, still under construction. All three are costing him more than he can earn in Massachusetts, something that didn't seem possible when he left ten years ago. The more dollars he sends, the more costly things become. It is beginning to dawn on Hermes Reis that as hard as he works in Framingham, he will never catch up.

For Timothy Whelan, the deputy director of the Boston office of the Immigration and Naturalization Service from 1977 through 1994, that dawning realization came years ago. A good old Irish Catholic, Whelan has more in common with New England's immigrants than most bureaucrats. He was born in Cambridge, the son of an immigrant from County Cork. He also married an immigrant from the Philippines. Still, he sees the Brazilian immigrant problem from a bureaucrat's point of view. Sympathy, sure, but laws are being broken everywhere you look—minimum wage laws, visa laws, tax laws, occupational safety laws, workman's compensation laws. Probably a hundred more laws covering everything from Social Security fraud to extortion. Like Hermes Reis, Tim Whelan also came to the realization he might never "catch up." In 1994, at the end of a thirty-three-year career, he described the onerous task that policing undocumented immigrants had become.

The immigration jail in Boston, with only fifty beds, has no space for all the illegals he sees every day. He doesn't even have the space for the offenders he wants jailed: the felons, the alien smugglers, even all the Chinese his office has nabbed running extortion rings as part of their enterprise. He laughed when he said that when he takes his son to play hockey in Marlborough—the town next to Framingham, with its own growing *brazuca* enclave —he knows the men serving his son's teammates pizza after practice are stone-cold illegals. A laugh and a shrug that says, What am I supposed to do? Whip out a badge and take them downtown? To where?

For years the INS has known how porous the suburban economy is for undocumented workers. Massachusetts, with a few other states, pioneered the use of the Social Security number on its driver's licenses. Now when a Brazilian wants a valid Social Security number, he simply gets a Massachusetts driver's license. He might copy the first nine numbers of his Brazilian license, or use his passport number, or simply make one up. A license can be shown to a prospective employer as "proof" of documentation. It's not legally recognizable under the law, but most employers don't realize this. They see a valid Massachusetts license, they assume the nine-digit identification number is a Social Security number, via which they assume the applicant is a legal resident. Usually, if taxes are withheld, the employee will file with this same number, assuming a "legal" identity he or she may share with another taxpayer somewhere else in America. It will take an Internal Revenue Service computer two years to discover the overlap and send a warning letter to both parties. By that time, the *brazuca* may be in another state, gone home, or be using another number to secure employment.

All of which is to say, stopping a peaceful invasion is next to impossible. The INS can, however, make life difficult. In 1994, over Labor Day weekend, Framingham hosted its first Brazilian Expo on a vacant lot across from the old General Motors plant. *Brazucas* with green cards and thriving businesses erected canvas pavilions, proud to display their wares. A Portuguese-speaking dentist proffered brochures, as did the Framingham Savings Bank, one of the few banks in the country whose automated teller machines deploy Portuguese-language screens. There was even an evangelical preacher, screaming salvation from a microphone. But no crowd. The day before, in a story "broken" by the *Middlesex News*, the INS indicated it would monitor the event. Although the organizers had spoken hopefully of as many as ten thousand patrons (and extracted an exhibitors' fee commensurate with a throng of that size), fewer than a thousand *brazucas* came to Framingham. In the end, although no busts were made, the expo was a disappointment.

"Look," Deputy Director Whelan insisted, "I don't do weddings, or soccer games, or demonstrations. It's not our policy." Several years ago the INS attempted a raid on a Salvadoran gathering on the Mall in Washington. Instead of a clean, effective demonstration of INS authority, they got chaos. "People ran wild," he recalled, shaking his head at the memory. "They were all over the reflecting pool, knocking tourists over, ruining picnics."

The INS may not do weddings, but it is not averse to a little psychological warfare—and if a well-timed scoop in the *Middlesex News* gets the point across that Framingham is not a haven for illegal *brazucas* and anyone else who enters this country on a tourist visa and decides to just stay, then so be it. For Whelan's small staff, the wake-up call came a few weeks before Labor Day, in July, during the World Cup soccer championship. For weeks, as Brazil advanced in the tournament with victories over Russia, Cameroon, and Sweden, downtown Framingham erupted with whistle-blowing, drum-pounding, and horn-honking *brazuca* delirium. Downtown Framingham—whose retail trade had been pronounced either "dying" or "dead" since Shopper's World opened decades ago—might have been grateful for any sign of vitality. But all that noise, all those girls dancing in their bikinis, all that traffic snarling the railroad crossing—and always just after 5 P.M., when the commuters were just starting to come home from Boston. It was too much! For Framingham, it translates into overtime pay for the cops, angry letters to the *Middlesex News,* and property owners standing up at town meeting demanding, *Who are these people?*

Framingham's immigrant problem can be defined in two words: bilingual education. It costs the town $1.4 million a year to service a polyglot student body, in 1994, just 3 percent of the town's education budget. However, with its bilingual needs growing every year, Framingham is spending more and more servicing immigrants. In 1994, town schools employed thirty-nine full-time bilingual educators, plus a bilingual support staff—guidance counselors, social workers, and school psychologists—of fifteen more.

The numbers, however, are deceptive. Although nearly five dozen different languages are spoken in the homes of Framingham students, only two—Spanish and Portuguese—receive full funding for "bilingual" instruction. Others—everything from Ibo to Urdu—are treated in "transitional" programs, usually in English as a Second Language course. In any given year, between 600 and 700 of some 7,400 kids will be receiving some form of transitional or bilingual instruction, or just under 10 percent of the total enrollment. Most pass into mainstream classes within a few years. But the "cost" of immigrants is hard to quantify because payment for things like building maintenance, busing, and support staff is amortized across entire schools' student bodies. What is more, in many ways immigrant students are a net benefit, at least in terms of state funding. Under the disbursement formula currently used in Massachusetts, foreign students garner $1.40 for every dollar doled out to local school districts for native-born kids. In that way, Framingham's immigrant costs are partially subsidized by neighboring towns, who pay the same state sales and income taxes, but receive less, per capita, for their students. Framingham officials also concede that, in cases where a critical mass of Portuguese or Spanish speakers allows them to group entire classes of immigrant kids together, the cost per capita is also reduced because any new educator hired is entering their system at a pay scale lower than veterans teaching identical classes for native-born children. Thus, the all-Brazilian kindergarten class at Framingham's Potter Road elementary school actually costs the town less than the "American" kindergarten down the hall—while the Brazilian kids "earn" Framingham more from the state.

Nonetheless, Framingham is sitting on a bilingual time bomb. Federal guidelines state that everything from science lab to music to after-school sports must be equally accessible to all students. It's not something Framingham can choose to do or not do. It's the law. In late 1974, the Supreme Court ruled in *Lau vs. Nichols* that "equal access" to a public school education meant non-English-speaking students had to receive service in a language they could learn in. States were free to establish their own guidelines, and Massachusetts, predictably, established bilingual standards that are among the most liberal in the nation. In Massachusetts, any school district with more than twenty students speaking a foreign language has to provide services in that language, systemwide. For bigger cities like Boston, Springfield, and Fall River, there are usually enough students in each language group to justify hiring native speakers as staff. Eugene Thayer, Framingham's school superintendent from 1987 until his retirement in 1996, was recruited from one of those cities, Lawrence, whose district has one of the largest bilingual staffs in the state. Compared to Framingham, Lawrence was relatively uncomplicated, since over 85 percent of its foreign-born students speak Spanish.

The "twenty or more" rule is not much of an obstacle for towns like Lawrence, Mr. Thayer explained in an interview. It can be a nightmare for smaller communities like Framingham with its diverse immigrant enclaves. In 1994, Framingham underwent a state audit of its bilingual and transitional programs. The review document, which runs sixty pages, rated the town school system on a bewildering array of requirements, and found the town lacking in more than a third of them. It found that Framingham was failing its Chinese and Russian students, not only by not instituting bilingual programs in these languages, but in not adequately surveying parents of Russian- and Chinese-speaking students with questionnaires written in their language. Framingham's middle school was cited for not providing access to science labs, "that is at least equal in all respects to those provided for monolingual English speaking students." The district was deemed insufficient in counseling services, despite the hiring of one bilingual psychologist, four bilingual guidance counselors, and three bilingual social workers. "However," the auditors wrote, "of these eight professionals, only one is *bilingual certified*" (emphasis added). Adding insult to injury, the town was told its bilingual recordkeeping was inadequate, and that it had failed to organize enough bilingual parent-teacher organizations.

The audit also left Framingham with a mandate to provide equal services for some twenty Chinese-speaking students. No matter that the twenty were distributed across ten grades or that almost all of them came from homes where English, while not the first language, was widely spoken. "The questionnaire says primary language," Thayer said. "And for most of these homes, Chinese was the primary language."

No matter, either, that the parents of these Chinese-English speakers expressed little desire to educate their children out of the mainstream. In fact, many "immigrant" parents were graduates of top local universities, and were holding engineering jobs in some of the region's new high-tech mills. No matter, either, that the

Russian and Indian parents had successfully steered their children away from bilingual programs. No matter that the 1993 high school valedictorian, Nital Patel, excelled without bilingual instruction. Under the twenty-or-more law, Framingham was compelled to provide services for its Chinese students—everything from kindergarten to physics to phys ed—to every child deemed to be denied "equal access" to the schools.

Ultimately, Framingham was spared the gouging of its budget. Based on the logic that there is not one "Chinese" language but many, Framingham said it lacked the critical mass of sameness that would dictate the provision of services. Superintendent Thayer argued, reasonably, that the same state bureaucrats who list Urdu, Hindi, Tamil, and Bengali—all "Indian" dialects—should recognize distinctions between Fukienese, Cantonese, and Mandarin Chinese. Framingham's "Chinese" students, like its "Indians," were simply too fragmented to merit separate services. "The state granted us the waiver," Thayer explained, with some relief, but left the door open on bilingual Chinese, and later Russian. Essentially, if enough parents stepped forward demanding these services, the town would be compelled to provide them—at a cost Thayer estimated at a minimum of $150,000 a year.

At a parents' organization meeting a few nights later, Superintendent Thayer further explained Framingham's dilemma. Thanks to Proposition 2½—a law Massachusetts voters passed in 1980 that held property tax increases to 2.5 percent of the previous year's assessment—the town's ability to raise tax dollars for its students is limited. At the same time, the post–baby-boom shrinkage that has lowered the population of teenagers means Framingham's student body is younger than ever—and compared to earlier years, heavily foreign-born. Thus, the cap on education spending runs headlong into the state's demand to provide "equal access" to all students, regardless of their background. That means having to find creative solutions to satisfy a body politic that resists spending money on someone else's kids. Particularly if the parents of those kids are undocumented.

One of those is the two-way program, in which elementary students spend seven full years in mixed English-Spanish instruction, in classrooms equally divided between American and immigrant children. The results are impressive, and local taxpayers are enthusiastic. In one third-grade classroom at the Barbieri School, eight year olds conversed easily in both languages. One boy, a Salvadoran immigrant, had become so fluent in English, he was embarrassed by his "bad" Spanish. His teachers said he was a straight-A student in two languages. Framingham runs the two-way program without outside funds, and it has proved so popular there is a waiting list for applicants. In 1995, Framingham planned to fund a second two-way program, in Portuguese.

Ironically, immigration provides Framingham with a tool, the two-way classes, in marketing its school system to affluent suburbanites. Fostering bilingual kids has become part of Framingham's quality-of-life appeal, even if the immigrants for whom special education programs are mandated are largely oblivious to these benefits. None of the Portuguese immigrant parents, the ones born in Portugal, seem to want their children taught in any language but English—they don't want them handicapped when they start work, and besides they don't approve of the Brazilian style of Portuguese being used. On the other hand, few of the Brazilians I spoke with were even aware that their kids, many already exposed to English through television, were being enrolled in Portuguese-only classes. A few parents at the Potter Road School, which I visited on opening day, actually were surprised to see the letters of the alphabet with Portuguese words ("A *avião,* B *barco,* C *carro,* D *dedo* . . .") underneath, and maps of Brazil on the bulletin boards. They weren't disappointed, just surprised. Some expressed annoyance that their kids' school, almost across town where Framingham bounds Sudbury, was so far from their own homes in South Framingham. Busing, it seems, is no more popular integrating Portuguese speakers than it is for anyone else. Clearly little of the push for bilingual aid comes from the community it is intended to serve. And virtually none comes from the *brazucas,* who are much too new in Framingham to lobby for much of anything, and certainly not for cultural sensitivity from the school system.

So where does it come from? The answer is from Americans, chiefly American-born Hispanics. Gene Thayer recalls that in Lawrence, the main long-term users of bilingual programs were Puerto Rican students, whose situation was very different from other Spanish speakers. "You had a situation where a lot of factories would ramp up in the fall, then lay off just before Christmas," he explained. "If you were laid off and qualified for unemployment, you could go home [to Puerto Rico] for the winter and live better on your unemployment check than you could in Lawrence. Then, when they were hiring again, you might come back with your family in the late spring. As a result we saw kids enrolled two or three times in different schools in a single year. They never got exposed to English long enough to not need bilingual instruction."

This, Thayer continued, was not the case with other Latinos, many of whom arrived illegally, who did not have the option of commuting back and forth from their native lands. Their progress was markedly better than the "boomerang" kids, and usually passed out of bilingual programs after only a few years. Out of this very real need of the Puerto Rican students, a bureaucracy was born, and like most bureaucracies, self-perpetuation became one of its goals. Juan Rodriguez, the principal at the Fuller Middle School in Framingham, points to another aspect of the same problem. As Puerto Rico's economy improved in the 1970s and 1980s, a different type of "immigrant" began coming north. Instead of single adults, coming to work and perhaps later sending for their families, a lower class of migrant came to dominate. Abused wives with their children, people trying to escape a drug dependency, misfits unable to find a place in Puerto Rico's emerging manufacturing and tourism-based industries, sought refuge in northern cities. Many of these migrants received public assistance on the island, and passed easily into welfare dependency up north. For these Puerto Ricans, Mr. Rodriguez explained, bilingual education is not only a transitional benefit but a necessary way children of dysfunctional families access a mentor. Others migrated among nearly a dozen Northeast cities where Puerto Rican enclaves provided temporary havens. "People not only go from country to country," Mr. Rodriguez explained. "But all around this area. From Framingham, to Lawrence to Lowell to Holyoke, Springfield, New York and back to Framingham."

Even those who excel in Massachusetts provide no guarantee that others, even from their own family, won't have problems. Mr. Rodriguez's family is a case in point. "Two of my sister's kids, who were born in Framingham, started in bilingual classes," he says, striking a tone somewhere between amused and embarrassed. The admission is startling, for Juan Rodriguez has been a Massachusetts resident for nearly thirty years, arriving in Framingham from Puerto Rico in the eighth grade. Back before *Lau vs. Nichols,* bilingual education was three hours a week, with a single instructor. For the handful of Latino students in Framingham schools at the time, it was a quick and crude passage into the mainstream—in Juan's case, more than enough to prepare him for undergraduate work at Framingham State College, then a master's degree from Fitchburg State. After working for Gene Thayer in Lawrence, he was recruited to come home to Framingham. Today, he sees Brazilian teens, arriving from tiny Minas Gerais towns, who haven't completed even a year of school. "They have normal intelligence, sometimes they are very intelligent," he says. "But no exposure. For them it's a twofold problem: no language and no school."

And yet, Principal Rodriguez says that many families, including Spanish speakers, simply refuse to send their children into bilingual programs. He says that the Russian, Chinese, Indian, and Korean kids whose transitional instruction more closely imitates his own experience—ad hoc tutoring several hours each week—tend to enter the mainstream sooner than students immersed in full bilingual programs.

For Framingham, the dilemma of bilingual education is, What works? Full immersion is cheaper and considered more "progressive," but it also engenders dependency, which makes it more costly in the long run. The Brazilians, few of whom are property owners, do not contribute as much as it costs to educate their children. On the other hand, they may be contributing more to the town's economy than the Puerto Rican families—many on welfare—who seem more adept than immigrants at wringing public services and tend to be more interested in having their kids taught in Spanish. No Brazilian I spoke with expects the school system to preserve his or her child's cultural integrity—yet immigrants are cited for inflating the cost of educating Framingham's children.

In a real sense, Framingham's immigrant dilemma is the same one faced by the immigrants themselves. It is a problem of an inefficient market. Framingham allows immigrants to profit from their labor, but cannot efficiently tap those profits for the town's own development. The immigrants, mostly undocumented, are unable to leave the underground cash economy. So, instead of leveraging earnings with a mortgage or a small-business loan in America, Hermes Reis is forced to spend his savings in Brazil—where credit is simply unavailable to common working families and where everyday dollar inflation outraces his earnings.

"It's what the Spaniards discovered in the sixteenth century," Abelardo Arantes, Boston's Brazilian consul, explains. "They were taking so much silver back from America, but Spain itself did not change. The result was silver inflation—more and more money chasing the same things. So everything got more expensive."

Arantes estimates that a hundred thousand Brazilians are caught in this syndrome. Brazil's reluctance to provide dual citizenship to expatriates compounds the problem. "It's the green card syndrome," he says. "They want to come to the surface, but it is not easy." The only Brazilians currently legalizing themselves are the children of immigrants—about seven hundred a year now. He has noticed that more parents are registering their children with American names—Tiffany instead of Terezhina, Johnny in place of João—a sign of America's pull. "If the parents could be citizens," Arantes says, "then you would see a permanent change. But for now, they say they will only stay until they have enough money to go home. But you can see, it is getting harder and harder to go home."

Hermes Reis's first son, Luiz Felipe, was born in 1992. Hermes Jr. followed two years later. Both pregnancies kept Jeni from working, but gave the Reis family a modicum of protection. Now, of four family members, three were legal. Nonetheless, in 1994 the INS came calling for Mrs. Reis and, despite appealing to an immigration court for special relief, deportation proceedings were begun against her. After almost ten years in America, despite two U.S.-born children and his own prospects of becoming a naturalized citizen, Hermes faced a difficult choice: stay and live underground, or leave. Appearing before an immigration court in August 1995, the Reis family was presented with one other choice. If Hermes would agree to become a naturalized citizen, he could sponsor his wife for a green card. She would be married to an American. On the spot, he accepted the deal.

But something happened, and later that year, Hermes, Jeni, and their two sons disappeared. His phone in Framingham was disconnected, and no one in town knew where to find him. The following February he turned up in Ipatinga.

As disappointing as the Reis family's departure may have been, it did not detract from the good things that were happening in Framingham. "Downtown" was still a euphemism for "ghetto," or "depressed," but business was picking up. The old Bancroft Cap factory, nearly vacant in 1994, was filled in 1996, with a waiting list of tenants eager to enter. Hollis Street, since the 1960s a name synonymous with "blight," was also without a vacancy, with many old-line businesses draping Brazilian flags in their windows, recognition of the immigrant revival. Across the street from Framingham's first Latino grocery, an old frame house had been freshly painted. Today it houses a clinic, started by a Cuban pediatrician who had transplanted his practice from Miami. A 1920s-era office building facing Concord Street, also mostly vacant for decades, was now full. There was a branch office of a Boston-based home-care referral agency, a big employer of immigrants, and two more Brazilian import shops. During 1995, two *mineira* women opened a tiny garment factory—stitching stacks of cut felt into mittens. "A Chinese woman brings them on Monday from Boston," one explained over the whir of a sewing machine. "We finish them and she pays us on Friday." Incredibly, manufacturing, albeit in sweatshop form, had returned.

Something else was returning to downtown—home ownership. On Torrey Street, one of those side streets within earshot of the Dennison plant, the Quintelas—Andre, Edwin, Xakvel, Flavio, Aguinello, Marcus, and Marcus, Jr., six brothers and one brother's son, are a veritable urban renewal project.

Like Hermes Reis, the Quintelas come from Ipatinga. Like Hermes, they clean homes—and offices and the multiscreen cinemas attached to the cluster of Route 9 malls. All told, some thirty members of an extended family are employed in seven different cleaning businesses, working from early dawn until just after midnight, somewhere. Active members of Padre Roque's parish at Saint Tarcisius, the Quintelas have become prolific home-buyers, acquiring rundown two-family duplexes out of foreclosure from a local bank. They bought three between 1994 and 1996. The Quintelas long realized downtown properties could be had at bargain prices, but they needed to be legalized before they could buy. By becoming citizens, they broke the cycle of repatriating dollars for homes they would never enjoy in Brazil. Thus, when they're not cleaning someone else's castle, they're on Torrey Street, putting sweat equity into one of their own. "We pay less to own than we would to rent," Marcus Jr. explained, shouting over the buzz of a power saw one hot summer evening.

Marcus Quintela, a former bank teller in Ipatinga, is a living example of the difference between the underground—and underdeveloped—immigrant economy and the prosperity waiting for all immigrants who join the mainstream. As long as the family was dealing in cash, sending dollars home to chase (and spawn) everinflating building costs, they could never catch up. But that same money, as a down payment, permits the Quintelas to buy on credit, and swiftly pay down a mortgage on terms—three hundred dollars a month—most in Framingham would consider pocket change. As the good news of citizenship spreads through Padre Roque's congregation, other Brazilian families are eyeing properties. As they start buying, and they are starting, depressed Framingham will disappear, practically overnight.

Out of the era of decline, something new is rising. Even the empty Dennison plant on Howard Street offers a potent reminder of what could come. Steve Herring, a researcher with the local Historical Society, points out that by the year Dennison arrived in Framingham, 1897, manufacturing in Framingham had already passed its peak. Yet Dennison Manufacturing endured long after the Robb-Mumford Boiler Company, the Framingham Chair Company, and the Minard Liniment Company (makers of the "King of Pain" balm) had passed from the scene. And even when Dennison was the world's biggest paper goods company, industries like transportation, construction, education, and health care were already overtaking manufacturing as contributors to Framingham's wealth. So it's intriguing today to stroll the main corridor of the Dennison building on Howard Street and see the last names stenciled in black letters on the frosted white glass of executive offices. It's a parade of Framingham ethnics, starting with K. M. O'Donohue and R. F. MacCahran in the middle suites, falling away to Sastavickas, Giglio, Minasian, and Zinck the farther one goes from the center of authority. The last, and smallest, office on the corridor belonged to H. F. Estrada, presumably Dennison's first Latino manager, installed only in the final years before the plant closed.

Somewhere in the next wave, a new product may emerge that will suddenly make this old plant—near a railroad, near a church, near a pool of workaholic *brazucas*—the perfect place to strike gold. One manager whose name does not appear on glass is Sushil Bhatia, an Indian immigrant born in the Punjab. Sushil worked at Dennison from 1976 to 1981 as a manager for new product development, then returned to India to establish Dennison's sales operations there. He returned to Framingham permanently four years later, primarily concerned with getting a proper education for his three children. While working at Dennison, he earned an M.B.A. at Suffolk University, Boston's legendary Bootstrap U. He was with Dennison when Avery International bought the company in 1990. When Avery began downsizing, he left, taking a piece of Dennison with him.

Today he runs JMD Manufacturing Inc., a tiny shop located in the old Bancroft Cap Company facility on Fountain Street. It had two employees in 1993; today it has seven—but has so many orders most of its work is farmed out to other factories in Framingham. Like the boss, all seven are foreign-born—two each from the Dominican Republic and India, three more from El Salvador, Belgium, and Cameroon.

The international nature of JMD is no afterthought. The business Sushil Bhatia took from Avery Dennison was low-tech labeling equipment, a simple spring-and-sprinkle apparatus that can slap a label onto a box rolling off an assembly line. "Most modern factories use a jet-ink spray," Bhatia explains, "and don't use this old technology. But in the Third World, there are hundreds of factories that still do."

Where Dennison saw obsolescence, Bhatia saw an opportunity. With the downsizing, he offered to buy the low-tech coding division from Dennison, and got his former employers to help finance the sale. "It was essentially a leveraged buyout," he recalls. Taking little more than the rights to various Dennison brand names and a few spring printers unassembled in boxes, JMD's real asset was the customer list, spread across four continents. Sushil himself hit the road to India and China, old haunts where he knew he could sell.

JMD has not only thrived in three years—with annual sales doubling to nearly $1 million by 1996—it has spawned a second firm: Imagex Technologies. This new company holds proprietary technology, developed by Bhatia himself, for an "office paper de-copier." Imagex uses a chemical-mechanical method to remove toner from photocopied white paper. Either as a paper-saver or as a security device—no more shredding sensitive documents— Imagex technology, Bhatia predicts, is the latest innovation in office technology, potentially as essential as the desktop computer or the facsimile machine. For Framingham, it could conceivably be the next Prime Computer or Bose or Genzyme Transgenics.

Or it could be an utter disaster. What matters is Sushil Bhatia and the human capital he represents. His knowledge of India and his confidence that an old product still could be marketed from Framingham kept a relic of Dennison Manufacturing alive. In November 1994, Sushil Bhatia was elected president of Framingham's Rotary Club. For a year he dedicated himself to organizing fund raisers for scholarships, joining Massachusetts trade missions on their forays abroad (including one to India), and presiding over the monthly Rotary luncheon at Ken's Steak House, a Framingham institution on Route 9. At one session, Sushil Bhatia kicked off a round of donations by stuffing a wad of cash into a plaster piggy bank. It's a tradition of Rotary chapters that requires the donor to cite the recent good news that inspires the offering. Sushil cited Devali, the Hindu "Festival of Lights," and start of Hindu year 2051.

How things had changed. In 1954, the year my parents helped found Framingham's Temple Beth Am, the Festival of Lights would have been Hanukkah, probably something exotic and strange to their Yankee neighbors. Today Hanukkah is a normal American holiday, as demonstrated by the construction-paper decorations in all the elementary school classrooms. Someday Devali will be, too.

How comforting, too, to know Framingham's tradition of religious inclusion endures. Sushil Bhatia attends the local Shri Lakshmi Temple, one of the largest Hindu temples in the East. On a picture-perfect fall afternoon, Shri Lakshmi emerged from a forest clearing bigger and brighter than any other "church" in town. Towering over the bright foliage were elaborately sculpted Krishnas and concrete elephant deities. Shri Lakshmi has four full-time priests living with their families on temple grounds. Inside the sanctuary, burning incense bathes a steady stream of worshipers in a warm mist. In 1994, as in 1954, as in 1844, a house of worship was smoothing the arrival of another of Framingham's immigrant enclaves. Downstairs, in a large kitchen, Hindu women prepared a

Devali feast, in a space identical to the one where Temple Beth Am's Sisterhood staged mass Passover seders for the kids attending religious classes on Saturday. The only difference was Temple Beth Am didn't have a rack of photocopied flyers, colored papers advertising everything from cheap long-distance calls back to India, to discount sarees, to private meditation services.

As the families began filling the sanctuary, Shri Lakshmi glowed in a soft New England sunset, the kind that turns the colors of a New England autumn into heartbreaking hues of gold and crimson. All over Framingham at that hour, kids were coming home to dinner. Later they would do homework and somewhere, even if it was just one kid, someone would learn that a child of Framingham was the first American to die in the Revolution. And no matter where they or their parents were born, they would know they belong here.

Which brings us back to Hermes Reis, new American. On the Fourth of July, 1996, an ecstatic telephone call from Massachusetts provided a happy ending to the Reis family saga. The day before, he was one of a hundred and ninety new citizens sworn in at a ceremony held at historic Fanueil Hall. "It was so beautiful," he gushed. "To be part of that room, just to hear we were all Americans now." There were Chinese, he said, and Russians and one or two Portuguese. As far as Hermes could tell, he was the only *mineiro* there that day, the lone Brazilian among immigrants from twenty-six countries represented in the ceremony. The keynote speech was delivered by Joyce London Alexander, chief U.S. magistrate judge for the state. "You have now been afforded the same rights, privileges, and immunities which every citizen of America possesses," she told Hermes and the 189 others. "But with these rights come responsibilities. You must vote. You must serve on juries. You must be involved in the uplifting of neighborhoods where you live and you must be involved for the 'common good' of all of America's citizens."

The "common good," the judge went on, found its roots in history. "This country opens its arms to you today, and you can give something back to it," the speech concluded. "That is to help someone else along the way. The notion that each of us has a responsibility to our fellow men and women is in fact a principle which will serve you well on your citizenship journey. Remember that this is the greatest nation in the world."

Outside, as representatives of the League of Women Voters passed out voter registration forms, Hermes searched for a familiar face. One brother had come to see him, but for now his wife and children remain in Brazil. He had waited for months for a letter confirming he had passed the citizenship test, he explained, but during the federal government's shutdown that January, the Immigration and Naturalization Service suspended many operations. The letter didn't come until May, long after Hermes had fled home. Hermes didn't even have time to sell his lists of home-cleaning customers.

Something no Brazilian at home would find unusual, government inefficiency, cost the Reis family thousands of dollars and months of anxiety. But on Independence Day there were no hard feelings. "As soon as I get my business back, I'm sending for Jeni and the boys," Hermes said that morning. He figured he needed twenty thousand dollars to reestablish himself in Framingham, about what he thought he could raise selling his holdings in Ipatinga. "This is what God wants for me," he concluded, sounding unsure whether to laugh or cry. "To be here."

CHAPTER EIGHT

Paranoia Redux:
California's New Majority

The troubles on what we might call the Eastern Pacific Rim raise the risk that fear will restrict the flow of people to the US from Asia. . . . Americans of all races understand that the US does not do immigrants a favour by issuing visas. Immigrants do the US the favour of their talents and skills.

Editorial response to the Rodney King riots,
Far East Economic Review, May 14, 1992

★

It was in 1992, just after the riots that swept Los Angeles in the wake of the verdict in the Rodney King trial. In the mayhem that followed the acquittal of the white police officers, hundreds of Korean- and Chinese-owned businesses were sacked and looted by a mostly African-American mob. It was not the reports of alien hooligans on the loose that gave Californians the borders-out-of-control shakes. It was something home grown, something of themselves. After the dust had settled, a Hong Kong magazine, the *Far East Economic Review*, weighed in with a bitter editorial. Woven between outrage over the acquittal of the white officers and sorrow for the riot's Asian victims was a judgmental tone that exuded the aloof attitude of the colonist; the tone was that of the German-born coffee planter in El Salvador, clucking at the brutality of "the natives." The message from Hong Kong was stern, even scolding, recalling a century's worth of Yankee editorials endorsing the dispatch of Marines to protect "our" interests in the Caribbean. It was titled "Eastern Pacific Troubles."

"For Asian business people, the rioting in Los Angeles was a grotesque case of being the wrong entrepreneurial group at the wrong place at the wrong time," the piece intoned. The rioters "made special targets of Korean groceries, Cambodian shops and Indian newsstands. Asians endured a disproportionate share of the killings, injuries and looting because they took the risk of operating in the tougher parts of the city."

The editorial issued a call for America to get its house in order or else endure the refusal of Asians to come to California. "This is not just a matter for white and black America, or even just for Americans," it continued. "The troubles on what we might call the Eastern Pacific Rim raise the risk that fear will restrict the flow of people to the US from Asia, the largest source of the country's immigrants in recent years. Just as free markets for capital require liberal financial rules, free markets for labour require the legal possibility of emigration, including the assurance of tolerance, starting with physical safety."

Was the writer threatening something here? Korean aircraft carriers riding at anchor off Long Beach? Gurkhas patrolling the streets of South Central? Now "our" interests were defined by foreigners demanding protection from American savages. Our banks support your fiscal deficit, the piece implied, our people colonize your ghettos. We are becoming you, the piece murmured under its breath, and you are not treating us right.

"Eastern Pacific Troubles" was a remarkable statement. "Asians will assess how welcome they feel in the US," it warned, adding that physical safety was not the only consideration now. America's prosperity relative to Asia's own was also becoming a factor. As Asia advances, the lure of Los Angeles wanes. Thus the Eastern Pacific Rim should worry about itself. "Americans of all races understand that the US does not do immigrants a favour by issuing visas," the piece concluded. "Immigrants do the US the favour of their talents and skills. A country built by recent arrivals for more than two centuries cannot afford to declare itself unsafe for today's most energetic, productive and valued immigrants."

Of course California is under no threat of military intervention, from Asia or from anywhere else. The warning in "Eastern Pacific Troubles" also signaled a great faith. "The economically or politically oppressed need America as a safety valve," the piece affirmed, placing a salve neatly between the "physical safety" and the "favour." California's colonization will take place as it always has—slowly, gradually, completely. Third- and fourth-generation immigrants won't be like the German coffee grower, who, even today, still keeps a German passport handy and is likely to send his children to German universities. Long before the gunboats arrive offshore, the Chinese, Cambodian, Indian, and Korean immigrants will have already become Americans.

In fact, Asians are among the quickest of all newcomers to become citizens, and have been for as long as they have been coming to America. As for sending their children home to study, that is almost unheard of. Indeed, sending their children to American universities is one rationale for Asian immigration in the first place. Throughout California, minicolonies of "parachute kids," dropped in as an advance guard of Asia's richest and most ambitious families, are populated by teenage scholars, working desperately to master English so they can apply for entrance to a prestigious U.S. institution. For all our inferiority complexes regarding Asians, it is the Asians who validate our lifestyle, becoming more American than the natives. They won't, as many Americans abroad do, refer to themselves as "ex-pats." How could they? Immigrants in America, by definition, are joiners.

Californians know this. They ride through cities where Asians have become the majority. Every day they see whole boulevards where all the businesses are owned by Chinese, Koreans, or Vietnamese. They see the names of candidates—Chan, Chen, Kim, Tanaka, Tran, and Nguyen—running for the schoolboard and city council. They sit in traffic, staring at the ads on bus benches that announce movies in Chinese. They sit behind buses staring at the ads for a newspaper whose text they cannot read—Sing Tao, a paper from Hong Kong—which has more than a million North American readers, almost as many as *USA Today* or *The Wall Street Journal*.

Whatever the pessimistic overtones of "Eastern Pacific Troubles," the Asian presence in California is less a warning than a reminder. A talented generation of Far Eastern immigrants has chosen California for renewal, their own and ours. Asia's prosperous middle class will not suddenly abandon its American dream. If anything, immigration is going to increase, and for all the best reasons.

California may be Latin America's safety valve, but it is also Asia's backyard. Not "backyard" in the imperial sense—a sphere of influence enforced by armed might. No, backyard in the American sense—a sphere of barbecue grills and swimming pools. Even as California becomes more crowded, as it endures another of its periodic "paranoia deluxe" crises over immigration, the immigrants themselves are optimistic. Despite the Rodney King riots, their comfort level with the state reached new highs in the 1990s. The evidence is everywhere, in the rise of dozens of new Asian towns spilling out from Los Angeles, San Francisco, San Diego, and San Jose.

The Carquinez Strait, the estuary that carries the Sacramento River down into the northern lobe of San Francisco Bay, is one of several streams carrying Asian colonization inland. Traveling upriver from Vallejo, at the mouth of the estuary, a wave of Asian settlement is passing through Benicia, then Martinez, Concord, Pittsburg, and Antioch, hopscotching back and forth across the water—in Contra Costa County on the south side, Solano County on the north. Beyond this central artery, a second wave is filling one-time farmland, in places like Brentwood, Suisun City, Fairfield, and Oakley. You need only study a map to see what is to become of the East Bay. Sometime in the next century the metropolis will stretch all the way east to meet other growing centers like Sacramento, San Jose, and Stockton, themselves swelling outward on a tide of Asian immigration. Sometime in the coming century, this wave of humanity will completely deisolate the San Francisco pen-

insula and create a new city that stretches from the Pacific Rim to
the heart of the Central Valley. In other words, a "city" more populous than most of the world's independent states, and bigger than
any other on the continent. A city, in other words, that looks like
one of the great Pacific cities—Manila, Jakarta, Bangkok, Hong
Kong, Los Angeles.

Until very recently, places like Pittsburg and Brentwood and
Antioch had more in common with rural centers like Napa or Davis
than cosmopolitan San Francisco. Yet, because of overcrowding
and California's addiction to the automobile, even these towns have
fallen into the category of "bedroom" community, with most of
their working adults commuting outside the county to their jobs.
Some days, the commute from Pittsburg to the peninsula can be
as long as three hours—almost an hour of which will be consumed
simply trying to get out of Pittsburg and onto the feeder express-
ways. After perhaps another thirty minutes driving at relatively high ,
speed past the brushed-felt pastures of cattle country, the motorist
can expect to crawl through a second endless hour down to one of
the cross-bay bridges.

In some ways, the Asian suburb is a purely California phenomenon, a new culture created almost whole between the freeway
exits. Even New York, which counts a handful of Japanese enclaves
in the suburbs, hasn't experienced this wave of immigrant sub-
urbanization—that is, of a suburb being absorbed by immigration
as opposed to immigrants being absorbed by the suburbs. Japanese
towns like Fort Lee, New Jersey, are not immigrant towns. They
are bedrooms for Japanese expatriates serving their companies'
New York offices. Fort Lee has Japanese stores and Japan-friendly
services like travel agencies and day-care centers, but little Japanese
involvement with the town.

However, this purely California phenomenon is not entirely
unprecedented. A similar transformation occurred along the East
Coast some fifty years ago, when white ethnics, especially Jews,
began leaving the cities for the suburbs. Just as the Chinese, Koreans, Filipinos, and Southeast Asians are doing today in California,
men and women of the postwar generation created whole new

"Jewish" suburbs, sometimes to the consternation of the original residents. The "Jewing" of the eastern suburbs would have seemed as threatening then as the Pacific wave seems today.

Like the Jewish exodus of decades past, today's Asian migration represents the great escape from the cities. What is different now is that the city is no longer simply Los Angeles, San Diego, or San Francisco. It may just as easily be Manila, Hong Kong, or Bangkok. Unlike the Jewish wave of the 1950s and 1960s, the Asian invasion that started in California in the 1970s and 1980s was unique because so many of its settlers were arriving directly from Asia itself. They were bypassing the stop-over in the American city. Los Angeles's "new" suburbs include Monterey Park, Long Beach, El Monte, and San Marino. In the Bay Area, Union City, Fremont, Daly City, Hercules, and Brisbane suddenly became places where Anglos begin to feel like an endangered species.

The new majority is often a single Asian group—Taiwanese in Monterey Park and Daly City, Vietnamese in Long Beach, Koreans in Hacienda Heights and Garden Grove. In 1980, Monterey Park, a majority Anglo suburb in the San Gabriel Valley, counted Asians as just 15 percent of its residents, according to that year's census, out of a population of just over fifty-four thousand. Blacks were practically nonexistent, but Hispanics outnumbered Asians by about two to one. By the summer of 1985, "Asianization" was in full swing. That summer, both Chinese and Anglos felt embattled, and threatened by the future each feared the other plotted for the town. In public hearings Anglo residents insisted on an "English only" agenda, not just in the schools and town offices, but on all commercial advertisement on city streets. The big Chinese billboards were garish, people complained, and distracting to motorists. The town's almost all-white police force worried about a rise in Asian gang activity. Asians accused police of needlessly harassing Asian businesses, conducting raids on several restaurants, and even staging a late-night bust of the town's leading Chinese-language newspaper.

Monterey Park had elected its first Chinese-born mayor, Lily Lee Chen, that year. But she was anything but a unifying figure.

An ugly smear campaign that began during the election campaign linked her to shadowy real estate speculators, often portrayed in Asian caricature, in crude handbills stuffed into mailboxes or inside screen doors. Even the Chinese, many of them ethnic Taiwanese opposed to the island's ruling Kuomintang Party, distrusted her. They said she was elected as a front for Taiwan's rulers, with money funneled to her father, a prominent Taiwanese businessman. All the infighting bewildered the Anglos, who sniped away at the new-comers on call-in radio shows and letters to area newspapers. "Will the last American to leave Monterey Park remember to take the flag?" demanded one angry citizen, in a bitter broadside printed in the local *Valley Daily Tribune*.

Yet Monterey Park was not changing as much as its old-time residents feared. Indeed, few of its old-timers could even claim to have been born in the town. Before 1965, Monterey Park was a sleepy village of orange groves about to become a bedroom com-munity feeding Los Angeles, just ten miles west. The Asians came because Monterey Park was only ten minutes from Chinatown, and because it had hills, especially prized by Chinese who regard ele-vation, virtually unknown to home buyers in Hong Kong or Taipei, as the next best thing to open space. They precipitated a land boom, and that made some locals rich. It's just that it happened so fast.

Ten years later the boom in Monterey Park had peaked. The town's population growth had leveled off at a little over sixty-one thousand, about the rate it had grown before the Asian invasion. Now, however, almost 65 percent of its residents claimed Chinese descent. The Anglo population was about half its former size, while the Hispanic population had actually increased. Yet the garish Chi-nese billboards along Atlantic Boulevard (note: not Pacific) were gone, as were the traffic jams and much of the ethnic rancor. Prob-ably the only lasting change was the run-up in home values, from a median price of just under $100,000 in 1980, to around $250,000 today. The schools remained American, the main streets were still Garvey and Garfield, not Guangdong or Guangzhou. By now the winds of change had already moved eastward, sweeping through towns like El Monte and Pomona. Monterey Park seemed like any of those other, older Los Angeles suburbs where residents pretend to remember when there were orange groves where the freeway is now. The population had changed, but not much else.

Monterey Park is one model, and there are others. Sometimes Asianization occurs like a rolling tide, the city simply extending itself over its boundaries. South of San Francisco, the suburbs of South San Francisco, Brisbane, and Daly City become almost indistinguishable from the metropolis. Their homes roll out in tight, dense rows, just like the city proper.

Sometimes the transformation occurs farther out from the urban core, where the new majority overwhelms a sleepy Anglo suburb, doubling its population in less than a decade. This second model is especially prevalent in the Bay Area, where the burst of population over the eastern hills began spilling into Contra Costa, Santa Clara, and Solano Counties during the 1970s. Twenty years later, the migration shows no sign of abating. The little town of Hercules, a haven for Filipinos in the northeast corner of the Bay, grew from less than seven thousand to just over twenty thousand people between 1980 and 1995. Benicia, a little farther out, grew from about fifteen thousand to almost twenty-eight thousand during that same period. In both places the Asian wave propelled growth.

Mass colonization is not entirely new. New towns had arrived, fully born, outside cities before. The famous Levittown tract-home communities that rose outside Philadelphia and New York in the 1940s and 1950s were similar in some ways. Like the Asian suburbs, they were marketed directly to ethnic migrants. William Levitt and the developers who followed him deliberately targeted Jewish World War II veterans who, with their G.I.-bill college degrees and access to federally backed mortgages, became instant candidates for home ownership in the suburbs. After the Korean War, a second wave of instant suburbanites was targeted.

The new Asian Levittowns of California are living off a similar postwar boom. The miracle economies of Asia emerged during the Cold War, their growth driven by what were essentially war industries. In suburbs like Long Beach and Westminster, where Cambodians and Vietnamese are the new majority, many of the newcomers are also, literally, war veterans. Like the World War II veterans back East, many Asian immigrants actually owe their professional training as engineers, doctors, and educators to America's long involvement in Asian wars. Which also explains why these instant suburbanites enjoyed visa preference when the wars ended.

So, just as the builders of the Eastern suburbs thrived on the benefits of one war boom, so do new boomers from Asia. Take Korea. In the decade after hostilities ended, Korean industry took off, largely thanks to U.S. economic and security assistance. Hundreds of villages disappeared under concrete and steel, and thousands of villagers entered cities for the first time. Most villagers were well compensated (who wanted another class struggle after warring with the Communists?), and quickly converted proceeds from the sale of farmland into educations for their children. The Korean immigrants working as storekeepers, dry cleaners, and wholesalers are all first-generation modernists, who trace their migration to families that made a killing selling farm property to the growing *chaebols,* the government-sponsored combines.

But the miracle was incomplete. In Korea, as elsewhere in Asia, wealth was growing under the security umbrella. Yet social development—democracy, individual expression, and consumerism— lagged far behind. These were, after all, war economies. Thus, the burst of consumer freedom Americans achieved in the 1950s and 1960s were unavailable to Asia's postwar baby boomers, unless they came to America to get it. That they came to open grocery stores and dry cleaning shops, forsaking "respectable" careers back home, is almost immaterial. These were boomers with middle-class expectations, seeking middle-class communities to fulfill them.

And Korea was lucky. Taiwan, until the early 1990s, was in a state of permanent war, not postwar. Vietnam was defeated. So it is not surprising that many in California's biggest Asian community

also were war veterans. Coming to America was the original passage
to the mother country. For this generation of Asians, as for the
Senegalese and Mexicans, America is the mother country of choice,
not law. For Filipinos it is a legal relationship. For fifty years the
Philippine islands were America's colony wrested away after centuries of Spanish rule. Many Filipinos, in fact, were U.S. servicemen, either uniformed soldiers and sailors, or stewards, cooks, and
other support staff on U.S. bases. Hundreds of Filipino women
became "war brides," married to U.S. servicemen stationed in Subic Bay Naval Station or Clark Air Base. War brides helped establish northern California's first Filipino beachheads, using the family
reunification provisions of the 1965 immigration law when their
husbands rotated stateside. The roots of Filipino towns like Vallejo
or Pittsburg are found in Vallejo's Mare Island Naval Shipyard
or Pittsburg's Camp Stoneman, where Filipinos ran the mess or
shined officers' boots. Eventually, these working-class Filipinos
grew to a mass of dollar-earning U.S. residents, attracting Filipino
elites eager to service the country's exported middle class.

The immigrants' propensity to save, and to treat home ownership as a savings mechanism, drew them to the Asian towns.
There development companies were building a new version of Levittown in planned townhouse communities, usually on recent farmland within easy reach of the freeway. Sometimes the builders
found Asian money had preceded them. Since the 1950s, wealthy
citizens of Taiwan and Hong Kong lived in fear of a Communist
takeover, and looked for safe haven in America. Since the mid-
1980s, Chinese, Korean, and Filipino developers have marketed
their Asians towns directly to buyers in Asia. In a reversal of the
Bairro Vale Verde phenomenon in Brazil, these towns became the
bank accounts of Asia's elite. The Philippines' Lopez and Ayala
clans sheltered millions of dollars in California real estate during
the turbulent 1980s, in effect creating offshore accounts managed
by offshore accountants, their "co-ethnic" tenants: expatriate Filipinos living in California. Like immigrant enclaves everywhere,
these towns grew as one immigrant followed another. Eventually,
the critical mass created its own gravitational pull. Asian banks

crossed the Pacific to serve their customers, and followed them from the city to the outlying towns—which fed more home-buying and brought more immigrants. In the process, a new kind of town emerged.

Nearly a quarter million Filipinos had settled in the Bay Area by 1990, about a third of their population nationwide. By 1994, they had surpassed Chinese Americans in the San Francisco metropolitan area. Everywhere they settled, Filipinos outworked their Asian counterparts, with women migrants heavily concentrated in nursing and related medical fields. A Filipino family is more likely to have two adult wage-earners working outside the home than either Korean, Indian, or Chinese families. All those two-income families began moving off the San Francisco peninsula in the late 1970s, first reclaiming slum districts in Oakland and surrounding Alameda County, then pushing out over the freeways into Contra Costa and Solano Counties. By the mid-1990s, some sixty thousand Filipino immigrants were entering Contra Costa County each year, enough to create a new Filipino town every twelve months. Hercules, the county's fastest growing town through the 1980s, was nearly one third Filipino. Vallejo, just across the estuary in Solano County, expanded by thirty thousand over a fifteen-year period. One of every three newcomers was a Filipino.

The Filipino wave is especially ironic, since, like the Mexicans and Central Americans who have swamped the state, Filipinos also share Spanish surnames. Reading a telephone or business directory in Vallejo, Hercules, Antioch, or Pittsburg, it's impossible to know whether Lopez or Valenzuela is Filipino or Latino.

Larry Shinigawa, a professor of Asian studies at Sonoma State University, has been studying the rise of the Asian towns. He divides them into two categories: the pan-Asian suburb, and the ethnic specific town. "These are self-sustaining Asian communities, which is different from what happens on the East Coast," he says. "On the West Coast they are self-sufficient. Part of it is the jobs they have here, part of it is the rise of transnational trade. There has been the creation of a critical mass. Once you get past fifteen percent of the population [in a town], people really notice. And that has its own juggernaut effect. It's not isolation, but it does create a community. So pretty soon you have a viable source of jobs. They have a middle class, lower class, and upper class. You have infrastructure, plus class composition. In other words, the creation of a new village."

Professor Shinigawa points to the East Bay Asian Local Development Corporation as a prime mover in what has become a widespread phenomenon. "They provide low-income housing, ten or twelve stories tall, below is parking and a slew of shopping centers," he says, adding that a place like Oakland, with its mixed Filipino-Chinese population, is becoming the quintessential modern Chinatown: a piece of America where over half the businesses are somehow involved in shipping product in and out of Asia. The shippers divide two ways: Chinese importers bringing cheap manufactured goods in, Filipino *balikbayan* sending expensive finished goods out. Housing above is for the old folks, parking below for their kids visiting from the suburbs. "The typical shopping mall in America doesn't look like that," he says. "That is Vallejo ten years from now."

The Filipino ethnic specific town may be the most complete multiclass village because Filipinos have had the luxury of being all things in America. The "typical" Filipino immigrant is the smiling houseboy to the admiral, or the West Point-trained officer. Or he is the *manong*, the Filipino farmworker forbidden by California race laws from marrying an Anglo woman, or the *pensionado*, enrolled at a U.S. university. Filipinos, in the 1950s and 1960s, were among the first Asian-American professionals—doctors, attorneys, engineers, and bankers. Then again, any punk knows the next best thing to a switchblade is a Filipino "butterfly," a fold-over weapon that cuts like a razor. Uniquely, Filipinos have existed within America's own confusion about place and race. Doctors and lawyers, but also boxers and dishwashers. Professor Shinigawa describes it as "living between competing paradigms." Like it or not, they have to live up to, or live down, the "model minority" image. "But Filipinos are at the cusp of a lot of identities: Hispanic, American, and also the paradigm of 'racial minority,' " he says. "Japanese and Koreans and Chinese did all those working-class jobs, too, but those weren't defining jobs. Filipinos are still stigmatized by images of the working class. There is the possibility of them associating with working-class racial minorities."

The possibility, in other words, of being Rafael Santos. Born during World War II, when Japan occupied the islands, Santos knew nothing but poverty in his little village of La Paz de Tarlac. When he was eighteen, he enlisted in the U.S. Navy, shipping out for basic training in San Diego. "Because I wasn't a citizen I had limited security clearance," he explains. "Now it's different, you do your basic training, you can do anything: seaman's apprentice, yeoman, corpsman. But not in my case. I did what the Filipinos and black Americans did: serve food and cook."

Half of Santos's fellow recruits at the Navy Steward School were like him, young "Flips" from the islands. After basic training, he was assigned to the Naval Air Station in Jacksonville, Florida. That was in 1961. Traveling by bus to his new duty station, he saw something he never could have imagined back home. "I thought America was heaven on earth," he says. "But by the time I passed Texas, the bathrooms were separate. The black people wanted me to go to the white bathroom, but I am not white! The white people said use the black one. That is the joke for Filipinos: we are white and black at the same time."

Santos spent twenty years in the military, mostly cleaning officers' rooms and serving meals on ships and bases. From Jacksonville he went to Bremerton, Washington, then to Hawaii and back to California. Along the way he managed officers' clubs and an enlisted men's mess. Everywhere he worked, "Flips" like Santos could expect to be, if not exactly scorned, then not exactly accepted, either. "You work there, but you enter through the service entrance," Santos says. "You don't use the front door."

By 1974, he had risen to a desk job, clerk in the navy's human resources division in Alameda. Ironically, his assignment was conducting surveys on military race relations. After retiring, Santos took a job with the postal service, availing himself of the veteran's preference in civil service hires. It's the same way hundreds of Filipino stewards and their families lifted themselves from greasy kitchens into California's burgeoning Asian middle class. Santos spent five years with the post office, launching a catering business on weekends. He settled outside Vallejo, where Rafael's Steak House and Bar became a popular nightspot for Filipino Americans, as well as for the servicemen at nearby Mare Island Naval Shipyard. He also bought two homes, and put four children through college, where they learned to use words, like "paradigm," that mean nothing to him after a lifetime in the kitchen. "It's just the policy of the navy," he shrugs. "Because we are not citizens, we are brought to do the jobs that citizens don't like. For me it was a blessing in disguise. I learned my trade and prospered."

Pittsburg, California, is one of many dying blue-collar towns on the Carquinez Strait that is coming to life with Filipino immigration. According to the 1990 census, about 10 percent of Pittsburg's twenty-one thousand households were Filipino-born, a percentage that probably doubled by mid-decade. For Pittsburg, an influx of Filipinos means a critical mass of commuting wage-earners. In a sense, the Filipino suburb mirrors the paradigm back home: it is a place that "exports" its labor to jobs outside the community, but that generates an enormous "remittance" income spent in the town. Pittsburg began its brief and unspectacular rise about a century and a half ago, during the Gold Rush. Like a lot of neighboring towns, Pittsburg was an off-loading port for men and supplies heading up the Sacramento River to the gold fields. As the Bay Area cities grew, Pittsburg's first big job magnets were fisheries and canneries. Later, Pittsburg became a depot for the produce raised in the farms outside Stockton. The same Sicilian immigrants who flocked to San Francisco's Fisherman's Wharf and Monterey's Cannery Row came to Pittsburg at the end of the last century, and fishing remained an important industry until heavier industry pushed it aside. As its name suggests, Pittsburg is a steel town, once the biggest on the West Coast. Its mammoth open-hearth furnace opened on five hundred acres in 1910 as the Columbia Steel Company, and employed up to ten thousand workers. But in the 1950s, Pittsburg began to fade. The loss of Camp Stoneman, once a thriving army base, and the rise of the big shopping malls outside Pittsburg sped its decline. By the 1980s, competition from cheap steel producers in Asia left Pittsburg's big plant on the verge of a shutdown. Its postwar peak came in 1965, when sixty-five hundred people worked at the plant. Today, it employs just twelve hundred men and women.

Like much of the East Bay, Pittsburg is poised between the end of a long period of decline and what may be the start of an even bigger one. A region that has spent the better part of thirty years climbing back to well-being lives in terror of what will happen over the next few years when the Bay Area loses some ten thousand jobs linked to the downsizing or closure of several U.S. Navy installations. Pittsburg already weathered a base closing once, when it lost Camp Stoneman. The nearby weapons station in Concord, the naval hospital in Alameda, the moth-balling of Vallejo's Mare Island Naval Shipyard look like storm clouds gathering over Pittsburg.

Or maybe not. "You got a real mix here," says Tom La Fleur, the head of the Pittsburg Economic and Housing Development Corporation. "You got your raging depression. But then, some people are making real money." The depression is evident along Railroad Avenue, Pittsburg's main street. Railroad Avenue is the strip supposedly enjoying a revival, yet much of it is abandoned. At one end, an old movie theater, The Vogue, sits on a lonely corner, a cream-colored stucco antique with an art-deco marquee recalling the old downtown theaters of the 1960s, the ones that disappeared after the multiplexes arrived at the malls. It's a piece of wholesome America just waiting for the wrecking ball—looking at it, one can imagine its glassed-in ticket kiosk, detached from the building in that old small-town style, smashed in an instant, then swept up like the shards of a broken mirror. When was the last time its auditorium was filled? La Fleur can't remember.

If this was Pittsburg in revival—every other storefront boarded over—then what had hard times been like? The answer: even worse. Downtown was deserted, day and night, except by criminals. Slum housing and bars were Pittsburg's only growth industries. La Fleur maintains a pleasant grin as he explains this. He is a pleasant man. His face is the color of white pine, his chestnut hair is straight and neat, and everything about him speaks of a conscientious man who just wants to do his job right. He is proud of his nothing-fancy town, and proud of his own past—working up from a blue-collar family, working in the steel mill to pay for college and earn a law degree. His oldest daughter goes to Harvard. La Fleur's drab office and drabber wardrobe are points of pride, the same way Pittsburg is proud to not be Walnut Creek or Mill Valley or any of those upscale suburbs whose names sound like Napa Valley vineyards. Those towns, living on the "soft" dollars of overpaid professionals, are blamed for draining off commerce in Pittsburg.

"We're not Walnut Creek" is an expression heard often in Pittsburg, a barb that pricks both Pittsburg and its posher rival. Not being Walnut Creek means not enjoying the big shoppers that drive sales tax revenues, an essential part of budgeting in California. Ever since Californians passed Proposition 13 limiting the amount of money cities and towns could raise through property taxes, sales tax is one of the indicators a town looks at to measure its economic health. So "We're not Walnut Creek" has a explanatory connotation, as in, we can't have computers for all of our schools, or new street lamps for our recovering downtown.

But not being Walnut Creek means homes start at sixty thousand dollars. Thus the town is attractive to younger families. The evidence is all over, in little "in-fill" housing developments blossoming on side streets off Railroad Avenue. Most of the homes are built presold, many to Filipino families. The nearby strip malls are part of a chain of commerce that link the new housing courts like beads on a necklace. Each offer the same mix of services: a laundromat, a video rental store, a fast-food outlet, a hair dresser. And a Filipino grocery, restaurant, or combination of the two. These are tiny businesses but serious ones: customers who have bounced checks see their names taped to the windows; a display of shame that suggests disapproval is a real motivator in keeping village commerce prosperous. Every store is a kind of outpost, a *puesto,* where community life is on display. An upcoming dance is publicized on colored flyers, a child's first communion is captured in Polaroid. Spare counterspace is for the plastic racks holding dozens of business cards, for realtors, plumbers, hair dressers, and the rest of the army of immigrant self-employed.

La Fleur's job is facilitating the entry of new businesses, which means shaking a lot of Filipino hands and loaning money at low interest rates. The little grocery stores aren't really the kinds of "new businesses" Tom La Fleur is after, but he cultivates them with zeal. The new businesses are run by young families, so they employ no more than a handful of workers, all of them immigrants. Pittsburg, then, knows the dilemma of the new Asian suburb: it wants the growth, but wishes it benefited the native-born.

An unabashed unionist, La Fleur is current on the new wave of economic thinking, which among other things holds that the loss of U.S. Navy jobs in the East Bay will trigger an economic boom for cities like Pittsburg. He is current, but not convinced. Not quite a roll-back-progress Luddite, he is skeptical of the "new economic order," which so far has been more threat to industrial Pittsburg than savior. "California is about change, and guess what? We're changing," he says with his wide grin. "Hey, you want an Asian connection story? I'll give you one that happened right here in Pittsburg."

Impulse Manufacturing, a local start-up, surfaced in the late 1970s when a retired navy engineer living in Walnut Creek devised an inexpensive gadget that combined a loran-C depth indicator with a fish-finder. It was soon the rage with sport fishermen and boaters. Retailing these for eight hundred dollars apiece, the little company was reeling in several thousand fishermen every month, until Impulse Manufacturing's Walnut Creek headquarters was bursting at the seams and the little company began looking for more space. In 1984, Impulse selected blue-collar Pittsburg, taking a row of buildings on Railroad Avenue. It put eighty-five Pittsburg residents to work on the assembly line.

But price pressure from abroad was relentless. The market for simple electronic gadgets is hard to protect, so the garage tinkerer, watching his margins shrink, decided to sell. Japan's Uniden Corporation bought Impulse in 1989. After agreeing to stay in Pittsburg, the new owners remained just eighteen months—the time remaining on Impulse's lease on its Railroad Avenue facility. Uniden closed the plant without warning in 1991, and now makes the same product it briefly made in Pittsburg in the Philippines. La Fleur's staff works out of the old Impulse showroom, on desks strewn with brochures where once a real product was displayed. Maybe some of Pittsburg's Filipino families have relatives assembling fish-finders back home. "We sure could use those eighty-five jobs," he says after a long pause. He is looking away as his grin fades.

The look on La Fleur's face suggests that was Pittsburg's last chance to restore its reputation as place where real things are made. But that's a defeatist view. Impulse Manufacturing was a legitimate employer with real prospects of success in the marketplace. But its products' simple assembly can be done almost anywhere today, thus it was never destined to be a major employer for Pittsburg. The town's base comes from its new population, and in that respect Pittsburg seemed to be very lucky indeed.

Self-employment is becoming the norm in Pittsburg, something that runs counter to the town's tradition. According to the 1980 census, there were around 9,000 jobs in a town of just over 15,000 households. By 1995, the number of in-town jobs had increased to over 16,000, despite the fading of the steel mill and the "raging depression." Yet the total population of Pittsburg grew by only 7,200 households between 1980 and 1995. That means there was one new job for every new household. What's more, the number of employed residents jumped those years from 17,000 to almost 30,000, a result of more two-income families and a sharp increase in the number of people working outside of town. Taken as a whole, these figures indicate that two-job homes largely replaced one-job homes over fifteen years, while actual employment in Pittsburg had outpaced population growth by two to one.

Just over six thousand business licenses were issued by the city in 1994, or one for every five households. Probably three quarters of these licenses were issued to individuals, many working out of their homes. Thus, it appears that more Pittsburg families were employing each other, either directly in family-owned businesses, or indirectly through higher demand for services and goods. Pittsburg families also got slightly larger (from just under two to just over three people per family), with children now about one third the town's population. In other words, a younger town, consuming more.

Quantifying the immigrants' precise role in these changes is impossible, of course, but circumstantial evidence suggests the newcomers brought the change with them. Immigrants tend to be more self-employed than native-born Americans. They tend to have bigger families, and they tend to serve each other within the enclave. Pittsburg was becoming less a city producing goods that outsiders buy, and more one where outside cash is driven home each night and spent in the community.

Although Americans are conditioned to admire manufacturing over service industries, unless that manufacturing is being done by a new industry with a long future ahead, service jobs provide a better base. Because Pittsburg is not Walnut Creek, its immigrant base is making it a better place to open a business. One indicator bears this out: the all-important sales tax. In this decade, sales tax revenues for the city of Pittsburg grew an average of 10 percent a year, over $1 million more per year in 1994 than in 1990. Per capita sales tax revenue had grown from fifty-eight to seventy dollars—indicating that more people were spending more of their money in Pittsburg. If the figures seem arcane, bear in mind that across the state sales-tax revenue declined by almost 10 percent during the early 1990s recession, and by more than 30 percent within Contra Costa County. It dropped in all of Pittsburg's neighbors—in Richmond, Clayton, Pleasant Hill, and Antioch. Even Concord, with its

enormous Sun Valley mall, and yuppie Walnut Creek took hits—
Walnut Hill dipping from $185 per person to $174 over five years.
In simple terms, Pittsburg was saving itself by spending on itself.

Where towns like Walnut Creek and Concord rely on aircraft-
carrier–class retailers like Nordstrom's and Macy's, Pittsburg
thrives deploying tiny U-boats. Take the Manila Kitchenette restaurant at the Save-Way Center mall off Harbor Street, a bold new
business launched by June Rullamas. At thirty-eight, June looks
much younger than his years, darting around his kitchen in a
T-shirt and floral shorts, loose sandals flapping as he sprints across
the tiles to serve customers lunch. As he bounces on his flapping
feet, the top of his head barely reaches Tom La Fleur's neck. His
hair is too long, too. Business is booming.

June was born five hours north of Manila, in Baguio City,
where he earned a degree in business and accounting and worked
as a purchasing officer for the local waterworks. In 1985, he came
to California, bypassing the city to settle in Pittsburg. It took just
two days to land a job as an accountant at the U.S. Army's purchasing office in San Francisco. Starting at eight dollars an hour,
he worked for the army until 1988, when the Pentagon moved the
purchasing office to Dallas. June decided it was time to strike out
on his own. By then he had married Mila, another immigrant, who
had been his classmate in Baguio City. Together with her brother,
the three began to save for a home in Pittsburg. June, not wishing
to be unemployed, joined a manufacturer of hospital equipment in
Brisbane, a Filipino suburb just south of San Francisco.

Less than a blip on Contra Costa's economic radar, June Rullamas's career nonetheless captures the change that is affecting
Pittsburg. Like his neighbors, June arrived an instant suburbanite.
Nine years later he not only had American skills, but savings. After
training for a month with the Unisys Corporation, June took a night
job in Concord, California, cutting his commute to fifteen minutes.
The Manila Kitchenette, which opened in 1994, brought the Rullamas family to the next phase of suburban life—building its
puesto. Today, June works the night shift at Unisys from 6 P.M. to
3 A.M., running his restaurant during the day.

Like a lot of immigrant businesses, the Manila Kitchenette was born with its customer base presold—those same housing developments whose families ordered the wife's dishes from home. Drawing on family members to staff the restaurant, and raising a bank loan of $40,000—plus $15,000 from Tom La Fleur—the restaurant was an instant success. On a good week, June and Mila gross a thousand dollars slinging coconut rice, longaniza, and lumpia rolls. After expenses, the restaurant generates less income than even one salary, yet employs three members of his family. It is, therefore, a consumption *puesto* more than an employment point, generating income for other Pittsburg businesses. June is already planning a second restaurant, in one of two other new Filipino towns, either in Hillcrest or in Antioch.

It may not seem like much, but little *puestos* like the Manila Kitchenette are what are saving Pittsburg. Here's why: June's *puesto* paved the way for the next step. The Rullamas family paid $139,000 for their home in Winter Way, an in-fill development, where Rullamas estimates more than half his neighbors are recent Filipino immigrants. They are themselves the basis for his business. "We started with catering," he recalls, "working out of our house."

More in-fill homes are going up just two hundred yards from June's restaurant. They, too, are going to be filled with more new customers, indeed some of those homes' owners chose to buy because they felt a "comfort level" in Pittsburg, inspired no doubt by the Filipino businesses nearby. The families in those homes will launch their own businesses, too, perhaps with June as a co-investor. In other words, a youthful new community, which is hard working and well paid, has chosen to restore Pittsburg. How long before the video cassettes of Filipino action movies, sold now in every tiny grocery store and café, give way to first-run reels from Manila? And how long before someone realizes the screen at the old Vogue theater on Railroad Avenue would be the perfect place to show them?

The answer is: soon. At Camp Stoneman, a few Filipino businesses have already expanded past the retail stage to manufacturing. Years ago, Pittsburg made the decision to attract businesses to the old base, offering discount rents to anyone who wanted a small space to mix chemicals or run a print shop or fix carburetors. Most of the small businesses had been operated out of people's homes and garages before the barracks were converted and, like June Rullamas's restaurant, barely exist in the universe of economic indicators. But that is changing. One sign of Pittsburg's future is Ramar Foods. Ramar smokes meats and sausages and cranks out lumpia rolls, the flute-shaped egg rolls Filipinos deep-fry then consume by the handful. Ramar has just twenty employees, but has recently expanded to a second room.

Overstating the importance of Ramar Foods in Pittsburg would be a mistake. But so would understating it. Based in Oakland, Ramar started in the early 1980s, producing tropical ice creams for the growing Filipino community. Ice cream, like meat, is one of those Old Country products that has to be produced in the United States in order to comply with U.S. Food and Drug Administration guidelines. It can't be imported easily, but it can be exported. Ramar's owner, Primo Quezada, was thinking of moving his ice cream plant up to Pittsburg. The lease on his Oakland factory was expiring, he said, and he had ambitious plans to expand. The Bay Area is not the only place Filipinos buy his ice cream. He exports to Guam, Tokyo, Hong Kong, and the Middle East, where Filipino workers in the oil monarchies of the Persian Gulf are among the highest paid Filipinos anywhere in the world. Filipinos live better in California, of course, but the grass is greener in Saudi Arabia and Kuwait, because no one else is making Filipino ice cream there. Quezada won't discuss how much he thinks he can make shipping ice cream to the Gulf ("Too many of my competitors want to know," he says), but he's sure he can make more shipping to them from California than he could from Manila. California is simply more in tune with a global market. "Besides," he says, "my best workers live in Pittsburg."

Twenty women in white smocks, rolling triangles of dough into lumpia rolls, does not a recovery make. Even calling Ramar a "plant" stretches credibility. It is barely a room.

Yet visions of Ramar as the seed of an industrial empire are not fantasy. Ramar is adding space in Pittsburg, and the owners are thinking of building their own factory close by. The ability to produce cheaply and efficiently in an old blue-collar town will permit Ramar to sell its produce anywhere Filipinos settle—across North America or across the Pacific. Unlike fish-finders, which are mass produced and price sensitive, Ramar's product is sensitive only to the proximity of its market. And without question, Ramar's market is proximate. In twenty years, Ramar Foods may be a division of Pillsbury or RJR Nabisco, employing thousands in its Pittsburg plant.

It could be Ramar, or any of the twenty thousand Asian firms launched each year in California. According to figures released by the Commerce Department, Asian-owned and -operated businesses grew in the state by nearly a hundred thousand from 1987 to 1992, mainly in towns dominated by Asian immigrants. Over forty separate towns, most of them smaller suburbs like Monterey Park and Vallejo, had at least a thousand businesses, twice the number they had in 1987. The number of new Asian businesses in Pittsburg grew by over 50 percent, to 205.

Whatever becomes of Ramar Foods, California's trade with Asia is inevitable, as is California's continued role as the gateway for Asian goods coming in. Which is why people like Primo Quezada, and even June Rullamas, give Pittsburg an important leg up on the future. "They are expanding beyond the ethnic enclave, to be part of Pan Asia," says Sonoma State's Larry Shinigawa. "They are in the right place at the right time. But they also make it the right place."

Just as the "Latinization" of south Florida turned Miami from a city of retirement homes and vacationers to the capital of Latin America, Asian immigrants are making California Asia's backyard. A critical mass of immigrants led to Miami's becoming a hub of financial services, trading, media, and development for the entire Caribbean basin. A Latin population made Latin trade inevitable. Asians are bringing the Pacific Rim to their new neighbors—and with it, all the opportunities to thrive at the meeting point.

Pittsburg's old-line steel mill has caught this change. After years teetering on the brink of closure, the mill was reborn in 1989 as U.S. Steel–Posco. Posco is South Korea's Pohang Iron and Steel Company. Officially a U.S.–Korean joint venture, it was essentially a buy-out by Posco, the Koreans sinking about $400 million into a plant overhaul. Without Korean participation, no steel man, either in Pittsburgh, Pennsylvania, or Pittsburg, California, imagines the plant would have survived. Again, it's an issue of markets. The California facility was only attractive to Posco as a finishing point for product bound for U.S. markets. Hot steel rolled at Posco's Kwangyang Works leaves Korea for finishing in Pittsburg. The venture allows the Koreans to streamline production to its biggest overseas market. A small California city keeps twelve hundred jobs. Instead of Korean aircraft carriers menacing the coast, Korean freighters steam up the Carquinez Strait and dock in Pittsburg four times a month. They are laden with Korean steel bound for automobiles, beverage cans, and office furniture, legitimately labeled "Made in the U.S.A."

While assets, not Asians, was what most attracted Posco to Pittsburg when the Koreans came, other sites also were being considered at the time. Pittsburg's growing Asian colony undoubtedly contributed to Posco's concept of a "comfort zone," and that will make it easier for other Asian companies to enter and feel at home. Besides keeping the town's biggest employer profitable, the Korean connection is opening other channels of commerce. Those Korean freighters leave Pittsburg empty, but maybe not for long. A team of investors in nearby Martinez is building a $30-million bulk cargo port near Posco's mill, designed to fill vessels for return voyages. Grain, cement, and crushed stone are the kinds of products a bulk facility is designed to handle. It won't mean very many new jobs, Tom La Fleur says, but it will open Pittsburg to the Pacific trade routes. And who knows where that will lead?

Like Sushil Bhatia's JMD in Framingham, or Tom Lam's baby bok choy in Oxnard, the leaders in America's trade future will be the entrepreneurs who can reach beyond borders—not just national borders, but borders of industry. Immigrants will have a clear advantage in overseas markets, because they will be more attuned to the subtle changes that make opportunities. People like Ed Orpina, a very large Filipino American, who operates a small computer firm called Hitech Information Systems.

Hitech is little more than a software program linked to a telephone line, but it will probably make Ed Orpina a millionaire. Big and gregarious, padding about his San Ramon office in tennis shoes, Orpina is the kind of transitional Asian who will thrive in California's future. He is thoroughly American, but still Filipino. California-born, Orpina heads Contra Costa's Tri-Valley chapter of the Filipino-American Chamber of Commerce, one of twelve chambers in California. The portraits in his office show a big family at a big Filipino barbecue—your basic American leisure-wear before an all-cholesterol buffet. Being both Filipino and American is part of what Ed Orpina sells. Hitech sells tax compliance to large American manufacturers. To do that cheaply he needs the Philippines.

Over the past decade, factories, through catalogues and other 1-800 sales networks, have become direct sellers to consumers instead of relying on distributors and retailers. As vendors, they are liable for sales taxes in every state they make a sale. Orpina's company sells software to crunch data from clients to monitor tax liability state by state. He is able to operate as a virtual (in both meanings of the word) one-man show because he uses programmers in the Philippines to service his customers. Programmers that cost $60,000 a year in San Jose costs less than $20,000 in Manila, even though they do identical jobs. Instead of recruiting out of San Jose State—then losing his best programmers to bigger competitors as soon as he trains them—Orpina reaches back across the Pacific. "Manila is my third floor," he smiles, swiveling a chair around his second-floor office. "I'm doing unto Manila what would have been done unto me."

Hitech Information Systems is what programmers call a "body shop," essentially labor contractors stealing onshore business by sending it to Asia where labor is cheaper. Large U.S. corporations bring foreign technicians to the U.S. for training, then send their own "third floor" work back to Asia. But Orpina's Filipino workers aren't "stealing" U.S. jobs. He built a new service around his ties to the Philippines and his ability to access Filipino capital in Manila.

Ed Orpina realized American factories, particularly those selling Asian electronics goods distributed from California, were facing a new world of tax problems by selling direct. He knew tax investigators could audit these business with impunity, fifty states at a time if need be. He also knew he could perfect a program that would monitor sales and that could be serviced by other programmers at remote work stations. And he knew how to put those work stations to work in Manila. Finally, he knew what it would cost customers like Hewlett Packard or Microsoft to keep their accounting departments and programmers waiting on stand-by to react to an auditor's call. "I did the math," Orpina smiles. "Two programmers at a hundred twenty thousand dollars a year, plus benefits, plus insurance, plus space in your parking lot, plus sucking down the company's coffee all day. It adds up. Maybe two hundred thousand dollars a year."

Hitech can do the job for a fifty-thousand-dollar initiation fee, plus a retainer renewable every twelve months. As the sun sets in California, the Manila shop is starting its day. Using the Internet, e-mail, fax, and modem, Hitech Information Systems can answer a service complaint from Michigan from half a world away. Customers like Hitech's programmers because their English is not only correct, it is colloquial. "I'm not sure they realize they are calling the Philippines," Orpina says. "If fact, I know they don't always realize it."

Being in San Ramon, an emerging pan-Asian suburb in Alameda County, Ed Orpina can market his product in two worlds. If a prospective client in San Jose wants to do lunch, Ed can be there in forty minutes. If his backers in Manila, the powerful Lopez family, want to see him, he can be there in six hours. Usually they come to see him. Orpina is the piece of America they need in order to compete in a global economy. "The thing I know about the Philippines is when you walk in, the first thing people think is you're scamming them," he says, recalling his early efforts to win a partner in a country he knew more by reputation than experience. "I come in and say, 'I don't care if you think I'm scamming you, I'm going to make money for you and money for me, and I'm going to sit on your people until they do the job right.' And they love it!" Orpina can do things that are unheard of in Filipino companies, where a family culture dominates. Things like fire a poor worker, or pay a good worker better than the boss's son-in-law. Hitech Information Systems not only makes U.S. customers cost-competitive here, but its Asian partners more competitive, too.

No town may be better positioned for California–Asia trade than Vallejo, home of the Mare Island Naval Shipyard. One of the biggest military installations decommissioned this decade, the base closure cost Vallejo thousands of jobs, but left a wealth of unused space for development. Because Vallejo was a navy town, it also has a huge Filipino community, which will be key to its rebirth.

In mid-1995, a new era dawned in Vallejo when its first Asian manufacturer, Meyer International, broke ground on a new factory. This fully computerized plant and distribution center will employ just a hundred Californians, but it is an important first step. Meyer International makes pots and pans. Expensive pots and pans, to be sure, the Circulon and Analon brands that come with a lifetime guarantee and cost three hundred dollars a set.

Meyer International goes back to the 1940s and a small cookware factory in Shanghai. After the Chinese Revolution, the business moved to Hong Kong, and eventually became so successful it expanded to Thailand, then back into mainland China, eagerly taking advantage of lower labor costs to source some of its lines. But as Meyer International began producing better quality pots and pans, it replaced cheap hands with sophisticated machinery. So, sourcing from Guangdong was limiting, and sourcing in California became inevitable. The Vallejo plant is the company's first in North America, but probably not the last. "My friends think I'm a visionary, to have the guts to invest in manufacturing in California," says Meyer's chairman, Stanley Cheng. "But I am sure when we become successful, we will be the example of what offshore companies can do."

Cheng, a graduate of Oregon State University, is the kind of visionary California needs, a green-card–carrying immigrant with kids in local schools and a vision of the United States as China's backyard. Yet there is nothing "Chinese" about the firm. But for the CEO, the staff is American-grown. Meyer makes a few woks, Cheng concedes, but its publicity materials don't include them, or any other oriental utensil. The company name, he adds, sounds Jewish, something he hopes will help sell products in America.

Cheng ticks off the reasons why the East Bay works for him. First of all, convenience in shipping, which allows Meyer to cut the high costs of freight from Asia. Second, compared to Hong Kong and Guangdong, real estate is cheap. Third, the availability of American know-how and spare parts for new machinery is unmatched anywhere in the world. Once a company makes a commitment to using top technology—whether it is in metallurgy or tooling or inventory control—it needs to know it can service that technology easily. A breakdown in Guangdong can idle a production line for weeks. In Vallejo, any glitch can be fixed in hours, at most a day.

Finally, there is the access to the market, the most important reason of all. North America represents 40 percent of Meyer's sales; and these days, for a producer to be competitive, it has to stay close to its customers. "U.S. retailers are very demanding," Cheng says. "They want the vendors to handle distribution, transport, financing, and inventory. They expect all this, which is impossible to do from an offshore facility."

Meyer sunk $20 million into its Vallejo site, buying the land and erecting a 180,000-square-foot factory on the waterfront. The shipping bays are already divided into team sectors, with pots and pans stacked to the rafters ready for swift departure. "We own this business all the way to the cash register," Ed Blackman, Meyer's Vallejo manager, explained during a tour of the plant. When a Macy's or a Nordstrom's orders product, they expect Meyer's managers to put the pots and pans into the stores, even onto the shelves, without the department store having to worry about how. If Meyer won't do it, Farberware will. So, it is no longer enough to perform cheaply in Asia. Today you have to perform in America.

Vallejo offers Meyer the same thing Pittsburg gives Posco, something Stanley Cheng defined as his "comfort level." It has to do with the people he will be working around, and a climate only California has—Chinese without being in China. Any day now, capitalists in Guangdong could suddenly fall from favor and have to sell. In Southeast Asia, where Chinese have historically been the victims of racial discrimination, even worse things could happen. At the same time, California is America without being too American. "Because of the ethnic mix in California, we have none of the racial tension. Also, we can recruit personnel [here] with multilingual skills, very very easily," Cheng says. "Guangdong people can't operate e-mail. And while Alabama or Arkansas has the technological support, they don't have the community."

Cheng calls the new facility a bargain considering all he is getting. Being in Vallejo, he adds, will make it easier to sell in Japan, where a "Made in the U.S.A." label is prized. Cheng's only regret is that he didn't wait a little longer to make his decision, long enough to get a slightly better deal. That would have happened by moving to Mare Island, of which Vallejo has become the landlord. With almost 10 million square feet of warehouse space, four dry docks, and berth space for twenty ocean-going freighters, Meyer would not have had to build its own plant. No matter, Cheng says, Mare Island will still be there when it comes time to expand.

But if he doesn't hurry, that opportunity may go by. Besides the warehouses and ship berths, Mare Island has another 10 million square feet of workspace, with every imaginable type of welding and tooling equipment already installed. It also has a hotel, movie theaters, officers' mansions, swimming pools, tennis courts, and a golf course. If Meyer is planning to invade Mare Island, it will likely have to fend off the rest of Hong Kong.

Far-fetched? Not really. Vallejo has already entertained thoughts of leasing the old Combat Systems Training school to a Manila university looking for a U.S. extension campus. "We got a

hundred thirty thousand square feet of space, two thousand dor-
mitory units on the island. Cafeterias, gyms, soccer fields," says
Alvaro da Silva, the Vallejo official charged with leasing space at
Mare Island. "You name it, they had it."

Both Vallejo and Alameda, another base slated for closure, are
in discussions with something called Pan-Asian University, "an education mall," one official described it, where campuses from across
the Pacific Rim will place extension "pods" around a central quadrangle. "Can you imagine what that can do for Vallejo's image?"
Da Silva asks. Hundreds of young Asian scholars coming to California for their junior year abroad, surrounded by business opportunity in every pan-Asian or ethnic specific suburb they visit. Any
one of those pods could spawn another Stanley Cheng, someone
who will go home to his family business with a scheme to make
Vallejo or Alameda or Pittsburg the American beachhead of a growing transpacific empire.

Can you imagine Mare Island itself becoming one those ethnic
specific towns? The streets are already laid out. Two generations
of Vallejo Filipinos already live there. Despite the shrinking of Vallejo's job base, or perhaps because of it, Filipino developers have
been promoting Vallejo as a kind of Manila Town, something between a theme park and shopping center, where Filipinos feel they
are running the show. Ten years from now, a visitor may wonder
which came first, Manila Town or all those new Asian factories out
at Mare Island? "It will happen sooner or later," Professor Shinigawa affirms. "There is enough of a professional class to form a
community. They'll have to follow nondiscriminatory ordinances
[allowing non-Asians to move in], and they will do so, but de facto
it will happen."

When the U.S. Navy pulled out of Subic Bay in 1992, the
Philippines quaked with fear. What would happen without all those
jobs? What happened was the surprise of the decade: Subic Bay
became a hub of transshipment in and out of Asia, a free port to
rival Colón, at the mouth of the Panama Canal. Filipinos earn less
than workers in Singapore, Taiwan, or Indonesia, yet they speak
English and are comfortable working with Americans. So Federal

Express chose Subic as its Far East hub. Those same advantages exist for the transplanted Filipino workforce in California. So, another not-so-far-fetched scenario is for Mare Island to reinvent itself as Subic Bay East, the mother of all *balikbayan* bases for the thousands of send-a-box-home-to-Manila outlets that thrive in Filipino communities everywhere.

Isidro Protasio, an executive at LBC Mabuhay, one of San Francisco's bigger *balikbayan* shippers, already sees a tie-in. He sees selling Mare Island to Filipino tourists coming to nearby Marine World, and to golfers flying in from Manila and Tokyo for a few rounds on the old officers' course. Between rounds, of course, of business meetings. Protasio and his partners have bid on five Mare Island buildings: the bachelor officers' quarters, the bachelor enlisted men's barracks, the gym, the bowling alley, and an on-base nightclub called Destinations. Protasio sees Little Manila on Mare Island, a place, he notes, with a single entrance at the old navy guard post, making it the perfect location for the most quintessential of California subdivisions—the gated private community.

One of Protasio's partners is Rafael Santos, the old navy cook who was forbidden to enter the officers' mess through the front door. Santos is now manager of Rafael's Farragut Inn, previously the base officers' club. Santos was the first outsider to take a piece of Mare Island, bidding on the 27,000-square-foot banquet palace as soon as the navy pulled out. He'll operate his catering business out of a kitchen where "Flips" once peeled potatoes. Only this time "Flips" won't be entering through the back door. "There are twenty-eight Filipino associations here. Just in Vallejo," he says. "And only fifty-two Saturdays. Tomorrow I could book this place for the year, and we haven't even opened."

CHAPTER NINE

Delray Beach, Florida: Import Substitution

Haitian people are different from African-American people. They have no fear of the white man. They compete as people.

Clay Wideman, African-American
business leader, Delray Beach, Florida

★

It is not only Asia's best and brightest that become the new majority, but also America's least and lowest. Surely the Haitian boat people of south Florida rank as our least wanted immigrants. No refugee mass has swollen more piteously, nor been more stigmatized. Was it coincidence that the Haitian link to AIDS—with homosexuals, heroin addicts, and hemophiliacs—rose at the same time Haitian bodies began washing ashore in Florida? Of course it was a coincidence, and of course it wasn't. If immigration is an infection without cure, then Haitians are the immigrants most infectious.

Yet even the Haitians have entered the great American marketplace eager, and able, to add value and prosper. Ragged and illiterate, many left villages barely emerged from the eighteenth century. Many arrived in Florida literally storm-tossed on rafts constructed from driftwood. Yet their entry has been as effortless as that of the most educated Korean or the most Americanized Filipino. If California's "model minority" suburbs are promising previews of America's twenty-first century, then south Florida's emerging Haitian havens are the renewed promise of all America could have been. And will be quite soon.

Delray Beach is such a haven. It lies in the southeast corner of Palm Beach County, between glitzy Boca Raton and middle-class Lake Worth, a mix of old and new. To the west, on the flat-lands stretching between Interstate 95 and Lake Okeechobee, is old Florida: farmland, lush with cucumber and pepper fields. Beyond the crops lies the spongy savannah of the Loxahatchee National Wildlife Refuge, the even older Florida of sawgrass and alligator trails. New Florida rises along a stretch of blinding white sand, the "beach" of Delray Beach. "New" here is repeated every generation, by whoever occupies the mansions with the ocean views. Ten years ago they belonged to the shopping mall developers, today to finance princes. Delray Beach's beach, compared to Palm Beach and Boca Raton, was always nouveau, at best a way station for the truly ambitious on their way up. That's because the rest of Delray Beach was always too low-rent for old money. Delray Beach, of course, always had Negroes.

In between old Florida and new Florida lay the decay—the Florida of the now, the Florida of massive relocation, of paved paradise, of the struggle for usable water and integrated schools. The Florida that lies in transition between tourist siren and mature matron. Palm Beach County was one of America's fastest growing communities in the 1980s, during peak years sucking in outsiders at a rate of almost one new resident every hour. So many newcomers arrived between 1985 and 1990 that being a newcomer is almost a reverse indicator of authenticity. "Real" residents here come from somewhere else. That's how it plays when every waitress, every doorman, and every baggage handler wears a two-line name tag, the top line for "Darcy" or "Dave" or "Ramesh"; the second for "Michigan," "New York" or "Toronto."

Or "Haiti." Delray Beach is Palm Beach County's most Haitian town, with something between a third and a quarter of its fifty-one thousand residents claiming some tie to that tragic island. Per capita, no district in the country is more Haitian, either. Delray Beach became America's most Haitian address almost overnight, from a handful of families in the late 1980s, to the mid-1990s, when more than half of Delray Beach's black population was either born in Haiti or claimed at least one parent who was.

History made the Haitians' arrival here inevitable. It starts with race, and a tradition of segregation called Jim Crow. Delray Beach was incorporated in 1911, after some twenty years of permanent settlement. The area's first residents came in 1894, a mixed community of black farmers from the Florida panhandle and followers of a couple of Yankee land speculators, a Mr. William S. Linton and a Mr. Henry Swinton. A boatload of black Bahamians rounded out the pioneer band—crossing over from Grand Bahama island just forty miles to the east. Delray Beach lies at the point where Florida juts farthest into the Atlantic before tapering west again toward the Keys. Bahamians were always arriving in these years, sometimes staying, sometimes not.

Mr. Linton did not stay. Although his name (and Mr. Swinton's) still grace two downtown thoroughfares, he skipped town, missing out on such local amenities as inch-long horseflies, voracious mosquitos, floods, hurricanes, and the Great Freeze of 1895, which wiped out the new settlement's first citrus crop. Farming was restored at the turn of the century, when a colony of Japanese settlers arrived. They established a prosperous pineapple plantation near a village called Yamato. A century later, the Yamato colony lies buried beneath a Boca Raton golfing club.

By 1960, on the eve of the central Florida land boom, Delray Beach's population was a mere 12,230—already double its 1950 size. Over the next quarter century, the town would double two more times, reaching 25,000 in 1980, then 47,000 in 1990. However, population growth did not make Delray Beach a prosperous place. If anything, it made it poorer. Delray Beach was a mixed community, with the blacks, Asians, and Latinos actually outnumbering whites. In the segregated South, "coloredness" doomed Delray Beach to underdevelopment. That became self-fulfilling with the land boom, when roadways were designed to sweep prosperity past the black parts of town. Ultimately, downtown Delray Beach fell within the "Blight Belt," a strip of eastern Florida lying just inside the Atlantic Intracoastal Waterway and extending from Dade County all the way north to Saint Augustine. Between the canal and congested Federal Highway 1 (later to uncongest to virtual abandonment with the laying of Interstate 95), a chain of aging downtowns began dying. By the late 1970s, most of Delray Beach's farmland had been bulldozed for retirement villages and the many tract-home developments sweeping south from West Palm Beach. Thus the Blight Belt was sealed inside Interstate 95—the same highway that whisked shoppers to malls in Boca Raton and took tourists to Fort Lauderdale and Miami.

Daniella Henry remembers the first time she drove through Delray Beach on that highway. It was a night in 1990 and she was visiting a friend who had recently moved to town. She exited the brightly lit interstate at Atlantic Avenue, the town's main drag, excited to be seeing someone else who had made a recent change in life. Daniella Henry was in Florida on vacation, something that was exciting in itself. Home was Brownsville, Brooklyn, where she had recently worked herself off welfare.

Born in Haiti, she emigrated to the United States as a child. Later, although graduating from the University of the District of Columbia, she accepted public assistance to qualify for Medicaid coverage after giving birth to an underweight, premature son. Eventually she was able to work herself off welfare, as it happened, with a job counseling other welfare mothers at a Brooklyn community center. Like many Haitians living up north, she had been hearing a lot about Delray Beach, and wanted to see it. Slim and bright and full of her own recent success, she was eager to visit a place she heard was sunny, laid-back, and friendly to Haitians. Speeding off the exit ramp toward the corner of Atlantic and Swinton Avenues, she was delighted to see streets filled with people in a festive mood, despite the late hour. "I thought it was a carnival," she said, recalling a night five years before. Her natural smile brightened with the memory. But the delight quickly turned to horror. "No carnival," she said, the smile crumbling the way it did that night. "They were selling drugs."

Delray Beach in 1990 was a notorious crack zone. Tourists may have bypassed its beaches on their way south, but everyone else knew where to dart off the freeway to score. Downtown businesses fled (they already had been fleeing for years), withering a tax base already overly dependent on the snowbirds commuting from Michigan and New York. Where the highway whooshed by overhead, emptiness echoed. By 1990, things had gotten so bad, elementary school playgrounds were guarded by ten-foot cyclone fences, tipped with barbed wire. Who cared, anyway? With all the newcomers filling in the western suburbs, school districts were building new schools beyond the interstate—and busing black kids in from the Blight Belt for "diversity." Inside the dying core, those who remained grew poorer still, and the core became a vacuum filling with crack.

Daniella Henry rolled up her windows and sped past the young men in the baggy jeans, mortified by their crotch-grabbing gestures, their angry hoots, and the kissee-kissee taunts they mouthed through her windshield. They took her slowing-down, where-am-I? driving style for the only thing they knew: a crackhead looking for her connection. She took their turned-around baseball caps, exposed boxer shorts, and obscene finger-play for what she knew: trashy dope peddlers—of whom she had seen plenty enough back in Brooklyn. Keeping her eyes straight ahead, she sped off Atlantic. Her heart didn't stop pounding until she arrived at her friend's new home. So this was the famous "Delray."

As shocking as Daniella Henry's first encounter with Haitian Haven was, she had only seen the surface corruption. Delray Beach's decline left intact a redneck power structure that enforced a tradition of segregation. Like a lot of coastal towns, blacks could work in the resorts and mansions on the beaches, but were expected to be back on the mainland by nightfall. Instead of a "wrong" side of the tracks, the Intracoastal Waterway served as Florida's line of Jim Crow demarcation. Blacks kept to "their" west bank of the waterway, in a low-lying ghetto of subdivisions lying along two thin corridors of Delray Beach's southeast and northeast quadrants. Besides drugs and crime, racial division fed civic rot. "The police chief collected rent on Friday night," Virginia Snyder, a local muckraker and private investigator recalls. "Black tenants fall behind? He made the rounds for the landlords."

But by 1990, Delray Beach was bottoming out. Only a few months before Daniella Henry's visit, voters had turned the old police chief from office, part of a clean sweep enacted by the re- form slate elected a year before. Delray Beach's new chief was Richard Overman, who had served twenty-five years in Orlando's police department, rising to deputy chief. The move to Delray Beach was a chance to manage his own department, and put into practice the techniques that in larger departments seldom advance past the "experimental" stage—after which they usually are shelved and forgotten. Overman was attracted to a town that wanted change. The drug dealing, the loitering, the all-night carnival on Atlantic Avenue, he decided, were symbols of neglect and aban- donment. For Delray Beach to take back its streets, police had to get out of their cars and work with the people.

Chief Overman made foot patrol a glamorous position, telling officers and their supervisors that certain parts of the city were theirs to operate, and that if they were successful in rooting out crime, they would be rewarded. Crime turf is a backyard overgrown with weeds, he told them. He expected those weeds to be chopped up and swept out. "Cocaine is about making money, it's about busi- ness," Chief Overman says today. "So we attacked the problem from that aspect. How can we ruin the business? What can we do to change things? One way was by assigning 'ownership' of an area. That means I hold them responsible for pulling a neighborhood together."

One area was West Atlantic, just off the interstate at a conve- nience store called Mario's Market. In the eighteen months before Chief Overman's arrival, police recorded more than three hundred complaints outside Mario's—complaints of loitering, heavy traffic, drug sales, fights. Police made dozens of arrests for cocaine pos- session, to little avail. But after a unit was given "ownership" of the block, the tide began to turn. First the officers convinced the store's owners to install new lights. Then the officers themselves arranged to spread a new layer of blacktop on the driveway. Small, cosmetic things, really, but part of an investment in reversing neglect. To keep drug dealers' cars away from the auto-borne casbah, Overman's cops added an unexpected wrinkle: "Handicapped Only" parking spots along the sidewalk. In a state overrun with drug peddlers—yet where the entitlements of elderly voters are taken with utmost seriousness—Chief Overman found the threat of a parking ticket more powerful as a deterrent than the threat of arrest. "Frankly, you get more punitive results for handicapped parking, a two-hundred-fifty-dollar fine, than for being arrested for possession," he says with a laugh. "The justice system is just glutted with drug cases, but if they know they'll get a ticket? They stay away."

Repeating the process up and down Atlantic Avenue, Delray Beach's cops made great strides in reducing crime. Today, Delray Beach is a model of civic restoration. In 1995, the state's top business monthly, *Florida Trend*, profiled Delray Beach in a cover feature titled "The Best Run Town in Florida." For eight pages, Delray Beach's rags-to-respectability saga was rendered in terms any reader could appreciate. On Atlantic Avenue, vacancies "went from almost half to near zero. Sidewalk cafes, nightclubs, and art galleries opened in empty storefronts. Young couples fixed up scores of old homes near downtown. And small businesses sprang up everywhere—including a healthy mix of minority ones."

Delray Beach's new tennis center brings Chris Evert and Martina Navratilova to an annual Virginia Slims of Florida tournament—on courts erected in the heart of the old black ghetto. But the ghetto is still there—a rare case of gentrification without displacement. As decades of middle-class flight began to reverse, more residents came in. A surge of new home-building since 1995 added new life to Delray Beach, and over a million more dollars a year in property taxes to pay for things like cops who "own" their strip of sidewalk.

Delray Beach deserves the accolades, and the story of how it changed is an inspiring one. Fighting crime was a first step, changing the mix of residents was a second. Daniella Henry returned to stay, moving her family to Delray Beach in 1992. When she drives along Atlantic Avenue today, she no longer sees a crack carnival. The strip has blossomed into Pineapple Grove, a pedestrian mall of restaurants and boutiques where formerly empty storefronts ruled.

By the mid-1990s, Palm Beach County, particularly Delray Beach, had replaced Brooklyn, then Miami, as the number-one destination of Haitian immigrants reaching the United States. The 1990 census recorded just 10,492 Haitians living in all of Palm Beach County. At least 60,000 live there today, with between 15,000 and 20,000 concentrated in Delray Beach. The town's Haitian enclave is still tiny compared with the Haitian community in Brooklyn, to say nothing of Miami's Little Haiti, each with over 100,000 residents. But its growth rate is exploding. And as a percentage of a single town's population, Delray Beach's Haitian immigrants compose the biggest presence of any Haitian-receiving city in the nation. Thus, the election of new leaders and the hiring of a new police chief coincided with another big change—in demographics.

Therefore, an obvious question: Did Delray Beach's rebirth happen in spite of the Haitians, or because of them? All evidence suggests it was because of the Haitians. The explanation lies in the history of the Blight Belt.

In Brownsville and East New York, West Indians replaced African Americans as workers in the hospitals and nursing homes. Florida's Haitians surged into the gap created by divisions in the local black community. But before that, profound changes occurred in the Jim Crow South. Civil rights was one of the changes; the arrival of new Floridians was another. Dr. Lance de Haven-Smith, a political scientist with the University of Florida's Institute of Government, has studied Delray Beach. Among his areas of inquiry is the effect modern appliances and a more mobile lifestyle have had on the working class, essentially how they contributed to the erosion of domestic jobs for black Floridians. "Look at the census," he says. "The category 'Domestic worker' dropped from about eight percent of *all* employment in Florida in 1964, to almost nothing in 1975. Now, a lot of those were black jobs. Fast food, microwaves, and dry cleaning was one reason for the drop-off. Blacks doing better was another."

Rising black expectations fueled the trend. So did physical mobility—to Miami, and to cities farther north like Atlanta, Washington, and New York. By the late 1970s, when Palm Beach County was on the verge of its population explosion, domestic work had essentially disappeared. The massive unemployment that resulted was the beginning of the Blight Belt.

The next step, de Haven-Smith determined, was homeowner abandonment and the replacement of the working middle class with the welfare class. Communities become poorer, younger, and less skilled. Government, either through welfare or other subsidies, paid an increasing share of the rent. Property taxes declined, but crime and addiction went up. "With the move to renter-occupied housing," the professor explains, "you see the urban blight take off. The residents don't invest in their homes anymore. Hell, even their relationships to each other change. They see themselves as temporary neighbors, so it's self-fulfilling. And it gets bad, fast."

The Blight Belt becomes a cancer, in some ways the purest embodiment of a free market's ability to destroy value as it attempts to maximize profits. Delray Beach and other Blight Belt towns established a pattern: a marginal neighborhood goes down, and that creates an opportunity for a forward-looking developer to make a killing—if he can get land cheap enough and fast enough to convert it into the next Gold Coast. "Developers sometimes go into areas to buy properties but don't treat them right. So property values go down so they can buy even more property so eventually they can clear the land, put in office space, and disperse the black population," de Haven-Smith explains. "You have to understand there are big bucks for the developer. Renting out to the worst people works for them: it drives the property values down next door, and they can buy more houses cheaper. It's like Monopoly; they want enough land to erect a luxury hotel."

De Haven-Smith says that through the 1980s, a typical Blight

Belt neighborhood could be destroyed inside five years. From stable, working-class districts they would deteriorate into festering
hellholes, practically overnight. The irony, of course, is that this
was occurring despite the surrounding real estate boom. After years
of decline, a developer finally would announce an "urban renewal"
plan (often funded with state and federal grants), amounting to
little more than a subsidy to bulldoze the wreckage for office parks
and shopping malls. There is slum clearance, but only at an incal-
culable human cost. The sad fact, de Haven-Smith says, is that the
Monopoly strategy is not only cynical, it is reckless. Making poor
areas poorer to prepare for "renewal" ignores the real costs of managing poor neighborhoods—in law enforcement, health care, and
education. Even when the Monopoly strategy succeeds, it forces
the displaced poor to pull up stakes and crowd into another hole
along the Blight Belt.

Professor de Haven-Smith's research suggests the Monopoly
strategy works only about half the time, the common pattern being
blight cleared for office development. Whites then move to the
western suburbs and the beach gets trendy. The black belt runs
right down the middle and, usually, it gets worse. "Once you get
in that downward spiral it is hard to reverse. And once the people
get pushed out, they take their problems with them. It's a very
expensive cycle and it causes an enormous amount of suffering for
the human beings involved," de Haven-Smith concludes. "You
drive from Jacksonville to Miami and about every five miles you
come across a place that is really scary: blight, vacant lots, abandoned gas stations, crack houses. The next time you read in the
newspaper about a tourist getting killed in Florida, he was probably
driving from one resort area to another. He stumbled into one of
these urban hovels and got robbed and killed."

Delray Beach was well along in the cycle de Haven-Smith describes when the Haitians started arriving. He believes their presence helps explain how the town became an exception. Counter to
everything happening everywhere else along the Blight Belt, a
middle-class community was returning. And it was black. "The Hai-

tians felt that America was about as great a place as you could ever find," de Haven-Smith says. "They are very good people; hardworking, church-going people who were looking for opportunity. They thought they had reached heaven. What happened to Delray Beach between 1980 and 1995 is just remarkable. That decline just stopped. And the Haitian in-migration was a big part of it."

On this the town is sharply divided. Chief Overman praises the Haitians and calls them a solid influence, especially in the black neighborhoods where they have been recruited into his civilian Crime Watch patrols. Many of Delray Beach's Haitians arrived in Florida illegally, yet the chief considers them among the town's best "citizens," even though most are years away from being citizens of any country but Haiti. However, Mayor Tom Lynch, whose record is the centerpiece of much of Delray Beach's favorable publicity, is rather cool to the suggestion of a Haitian connection to the town's renaissance. In 1995, he dismissed the analysis that Haitians played an essential role in saving the town. "The Haitian community has not been active," he said flatly, explaining that he never sees them at community meetings, or hears of very many calls that his office receives from Haitian residents. Compared to the black groups who are vocal, the Haitians are the invisible minority, a factor Mayor Lynch seemed to believe was limiting Delray Beach's fame, not enhancing it. "They are working hard to save their money and buy a home," he surmised. "Many send their money back to their families in Haiti."

From the top down, the Haitian influence looks negligible. But the view at street level is more compelling. Those small businesses that *Florida Trend* reported are springing up "everywhere—including a healthy mix of minority ones"? Many belong to Haitian entrepreneurs: a grocery store, a plumber's shop, a silk-screen textile boutique, a cosmetology school. Here and there, you can spot that most Haitian of all establishments—the combination money-remittance outlet/international phone-call kiosk/travel agency/dry cleaner's—all in one space. Along Pineapple Grove, by those once-empty storefronts that *Florida Trend* reported now house "sidewalk cafes, nightclubs and art galleries," many of the new places are owned or run by Haitians or employ them. The rest count Haitians among their clientele.

"You have people saying they are their best customers, and some saying they're their worst customers," says Tom Fleming, the coordinator of Delray Beach's Main Street Association, the group that converted Atlantic Avenue into Pineapple Grove. He does know that the more working people inhabit Delray Beach, the easier it is to gentrify. And with the Haitian zone abutting Pineapple Grove, the connection between Haitian jobs and Delray Beach's stability is an obvious one to make. "A broken home supported by welfare is not an attractive target consumer," Fleming says. "I want the household that is one-family, employed, and growing its income. That's the family a business will target."

Although Fleming, like Mayor Lynch, is personally identified with Delray Beach's turnaround, he admits that simply sponsoring a tennis tournament or slapping a new name on a troubled strip won't revive a city. If that were the case, the Virginia Slims of Detroit would be world-famous today and that old New Orleans ghetto that was so crime-ridden way back when now would be called Gumbo Grove. "All areas have to come back together, it is synergistic," Fleming concludes. "If you have just one area improving and the rest isn't, what you improved will eventually decay."

What Fleming doesn't say (and few in Delray Beach will) is that for a town to truly change, something has to change in the citizenry—either who they are, or the way they behave. That has happened in Delray Beach, dramatically.

It's obvious driving in Delray Beach's black quarter any late afternoon. Traffic crawls by as cars filled with young men weave down the street. In another city, a car filled with joyous, loud black men may seem threatening, trouble on wheels ready to erupt. In black Delray Beach, it's trouble's antidote. As one old Pontiac went by, it stopped nine times on one block, a stop-and-start ritual repeating itself every ten yards, and always for the same reason: the men were coming home from work in their car pool. As each man got out, sweaty and tired in bib overalls or a mechanic's jumpsuit, a range of jobs were revealed. Paint stains meant construction work, grass shavings on pants legs indicated landscaping, wrenches dangling from tool belts meant auto repair or electrical work. Nine guys in nine entry-level jobs.

Together they make a picture of a neighborhood's transformation. The Pontiac was more than a car pool, it was the village bus making all local stops to and from work. The village itself was something rather unique in modern America: an extended family where work habits were so similar a gang of nine could live on the same street, commuting together to the same job. As it happened they were all working as laborers scouring the bottom of Palm Beach County's residential building trade. But they could have been cane cutters or cucumber pickers. Probably, at least for some years, a few of them were.

Outside their community, the Haitians' contribution to gentrification is barely recognized. But it is undeniable. While it is hard to comprehend how a population so lumpen—so lumpen nine men in a battered Pontiac might be the homeowning "middle class"— can be a gentrifying force, the evidence is in the numbers. According to the census, Delray Beach had just over twelve thousand blacks in 1990, out of a total population of forty-seven thousand. Even if the Haitians already living in Palm Beach County had been undercounted by several thousand, the census wouldn't have missed very many in Delray Beach, because by 1990, few had found their way there from West Palm Beach. Yet by 1995, the town's official population had grown to just fifty-one thousand— despite the surge of newcomers, white and black, and the several thousand Mexicans migrating in from the vegetable fields.

How many of these newcomers were Haitian? Even if the entire increase derived from this one group, the uptick would not account for the tripling of Haitians residents since 1990. It's virtually certain that the Haitians' arrival corresponded with an exodus of older black families. If, as Haitian leaders like Daniella Henry say, there are twenty thousand Haitians in town—and if at least half of them arrived after 1990—then the newcomers simply displaced the older population. Displaced and effectively replaced: a wholesale substitution of one black community for another. That's what the numbers suggest, but that conclusion is subjective. Again, the real evidence is at ground level, visible in the old Blight Belt where a new middle class has emerged. In effect, what the Monopoly strategy did painfully—driving local blacks out by deepening poverty—the Haitians did painlessly, with prosperity, replacing families house by house as they bought their own homes.

Gripping I-95 like a vise, the Haitian army helped police choke off the drug trade. Essentially, it occupied a no-man's-land held by absentee landlords and their tenants, and filled it with loyal troops. By occupying and owning, the Haitians effectively eliminated vice's habitat, reducing the number of potential crack houses with every purchase. The Haitians didn't only occupy, they deployed. In one depressed neighborhood in the southeast quadrant, twenty-four of twenty-six new "in-fill" homes erected in the early 1990s were built by Haitian immigrants.

"Our biggest problem is with absentee landlords who will rent to anyone," Chief Overman says, adding that the rental process cuts two ways. It allows drug dealers to harass the neighborhood, and it guarantees that anyone who can leave, will. "If you rent and you don't like the neighborhood, you are going to move. You have freedom to relocate," Overman explains. Ownership isn't just about cops controlling their beat, but residents controlling their neighborhood. Fanatic workers and savers, Haitians swept through black Delray Beach like a conquering army, buying homes and repairing them, and transforming the Blight Belt into a stable, drug-free neighborhood. Chief Overman doesn't know what percentage of new owners are Haitian, nor does he care. In fact, on block after block, the Haitian wave is gradually turning crime out of Delray Beach. As Chief Overman concludes, "Wherever you create ownership, things get better. People have more of a stake where they own. They have their life savings invested, they become very emotional, passionate about change. And where you have owners who have a stake, they *want* change. Very few people come in, invest a lot of money to build a home and then sell crack out of it."

Between 1990 and early 1995, more than a thousand new homes were commissioned and built in Delray Beach. Almost a third of the total—292 new homes—went up across a wide swath of ghetto neighborhoods hugging I-95. Most of these were homes occupied by Haitian immigrants. Palm Beach County housing officials who never spoke to a Haitian outside an immigration court or an AIDS clinic were delighted to see new families step forward to participate in the county's Restore Our Neighborhoods program to rehabilitate derelict housing. "We're used to single-parent families," says Chauncey Taylor, a Palm Beach County housing official. "It's super when you see mom, dad, and the entire family come in together for an application."

Palm Beach County's property appraiser's office tracks the Haitians' campaign in Delray Beach, charting home purchases lot by lot across town. In the subdivision of Southridge, Haitian families have filled whole streets. Take Reigel Avenue, where the block between First and Second Avenues is all Haitian. The property rolls show homeowners named Boliere (Roland and Marie Dorsonne), Belony (Monotte and Marie Etienne), Paul (Gedene, Chrismene, and Colomb Petitienne), Louverture (Jean, Anne, and Gerard Joseph), Eugene (Jeanette and Muscadin), Raymond (Jean and Gigelle). From the computerized rolls, this appears to be an early beachhead, two-, three- and four-income families arriving en masse during the last three months of 1987, each paying $68,500 for homes. Around the corner, on Sterling Avenue, another wave swept through around the same time, lots more Toussaints, Jeans, Assantes, and Duplessys. In all, a total of thirty-six Haitian families have arrived on Sterling, a street that was a wasteland before the Haitians came. What is striking is not just the consistency of purchase price and sale dates—$68,000, almost every home purchased between 1987 and 1991—but the apparent practice of bonding several families to each purchase. Not all the Haitians live this way, but they clearly are joining forces to buy. "People sold out and they just bought in," says Jackie MacKenzie, whose family is one of just three non-Haitian families left on Sterling Avenue. "It's become a very busy street," she adds. "But no one's complaining."

No one's complaining because Sterling Avenue is a safe street. Fanning out from Southridge, similar conquests have taken place in Carver Square, Atlantic Gardens, and Jefferson Manor, all of which are in districts that, according to the 1990 census, are more than 80 percent black—sometimes over 95 percent black in the ghetto's core. There the purchases are more recent, sometimes for quite a bit less money. Haitians apparently are driving into even more depressed zones, bottom fishing along rougher streets earlier arrivals were able to avoid. Now the bargain pickings are gone, but the mass of Haitians is growing. Deploying its considerable strength in numbers, the mass is venturing farther into no-man's-land. The army is moving into tougher terrain.

At the same time, Haitians were venturing into another hostile area: white districts. If black flight decimated the Blight Belt, corners of previously white-only Delray Beach were also in decline. The Haitians saw value there, entering neighborhoods that would have declined after "going colored," but only if they went to renters. By beating the absentee landlords to the next area of decay, the Haitians replaced aging whites. They created stable, multiracial districts like Osceola Park (according to the census, the most integrated neighborhood in Palm Beach County: 33 percent white, 46 percent black, and 10 percent Hispanic) before white flight became white rout. Thus, even more important than reversing the trend of home abandonment, the Haitian wave broke Delray Beach's tradition of apartheid. "The Haitians broke the color line," community activist Carolyn Zimmerman says. "They didn't know blacks lived on one side and whites on the other."

In any of these new neighborhoods, it's easy to find the Haitians. Their homes are well kept, but have twice as many cars outside—the better to deploy the many wage-earners inside. Sunday afternoon is the day even the hard-working Haitians don't work, at least not for pay. The homes along Southwest Sixth Avenue buzz with suburban renewal, the sounds of carpentry and hedge chopping and the swish-swish of the lawn mower, island-style, one man swiping away with a machete. In front of one house a burly man led a gang of sons and nephews clipping bushes and hauling tar in bucket-brigade style up to a shirtless Sampson balancing himself on the sticky roof. "I bought this house in 1983," Nicholas Legenord says, pointing to the tall ficus tree in his front yard. "That was just a little thing when I came."

One of the first Haitians to buy a home in the area, Legenord came from Atibonette. He settled in Miami in 1980, working construction by day and restaurant kitchens by night to raise the down payment on a $50,000 fixer-upper in Osceola Park. Legenord chose Delray Beach because it was where he came for church every Sunday, commuting up from Miami to worship with a small evangelical congregation founded by members of his church back home in Atibonette. With his wife now working as a nurse's aide, life has been sweet in Delray Beach. His oldest son, Chamard, has excelled at Olympic Heights High School in Boca Raton, where Haitians are bused in to satisfy federal integration guidelines. Chamard was the county's leading defensive back in football last season, and was later accepted at Indiana State University in Terre Haute on a football scholarship. Still, Legenord acknowledges, the welcome has been uneven at times. "Some white Americans moved away when we came," he admits. "Some of the young blacks still throw rocks at us." Kids at the middle school call his eleven-year-old, Daniel, "Banana Boat."

Replacement or displacement? If the Haitian wave represents the triumph of "good" black families over "dysfunctional" ones, where does that lead? At the crux of the immigration debate lies poverty and the concern that immigrants who take jobs make it more difficult for poor Americans (read: poor *black* Americans) to enter the employment mainstream. In the case of Delray Beach's Haitians, it is a false argument. Haitians entered a place where labor shortage, not excess, was the rule. Indeed, it was the demand for Haitian labor that caused the shift of immigration from Miami and New York into Palm Beach County.

The Haitian wave to Palm Beach County was spurred first by demand for farm laborers, desperately needed in the fields between

Lake Okeechobee and Interstate 95. Thus, the Haitians who were arriving in Delray Beach in the mid-1980s came from two sources. Most came from somewhere else in south Florida, either Miami's Little Haiti or from farm centers like Belle Glade, Indian Town, and Okeechobee, all places with sizeable black ghettos surrounded by lots of low-paying jobs in the vegetable fields. Jobs that were going unfilled.

In the curious way race defines place in America, the Haitian farmworkers became conspicuous outsiders the moment the crops were harvested. Yet they were invisible once they relocated into the towns along the coast. They chose places like Delray Beach, Riviera Beach, and Fort Pierce—segregated "over the water" districts, the sleeping quarters for servants who worked by day along the shoreline. Delray Beach offered proximity to Boca Raton to the south and Palm Beach to the north. Renting from absentee landlords, and taking traditionally "black" service jobs, Haitians melted easily into the tropical ghetto. There they discovered that being invisible is the first step to prosperity.

The second source of migration was the Bahamas, just forty miles away across the Straits of Florida. Since the 1880s, Bahamians have crossed over to the mainland. In the 1980s, the Bahamas became a back-door entrance for Haitian boat people. By 1990, some five thousand Haitian refugees were living near Marsh Harbor in two squalid refugee camps called Pigeon Peas and Du Mode. Daniella Henry, now director of Delray Beach's Haitian American Community Council, visited Pigeon Peas as part of a Florida delegation researching Haitian immigration. Haitians were living in makeshift shelters, little more than the wreckage of the leaky boats they trekked up from Haiti on. Drug use was rampant, prostitution was one of the few industries employing Haitian refugees. Fed up with their own "illegal alien" problem, Bahamians began evicting the Haitians in 1991. Many rode smugglers' skiffs to Delray Beach.

Daniella Henry describes the morning drill whenever refugees wandered in. "They knew to come to the office," she says with a conspiratorial smirk. "Sometimes I let them shower and have breakfast, then I took them to find their people." By then the local Haitian zones reflected clear lines of emigration from a chain of villages running along Haiti's northern coast. Starting with Port-de-Paix on the northwestern tip of the island, the coastline faced north toward the Bahamas. That was the launching point for the exodus.

Most of the Haitians who found their way to Delray Beach came from the interior, rural people used to hard work, who hocked everything they owned to get on board a vessel sailing toward Florida. If the smugglers slipped past the Coast Guard cutters and got within sight of the Palm Beach shoreline, there were fifty miles of beaches to drop their passengers. Unlike drugs, immigrants are any smuggler's easiest cargo—the bounty pays its own passage and has legs to run in the unlikely event of an ambush or detection. Sometimes the refugees hit the beaches, then found themselves wandering amid the garden estates of celebrities—Estée Lauder, Donald Trump, the Kennedys—who won't even let local cops onto their properties, much less illegal aliens. If they slipped through the gauntlet and could get to Delray Beach, they were home free. "If the man says he comes from Port-de-Paix, I drop them in southeast," Henry explains. "From Leogane, I drop them in southwest. Someone will know them, and help them find their people."

If the man came from Atibonette, Henry drove north to Lake Worth, another emerging enclave, or to Jupiter, Mangonia Park, West Palm Beach—all places where Haitians knew someone who would know them, and help them find a job. After a night at sea or on a public beach, they arrived dazed and disoriented. But by sundown many would be in uniform—laundering sheets at a hotel, scrubbing floors, or busing tables.

The smuggling goes on, although on nowhere near the scale of years past. Most vessels are stopped on the high seas by Coast Guard cutters and turned back toward Haiti or, if they are judged unseaworthy, are sunk and their cargo transported to the refugee camp at the naval base on Cuba's Guantanamo Bay. There, many begin the long process of applying for legal entry. Although smuggling continues, the nearest border patrol station, Riviera Beach, no longer patrols the beaches on weekends, due to government budget cuts, so that is when most landings occur. Officials in 1995 estimated there was at least one successful landing every week, with an average of two dozen Haitians hitting the beaches undetected each time.

Although Floridians decry the immigrant onslaught, their taxes pay Daniella Henry's salary. The effort to assimilate Haitians includes publishing information in Creole on food stamps, prenatal health care, and AIDS prevention. The Boca Raton Resort and Club, the county's most exclusive hotel, employs more than five hundred Haitian immigrants—and provides classes in "hospitality English." Palm Beach County provides the teachers, free of charge. Few in Palm Beach County seemed to be aware of the contradictions in these policies. Nor was there any sense that officials were abetting Haitian migration as part of an overall development plan. But whether it is by accident or by design, the inflow is having that effect.

The speed with which the Haitians assimilated is more than remarkable—in less than five years they have made Delray Beach their own. Compared to Brooklyn's West Indians, who didn't emerge as a force until a community had been in place for decades, or California's Mexican farmers (some of whom, it could be argued, have roots dating back centuries), the Haitians had come on like a whirlwind. Why? In part because of location: these Haitians were close to Haiti and even closer to Miami's Little Haiti; thus Delray Beach became a community quick to replenish itself. In part, too, it was because of a third source of Haitian migration, the older Haitian-American community. By the mid-1990s, many of the "new" Haitians in Delray Beach were actually long-term immigrants, people like Daniella Henry, who were undertaking a second migration within the United States.

And, in part, it was because everything clicked: service jobs were abundant close by in growing tourist communities; a depressed community had housing stock going begging; and a critical mass of new immigrants was arriving over a few short years. Haitian immigrants from as far away as Canada and New England are flocking to Florida. They are what Haitians call the "Boeing people" (as opposed to "boat people"), who arrived during the long reign of the Duvaliers. They are the doctors and dentists looking to serve Haiti's expatriate middle class. "The first month I opened, I had at least twenty new patients," says Robert Victome, a snowbird from Brooklyn who opened Delray Dental Associates in September 1995. Another recent arrival is Patrick Le Conte, also a dentist. Le Conte arrived from Gainesville and was born in Haiti. He had been raised in Senegal, where his father was chief of oral surgery at Cheikh Anta Diop University. Le Conte says before certified Haitian dentists came to Delray Beach, "private" specialists from Haiti went door to door in the black zones, knocking on windows and opening mouths on the spot. They're still shaking out jobs, like Fuller brush salesmen or itinerant handymen. As soon as those gypsies are certified in Florida, they'll be knocking on his door, looking for better-paying work and a permanent address.

The experiences of professionals like Dr. Le Conte and Dr. Victome demonstrate how immigration's energy converts to upward mobility for everyone. The boat people are the critical mass that draws the Boeing people to Delray Beach. Doctors Le Conte and Victome can make a living anywhere; they come to Delray Beach because by getting to the Haitians first, they can make a better living more easily. As agents of change, the Haitians are miles ahead of the politicians; but as noncitizens, they still lag behind the rest of Delray Beach in terms of using their strength. Bob Trescott, the University of Florida urban planner who helped launch Delray Beach's startling reform movement, sees the Haitians' upward mobility as a key element in stabilizing the community. He's not bothered by the fact that most local politicians have missed what is right under their noses. "Their reaction is not too surprising; if you're being stroked every day, why dig to find the reason why things are going well? They know some energy is there, but they don't know where the hell it comes from," he says. "One, they can't measure it, and, two, they don't know. It's like lifting a barbell: you think you can lift four hundred pounds, and then you turn around and see someone is holding up one side of the barbell. I don't think they have a handle on it."

The Haitians, Trescott says, don't "know" either. They don't
know they should shun neighborhoods like Atlantic Gardens and
Southridge, or reject jobs busing tables at the Boca Raton Resort.
They don't know that it offends African Americans that Haitians
are converting the worst jobs in America into middle-class incomes.
They don't know they "deserve" to participate in subsidized housing schemes, so they buy or build their own. "They don't know all
those psychological hang-ups," Trescott explains. "They just see it
in market terms. They didn't know the neighborhood had this history or that certain people were 'in line' or certain people had
'earned' their right to these things. They say, 'Why are you jumping
on us? We just saw an opportunity and we took it.' "

Lance de Haven-Smith sees a more profound sequence of
events unfolding, a kind of back-to-the-future plan whereby Haitians are repeating the steps taken by black Americans half a century ago, this time without suffering the overt and institutional
racism of that earlier era. "It's gentrification with blacks still there,"
he concludes. "Delray Beach is truly exceptional."

The Blight Belt offered Haitians a ready-made niche in Florida's land grab, allowing them to be the black newcomers. In a state
where "newcomer" is practically synonymous with "resident," Haitians were simply the black side of the Florida looking-glass. By
colonizing in Delray Beach, Haitians have become the county's
"good" blacks, snapping up the menial jobs in Boca Raton, even
sending their strapping teenage sons to play football for the better
high schools—one rung of the upward-mobility ladder especially
prized by resident African Americans. Thus, Haitian success is
something that confuses, and rankles, older African Americans.
Clay Wideman, an African-American businessman and community
activist, admits the Haitians have simply outcompeted locals by being reliable, energetic, and willing to work cheap. Like a lot of older
blacks in town, he is ambivalent about the Haitians. Like Mayor
Tom Lynch, he says they don't invest in the community, but instead
send all their money home to their families in Haiti. Yet, like the
mayor, he acknowledges that some, indeed many, are buying
homes and starting businesses. "Ninety percent of them have at

least two jobs, so the minimum wage doesn't mean as much to them," Wideman says. "They take on jobs we used to take, and if they weren't here, to be truthful, we probably still would be doing those jobs."

But that cuts two ways, Wideman says, explaining that Delray Beach without Haitians would not necessarily be a better place. Haitians may work for less than other blacks, but the kinds of jobs Haitians do—landscaping, dish-washing, picking cucumbers— aren't the jobs Florida blacks should *want* to do in the late twentieth century. Nor are they the kinds of jobs anyone in Florida who manages to finish high school and prepare for a career *has* to do. Wideman admits that at his own shop, a beauty parlor, four of the five girls who work for him are Haitian immigrants. "If they don't come, it's for a real good reason," Wideman says. What he doesn't say is implicit: other workers he's hired in the past, well, if they didn't come to work, a "real good reason" was not always provided.

Most Haitians consider farmwork, landscaping, and restaurant work as jobs to escape, not preserve. While it is true Haitians, as well as Mexican and Central American migrants, dominate the workforce in the fields, few imagine making a career of harvesting crops. It's not that they are used to better—they most definitely are not—but that, once in Florida, they discover so much better work lies so close by. Haitians are drawn to the hotels for the fringe benefits, like night school, but also the environment—air conditioned and elegant. Serving white tourists is not demeaning but rather an opportunity to share a piece of the America they dream of. The longer Haitians stay in Palm Beach County, the more baffled they are with black American mores—the more shocked that in a land of plenty, blacks seem drawn to crime and drugs instead of work. In some ways they are learning the same racism their white neighbors are learning to forget. The longer they stay, the more determined Haitians are that their children not attend black schools or live in black ghettos. "People say Haitians don't know they are black," says Daniella Henry firmly. "Haitians know they are Haitian."

The ghetto bisected by Martin Luther King Boulevard in Boyn-

ton Beach, just north of Delray Beach, is one place Daniella Henry
shuns, yet one she cannot avoid. Six years ago the congregation she
worships with, the Bethanie de Boynton Seventh Day Adventist
Church, bought two buildings in the neighborhood, one for a
church and one for a school. The buildings lie at the end of the
block, right where Martin Luther King bumps into I-95. "We were
so wrong about the neighborhood, but we didn't know," Henry
complains. "Drug people in all the houses. Sometimes people are
scared to come."

Like most Haitian churches, the Bethanie de Boynton SDA
Church is also a community center. Bible classes, choir practice,
and any number of club activities are scheduled through the week,
always after working hours, often until midnight. On Saturday (the
"seventh day" the sect keeps as Sabbath), so many cars are parked
outside the church, the spillover extends two-deep along the hillside reaching up to the interstate. During weeknights there aren't
quite so many cars, but enough to be attractive targets for local
kids to break into and rob. Most of the congregation commutes to
church from the newly reclaimed blocks of Delray Beach. Undoubtedly some of the vandals who victimize them are recent arrivals, perhaps replants from those same neighborhoods, now living
in Boynton Beach. There's nothing the Haitians can do about the
problem: they have a mortgage to finish paying on the church
buildings, and can't afford to sell or move. Their only hope is that
a similar gentrification will occur nearby, repeating the process that
occurred in Delray Beach.

In that way, time is on the Haitians' side.

Although Boynton Beach looks unwelcoming now, the tide of
Haitian migration to Delray Beach and surrounding towns will one
day do to the neighborhood around Martin Luther King Boulevard
what transplanted newcomers like Daniella Henry did for Pineapple Grove earlier this decade. Quite a few transplants attend services with Daniella Henry on Saturdays. All chose Delray Beach to
buy first homes, and all plan to stay. "I didn't want to raise my kids
in Miami," explained Kesnel Exantus, one parishioner. He left Miami's Little Haiti in 1988, and now works as a salesman at a Delray

Beach Volvo dealership. "Miami is too different from life in Haiti," said another parishioner, Weisner St. Ville, a tall man, looking cool in a white shirt and dark blazer. Weisner St. Ville bounced from Brooklyn to Miami before coming to Delray Beach. Today he runs his own textile screen-printing shop, a job he trained for in Haiti. Like a lot of immigrant businesses, his started in the house and has only recently expanded to an outside address with four employees.

"You hear this fear, that there's 'too much' immigration," Chief Overman says. "We work with these people day to day, and I have so much admiration for them. I try to imagine if I had just floated up on the shoreline, and if I had an opportunity to own a house and work hard. They see it that way. They wash up on the beach, but they are here after the dream: own a house and work and raise their kids. Maybe I'm a softy, but I just feel if people work hard all day they deserve a break."

Haitians are making it in Palm Beach County, but they are also making waves. In one Delray Beach neighborhood in 1995, over three hundred residents signed a petition protesting construction of the Emanuel Evangelical Lutheran Church. All the signers were black. They complained their streets would be spill-over parking lots, and that choir practice and Bible thumping would disturb their evenings. Others said the services attract crime: those cars routinely vandalized while the owners are praying. Chief Overman says he was never consulted about whether another Haitian church would, or would not, increase crime. He says if he had been, he would have said "no." Nonetheless, the city council voted against construction, leaving the congregation of Emanuel Evangelical Lutheran angry and confused.

Where drugs had reigned, who could refuse a church? Haitian services are raucous, says the Reverend Alberto Busby, an immigrant from Curaçao and rector of the Calvary Bible Baptist Church. "But all that was an excuse. There are jobs black Americans won't do. But it gets around 'your father took my father's job.' Or they say that Haitian people make it hard for American blacks to find jobs."

Like all immigrants, Haitians are resented by poorer Americans

for not being, or not behaving, poor. As fellow blacks, they are seen
to be validating roles many, especially Southern blacks, want to
forget. Clay Wideman sees a different, deeper phenomenon. Haitians are not simply doing "black" jobs, they are doing the jobs
from yesteryear. And they are doing them right. They are showing
up on time and saving their money and going to church and helping
each other out with leads on jobs and loans when buying their first
cars and houses. Accepting welfare, which automatically disqualifies
an immigrant from sponsoring a relative's visa to enter the United
States, is almost unheard of in the local Haitian community. In
fact, in no segment of America—black, white, red, Latino, or
Asian—do families pitch in and help each other the way immigrant
families do. However, a sad truth emerges in confessions like
Wideman's: that Haitians make American blacks feel like failures
only because they, too, are black.

Clay Wideman may be the only local black leader willing to
discuss the Haitian presence honestly. Wideman's portrait appears
in *Florida Trend*'s spread on Delray Beach, giving him a kind of
parity with Mayor Lynch, Carolyn Zimmerman, and Christopher
Brown, head of Delray Beach's Community Redevelopment
Agency. All except Wideman are white. And where the others'
quotes are rendered in pithy, T.V.-newsworthy sound bites, Wideman's quote seems deliberately hokey, almost as if it is meant to
convey the black man's simplicity. In the photo, Wideman's elderly
profile is set against what looks like a white clapboard steeple. Perhaps this, too, was meant to convey Old South ways. "We're doing
it in Delray Beach like America ought to do it," Wideman's quote
reads. "We're breaking down the barriers."

What Clay Wideman conveys in person is neither simple nor
hokey. "I grew up in south Georgia," he relates. "And it would just
irk me to death to listen to my grandfather with all his 'yes, sir,'
and 'no, sir' stuff to white people. One day he took me aside and
he said, 'Son, you keep living and you'll understand who I was
doing this for.'" Wideman pauses for a moment and then continues, "And now I do understand. He was making it possible for me
to be where I am today. I am an entrepreneur, I own a home in

Boca Raton, and a building worth three hundred fifty thousand dollars."

As poignant as his grandfather's quote was to hear some fifty years later, what Wideman had to say next was positively heart-breaking. "Haitian people are different from African-American people. They have no fear of the white man. They compete as people," he said. "When they apply for a job, they expect to get it." In other words, when they come in they don't look down at the floor, glance at the door, and give every indication that they hope they *don't* get this job so they can just go away. And when they buy homes in "white" areas, they intend to live in them like anyone else. Thus, they remind other blacks, Wideman indicated, that racism often is self-applied.

Like the Filipinos of Pittsburg or the Chinese of Monterey Park, Haitians in Palm Beach County are discovering the joys of being the new majority. They employ each other and create wealth for their neighbors simply by preserving home values on the streets where they live. And they have no fear. In that way the Haitians are a good thing for Delray Beach, where blacks held on to an unhealthy fear of the white man long after such fears were unfash-ionable in the rest of the country. Daniella Henry sees the conflict between Delray Beach's old African-American community and the Haitians as a problem of assimilation, one that black Delray Beach will overcome, just as white Delray Beach did. "When we first came, the white people never made us feel welcome," she says. "Now the blacks are scared. They think we're going to take over. Like the Cubans."

Assimilation has become her personal challenge. Daniella Henry has already attended one of Chief Overman's "Police Acad-emies," a training course in public safety. In the five years since she first visited Delray Beach, dozens of Haitian immigrants have joined the public payroll as teachers, police officers, code enforce-ment inspectors, sanitation men. And every day others enter the mainstream. Daniella Henry plans to run for city council, she says, a post a Haitian will win by the end of the century. As if to make her point, she says over five thousand Haitian immigrants have stopped by her office asking for naturalization forms. "If just three thousand vote," she affirms, "that will make a difference."

And if they vote with African Americans, something will happen that no one could have anticipated in the old Jim Crow days: blacks will run the town. "I want to be the bridge," Daniella Henry says. "Nobody recognizes the Haitian contribution today. But they will."

Postscript: American Alchemy—
Why the Mass Matters

N o other country in history has been as successful as the
United States has been in converting its poor into its rich.
No other society has managed this alchemy as continually
or as consistently or as completely. Even Europe, with its high
standard of living, cannot claim America's success in defying class
as national wealth is distributed. Indeed, it has been that European
policy, repeated across the continent, to import their poor, and
keep them poor, which has accounted for much of the native population's prosperity. And while this is not yet the case with Asia,
even its booming free-market economies—few more than a generation old—have not created as much wealth from poverty as
America has. Nor have Asians proven they can repeat the pattern
in generations to come.

This American Alchemy, the essence of our world dominance,
is essentially foreign in its composition. For most of American history, indeed for all of it with the exception of two post–World
War II decades, the poor who made it rich were largely imported.
That is, immigrants. The 1945–65 rule-proving exception, moreover, occurred during a time of deepening poverty for many American-born blacks, precisely the group believed to be victimized by
immigration through the years. It wasn't true from 1945 to 1965,
when immigrants were not coming, and it's not true now.

As the changes occurring in places like Brownsville, Brooklyn,
and in Delray Beach show, blacks are as likely to benefit from
increased immigration as anyone. Perhaps not immediately, as the

poorest Americans compete for low-end "starter" jobs, but inevitably, as neighborhoods and schools are improved, and as a new middle class rises. Immigrants are our oldest and most dependable pool of "riser," a kind of demographic yeast that guarantees shared prosperity. They are the villagers entering and renewing our cities, repeating a pattern of self-cleansing as old as civilization itself. Essentially, we could not be Americans if we were not foreigners first.

In American terms we call this pattern "upward mobility." In an era of stagnant workers' wages, corporate downsizing, and the "embattled" middle class, many Americans believe that upward mobility has stalled. It has not. Immigrant workers' wages have been rising without pause for thirty years. And while larger, maturing industries are shucking off excess manpower, there is no "downsizing" in the immigrant economy. As the immigrant economy joins the mainstream, it brings with it the new middle class. Thus America's middle class is neither disappearing nor "embattled." It is imported.

There lies the uncertainty of immigration for America, and its dilemma. Poor Americans find mobility more difficult, and an aging middle class finds security harder to hold on to. But the solution to these problems comes not in protecting the struggling classes from youthful foreign competition, but in assimilating those competitors as quickly as possible. The dilemma isn't Jamaicans dreaming up schemes to run off-the-books car services in ghetto neighborhoods, and siphoning revenues from "official" transit providers. The dilemma is how to draw the guerrilla services into a partnership that complements the city's service. The solution has been assimilation: converting an open space at the end of one commuter line as a terminus for the gypsies—the same place they were bound for in any case, now without the threat of police harassment. Instead of siphoning revenue, the van services funnel thousands of extra passengers into the subway lines, more quickly and more efficiently than city buses can manage to do by themselves.

The same goes for the renewal of neighborhoods. The dilemma isn't that Brazilians choose aging New England mill towns for their cheap, declining housing stock. The dilemma is how to convince

Brazilians to stop sending their earnings home and use their money to buy homes here. In city after city, immigrant home buying is the key to renewal—and it doesn't matter if they are Brazilians in Massachusetts, Haitians in Delray Beach, or Senegalese in Harlem. "As a general observation, immigrants bring a lot of optimism and energy. And if you focus that energy on one area, good things happen," says Bill Apgar, a researcher with Harvard University's Joint Center for Housing Studies. By tracking the rise of immigrants' incomes and those incomes' conversion into home ownership, he has been able to quantify the upward mobility of the future. "Immigrants are more optimistic," he explains. "They start with a home-ownership deficit, then they close that deficit. That upward mobility is the 'energy' we talk about. You focus that on a city, and you see the difference. It's the difference, say, between New York and Detroit."

The comparison is apt. Detroit, a city largely "free" of immigrants, is hardly a model for economic growth. In fact, it has been the epitome of everything that has gone wrong with America's cities—white flight, the decline of manufacturing, and runaway public expenditures, mainly funded by taxpayers who live far from the city limits. New York, too, has experienced white flight and a dwindling manufacturing base, but it is experiencing a spectacular boom as the century draws to a close. Immigrants are not the only reason, but they are part of a complex reshuffling of the city's resources that has allowed other investment to occur. At the city's base, the great immigrant arbitrage game—the simple ability to convert Third World sweat and muscle into First World hard-currency earnings—created much of the seed capital that funded New York's turnaround. An apartment full of *"pizzeros,"* Mexican migrants who deliver pizza for cash tips only, gives a landlord in a decrepit tenement the beginning of a stable, predictable revenue stream. A building full of *pizzeros* draws more tenants to surrounding buildings. Those tenants stock a neighborhood with consumers who, in turn, inspire a *tortilleria* owner to buy an empty lot next to his factory, and to open a store to sell other items to his growing customer base. His purchase inspires another's and, suddenly, a neighborhood where real estate had been abandoned to the city in lieu of property taxes becomes a neighborhood where bottom fishers are bidding up prices for lots at the city's property auction. Whether those bidders are immigrants or not no longer matters— the immigrants' initial presence created the spark that lit the fire that brought the change.

Not all of those *pizzeros* need become businessmen or home buyers for the American Alchemy to take place. The promise of immigration is that it allows the most talented to rise without punishing those with lesser talents. Immigrants who "fail" often simply go home—about a third of all legal and illegal immigrants, a proportion of returnees that has remained remarkably consistent for the past 150 years. A few "failures" do drift downward to become the new underclass, a phenomenon that has convinced several researchers that the immigration formula has changed. While it is possible to find Jamaican-born drug dealers in city prisons and Southeast Asian refugees struggling to escape welfare, there is absolutely no evidence to suggest that these cases are more than unfortunate exceptions to the immigration boom. Moreover, while many of today's immigrant enclaves have harbored criminal networks—Dominican cocaine rings, Chinese smugglers, Nigerian loan-fraud artists among them—there is no compelling reason to see these groups as anything other than aberrations, even within their own communities. Criminal enterprises have always been part of the immigrant saga, created by sinister opportunists availing themselves of the same market opportunities that the law-abiding majority exploits.

We have no choice other than to accept immigrants—for one reason, because our background demands it. For another, we cannot stop the flow. Criminalizing the world's poor simply for its desire to enter the American market is self-defeating. It creates a "failed" immigration policy that succeeds only in deepening our resolve to "protect our borders." That usually means spending more resources on more police actions that don't work, which creates more "failure," thus more resolve to repeat the cycle. "It doesn't have to be this way," says Timothy Whelan, a former Immigration and Naturalization Service officer in Boston. "Temporary workers can be licensed to do all kinds of jobs. They enter with papers, they work, and they leave," he explains. "Other countries do it, and so can we."

In other words, the alternative to "protecting" our borders need not be surrender, but assimilation. Any and all immigrants can be licensed to work on a temporary basis. And "temporary" can be anything from a six-week harvest season, to a four-year university career, to a ten-year "apprenticeship." It shouldn't matter what industry the worker chooses—just as it wouldn't matter which course of study the university offered, or what fruit or vegetable was being picked. Everyone from construction workers to dishwashers to *pizzeros* could hold papers, and allow the market to set his or her wages. At the end of each period temporary residents would have the right to renew their status or to move up to something better. Ideally, the goal of full citizenship would be attained.

The argument that this would create unfair competition to existing citizens is no argument at all. Americans already face stiff competition, both at home and abroad. The surest route to prosperity is to bring the competition here, and find a way to get "their" best players onto the home team. To do otherwise is to do nothing, and let the current uncertainty about immigrants and their role in American society deteriorate into something worse—xenophobia, racism, the clamor for policies that overtly discriminate on the basis of ethnicity or origin. That has already begun to happen in some places, and will always be a threat to the American antitribe. We have resisted that threat before, and we must resist it now.

Our future is being born today in a village somewhere far away. Our welfare depends on the quality of our welcome when that future arrives.

NOTES

Introduction

Page 1 Epigraph: Richard Critchfield, *Villages* (Garden City, N.Y.: Anchor Books, 1983), p. 334.

Page 3 ". . . Roman Empire": United Nations Population Fund, *The State of World Population*, 1993, New York, July 1993.

Page 8 Grupo Mexico, the Mexican conglomerate at least indirectly responsible for sending thousands of Poblanos to New York, lists shares on the New York Stock Exchange. In the summer of 1994 those shares peaked, surpassing $1 billion in value. An investor shrewd enough to have bought shares at the time of the Calipan and Izúcar de Matamoros privatizations would have reaped enormous gains from his stock.

ONE New York: The Critical Mass

Page 19 "The Well" was described in two 1992 articles in *The New York Times*, by Mary B. W. Tabor: "The World of a Drug Bazaar, Where Hope Has Burned Out" (October 1, p. A1) and "Where the Drug Culture Rules" (October 2, p. B1). The series did not mention Mexican immigrants, but one photograph showed crack cocaine dealers milling in front of a bodega on Knickerbocker Street, "the most notorious drug bazaar in Brooklyn." The name of the bodega: Puebla Grocery.

Page 24 Telephone rates comparison is based on a rate sheet sent to all MCI customers in the spring of 1995. A few months later, the Sprint service advertised its 10-cents-a-minute plan, matching the cheapest of the street fares. The big difference between these and the all-cash prices are that Sprint and MCI customers are required to have in-home

phones installed, and pay federal tax on all charges. Street phones are
still the cheapest in the country. All street prices are from the winter of
1994–95. Depending on the volume at any given location, prices vary
considerably from neighborhood to neighborhood. One trend was consistent everywhere: the bigger the community, the lower the price. In
the 1990s no place was as cheap to call as the Dominican Republic.

Pages 27–28 Immigrant specialization is of particular interest to aca-
demicians and city officials alike. In 1992, *The New York Times* reported
at least 85 percent of the city's greengrocer stores were run by Koreans,
and 40 percent of its gas stations by Indians. Citing local sociologists,
the *Times* reported that Afghans, who number fewer than four thousand
in the city, own more than two hundred fried-chicken outlets, while
Guyanese dominate the city's pharmacies and machinery repair shops.
See Donatella Lorch, "An Ethnic Road to Riches: The Immigrant Job
Specialty," *The New York Times*, January 12, 1992, p. A1.

Page 33 In just one census tract in the heart of the Gift District—
#58, the fourteen square blocks from West Twenty-eighth Street and
West Twenty-first, between Fifth and Sixth Avenues—some three thousand new jobs were created between 1980 and 1990. Conceivably there
would have been more, since so many of the immigrants who "work" in
the area go uncounted in the census. Gift District employment figures
are based on the New York Metropolitan Transportation Council, which
gathers data from the census on the number of respondents who commute out of the tract they live in and into the one they work in. In New
York the amount of commuting is considerable, but since practically no
one lives in the Gift District, it is fair to compare figures for commuters
in 1980 and 1990 to determine the minimum amount of job growth.
Certainly there were no fewer jobs than before the boom. Hundreds of
other "workers" would be buyers, like Africans arriving on tourist visas,
who wouldn't be registered in any census tract. Another indicator comes
from the Metropolitan Transportation Authority, which counts turnstile
traffic at all the subway stations in the Gift District. One station, at West
Twenty-third Street and Broadway, saw turnstile traffic grow 15 percent
in one year, from 1993 to 1994—almost half a million extra fares—a
rate of growth more than three times that of the system-wide average.

Pages 33–34 The numbers of minority-owned businesses and the
percentage of foreign-born proprietors are derived from the New York
City Department of City Planning's 1992 study *The Newest New Yorkers*,

which lists the numerical growth of businesses, based on data taken from the 1990 census. The U.S. Department of Commerce published a survey of minority-owned businesses in mid-1996, further refining the 1990 figures. In addition, the Census Bureau's Center for Economic Studies refined the same data to separate native-born from foreign-born respondents to its Characteristics of Business Owners report.

Page 36 Yoon Dam Construction, which was listed in the New York telephone directory in 1992, denied it ever contracted illegal workers. It disappeared sometime in 1993.

Page 38 Square footage of new construction is taken from the 1994 *Annual Report on Social Indicators*, published by the Department of City Planning, City of New York, based on data from the New York City Department of Buildings. Construction employment figures are from the same volume, based on census data broken out by the New York State Department of Labor.

Page 39 Mexicans began appearing in Korean stores in the late 1980s, and continue to be the only nonfamily help most of these stores employ today. Many Korean stores are open twenty-four hours, so the Mexicans who staff them have to be paid well enough to work long hours, yet cheaply enough to keep costs low. The solution is hiring within families, relying on informal networks to manage the workforce. By the mid-1990s, it was possible to find Korean stores that hired Mexicans only from Tulcingo or Zapotitlán Salinas or any of the other Mixteca villages of Puebla and Oaxaca. Dozens of these workers confirmed their salaries in interviews.

Page 41 In computing taxi figures: the cost of living has risen 85 percent during that 15-year period, a compounded rate of 4.2 percent a year. Change occurred in the valuation of individual medallions, the entry-level cost of which actually dropped. Medallions were bid up from about $60,000 in 1975, to about $140,000 in the mid-1980s, to just over $200,000 in 1995. In the course of twenty years, the cost of owning a cab business seemingly tripled. But those numbers don't account for usage—the amount of income earned per cab. According to the city's Taxi and Limousine Commission, the average annual profit per medallion grew from about $7,000 in the mid-1980s to nearly $19,000 in 1995—profits grew at four times the rate of inflation in the cost of a medallion. A medallion that traded for twenty times annual profits in 1985, trades for just twelve times profits ten years later. See Richard

Phalon's study in *Forbes* (June 22, 1994); Sheryl Fragin, *The Atlantic Monthly* (May 1994); and Richard Perez-Pena, *The New York Times* (August 9, 1995), for figures on the earnings per taxi, lease prices, and the net worth of medallions over the years.

Page 44 Subway ridership statistics are from the Metropolitan Transportation Authority, *Subway Registration and Bus Report, 1994*.

Page 46 The 1990 census revealed that 29 percent of Jersey City's residents are foreign-born, a figure that is probably higher now. Among big cities Miami is the leader, with 46 percent foreign-born, followed by Los Angeles, with 33 percent (Jeffrey S. Passel and Michael Fix, *Setting the Record Straight*, The Urban Institute, Washington, D.C., 1993).

Pages 46–49 Income data for native-born and immigrant New Yorkers are from the 1994 *Annual Report on Social Indicators*, published by the Department of City Planning, City of New York, based on information gathered in the 1990 census. Professor John Mollenkopf of the City University of New York shared his data on labor force participation, which is also based on 1990 census information. Jeffrey S. Passel, in his *Immigrants and Taxes: A Reappraisal of Huddle's "The Cost of Immigrants"* (The Urban Institute, January 1994), makes the observation that most studies on immigrants and fiscal burdens have consistently shown immigrants to be *not* a net fiscal burden on the national level, sometimes a burden on the state level, and almost always a burden on the local level. Passel adds, "Often, however, the studies found that native populations are also a fiscal burden on the local level."

Page 50 Figures on housing costs are low estimates. Officially, New York City spends at least $220 million a year managing derelict buildings. In order not to deepen that deficit, the city ended the practice of seizing foreclosed buildings in 1993. The cost of tax delinquency of all buildings was over $400 million in fiscal year 1994, which means the actual cost of foreclosure was anywhere between the $220 million the city says it loses managing seized property and over $600 million, counting the $400 million that it is losing on buildings it will not seize. See Shawn G. Kennedy, "New York City Stops Foreclosing on Tax-Delinquent Buildings," *The New York Times*, March 13, 1995.

Page 52 The "simply breathtaking" quotation is from Clifford Krauss, "Mystery of New York, the Suddenly Safer City," *The New York Times*, Sunday, July 23, 1995, p. E1.

Crime statistics for New York City, 1989–93, are based on the New

York City FBI Index Crime Reports (Uniform Crime Reports), published in the 1994 *Annual Report on Social Indicators*, by the Department of City Planning, City of New York.

Page 53 The Korean grocery job—perhaps 40,000 positions citywide—actually represents increased spending on labor, not a decrease. These stores didn't begin hiring Mexicans until about 1990, more than a decade after Korean stores first appeared in New York. Essentially the owners were replacing two generations of family members—their children and their parents—who worked part-time. Now that the owners' debt was paid and the stores were prosperous, the kids went to college and the grandparents retired. If anything, prosperity generated new employment, with three or four thousand "volunteer" positions being replaced by salaried workers. Professor John Mollenkopf of the City University of New York provided the author with a fascinating statistic on immigrant self-employment. More than 25 percent of all Korean immigrants arriving before 1980 are self-employed today, a level not matched by any other group, native-born or foreign. Those arriving after 1980 also have a rate of self-employment higher than any other group's: 14 percent.

TWO **The City Without Immigrants**

Page 57 The Diversity Lottery was the result of the Immigration and Naturalization Act of 1990, which offered green cards to 55,000 lottery applicants from all but the biggest "sender" countries. Africans were the second-most favored applicants, following Western Europeans, but leading Asians, Latin Americans, and Caribbeans. According to Joseph Salvo of the New York City Department of City Planning, the Diversity Lottery brought 95 percent of the city's new Irish and 64 percent of its new Polish immigrants, a total of about 18,000 city residents and their families. See Rachel L. Swarns, "Polish and Irish Immigrants Benefit from Visa Lottery," *The New York Times*, January 30, 1996.

Page 57 The quotation from the Senegalese visa applicant comes from a Fulbright grant dossier, shown to the author by the U.S. embassy in Senegal.

Pages 62–64 Details on steamship passage in the late nineteenth century are provided in Philip Taylor's classic 1936 study, *The Distant*

Magnet: European Emigration to the U.S.A, published in London. Details of the *padrone* system come from Robert F. Harney's fine research article "The Padrone and the Immigrant (*The Canadian Review of American Studies*, vol. V, no. 2 [1974]). Another fascinating study, which also details the *padrone* network, is John E. Zucchi's *The Little Slaves of the Harp: Italian Street Musicians in Nineteenth-Century Paris, London and New York* (Montreal and Buffalo: McGill-Queens University Press, 1992). The following scholars lent their insights into this aspect of immigration history: Virginia Yans-McGloughlin of Rutgers University; Humbert Nelli of the University of Kentucky; David Reimers of New York University; Rudolf Vecoli, University of Minnesota; and Tom Archdeacon, University of Wisconsin.

Pages 63–64 Compared to today, immigration was cheaper in 1898. Teenage Pelegrino Rodino would have remained in debt into his twenties, but only because he was raising a family. Most immigrants could expect to repay their travel debt within a few months of arrival; indeed, travel was so cheap on the new steamships that thousands of Italian workers were able to make the round trip annually. Today's Chinese immigrants are notoriously dedicated savers, yet few are able to repay their debts—upwards of $30,000, according to testimony offered in trials of smugglers—in less than three or four years. One man, according to his employer, paid his debt in twelve months. After arriving in New York, he accepted a job as a cook in a Chinese restaurant in Alaska. He flew halfway back to Asia to work for $3,000 a month, with his room and board included. With no reason to spend money, and no reason to leave the warm kitchen during much of his stay there, he returned to New York's Chinatown debt-free after one year. Today he owns two restaurants in the suburbs.

Page 65 On his fellow Newark congressman, Mr. Rodino recalled, "Minish let Jewish voters think he was Jewish. But he was more Italian that I was. His father's name was Minisi. And his mother was born in Italy, whereas mine was born here."

Pages 66–67 The quotations from Lyndon Johnson, Sam Ervin, and Maston O'Neal are from the *1965 Congressional Quarterly Almanac*, pp. 466–67 and pp. 459–82.

THREE Brownsville, Brooklyn:
Mass Plus Energy Equals Upward Mobility

Page 70 "Plymouth Rock" quotation: Alter Landesman, *Brownsville* (New York: Bloch Publishing Corp., 1969), pp. 65–66.

Pages 70–72 Growth of Brooklyn: Elliot Willensky, *When Brooklyn Was the World, 1920–1957* (New York: Harmony Books, 1986), and David W. McCullough, *Brooklyn—And How It Got That Way* (New York: Dial, 1983). The $90 million sales figure is from Landesman's *Brownsville;* the calculation of $400 million current dollars is from Ibbotson and Associates, an econometric analysis firm in Chicago.

Page 74 Thomas Muller's excellent book *Immigrants and the American City* (New York: New York University Press/Twentieth Century Fund, 1993) has several well-documented passages on the relations between African-American immigrants. In Chapter 5, "The Price of Immigration," Muller argues his point convincingly: "Applying 1980 data, [an earlier analysis by the author] found that black unemployment rates were not increased—in fact they were marginally lowered—by a rise in the proportion of Mexican immigrants in metropolitan labor markets across the nation. . . . In addition, the research examined links, if any, between Korean immigration (a proxy for Asians) and black joblessness. It found a statistically significant *negative* correlation. . . . These results can be interpreted to mean that Mexicans and Asians are attracted to urban areas, where employment opportunities for all groups, blacks as well as Hispanics and Asians, are favorable. A plausible, but less certain interpretation of the data is that immigrants create economic growth, which, in turn, improves job prospects for blacks" (pp. 172–73, italics in the original).

Page 75 "Caribbean" refers to any of the non-Hispanic peoples of the Caribbean basin, a total of thirty-five independent states, plus the U.S. Virgin Islands. The majority are citizens of present and former British colonies: Anguilla, Antigua and Barbuda, Bahama Islands, Barbados, Belize, Bermuda, British Virgin Islands, Cayman Islands, Dominica, Grenada, Guyana, Jamaica, Montserrat, Saint Kitts–Nevis, Saint Lucia, Saint Vincent and the Grenadines, Trinidad and Tobago, and Turks and Caicos. "Caribbean" may also refer to immigrants from the Dutch West Indies (Aruba, Bonaire, Curaçao, Saba, Saint Martin, Saint Eustatius, and Suriname) and to francophones from French Guiana, Guadeloupe, Haiti, and Martinique. "Caribbean" may also include citizens of those South and Central American nations where Spanish is the official language, but where a population of black coast dwellers has traditionally been English-speaking. Those countries are Colombia, Costa Rica, Guatemala, Honduras, Nicaragua, and Panama. Caribbeans from the U.S. Virgin Islands of Saint Croix and Saint Thomas are, of course, not immigrants. See Philip Kasinitz's *Caribbean New York: Black Immigrants and the Politics of Race* (Ithaca, N.Y.: Cornell University Press, 1992).

Page 76 The United Hospital Fund of New York counts nearly 300,000 employees in all private health-care providers, plus another 100,000 in the public sector. Ronnie Lowenstein's report in the Federal Reserve Board of New York's publication *Current Issues in Economics and Finance*, "The Health Sector's Role in New York's Regional Economy" (vol. 1, no. 5 [August 1995]), puts the figure at almost 700,000, counting "health related" fields like pharmacy, health insurance, and wholesalers of medical instruments and supplies throughout the metropolitan region. It is impossible to know how many Caribbean immigrants are employed locally in the health field, but the number is substantial. According to the Public Use Microdata Survey (PUMS), health care is the number-one occupation for Caribbean New Yorkers. For example, among 71,000 Haitians in New York, almost a third of all households have at least one member employed in some aspect of health care, for some 10,000 jobs. Among Jamaicans, 9 percent of working men and 37 percent of working women are in health care, for another 20,000 jobs. Dr. Marco Mason of the Caribbean Women's Health Association of Brooklyn estimates that by 1980, more than 20,000 Caribbean women were working in just two jobs, nurse's aide and registered nurse, with another 4,000 as secretaries, 3,000 as cleaning women, 3,000 as general office workers, and 2,600 as hospital maids. Thousands more male immigrants worked as janitors, security guards, and nurse's aides. Given the large surge of Caribbean immigrants through the 1980s and 1990s, a conservative guess would be that at least 200,000 Caribbeans today work in some aspect of the health-care field. "Once you are in there, and you are my cousin, I'm going to get that job," Dr. Mason says, "even though this industry is still not the industry of choice."

Page 77 During the writing of this chapter two long-time civil rights activists died within days of each other in New York. Both were West Indian–born. Cleveland Robinson, former president of the Negro American Labor Council and chairman of the 1963 March on Washington, emigrated from Jamaica in 1944 (*The New York Times*, August 26, 1995). Dr. Benjamin W. Watkins, who emigrated from Barbados, to New York, in 1948, was the unofficial "Mayor of Harlem" from 1968 through 1974, and a leading figure in public health in the city (*The New York Times*, August 27, 1995).

Page 77 By 1965 only two former English colonies had become independent nations—Jamaica, and Trinidad and Tobago; both received quotas of 20,000 visas per year, like all other Western Hemisphere nations. In 1966 Barbados and Guyana were added to the quota list, to be followed in the 1970s by Antigua and Barbuda, Saint Kitts–Nevis, Grenada, Dominica, Saint Lucia, Bahama Islands, and Saint Vincent. The last of the British colonies to become independent was Belize, in 1985.

Page 78 The 1990 census reported 113,000 Jamaican New Yorkers; however, that is considered a low estimate, undercounting tens of thousands of undocumented aliens, as well as the many thousands who have arrived since the 1990 census was completed. It is widely believed that virtually every Jamaican household has at least one member who is undocumented—that is, someone who may have overstayed a tourist visa or simply a newborn child whose "immigration" status is that of a U.S. citizen. Thus it is safe to estimate there were as many as 30,000 uncounted Jamaicans in 1990, for a total in New York today, conservatively estimated, closer to 200,000.

Pages 80–81 Statistics on Brooklyn's neighborhoods come from several sources. The City of New York's Department of City Planning lists population growth by Community Board in its 1992 report, *Demographic Profiles: A Portrait of New York City's Community Districts from the 1980 and 1990 Censuses of Population and Housing*, pp. 98–153, designating racial composition for each district. "Black Brooklyn" is identified as those districts with a majority black population.

Page 82 The Pitkin Avenue descriptions are from Francis X. Clines, "Down These Mean Streets," *The New York Times*, Friday, July 16, 1977, p. A16.

Pages 82–83 On the use of the word "underclass," purists may disagree that the term "the underclass" stems from the 1977 riots. Its origins date back to at least 1963, to the Swedish sociologist Gunnar Myrdal, who defined the underclass as "an underprivileged class of unemployed, unemployables and underemployed who were hopelessly set apart from the nation." However, the term achieved greater currency following the 1977 blackout, especially when *Time* magazine ran a post-riot cover story: "The American Underclass: Destitute and Desperate in the Land of Plenty" (August 29, 1977). Five years later, Ken Auletta published the book *The Underclass;* by that time the word had become an accepted code term for ghetto blacks. See Herbert J. Gans, *The War Against the Poor: The Underclass and Antipoverty Policy* (New York: Basic Books, 1995).

Page 84 According to union officials and the personnel director at Wartburg Lutheran, $13,000 was top scale for a dietary aide in 1983, the rate set by a coalition of religious hospitals in collective bargaining with the Service Employees International Union. By 1995, dietary aides were making salaries between $18,000 and $20,000 a year. Alexander Greenwood, who was still employed at Wartburg Lutheran in 1995, made top scale.

Pages 85–86 The quotations from Dr. Waldaba Stewart are part of material quoted from or information developed for a story appearing in the February 12, 1996, issue of FORBES Magazine entitled "Ghetto Blasters," reprinted with permission of Forbes Inc.

Pages 87–88 Hospital Row is four facilities: Kings County Hospital, the State University of New York Health Science Center, Kingsborough Psychiatric Hospital and the Kingsbrook Jewish Medical Center. Combined, they employ close to 14,000 workers, the vast majority of whom are Caribbean immigrants. They generate more than $450 million in paychecks each year, part of the $25 billion in annual salaries generated by health-care jobs citywide. See Ronnie Lowenstein, "The Health Sector's Role in New York's Regional Economy," *Current Issues in Economics and Finance* (vol. 1, no. 5 [August 1995]), which reports that the average weekly wage in health care is about $700, citywide, ranging from the low end with home health care (under $350 per week) to medical doctors and pharmacists (more than $1,000/week).

Page 88 In 1990, there were 69,728 new residents of Brooklyn, but nearly 80,000 entered the majority-black districts of Bedford-Stuyvesant (5,317); Bushwick (10,075); Crown Heights (22,146); Brownsville (11,122); Fort Greene (1,802); East New York (6,419); East Flatbush (6,665); and Flatbush-Midwood (15,966). Therefore, black "inflight" not only accounted for virtually the entire new population, it more than compensated for the continued white flight out of Brooklyn. The estimate of 25,000 additional new residents in these districts by 1995 comes from Ken Hodges of the Claritas Group in Ithaca, New York.

Page 89 On home ownership: In the seven majority-black districts, stretching from Bushwick in northwest Brooklyn to East New York in the south, home ownership by existing tenants rose from 1980 to 1990. This increase was uneven—just 0.2 percent in East New York, for example, but more than 60 percent in Brownsville—although no area showed a decline. Home ownership was up 5 percent in Bushwick, 11 percent in Flatbush-Midwood, 28 percent in Crown Heights, 21 percent in Bedford-Stuyvesant. More than 1,500 home owners were added in the 1980s, meaning that whereas fewer than one in six residents owned their homes in 1980, slightly more than one in five did in 1990. In Brownsville, where fewer than one in ten owned a home in 1980, that figure by 1990 had become one in seven. How many more homes are being added currently won't be knowable until the 2000 census, but all indications are that home ownership has increased in black Brooklyn through the 1990s. See *Demographic Profiles*, pp. 98–153.

Page 89 Whereas groups such as Nehemiah and the New York City Housing Partnership have received favorable publicity for restoring communities in Brooklyn and the Bronx, few newspaper or magazine accounts discuss the immigrant connection to home buying. A report in *The New York Times* in 1995 noted that over 39,000 new apartments and 12,000 new one-, two-, and three-family town houses had been built in New York on vacant city-owned land. Yet, nowhere in the 2,000-plus-word article did the word "immigrant" (much less "Caribbean") appear. And yet, several housing activists quoted in the article, when interviewed for this book, confirmed that at least half of the Brooklyn and Bronx homes were purchased by owners who were born outside the United States, the vast majority from the Caribbean. See Alan Finder, "New York Pledge to House Poor Works a Quiet, Rare Revolution," *The New York Times*, April 30, 1995, p. A1.

Page 89 "a thriving commercial ship": On Brooklyn's restored retail activity, an organization called ProphetPoint tried in 1995 to determine just how much commerce had come back to Pitkin Avenue and the surrounding streets. Using only what it could glean from major distributors and phone-book listings, ProphetPoint found retail sales increased in Brownsville from $110 million in 1990 to $162 million in 1995, an increase of 42 percent, despite a citywide recession. ProphetPoint found the trend repeated throughout black Brooklyn. Retail sales were up, at a minimum, over 40 percent in East Flatbush, East New York, New Lots, Crown Heights, and Midwood. So, the outfit learned, were revenues from construction and services. The true increase—one reached by including all the tiny immigrant businesses that don't buy listings in the phone book—is probably closer to 100 percent.

Page 90 The area where Elon Gibson lives was restored under something called the Marcus Garvey Urban Renewal Plan. Ironically Marcus Garvey, a West Indian considered the father of Black Nationalism in New York, was deported in 1927. Now his descendants are among the prime beneficiaries of black-only set-aside policies. Says Phil Kasinitz of Hunter College, "This is Garvey's revenge."

Page 92 Su-su is hardly unique to Caribbean immigrants. Senegalese call such savings circles *tontine*, Dominicans call theirs *san* or *asociación*, Nigerians *ajo*. Korean immigrants use something similar, although usually more elaborate, called *keh*. Korean men join together to raise stakes to start a business. *Keh* circles may require contributions of $10,000 and even $20,000—enough to fill a warehouse with inventory or open a dentist's office or buy a grocery. *Keh* financed the bustling Gift District in Midtown Manhattan and a legion of Korean retail shops during the 1980s.

Page 93 According to a recent publication, there are nearly 150,000 foreign-born blacks in Dade County, about two thirds of them Haitian. Because live births among the native-born black population have failed to keep pace with deaths and out-migration, immigrants account for almost the entire growth of Miami's black community. In other words, had black immigrants not come to Miami, the existing black community would have shrunk to less than one-in-ten residents, instead of the one-in-five of 1995. See *Profile of the Black Community, 1990* (Metropolitan Dade County Planning Commission, 1996). Estimates of new businesses were provided by Claritas Business Information Services.

Pages 96–97 Golden Krust and revival of Pitkin Avenue are part of material quoted from or information developed for a story appearing in the November 6, 1995, issue of FORBES Magazine entitled "Imported Entrepreneurs," reprinted with permission of Forbes Inc.

Page 98 The best example of the improvement in public schools is Medgar Evers College, part of the City University of New York system in Brooklyn. Named for the slain civil rights leader, Medgar Evers was the first of the "black" borough schools to adopt a militant Afrocentric stance, defending open admissions, no matter how poorly students performed. During the 1970s fiscal crisis the school was downgraded to the status of a two-year community college. In the 1980s it became a majority West Indian school and encouraged immigrant students, accepting transfer credits from Caribbean schools like Jamaica's University of the West Indies. In the 1990s, as academic standards improved, it became the first CUNY community college to re-earn a four-year accreditation. Today its nursing program is considered among the best in the country.

FOUR California: "Land and Liberty"

Page 104 Mexican consulates are located in California (Calexico, Fresno, Los Angeles, Oxnard, Sacramento, San Bernardino, San Diego, San Francisco, San Jose, Santa Ana); Texas (Austin, Brownsville, Corpus Christi, Dallas, Del Rio, Eagle Pass, El Paso, Houston, Laredo, McAllen, Midland, San Antonio); Albuquerque, Atlanta, Boston, Chicago, Denver, Detroit, Douglas (Arizona), Miami, New Orleans, New York, Nogales, Orlando, Phoenix, Philadelphia, Portland, Saint Louis, Salt Lake City, Seattle, Tuscon. A forty-second consulate is attached to Mexico's embassy in Washington, D.C., and a forty-third is in San Juan, Puerto Rico. Mexico's 1994 economic crisis postponed the opening of new consulates planned for Las Vegas, Nevada, and for Boise, Idaho. By comparison, the country with the second-highest number of consulates in the United States is Canada. It has eleven.

Pages 106–107 Simpson and the Republicans lacked the votes in 1986 to pass a reform bill without making a compromise: a "one time only" amnesty. Rodino's side gave in on the terms of the amnesty, from being able to prove just two years of continuous residency to four years. Rodino got unexpected support from the Reagan White House, which also had an interest in protecting recent immigrants. During the 1980s nearly a million refugees from El Salvador, remitting more than 3 million dollars a day back home, played an essential role in propping up an ally defending itself from Marxist insurgents. In order to support a Cold War objective, the White House tacitly backed Rodino over Simpson on IRCA.

Page 110 Starting in the 1940s, despite restrictions imposed under the 1924 National Origins Act, Mexican farm workers were permitted entry under the Emergency Labor Program, also called the Bracero Program. Under what was essentially a "guest worker" program, the *braceros* weren't abolished until 1964, making the program one of the longest "emergency" measures ever instituted. After IRCA, Mexican farm labor entered under a variety of different specialty clauses. The law included the SAW, the Special Agricultural Worker, which allowed any undocumented worker who put in at least ninety days between May 1, 1985, and May 1, 1986, to apply for legal permanent residency, an amnesty even broader than the pre-compromise terms sought by Rodino. Added to this was a second, supplementary provision called RAW, for Replenish Agricultural Worker program, which went into effect in 1990. RAW was enacted with the understanding that many farm workers, once legalized, would abandon farming for better jobs. RAW allowed new immigrant workers to enter between 1990 and 1993. Both RAW and SAW were widely abused by employer and employee alike. A simple letter attesting to having employed an alien over a three-month period at some previous date was often enough, in many jurisdictions, to grant the bearer of that letter temporary work authorization or even a green card. In 1995 at least one "employer" admitted to having written over a thousand fraudulent letters of this kind.

Page 111 The Alien Land Laws of 1913, 1920, and 1921 prevented foreign-born Japanese from legally owning agricultural land. The laws were repealed in 1952. Miriam Wells, a California scholar who has researched the strawberry industry, wrote in 1984, "As did the Japanese with regard to other crops, many berry-growers circumvented the laws by securing land in the names of their native-born children, who could own the land after they reached the age of majority. Others paid American citizens to purchase land for them. Some Japanese owners and renters themselves hosted sharecroppers. . . . The system was disrupted in 1942 when the Japanese were forcibly relocated in detention camps for the duration of the war. During World War II berry production in the state practically ceased. After their release in 1945 many Japanese went back to share and cash tenancy, often with the same landowners." See Miriam J. Wells, "The Resurgence of Sharecropping: Historical Anomaly or Political Strategy?" *American Journal of Sociology*, vol. 90, no. 1 (1984), pp. 1–29.

Pages 114–115 By the mid-1990s, it had already become clear to demographers that the decline of rural America that occurred in the 1970s and 1980s had been reversed. Kenneth Johnson of Loyola University of Chicago and Calvin Beale of the USDA's Economic Research Service reported in 1995, "Since 1990, nonmetropolitan population growth rates have rebounded from the low levels of the 1980s. Population growth is now widespread geographically and is occurring in counties with a variety of economic specialties. The estimated nonmetropolitan gain of 2 million between April of 1990 and July of 1994 already exceeds the gain of 1.3 million during the 1980s. Nearly 74 percent of the 2,304 nonmetropolitan counties grew between 1990 and 1994, compared to 45 percent in the 1980s." See "Nonmetropolitan Demographic Trends in the 1990s: The Revival of Widespread Population Growth in Rural America," paper presented by Beale and Johnson, August 19, 1995, at the annual meeting of the Rural Sociology Society in Washington.

Pages 115–16 The largest increase in Asian and Hispanic-American small farmers has occurred since 1987, but the beginning of the rise can be traced from the 1982 census. A sampling of the earlier census figures tracks part of the Hispanic increase between 1982 and 1987 as follows:

	1982		**1987**
Colorado:	632	to	710
Idaho:	150	to	282
Missouri:	152	to	197
New Mexico:	2,728	to	3,013
Oklahoma:	128	to	143
Oregon:	209	to	238
Texas:	5,197	to	5,427

The Asian sample is as follows:

	1982		**1987**
Florida:	66	to	118
Iowa:	10	to	15
New Mexico:	8	to	19
Texas:	71	to	82
Virginia:	13	to	21

Page 120 One new manager, Joey Hernandez, settled in the little town of Mountain Home, and now farms 300 acres under the sponsorship of a retired farmer still living nearby. Hernandez, like Alberto Solis in Carruthers, California, has emerged as a Hispanic leader in Mountain Home, helping to establish a migrant workers' camp and improving working conditions for Mexican migrants. Nonetheless, he is also critical

of the surge of Mexican immigration to Idaho, sounding more like an old Anglo restrictionist than a Pan-Hispanic activist: "There are too many of them coming," he says, "and they don't want to work as hard as we did."

Page 123 Roger Ankrom, the cooperative extension agent for Polk County, Missouri (where the census recorded eight new farms), knew of very few Hispanic growers, but he did know of one rather unexpected development: Romanian immigrants have entered the county, nearly a dozen families growing beef cattle. The Romanians left Europe after the fall of Nicolae Ceaucescu in 1990, settling first in Dallas, where they found factory jobs. Saving their money, they were able to buy their first ranch, outside the town of Bolivar, on land going for the bargain-basement price of $800 an acre. "They are pretty independent people, they bring their old-style habits," Ankrom said. "We set up grazing systems, teach them how to get more out of the land."

Page 125 Both Alberto Solis and Manuel Gomez, like many Rodinos testing new lives as gringo growers in California, tried, once, to go home again. Gomez went back to Pabellon, he says, with a plan to make a living as a plow-for-hire. "I tried to work for myself," he recalls. "I bought one tractor and I tried to plant beans. But people can't pay. Every place I go, the places I plowed, they never paid me back. I had to come back to the U.S. to work again." Alberto Solis had a similar experience in Zacatecas.

Page 130 Figures of annual loss of farm acreage in Fresno County are from Greg Kirkpatrick of the American Farmland Trust office in Visalia, California.

Page 130 Statement made at a seminar on immigration at the New School for Social Research, New York, June 1995. Simpson also said that in 1986, when Governor Wilson was Senator Wilson, he worked vigorously for the loopholes in SAW and RAW in the IRCA law that permitted so many Mexican farm workers to legalize their status.

Page 131 The Hmong are hill tribesmen from Indochina who fought as mercenaries against various Communist armies from 1956 through the end of the United States–Vietnam War, around 1975. Almost the entire population fled ancestral homelands after the fall of Vietnam and Cambodia, most settling in refugee camps in Thailand or coming as individual refugee families to the United States. The Hmong are among the least successful of all immigrant groups and are often held up as examples of everything that is going wrong with America's immigration policy, particularly the abuse of the welfare system. *The Atlantic Monthly* chose the plight of the Hmong in Wausau, Wisconsin, to slam immigration policy ("For a look at a possible American future, consider the fate of a small midwestern city," the piece begins), in a particularly shrill article later repackaged by Morely Safer on CBS's *Sixty Minutes*. To be fair, the Hmong are not immigrants in any traditional sense. They were evacuated from Southeast Asia by force, taken from a traditional culture and thrust into hostile communities on a far-off continent. Even if they were inclined to migrate, under no circumstances imaginable would they have come in such numbers to the United States, much less have so easily accessed public welfare programs. Unlike most immigrants, the Hmong are refugees, and under U.S. resettlement programs were deliberately provided welfare assistance. Soviet Jews, it should be said, are also refugees, and also notorious abusers of welfare. Even worse for the Hmong was the way U.S. resettlement policy was implemented. Rather than "burden" any single community with a "Hmong problem," U.S. officials scattered Hmong in many states. For tightly knit Hmong families, this only deepened their welfare dependency and probably set them back a generation in their progress. All that said, twenty years after fleeing their mountain villages even the Hmong are showing they can be successful "immigrants." In the mid-1980s the Hmong started their own, internal migration toward California. There families were reunited and the beginnings of a real assimilation took place. Fresno officials interviewed by the author indicated in 1995 that welfare use among the Hmong had peaked, and that many Hmong teenagers were entering adulthood as fully self-sufficient citizens. Farming was only one industry they were excelling in. See Roy Beck, "The Ordeal of Immigration in Wausau," *The Atlantic Monthly*, April 1994, p. 84, and *Sixty Minutes*, October 16, 1994.

Of some 150,000 Hmong in America, almost a third live in California, some 40,000, just in Fresno County. See "Hmong at the Crossroads," a series in *The Fresno Bee*, January 1–3, 1995.

Page 131 A "metropolitan center" is defined as any county that has at least one municipality with 50,000 or more inhabitants. The number 50,000 is a small threshold, but some of the cities on the list have as many as a million or more. Villarejo's top twenty, in order of output, are:

		Output 1992
1	Fresno County, Calif. (Fresno)	$2 billion
2	Tulare County, Calif. (Visalia)	$1.38 billion
3	Kern County, Calif. (Bakersfield)	$1.33 billion
4	Monterey County, Calif. (Salinas)	$1.20 billion
5	Weld County, Colo. (Greeley)	$1.18 billion
6	Merced County, Calif. (Merced)	$907 million
7	Stanislaus County, Calif. (Modesto)	$897 million
8	Palm Beach County, Fla. (West Palm Beach)	$891 million
9	Riverside County, Calif. (Riverside)	$846 million
10	San Joaquin County, Calif. (Stockton)	$785 million
11	Imperial County, Calif. (NON METRO)	$753 million
12	Yakima County, Wash. (Yakima)	$689 million
13	Lancaster County, Pa. (Lancaster)	$681 million
14	Ventura County, Calif. (Oxnard)	$668 million
15	Deaf Smith County, Tex. (NON METRO)	$645 million
16	Kings County, Calif. (NON METRO)	$581 million
17	San Bernardino County, Calif. (San Bernadino)	$567 million
18	Maricopa County, Ariz. (Phoenix)	$505 million
19	Texas County, Okla., NON METRO	$504 million
20	San Diego County, Calif. (San Diego)	$496 million

Source: 1992 Census of Agriculture.

Page 134 The Asian connection is particularly dynamic in places where "urban" is a newer concept. Fresno, despite a long history of Japanese and Filipino farming in the county, actually lost four of its larger Asian farms from 1987 to 1992, according to the census. However, as the city grew and immigrants entered, Fresno County's Asians actually added 20,000 new acres and increased the value of all Asian farming in the county. The reason: While larger farms were dying off (presumably due to the aging of Japanese and Filipino growers, whose children had left farming), more than 264 "micro" farms were in operation. Micro farmers, who average just about 10 acres each, were adding acreage five times as fast as the larger farm category. Farther south, in Los Angeles County, the average Asian farm had no more than 18 acres, yet almost three fourths earned at least $10,000 a year, the census designation for a commercial farm. The remaining micro farms had an average size of just 6.5 acres, and even those are viable commercial enterprises.

Page 135 On exports: According to the California State Department of Food and Agriculture's Export Section, Japan was the leading Asian recipient in 1995, with $3 billion. Korea was next, with $1 billion; followed by Hong Kong, with $727 million; Taiwan, with $546 million; Singapore, with $505 million; Indonesia, with $275 million; and China, with $256 million.

Page 135 Farmland is disappearing so quickly in parts of Asia that it is quite likely that, early in the coming century, the majority of food consumed in some countries will be imported. This is true not only for smaller countries like Taiwan and Singapore, where almost all of the arable land is finite, but in bigger ones like Malaysia, Indonesia, Korea, and Thailand. In 1994 alone, Indonesia's most populous island, Java, converted more than 10,000 acres of rice paddies to accommodate industrial development. As a consequence, Indonesia began developing agriculture on the island of Borneo. But, even where farmland is available within national boundaries, infrastructure that can connect fields to consumers is often lacking. Thus, it will be easier to access such markets flying fresh produce from California than from rural areas far from population centers. See Manuel Saragosa, "Fears for Indonesian Rice Fields," *Financial Times*, February 9, 1996, p. 7.

Pages 135–38 Thomas Lam's story is part of material quoted from or information developed for a story appearing in the November 6, 1995, issue of FORBES Magazine entitled "Imported Entrepreneurs," reprinted with permission of Forbes Inc.

FIVE **Interstate Commerce**

Page 141 For a history of Chattanooga and the Shallowford Road, see Gilbert E. Govan and James W. Livingood, *The Chattanooga Country, 1540–1976*, third ed. (Knoxville: University of Tennessee Press, 1977).

Pages 145–46 Besides Athens, Canton, and Burlington, other similarly named towns with multiple Patels are Albany (Georgia, Oregon, and New York); Cleveland (Ohio and Tennessee); Troy (Alabama, Ohio, and Michigan); Jacksonville (Florida, Arkansas, and North Carolina); Rome (Georgia and New York); Columbus (Georgia, Indiana, North Carolina, and Ohio); Monroe (Ohio, Louisiana, and North Carolina); Manchester (Tennessee, Missouri, and New Hampshire); Decatur (Texas and Georgia); Florence (Arizona and South Carolina); and Richmond (Kentucky and Virginia). Bombay, New York, a town of 400 near the Saint Regis Indian reservation, has neither motels nor Patels. But Ramesh Patel runs Bob's Motel in Massena on State Highway 37.

Page 146 Dahyabhai Patel holds the record for longevity in the lodging business—more than thirty years with the Empress Hotel in San Francisco. This original "Motel Patel" is still in business at age seventy-two, today operating thirteen motels in California. But was he the first? He admits an early mentor was Kanjibhai Desai, whose surname is synonymous with Patel. Desai operated motels at least since 1952. See David DeVoss, "Hotel, Motel, Patel," *Asia, Inc.*, January 1994.

Page 146 Description of the "tradition" of Gujaratis in lodging comes from the *India Post*, vol. 1, no. 52 (June 30, 1995), p. Al.

Page 147 The $40,000 visa-for-business offer lasted until 1978. Today the requirement is $200,000.

Pages 151–53 For Patels in the mainstream media see Gale Scott, *The Washington Post*, May 7, 1979. Another early classic is Steven A. Marquez, "Indians Own at Least Eight Motels in Pinellas," *Saint Petersburg Times*, September 6, 1982, which begins: "A slight whiff of curry lends an exotic flavor to the small, spartan office of the Blue Moon Motel."

Pages 159–61 Although Silverman and Pettit downplay the role of ethnicity, most analysts believe their companies could not have grown as quickly as they did without Patels. Silverman's Hospitality Franchise System had practically no Indian franchisees in 1990. Over the next five years it added more than 2,000 properties, and boasted that some 40 percent of its ownership was in Patel hands. In other words, virtually all the growth after 1990 came from Patels.

Page 160 The economics of the lodging industry, hotel operators say, requires that a property make a dollar per night per room per one thousand dollars spent on construction. A luxury hotel costs about $250,000 per room. That means it must charge an average of $250 per night. A mid-level hotel is built for $100,000 per room, or $100 per room per night. Only the Patels building budget motels could charge full price and attract lodgers.

Page 161 All prices for the Choice chain are from the 1993 Choice Hotel International press kit. Prices have risen slightly since then.

Page 164 Rib-Roof and Smart Flapper are both registered trademarks.

Page 167 Another advantage Patels had in building their motel groups was special Small Business Administration set-asides that allow minority businessmen to qualify for subsidized loans of up to $750,000 in starting a new business. Although the Patels are in no way disadvantaged, they qualify as an Asian minority.

Page 168 Almost a year after its presence was denounced at the AAHOA convention, the "American Owned" sign remained in place. In retaliation, the chain prescribed "capital punishment," or expulsion, from the system. The owner of the Rodeway Inn at Exit 91 in Elizabethtown, Kentucky, a Mr. Gilbert, refused comment on two occasions, first in March, then in September 1995.

six *Boubous* over Broadway: The New African Americans

Pages 179–80 Mass migration: This is not as startling as it sounds. Air travel has opened transatlantic passage to thousands of black Africans, and perhaps 10,000 cross the Atlantic each month. Of course, only a fraction stay permanently. By contrast, some 4.7 million Africans are estimated to have been sold as slaves in the Americas over a 200-year period. However, according to Phillip D. Curtin's authoritative study, *The Atlantic Slave Trade: A Census* (Madison: University of Wisconsin Press, 1969), a total of 400,000 Africans entered North America between 1619 and 1860. Gwendolyn Midlo Hall's *Africans in Colonial Louisiana; The Development of Afro-Creole Culture in the Eighteenth Century* (Baton Rouge: Louisiana State University Press, 1992) reports that 3,250 Senegalese slaves came to Louisiana between 1726 and 1731, peak years of African "immigration" to Louisiana. In other words, even at the height of the Atlantic slave trade, North Americans rarely imported more than 10,000 Africans a year. See also Ronald Segal, *The Black Diaspora: Five Centuries of the Black Experience Outside Africa* (New York: Farrar, Straus and Giroux, 1995).

Page 179 The estimate of the U.S. African population comes from spokesmen at several African embassies in Washington. The largest "sender" countries from French Africa are Zaire, Ivory Coast, and Senegal, which, combined, have sent no more than 70,000 immigrants. Smaller countries, such as Rwanda, Guinea, Mali, and the Congo have sent fewer than 10,000 immigrants each. Like all official estimates, these may be low. The case of the Senegalese demonstrates. Six thousand is the estimate offered by Senegal's consul in Washington. However, the government-owned Banque de l'Habitat du Sénégal in New York says

that more than 15,000 Senegalese residents in the United States responded to a questionnaire it circulated in 1993. Ultimately, 5,000 expatriate Senegalese became regular bank customers. The most reliable
estimate by the mid-1990s was close to 30,000 Senegalese living in the
United States, more than half living in New York. Figures on Senegalese
entry are from the *Statistical Yearbook of the Immigration and Naturalization Service*, 1991 and 1994 volumes.

Page 183 Despite the growing number of Senegalese, since the late
1980s getting visas has been much more difficult for Senegalese. In
1980, only 3 percent of visa applications were rejected; by the end of
the decade more than 90 percent were rejected. At the same time, not
every Senegalese applies from Senegal. Many emigrate from Europe or
elsewhere in Africa. A Senegalese who has his application rejected in
Dakar may go to Mali, Guinea, or Gambia—all places with large
Senegalese colonies, where a blood relative may be established. New
documents can be obtained, perhaps even a new identity. After the
Senegalese, Guineans and Gambians constitute the fastest-growing West
African groups in America, although many may actually be transplanted
Senegalese.

Page 183 In 1996 Air Afrique had five weekly nonstops connecting
Dakar with New York. Senegal's national airline is also the airline of
nine other states: Ivory Coast, Congo, Niger, Chad, Burkina Faso, Togo,
Benin, Mauritania, and the Central African Republic.

Page 184 Coumba, the street peddler, insisted she spent three days
in the women's jail in Brooklyn, something that the author could not
confirm. She said peddlers are offered a choice of paying a $50 fine or
doing time. She decided to save her money, adding that the police made
no inquiry about her visa status, which by law they cannot do, except in
felony cases. She said that if they had asked, her alibi to explain her long
stay in America would be that she lost her passport and doesn't know
when her visa expired.

Page 185 The Pakistani-Senegalese connection extends across the
city. Besides newsstands, Senegalese colonize corners of Pakistani delicatessens, convenience stores, and smoke shops. Explanations for these
ad hoc alliances are varied. Two are often given: Senegalese and Pakistanis are both Muslims, thus often meet in mosques; adult Senegalese
males provide security for the Pakistanis against shoplifters, as well as
escorts in and out of the neighborhood where they work.

Page 198 In 1994 Senegal's Foreign Affairs Ministry released the following chart listing the top ten expatriate communities. All numbers are thought to be low estimates:

Ivory Coast	150,000
Gambia	80,000
France	60,000
Italy	40,000
Mali	30,000
Spain/Portugal	15,000
Gabon	15,000
Cameroon	15,000
Guinea	10,000
Zaire	5,000

Other countries, which recorded at least 1,000 Senegalese, include: United States (6,000), Egypt (3,000), Morocco (1,000), Saudi Arabia (1,600), Nigeria (1,500), Germany (2,000), and Mauritania (3,000).

Page 199 The cable on disaffected youth was titled "Dreaming of America: Senegalese Turn to the United States." It was prepared March 29, 1993, for Ambassador Mark Johnson, and was reviewed by the author in January 1995.

Page 199 The word "captive," *captif*, was a legalistic fiction used by the French to blur the moral stigma of the trade. The Bambara, they rationalized, were "war prisoners" from the interior. They were prisoners only of the "war" between tribes competing to sell "captives" to European slave traders.

Pages 199–200 Few Senegalese slaves arrived in America, for two reasons. In 1803 Louisiana became part of the growing United States of America under the Louisiana Purchase. In 1808 Congress banned slave importation, meaning any new slaves entering the region had to be brought from other states. In fact, the term "sold down the river" stems from the business of shipping American-born slaves down the Mississippi from Tennessee and Kentucky to the slave market in New Orleans. Although Senegal's historic link to North America is tenuous, it is real. Today the surname "Senegal" endures in southwestern Louisiana, particularly in Lafayette Parish, which has over thirty listings for "Senegal" and "Sinegal" in each of two cities, Lafayette and Carencro.

According to Carl A. Brasseaux of the University of Southwestern Louisiana, the surname surfaced among freed slaves sometime in the 1700s, together with at least one other African name, "Ebow" (derived from a French rendering, "Hibou"), for Nigeria's Ibo tribe. He adds that while many freed slaves and so-called Creoles of color owned slaves, slave ownership in the Senegal clan was more a rescue operation. These Senegalese "owned" slaves not for work on their plantations, but to free family members from others' ownership.

Pages 200–203 The word "Mouride" comes from the Arabic *Murid d'lahi*, or the "slaves of God." Spelled several ways in the West, Murid is a term known to Muslims everywhere, referring to the ultra-devout. Separatists in Chechnya call themselves Murids. The French word "Mouride" almost always refers to Senegal's Bamba cult. Mourides are "fundamentalists," but unlike Hamas and Hezbollah in the Middle East, not "extremist." Politically Mourides tend to be ultra-conservative. Some refer to overseas migration as *"jihad,"*: in the traditional Muslim meaning of the word, something between "colonize" and "proselytize"—in other words, a peaceful campaign devoid of the Great Satan rhetoric associated with Muslim fundamentalism of North Africa and the Middle East. The best text on Ahamadou Bamba and the Mourides is Donal B. Cruise O'Brien's *The Mourides of Senegal: The Political and Economic Organization of an Islamic Brotherhood* (Oxford: Clarendon Press, 1971).

Disagreements between Mourides and traditional Muslims are great, and obvious: "You ask a Moroccan? It's not Islam," Moustapha El Khadowi, Dakar correspondent for the Casablanca-based Maghreb News Service, told the author. "Take Ramadan. We fast. Here the *marabout* says, 'You don't have to fast. Pay me, and I fast for you!' In Islam this is forbidden. We have *marabout* in Morocco, but not like here! Like in a cemetery, you have a mausoleum for a really religious man; you point to it and say, 'Pray to God, be like this man.' But to be a *marabout*, you should be dead. Here the *marabout* is like a king; it's hereditary." In fact, Ahamadou Bamba's last living son, eighty-three-year-old Serigne Saliou Mbacke, was Khalifa General of the Mourides in the mid-1990s, the sect's supreme cleric. Three of Bamba's sons have served as Khalifa since his death seventy years ago. In that way, too, Mouridism is unique—a medieval Islamic movement only a generation removed from the founder.

Page 205 As the Senegalese community grows, eventually return trips by traders become unnecessary. When it's time to ship money home, Mourides simply send a *marabout* to New York. During a week's worth of spiritual consultation, he collects dollars to buy televisions or other appliances, usually from another Mouride running a wholesale outlet. He would then arrange for the purchases to be shipped as cargo on his return flight. Back in the Sandaga, a $500 television might fetch $800 at retail; that money, now converted into West African francs, is then parceled out to family members. Thus, the work of one peddler grows into the work of hundreds, who in turn support thousands of Senegalese back home, many constituting the next generation of emigrants.

Pages 206–7 A search of U.S. telephone directories in 1996 yielded a partial list of Mouride businesses. Among them: Touba African Arts, Touba Guede, Touba World of Elegancy (Atlanta), Touba Gold (Decatur, Georgia), Touba Mbacke Art (New Orleans), Touba African Business Center (Washington, D.C.), Touba African (Los Angeles), Touba-Bagdad Hair Fashion (Trotwood, Ohio), Touba African-American Shop (Providence, Rhode Island). By far the most Toubas are in New York City, including: Touba Jewelry and Fabrics, Touba Tropical Hats, Touba International Flavor, Touba International Calls, Touba African Jewelry (Bronx), Touba African Grocery, Touba Trading Inc., Touba Mbacke Trading, Touba Darou Salam (Queens).

Page 208 There has also been growing anti-Senegalese sentiment at the out-of-town festivals. At Detroit's African World Festival, vendors' fees advanced from $200 in 1984 to $800 ten years later. Senegalese were more than willing to pay, but locals protested. The African World Festival Vendors Association forced the sponsors to give their group a special discount. Their leader, Abdul Raheem of the Pan Afrikan Resource Network, told the author, "The Senegalese, with their capitalistic ways, are against the spirit of the festival. They're just doing the bidding of the Koreans, who we already kicked out."

Pages 208–9 The reaction to this overseas migration is positive. In Dakar, the director of expatriate affairs at Senegal's foreign ministry, Ibrahima Diallo, added this insight: "For us this migration is an economic movement. They come to America to work, to develop their villages and towns, to make joint ventures. For us it's an opportunity to develop our country. We are happy to notice this is a quiet emigration, which will influence positively the balance of payments. . . . If Senegalese establish themselves and find a way to become American, that's no problem for us."

SEVEN Typicalness: Massachusetts and Minas Gerais

Page 212 Brazil's present currency, the *real* ("royal"), was introduced in 1994 and has proved remarkably stable. Over the previous eight years, Brazil issued at least four different tenders—the *cruzeiro,* the *cruzado,* the *reais,* and the *cruzado novo.* During those years Brazilians abroad became an important source of foreign exchange. Between 1987 and 1992, remittances from *"dekasegi,"* Brazilians of Japanese descent hired as guest workers in Japan, rose from $70 million to almost $2 billion. By 1994 remittances from all Brazilians living abroad totalled $2.7 billion; in 1995 almost $5 billion, 70 percent of that amount coming from the United States and Japan. See *Gazeta Mercantil,* international weekly edition, November 23, 1992, and November 27, 1995.

Page 213 The excerpt from *States News,* of June 26, 1994, is one of dozens. Fascinating for their simplicity, they read like the cryptic messages scratched in rail yards by hoboes during the Depression or left along the guard rails on interstate highways by hitchhikers years later. *"Sidney, vocé vem o não vem? . . . João Carlos"* ("Sidney, you coming or aren't you?") reads one. Another: *"José Lauro, não vem agora que o clima aqui esta gostoso, mas emprego esta a maior fria, Claudio"* ("I'm not coming now because the weather is agreeable. But I probably will when it gets colder"). Others capture the poetry of a pioneer experience: *"Rita, aqui é mais do que maravilhoso, é fantastico. Estou adorando, é breve comecarei a estudar. . . . Saudades da amiga, Rejane, Boston."* ("Rita, here is more than marvelous, it's fantastic. I am adoring it and soon will start my studies.")

Page 213 For statistics see "1992, Minas Gerais in Figures," published by the Industrial Development Institute of Minas Gerais.

Pages 213–14 Joseph A. Page, a Latin American scholar, writes, "Just as fun-loving *cariocas* (Rio de Janeirans) are a product of their lush environment, *mineiros* bear the imprint of the mountains that fill their home state and isolate its communities. *Mineiros* tend to be cautious, steady, distrustful, and averse to emotional extremes. They also shun extravagance, a trait that has earned for them the reputation of being tight-fisted or *'pão duro'* (an expression referring to people who keep bread until it hardens)." In other words, the perfect immigrant. See *The Brazilians* (Reading, Mass.: Addison-Wesley, 1995), p. 441.

Page 214 Like most immigrant groups, Brazilians are undercounted. Fewer than 95,000 were counted in the 1990 census, about 25 percent of the estimate researchers give. By 1993, the Roman Catholic Archdiocese of Boston was reporting that some 158,000 Brazilians were living in Massachusetts alone. See Doreen Iudica Vigue, "A Brazilian Community Thrives in Marlborough," *Boston Globe,* April 11, 1993; *West Weekly,* p. 1; and Marcos Sa Correa, "O Brasil se Expande," *Veja,* September 7, 1994, pp. 70–77. The best research on Brazilian immigration is compiled in Maxine L. Margolis, *Little Brazil* (Princeton, N.J.: Princeton University Press, 1994). One footnote states, "There is no doubt that people from Minas Gerais are overrepresented among Brazilians in the United States. Virtually all accounts of *brazucas* in the Brazilian media mention this. Forty-one percent of my own sample are *mineiros,* as were 87 percent of Bicalho's [a Brazilian researcher]" (p. 281).

Page 219 The statistic on Portuguese speakers, provided by the Massachusetts Association of Portuguese Speakers, or MAPS, includes the children and grandchildren of immigrants.

Pages 219–20 The link between Governador Valadares and Massachusetts was forged during World War II, at a time when Brazil's loyalty to the Allied cause was dubious at best. Officially neutral, Brazil's military leaders sympathized with the Fascist dictatorships; thus there was concern that certain strategic materials would become unavailable. One was mica, used in radio tubes and the detonators of airborne explosives. A mica mine near Governador Valadares was militarized during World War II as a preemptive strike against Nazi saboteurs. It was managed by U.S. Army engineers, some of whom came from the Massachusetts Institute of Technology. Military service begot wartime marriages, which brought the first Amero-Brazilian families to Massachusetts. However, by 1996 the one-way travel toward the United States appeared to have peaked. The reasons for the drop-off are varied. For one thing, it is getting harder to get tourist visas, as U.S. consular officials are especially wary of anyone with a Valadares address. According to a Brazilian chamber of commerce publication, approximately 20,000 Valadarenses were living in the United States by 1989. That figure has increased over the last eight years. See "Caminho das Americas," *Revista Municipios do Brasil,* February 1990, p. 29.

Page 220 Framingham as Edge City was described by Joel Garreau in his book *Edge City.* Of eastern Massachusetts he writes, "Beyond [Route] 128, there are two Edge Cities emerging, and they are both on the same spikelike road: the Massachusetts Turnpike heading west toward the Berkshires and Albany. One is located where the highway crosses the outer beltway, at 495 and the Pike, sometimes known by the name of the nearby town of Westborough. The other emerging Mass Pike Edge City is between the first and second beltways, near Framingham." See *Edge City: Life on the New Frontier* (New York: Doubleday, 1991), p. 81.

Page 221 Horace Mann moved his normal school, which was founded in nearby Newton, to land donated in Framingham in 1853. This and other items are covered in Josiah H. Temple, *History of Framingham, Massachusetts, 1640–1885,* a reprinting of the 1887 edition (the original frontispiece has the title *History of Framingham, Massachusetts, early known as DANFORTH'S FARMS, 1640–1889, with a GENEALOGICAL REGISTER*). A book published in 1909, *Certain Towns and Cities Adjacent to Boston and the Boston Edison System* (Boston: The Edison Electric Illuminating Company), reports on Framingham, "At South Framingham are Baptist, Episcopal, Congregational, Universalist, Methodist Episcopal [sic], Presbyterian and Roman Catholic Churches, while there is a Roman Catholic mission for Italians" (pp. 17–18).

Page 223 The term "wop gang" was not an insult, at least not among immigrants. It comes from a Sicilian word, *guappu,* which means "dandy" or "good-looking," what bosses who recruited immigrant laborers called themselves—probably because they could afford better clothes. People who did a *guappu's* work were "wops," or worked on "wop gangs."

Page 229 One of the more ingenious businesses is *Diário do Brasil,* a desktop cousin to *States News.* Composed daily in Minas Gerais and Chelsea, Massachusetts, *Diário do Brasil* can be read via Internet or in dozens of Massachusetts shops catering to Brazilians. *Diário do Brasil* packs a lot into eight pages—everything from the daily dollar exchange rate in Brazil (in 1994 that meant three different rates: bank, tourist, and black market) to a news summary of the headlines in Belo Horizonte newspapers. It also runs classified ads, sports scores, and a horoscope, which usually runs across the page from a summary of the evening-before's most popular soap operas.

Pages 231–32 All corporate descriptions come from the companies' own 1996 press releases.

Page 232 An article published in 1991 described the plight of Framingham. Unemployment, just 2.4 percent statewide in the booming, pre–1987 era of the Massachusetts Miracle, was a "nearly invisible

1.7 percent" in Framingham. Just months before the bubble burst, Framingham voted against a zoning variance that would have allowed the General Motors plant to expand to build family-size mini-vans. Three years later, GM closed the plant, terminating 3,700 jobs. By 1994, with the local economy beginning its recovery, unemployment in the town was around 4.5 percent, about three times what it had been during the Massachusetts Miracle. Yet, during that same period, from 1987 to 1990, at least 5,000 Brazilians entered the town, obviously unconcerned by the apparent lack of opportunity. See Brian O'Reilly, "How Recession Swept a Town," *Fortune*, January 14, 1991, pp. 83–84.

Pages 239–40 According to the November 1994 Framingham Public Schools expenditure report, all bilingual programs were budgeted at $1,406,893.38, compared to a total budget of $42,638,852.16. For an idea of just how diverse Framingham schools are, here is the language list for one elementary school, the Charlotte Dunning School, in October 1994: Arabic, Armenian, Bengali, Chinese, Farsi, Greek, Gujarati, Haitian Creole, Hindi, Ibo, Japanese, Khmer, Korean, Portuguese, Russian, Spanish, Tamil, Thai, Urdu, and Vietnamese. The teachers' salary schedule for 1995–96, the formula used by Framingham Public Schools, shows compensation ranges from $26,140 a year to $54,360, depending on years of service and level of education. Thus a new bilingual educator could cost the town less than half the salary paid a veteran educator.

Page 240 Lau vs. Nichols: Supreme Court (414 U.S. 563, 1974). The decision drew from the Title VI of the 1966 civil rights act and ruled that, in the absence of treatment, students lacking English proficiency were "effectively foreclosed from any meaningful education."

Page 241 The total number of "linguistic minority" students in Framingham public schools in 1994 was 1,327. In other words, only about 45 percent of the immigrant students were partaking of bilingual programs. Despite Framingham's progress in assimilating immigrants, the burden was growing. In 1984, there were just 725 linguistic minority students enrolled in Framingham schools out of a total enrollment of 8,304. Ten years later, the student body had shrunk by nearly 1,000 students, but the linguistic minority had more than doubled, from 8.7 percent to 18 percent.

Page 241 The Bilingual Program Review Report of Findings was issued in May 1994 by the Commonwealth of Massachusetts Department of Education. It cites a total of 65 criteria in four categories: Administration (21 criteria); Identification, Placement, and Transfer (20);

Program Delivery (14); and Parent Involvement (10), and rates the district in each with scores of Commendable, Implemented, Partially Implemented, and Not Implemented. Framingham's schools received no Commendable rating, and only a handful of Implemented ratings, with the majority earning Partially Implemented and Not Implemented scores.

Page 242 In his letter to the state, dated September 30, 1994, Superintendent Thayer turned bureaucratic logic back on itself, quoting law like biblical scripture. While conceding that Framingham had twenty Chinese speakers (under the guidelines of M.G.L. Chapter 71 A, Section 2), he cited the provisions of Regulation 603 CMR, which "specifically preclude a school district from enrolling children of limited English-speaking ability of different primary language backgrounds in the same Transitional Bilingual Education class. Simply put, all of our Chinese students are not able to communicate with one another because each dialect effectively constitutes a separate primary language. No one teacher could communicate with all of the students." Two years later the state agreed with Thayer and dropped the requirement.

Page 243 Framingham's two-way program for Spanish starts in kindergarten; Framingham was in its seventh year of the program in 1994.

Page 247 While family unification remains a goal of U.S. immigration policy, family preservation is not a reason to waive violations of visa law. If it were, every undocumented alien would be able to use his or her children as a shield against deportation.

Page 248 The Quintelas are pioneers, but they are not alone. Among the other names turning up in a search of Framingham property records are Alameida, Alvares, Alves (6 families), Araujo, Amaral (2), Soares Batista (3), Carvalho (2), Des Marais, Dias (4), Fernandes (4), Martins (8), Pereira (2), Ramos (6), and Oliveira (2).

EIGHT **Paranoia Redux: California's New Majority**

Page 254 Editorial: See "Eastern Pacific Troubles," *Far East Economic Review*, May 14, 1992, p. 3.

Page 258 Despite sending their children to local schools, for example, no Japanese resident serves on Fort Lee's nine-member school board.

Pages 259–61 Monterey Park is believed to be the first city on the

U.S. mainland to achieve an Asian majority, which occurred sometime during the 1980s. See Seth Mydans, "Asian Investors Create a Pocket of Prosperity," *The New York Times,* October 17, 1994, p. A12. Chino, California, is another new Asian suburb. To be *"chino,"* in Spanish, is to either look or be "Chinese." Considering California's past as a colony of Spain, and its future on the Pacific Rim, it is only fitting that Chino, California, be a Chinese suburb with a Spanish name.

Page 260 One realtor, Don Georgino, told the author that in 1985 he sold a hillside property for $300,000, property he had purchased just a few months before for $60,000.

Page 261 Certain Massachusetts towns swelled as quickly with out-bound urban folk in the 1950s as some California suburbs are doing today. For example, Framingham's population grew from 28,086 to 44,526 between 1950 and 1960; Needham's grew from 16,313 to 25,793, and Natick's from 19,838 to 28,831, all gains of over 50 percent, with much of the growth driven by Jewish families. Sharon, probably Massachusetts's most Jewish suburb, saw its population more than double, from 4,847 to 10,070 residents between 1950 and 1960.

Page 263 Camp Stoneman was more than a War Brides' post. Along with Monterey's Fort Ord, it was a training ground for the First and Second Filipino Infantry regiments mustered in California after the outbreak of World War II. Even though the U.S. Army remained segregated until nearly the end of the war, Filipinos enlisted by the thousands to serve. One of the consequences of their service was that antinaturalization laws (which applied even to the children of Asians born in this country) were relaxed. The number of Filipinos entering service in the U.S. Navy is astonishing. According to Yen Le Espiritu, a Filipino-American scholar in California, more than a million Filipinos applied for navy service during the decade of the 1960s, although relatively few actually were inducted, because of the 94–99 percent reenlistment rate of those already in service. By 1970, Professor Espiritu notes, the U.S. Navy, with about 14,000 Philippines-born enlistees, employed more Filipinos than the entire Philippine navy. See Yen Le Espiritu, *Filipino American Lives* (Philadelphia: Temple University Press, 1995), p. 15.

Page 263 The Philippines, like Ireland, Armenia, Greece, and Senegal, is a "sender" country, with a high proportion of its people living abroad. In all of Asia, only China sends more immigrants than the Philippines. Filipinos are also the great intra-Asia migrants, with settlements stretching from Kuwait and Saudi Arabia to Singapore and Tokyo. More than 140,000 Filipino nurses and house maids, for example, live in Hong Kong alone.

Page 263 At least one old-line Filipino family, the Lopezes, has ventured across the Pacific. In 1972 the Lopez family had its holdings seized by dictator Fernando Marcos, while two of its scions (including the grandson of the islands' World War II president) were thrown into a military prison. Eugenio "Geny" Lopez, Jr., escaped, and spent nine years in exile in San Francisco. He returned after Marcos fell, but left substantial new holdings behind in California. See Beth Day Roulo, "Geny Lopez's Revenge" *Asia, Inc.*, July 1994, p. 50.

Page 264 For statistics on Filipinos in Contra Costa, see Wylie Wong, "A Place to Call Home: The Number of Filipino-Americans Is Growing in West County and Vallejo, and That Should Translate into More Clout," *Contra Costa Times*, November 12, 1995, p. 1A.

Page 264 Filipino immigrants, like most immigrant groups, tend to out-earn the U.S. average. Filipinos also tend to have a higher income level than most immigrant households, nearly $22,000 per year nation-wide in 1990. They also have among the highest labor participation, 73 percent male and female, due to the fact that so many Filipino women work full-time, full-year jobs, more so than any other Asian immigrant group. One in five Filipino families has at least three full-time workers; one in three has at least one university graduate. See California Coalition of Fil-American Chambers of Commerce, *Numbers That Make a Difference: The Filipino-American Community of the 1990s.*

Page 265 "*Balikbayan*" is Tagalog for "what you bring home when you're going home," but has earned a generic Filipino meaning: express mail home. A *balikbayan* box, usually 18 × 18 × 18 inches, is a fixture in every Filipino household, and can be shipped door-to-door from California to any town in the Philippines for a fraction of what Federal Express or DHL charges. The San Francisco Bay Area now has so many Filipino enclaves that *balikbayan* is practically an industry, employing hundreds of shippers, packers, inventory clerks, and drivers moving cardboard cubes like miniature container blocks across the ocean.

Page 267 Today Filipinos dominate the low end of the state's bureaucracy, especially in the Bay Area, holding down the secure jobs that pay for the neat town houses in places like Hercules and El Cerito.

Filipinos have availed themselves of civil service jobs in California much as Jamaicans have chosen public-sector work in New York. Like the West Indians, they take advantage of English proficiency and the desire of cities like San Francisco and New York to pursue an aggressive "diversity" policy in public employment. Filipinos fill an Asian "quota" that Chinese are reluctant to fill, just as Jamaicans out-compete African Americans in New York jobs. In 1985, a class action suit, Filipino Municipal Employees vs. Diane Feinstein, was presented to the Equal Employment Opportunity Commission (EEOC) for consideration. Public-interest lawyers complained Filipino Americans represented 12 percent of the City of San Francisco's municipal workforce, but less than 1 percent of its managers. The EEOC said the 3,000-odd Filipino Americans working for the city filed too few complaints to merit hearing the suit. Since then the size of the Filipino workforce in the public sector has grown.

Pages 270–71 The details of the Impulse story and its removal by Uniden were confirmed by Impulse's founder, Gary De Kat, in a telephone interview with the author, November 1995.

Page 271 The figures on employed residents, jobs, and population come from the Association of Bay Area Governments (ABAG) data collection center. The population of Pittsburg in 1995 was 51,000, according to city officials. ABAG cites a figure of 72,000, which includes Pittsburg's own suburbs, like Bay Point. The number of business licenses includes Pittsburg and outlying cities. The word "households" is used instead of "residents" to reflect the agglomerative effect of all the jobs in the greater Pittsburg area.

Pages 272–73 Sales tax figures are from the California State Controller Report of 1995. As if to prove the power of the Filipino consumer, the only town that approached Pittsburg's spending jump was Hercules, another immigrant boom town. Sales tax revenues jumped from $287,000 to $480,000 in four years, although population growth had leveled off by that time. Per capita, sales tax revenue leaped more than 50 percent, from $17 to nearly $26.

Page 276 The figure of 100,000 new businesses is an extrapolation, based on the 94,937 new Asian firms that opened in the state between 1987 and 1992, as reported in the U.S. Department of Commerce's 1992 Economic Census. The number now is probably much higher. The Commerce Department's list, published during the summer of 1996, counts

Asian and other minority firms recorded in the 1990 census. Among the "pan-Asian" and "Ethnic Specific Towns" recording growth were the following:

Difference	1987		1992
Alhambra (Taiwanese)	1,843	2,527	+716
Ceritos (Taiwanese)	1,597	2,162	+575
Daly City (Taiwanese)	1,389	2,004	+615
Fremont (mixed)	1,379	2,816	+1,437
Garden Grove (Korean)	1,831	3,386	+1,555
Gardena (Korean)	1,301	1,817	+516
Hayward (Vietnamese)	763	1,258	+595
San Gabriel (Cambodian)	687	1,529	+842
Torrance (Taiwanese)	1,845	2,832	+987
Westminster (Vietnamese)	1,086	1,663	+577

Each of these communities added new businesses at a rate of more than 100 per year—or at least two every week.

Page 276 For Miami see Alejandro Portes and Alex Stepick's fine book, *City on the Edge: The Transformation of Miami* (University of California Press, 1993). Employment patterns changed between the 1950s and the late 1980s. Prior to the big immigration waves, about one in five Miamians was employed in tourism; by 1987 that had shrunk to one in eleven. By contrast, the proportion of Miamians employed in banking had nearly tripled, while those engaged in finance, insurance, or real estate had risen 50 percent (p. 209).

Page 277 Ironically, the Koreans were repaid for their efforts when the U.S. Commerce Department slapped steel producers like POSCO with 35 percent punitive duties for allegedly dumping product in the United States. POSCO admitted it was selling steel to the Pittsburg plant for less than it could earn in Asia, but only because that was an original condition of the deal to keep the California plant operating. See Damon Darlin, "Protecting Whom?" *Forbes*, March 29, 1993.

Page 277 Pittsburg and the entire Sacramento River region is poised on the verge of a transpacific boom, starting with Vallejo at the mouth of the estuary, and following the shoreline all the way to Pittsburg. Over the last fifteen years Toyota has selected Benicia, a town just west of Pittsburg, as its intake point for cars and parts entering from Japan. Honda has selected the city of Richmond, due south. Down in Fremont,

Mitsubishi builds cars with General Motors, essentially repeating the Posco–U.S. Steel equation: Asian finance plus American assets. All three towns have growing Asian populations.

Page 278 There were twelve FACCs (Filipino-American Chambers of Commerce) on a list compiled by the Philippines Consulate in San Francisco in 1995, not including the Fil-Am Business and Professional Association of Salinas and the Fil-Am associations of Fresno, Roseville, Milpitas, and Pittsburg, as well as three Fil-Am Catholic Associations in Vallejo, Watsonville, Salinas, Marina, and San Francisco.

Page 280 The navy announced in 1993 it would decommission Mare Island. Then, more than 7,000 Vallejo-area residents worked on the base. Two years later that number had shrunk to 1,200.

NINE Delray Beach, Florida: Import Substitution

Page 285 Other groups are as prone or more prone to testing HIV-positive than Haitians. Zairians, Ugandans, and Zimbabweans all come from countries where the AIDS virus originated. They are, on balance, more likely to be AIDS carriers. But Africans are less likely to be immigrants. Singling out 4 million Haitians (and not, say, the 7 million residents of Rio de Janeiro) as likely carriers was not simply a matter of science. It was a also a reaction to immigration.

Pages 286–87 Historic details are recorded in *Delray Beach: The Early Years*, produced in 1986 by the Greater Delray Beach Chamber of Commerce, in honor of the city's seventy-fifth anniversary.

Page 291 Renaissance: Otis White, "The Best Run Town in Florida," *Florida Trend*, February 1995, p. 36. Neither the word "Haitian" nor "immigrant" appears in *Florida Trend*'s eight-page spread.

Page 292 The 1990 census recorded about 60,000 Haitians in Dade County. A recent study by the Research Department of the Metropolitan Dade County Planning Department indicated the census may have undercounted Haitians by as much as 50 percent. Using birth and school enrollment data, the authors updated the figure to 90,000. Moreover, Little Haiti has begun to spin off its own "suburbs" of El Portal, Opa Locka, and North Miami Beach. See Metropolitan Dade County Planning Department, *Profile of the Black Population, 1990*, December 1995, pp. 17–21.

Pages 292–93 As Professor de Haven Smith points out, although Domestic Worker declined as a job category, similar work was booming

in the hotels, restaurants, and resorts. But by that time thousands of
blacks had abandoned these jobs for better work, while those least
equipped to compete shunned them.

Page 299 According to the Palm Beach County Property Appraiser,
a total of 1,075 new residences was built in Delray Beach between 1990
to 1995. How many belonged to Haitian families is not recorded. However, Dan Marfino, of the City of Delray Beach Planning Department,
identified parts of the city that had large concentrations of Haitian immigrants and their corresponding census tracts. Using something called
the "Population Disaggregation Model," Palm Beach County planners
break all of the county's census tracts into smaller units called "Transportation Analysis Zones," or TAZs. While the census describes population and residential change over a ten-year period, the county is able
to monitor TAZs year to year to determine which TAZs showed the most
new housing activity, and whether those TAZs were in black and/or Haitian districts. Six areas where Haitians have settled accounted for 80
percent of the new home construction in Delray Beach, while a seventh
(where Haitians are a relatively small minority) accounted for almost all
of the rest. In three of these tracts, black residents make up at least 82
percent of all households. A total of 292 new homes was added to property rolls in these areas since 1990. It is believed that almost all of them
were built for Haitian owners.

The table below indicates the six census tracts where Haitians have
settled in Delray Beach, the number of new homes by 1995, and the
percentage of black households recorded in the 1990 census.

Tract 65.02	13 new homes	47% black
Tract 66.04	153 new homes	13% black
Tract 66.05	403 new homes	31% black
Tract 67	132 new homes	95% black
Tract 68.01	101 new homes	82% black
Tract 68.02	59 new homes	89% black

Page 299 The other Sterling Avenue names are: Carry (Luckner and
Renand), Duplessy (Joseph and Marcia), Assantes (Robert and Fred
Wenisch), Illait (Reserve and Nadiana Hilaire), Etienne (Alfred and Ve-
nus), Jean (Eveque, Elodie, and Francois Cleristor), Anfriany (Waltoguy,
Mirelle, and Wilson Ulysee), Augustin (Vierge), Pierre (Dufrely, Mom-
premier, and Terrible), Salomon (Joseph and Premise), Dorceus (Anne,

Jean, Jeune and, Jude Desin), Toussaint (Judith), Jean (Gardien and Marie), Polissaint (Marcel and Vierginie), Desir (Virgilant, Guerda, and Roland Dort), Elie (Jacques and Gilbert Occean), Floreal (Marilene and Jean Louis Francois), Achelus (Madeleine and Michael), Alexis (Louverture and Nicole), Cavalier (Victor and Marie), and Mascary (Vilbert, Evenalie Racine, "et al").

Page 309 Additional interviews were conducted with the Reverend Edouane Jean, the pastor of Emanuel Evangelical Lutheran Church, and with Robert Braver, of a Lutheran church in Boynton Beach where the Haitian congregation had been meeting. Both emphasized the anti-Haitian characteristic of the protest, and both expressed their beliefs that black Americans were their antagonists on the issue. Attempts to reach the leader of the petitioners' group, Pauline Williams, were unsuccessful.

INDEX